Collins

GCSE STATISTICS

AQA

Fully supports the AQA GCSE Specification for 2009 onwards

Student Book

Delivering the AQA specification

Anne Busby • Rob Ellis • Rachael Harris • Andrew Manning • Jayne Roper

William Collins' dream of knowledge for all began with the publication of his first book in 1819. A self-educated mill worker, he not only enriched millions of lives, but also founded a flourishing publishing house. Today, staying true to this spirit, Collins books are packed with inspiration, innovation and practical expertise. They place you at the centre of a world of possibility and give you exactly what you need to explore it.

Collins. Freedom to teach.

Published by Collins
An imprint of HarperCollins*Publishers*
77–85 Fulham Palace Road
Hammersmith
London
W6 8JB

© HarperCollins*Publishers* Limited 2011

10 9 8 7 6 5 4 3 2 1

ISBN-13 978-0-00-741009-5

Anne Busby, Rob Ellis, Rachael Harris, Andrew Manning and Jayne Roper assert their moral rights to be identified as the authors of this work.

The publishers have sought permission from AQA to reproduce questions from past GCSE Statistics and GCSE Mathematics papers.

All rights reserved. No part of this publication may be reproduced, stored in a retrieval system, or transmitted in any form or by any means, electronic, mechanical, photocopying, recording or otherwise, without the prior written permission of the Publisher or a licence permitting restricted copying in the United Kingdom issued by the Copyright Licensing Agency Ltd., 90 Tottenham Court Road, London W1T 4LP.

British Library Cataloguing in Publication Data
A Catalogue record for this publication is available from the British Library.

Commissioned by Katie Sergeant
Project managed by Emma Braithwaite and Patricia Briggs
Edited by Joan Miller and Susan Gardner
Proofread by Patrick Roberts
Answers checked by Wearset
Design and typesetting by Wearset
Concept design by Nigel Jordan
Illustrations by Ann Paganuzzi and Wearset
Cover design by Angela English
Index by Michael Forder
Production by Kerry Howie
Printed and bound by Gráficas Estella, España

Browse the complete Collins catalogue at:
www.collinseducation.com

Acknowledgements
The publishers wish to thank the following for permission to reproduce photographs. Every effort has been made to trace copyright holders and to obtain their permission for the use of copyright material. The publishers will gladly receive any information enabling them to rectify any error or omission at the first opportunity.

p.6 Business man making a presentation ©shutterstock.com/Andresr; p.6 Graph analysis ©shutterstock.com/fernando blanco calzada; p.7 Torn newspaper headlines ©shutterstock.com/Brian A Jackson; p.7 Glass cup of tea ©shutterstock.com/Tanya Ien; p.14 Ishango bone ©Science Museum of Brussels; p.14 Tally sticks ©Marion Drennen, artist, 'Three', www.quantumconnectionsart.blogspot.com Represented by Brunner Gallery, Covington, Louisiana, www.brunnergallery.com; p.15 Colourful abacus 2 ©istock.com/Kun Jiang; p.38 India sari ©istock.com/Robert Churchill ; p.38 Paint sample ©shutterstock.com/pjcross; p.38 DNA samples ©shutterstock.com/Vasiliy Koval; p.38 Black sliders on DJ console ©shutterstock.com/wronaavd; p.39 Open Pantone sample colours ©shutterstock.com/scyther5; p.58 Online customer survey ©shutterstock.com/Lasse Kristensen; p.59 Customer satisfaction survey ©shutterstock.com/Chad McDermott; p.78 Blue pills ©istock.com/fotografiaBasica; p.79 Flight information board ©shutterstock.com/Tatiana Popova; p.96 Osiris graph. From H Gray Funkhauser, "A note on a tenth century graph", *Osiris* **1** (1936), 260–262, reproduced on p.28 of E R Tufte, *The Visual Display of Quantitative Information*, Cheshire, CT: Graphics Press 1983.; p.97 Business still life with blue charts and numbers ©shutterstock.com/S. Dashkevych; p.172 Growth tomato ©shutterstock.com/Fotokostic; p.173 Highlighted ten mark on measuring tape ©shutterstock.com/Alexandru Cristian Ciobanu; p.175 PeaPod with peas ©shutterstock.com/ribeiroantonio; p.202 Colorfull shirts ©istock.com/Tomaz Levstek; p.203 High class dresses ©istock.com/Juanmonino; p.233 Newspaper headlines – financial crises 2008 ©shutterstock.com/Norman Chan; p.249 Blue toned calendar page ©shutterstock.com/Korn; p.288 The Four Seasons ©istock.com/Frank Van Den Berg; p.289 Blue sea ©shutterstock.com/Tatjana Strelkova; p.316 Roulette wheel closeup ©istock.com/Lise Gagne; p.316 Rush hour – soft focus ©shutterstock.com/Natalia Bratslavsky; p.317 Two dice ©shutterstock.com/S.M.

INTRODUCTION

Welcome to Collins GCSE Statistics AQA Student Book. This book provides all the Foundation and Higher content that you need to study for the GCSE Statistics examination. The content is divided into the six main sections of your course. These sections are colour-coded:

- Planning a strategy
- Data collection
- Tabulation
- Diagrammatic representation
- Data analysis
- Probability

Throughout the book you will also learn how to interpret data and draw conclusions from your findings; realising the usefulness, as well as the limitations of Statistics.

Chapter overviews
Find out why each chapter is important and how Statistics is used in all aspects of our daily life. Look ahead to see what maths you will be doing and how you can build on what you already know.

Colour-coded grades
Know what target grade you are working at and track your progress with the colour-coded grade panels at the side of the page.

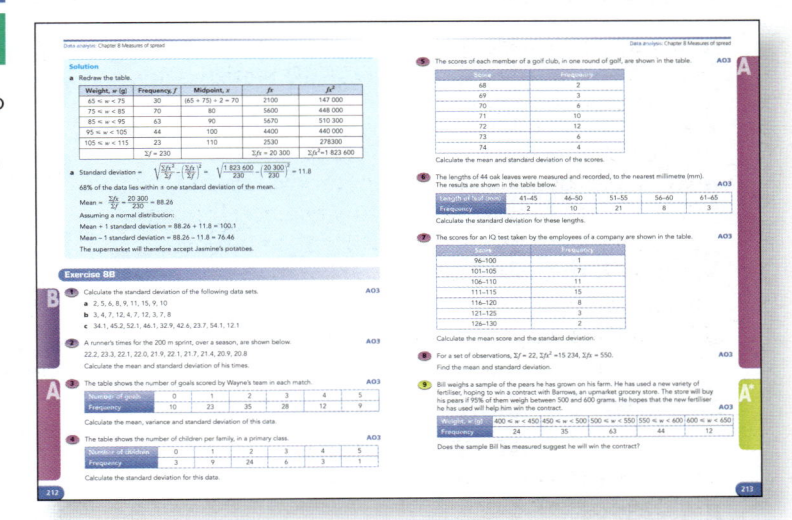

Worked examples
Before you start an exercise, take a look at the examples in the blue boxes. These take you through questions step-by-step and help you understand the topic.

Grade booster
Review what you have learnt and find out how to improve your grade with the Grade Booster panel at the end of each chapter.

GCSE Statistics Assessment Objectives
Practise the parts of the curriculum, where you can achieve the most marks (Assessment Objectives AO3 and AO4) with questions that assess whether you can process, analyse and present data appropriately **AO3** and questions that test if you can make deductions and draw conclusions from the data you have collected **AO4**. There are also plenty of questions that test your basic Statistics skills (AO1 and AO2).

Exam practice
Prepare for your exams with examination-style questions and detailed worked examination questions. Find extra hints and tips to help you score maximum marks.

CONTENTS

Planning a strategy

Chapter 1 – Planning a strategy — 6
- 1.1 Data handling cycle — 8
- 1.2 Planning an investigation — 10

Data collection

Chapter 2 – Collection of data — 14
- 2.1 Types of data — 16
- 2.2 Grouping data — 20
- 2.3 Data sources — 26

Chapter 3 – Sampling — 38
- 3.1 Sampling — 40

Chapter 4 – Conducting a survey or experiment — 58
- 4.1 Surveys — 60
- 4.2 Questionnaires — 64
- 4.3 Experimental design — 70

Tabulation

Chapter 5 – Tabulation — 78
- 5.1 Tally charts and frequency tables — 80
- 5.2 Grouped frequency tables — 83
- 5.3 Two-way tables — 87

Diagrammatic representation

Chapter 6 – Diagrammatic representation — 96
- 6.1 Pictograms, line graphs and bar charts — 98
- 6.2 Pie charts — 115
- 6.3 Misleading graphs — 122
- 6.4 Choropleth maps — 128
- 6.5 Stem-and-leaf diagrams — 135
- 6.6 Histograms and frequency polygons — 140
- 6.7 Cumulative frequency graphs — 150

Data analysis

Chapter 7 – Measures of location — 172
- 7.1 The mode — 174
- 7.2 The median — 176
- 7.3 The mean — 181
- 7.4 Which average to use — 185
- 7.5 Grouped data — 190
- 7.6 The geometric mean — 194

Chapter 8 – Measures of spread — 202

- 8.1 Box-and-whisker plots — 204
- 8.2 Variance and standard deviation — 210
- 8.3 Using a calculator to work out standard deviation — 214
- 8.4 Properties of frequency distributions — 217

Chapter 9 – Statistics used in everyday life — 232

- 9.1 Statistics used in everyday life — 234

Chapter 10 – Times series and quality assurance — 248

- 10.1 Moving averages — 250
- 10.2 Time series — 258
- 10.3 Quality assurance — 268

Chapter 11 – Correlation and regression — 288

- 11.1 Scatter diagrams and correlation — 290
- 11.2 Spearman's rank and product moment correlation coefficients — 299

Probability

Chapter 12 – Probability — 314

- 12.1 Probability scale — 316
- 12.2 Equally likely outcomes — 318
- 12.3 The addition rule for events — 323
- 12.4 Experimental probability — 328
- 12.5 Combined events — 334
- 12.6 Expectation — 338
- 12.7 Two-way tables and Venn diagrams — 341
- 12.8 Tree diagrams — 348
- 12.9 Conditional probability — 355

Answers — 366
Glossary — 405
Index — 408

1 Planning a strategy

This book will show you how to collect and analyse data and also how to interpret the meaning of your results. In order to get accurate, reliable results from a data gathering exercise we need firstly to plan the process of collection, analysis and how the results will be represented.

1.1 Data handling cycle

1.2 Planning an investigation

This chapter will show you how to:

- understand the data handling cycle
- understand what a hypothesis is
- learn how to plan and perform a statistical investigation

Higher tier only

- understand strategies for dealing with problems when performing a statistical investigation.

The exercise questions in this chapter are given individual target grades as a guide.

Visual overview

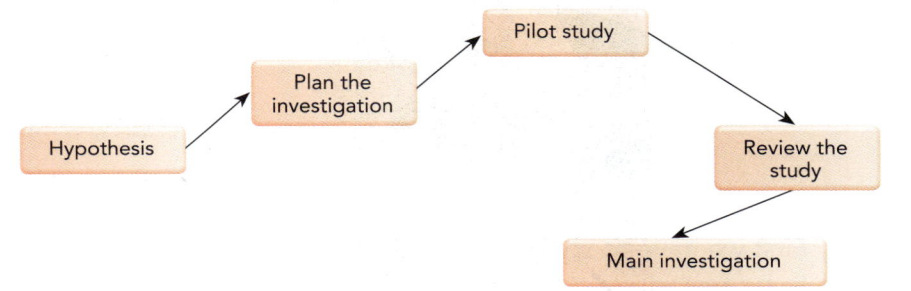

Hypothesis → Plan the investigation → Pilot study → Review the study → Main investigation

What you should already know

F How to make a plan in order to complete a task, such as a revision program or a piece of coursework (KS3, level 4).

Quick check

Design a plan to make a cup of tea in the shortest time possible.

Hints and tips

Remember that some things can take place at the same time.

1.1 Data handling cycle

This section will show you how to:
- use the data handling cycle and state a hypothesis.

KEY WORDS

Data handling cycle
Hypothesis

The **data handing cycle** underpins the process of planning a strategy.

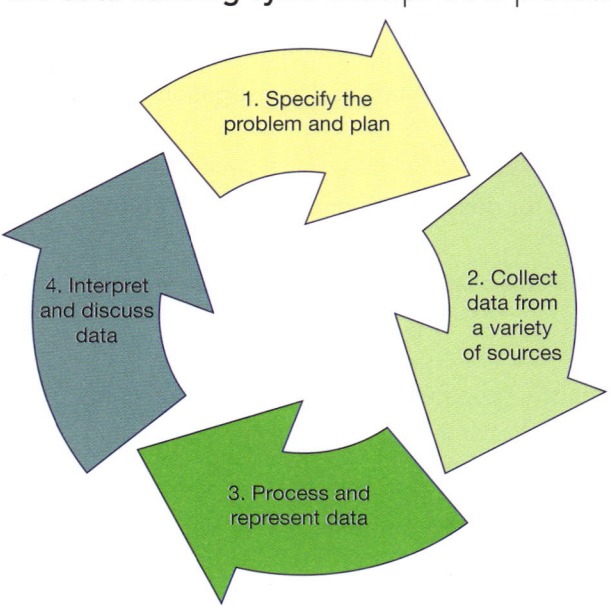

1. Specify the problem and plan
2. Collect data from a variety of sources
3. Process and represent data
4. Interpret and discuss data

1. First we have to specify the problem and plan. This will lead to deciding upon a **hypothesis** to be tested.

2. Once we have a hypothesis, we then need to collect the data. This might initially involve a pilot study, which is a kind of study that is used to give an indication of the type of responses likely, before a main study is undertaken. There are many different ways of collecting data which will be discussed in depth in later chapters and we must decide which will lead to the most reliable results. Data can sometimes be collected from a variety of sources.

3. Once we have the data we need to process, analyse and then represent it. We will learn many different ways to do this in later chapters.

4. Finally, we need to interpret and discuss the data. If this first stage is a pilot study, we may need to refine this process by adjusting the hypothesis or the data collection methods and possibly do a further pilot study. It is not unusual to go through the cycle more than once in order to prove or disprove a hypothesis.

What is a hypothesis?

A hypothesis is a statement that we think might be true. It mustn't be confused with a question. A good hypothesis is a statement that can be tested and might include a prediction.

Often a hypothesis is based on an observation such as noticing that the letter 'e' appears often in sentences. This might lead to the hypothesis:

> The letter 'e' is the most commonly used letter in sentences.

Examples of hypothesis statements could be:

- There are more silver cars on the road than cars of other colours
- Using fertilizer on my potatoes makes them grow bigger.
- Smoking damages your health.
- Women look after their health better than men.

Example 1

A gardener grows tomatoes, both in a greenhouse and outside.

He wants to investigate whether tomato plants grown in the greenhouse produce more tomatoes than those grown outside.

Describe the data handling cycle that may be applied to this problem.

Solution

- *State the hypothesis.* 'Tomato plants grown in the greenhouse produce more tomatoes than those grown outside.'
- *Plan the data collection and collect the data.* Consider 10 tomato plants grown in the greenhouse, and 10 plants grown outside. Count the tomatoes on each plant. Record the numbers of tomatoes collected from the plants between June and September. Only count those that are 'fit for purpose'.
- *Choose the best way to process and represent the data.* Calculate the mean number collected per plant as well as the range.
- *Interpret the data and make conclusions.* Look at the statistics. What do they show? Is there a clear conclusion or do you need to alter the hypothesis in any way? Discuss results, refine the method and continue the cycle.

As you see, when following the data handling cycle, you must use each of the four parts.

Planning a strategy: Chapter 1 Planning a strategy

Exercise 1A

1 Use the data handling cycle to describe how you would test each of the following statements or scenarios. Write your own hypothesis to suit the situation. In each case, state whether you would use primary or secondary data (see section 2.3).

  a Oliver is investigating which month of the year is the hottest.

  b Andrew wants to compare how good boys and girls are at estimating distances.

  c Joy thinks that more men than women go to football matches.

  d Sheehab wants to know if tennis is watched by more women than men.

  e A headteacher said that the more revision you do, the better your examination results.

  f A newspaper suggested that the older you are, the more likely you are to shop at Marks and Spencers.

2 You are asked to compare the number of news programmes on different TV channels.

  a Write down a suitable hypothesis that you could test.

  b Design a suitable observation sheet to record the data.

  c Show how the data handling cycle would be used in this investigation.

3 Kath thinks that girls are better at mental arithmetic than boys.

Explain how Kath could test this. Use the stages of the data handling cycle in your answer.

1.2 Planning an investigation

This section will show you how to:
- determine what is the most appropriate data required to address the hypothesis
- select a method for obtaining the data including deciding between a survey and an experiment
- deal with the problems of constraints.

KEY WORDS
Experiment
Hypothesis
Pilot study
Survey

Now take the hypothesis from the previous section 'women look after their health better than men'. We now need to decide whether the investigation will be a survey – whether we get information by asking questions, or by observing, or by an experiment.

If we decide upon a survey we could collect data on:
- the number of visits made by males and females to the doctor.
- the amount of alcohol drunk by males and females.
- whether males smoke more the females.
- whether females live, on average longer than males.

If we decide upon an experiment we could collect data on:
- blood pressure.
- cholesterol levels.
- blood test results.

All of this data will give interesting results which will be related to the relative health of males and females. Careful consideration of the many factors that need to be addressed before the study is undertaken is required. For example:
- the ages of the sample of people.
- where they live.
- their diet and exercise routines.
- their family history of illness – i.e. hereditary heart problems, etc.

There is always the danger of going into too much detail, thus making the data impossible to collect. It is always useful to do a pilot study first where a small sample of data is collected and analysed to see if you get meaningful results. It is also possible that the data has already been collected by someone else.

Example 2

David is 17 and wants to purchase a car. Before he buys he wants to compare the price of insurance policies.

a State a hypothesis that he could use.

b What data would he need to collect?

c What other factors could he consider?

d What problems might he have in collecting his data?

Solution

a David could come up with several hypotheses. For example:
- cars with smaller engines are cheaper to insure.
- citroen cars are cheaper to insure than other makes.
- a limited mileage insurance policy is cheaper.

b David would need to collect data on the cost of insurance. He would do this by phoning insurers or comparing prices on an internet comparison website.

c Other factors would include items that could change the cost of the policy such as:
- type of cover i.e. fully comprehensive, third party, etc.
- additional items on the policy such as no claims protection, breakdown insurance, etc.
- amount of excess he is willing to pay. (An 'excess' is a specified amount that you agree to pay towards the cost of an insurance claim. The higher the excess, the cheaper the policy.)

d Problems he might encounter would include:
- unable to get quotes on many vehicles due to his age.
- he might be restricted to certain policies, thus reducing the breadth of his survey.

Planning a strategy: Chapter 1 Planning a strategy

Exercise 1B

1 Lucy wants to compare the cost of books bought from the Apple iBook store with Amazon kindle store.

   a State a hypothesis that she could use.

   b What data would she collect?

   c What other factors could she consider?

2 Katie's mobile phone contract is up for renewal. She wants to do a statistical investigation to find out what would-be provider, phone tariff, etc. would best suit her before she makes a decision.

Design a simple statistical investigation that Katie could use. Make reference to the data handling cycle in your answer.

3 Dave's hypothesis is:

'Boys are better at maths than girls'.

Explain how Dave could investigate this problem.

4 John states the hypothesis

   'Wales has the more rain than other parts of the UK'.

   a What data would he need to collect?

   b What other factors could he consider?

   c What problems might he have in collecting his data?

5 Angharad thinks that certain TV shows have more adverts than others.

   a State a hypothesis that she could use.

   b What data would she need to collect?

   c Are there other factors she might consider?

   d What problems might she have in collecting this data?

GRADE BOOSTER

What you need to do to get this grade

C	Write a hypothesis
	Use the data handling cycle
	Know when to use a survey or an experiment
	Plan an investigation
B	Be aware of problems and how to overcome them when planning an investigation

What you should now know

- What the the data handling cycle is.
- How to write a hypothesis.

Higher tier only

- How to plan and carry out a statistical investigation overcoming any problems.

STATISTICS IN PRACTICE

You will have to complete at least one Controlled Assessment task for your GCSE Statistics qualification. One of these tasks is an investigation. You will have to carry out and write up this task. This section focuses on the hypothesis refinement for the investigation.

You will be given a task sheet that will outline the broad theme for the investigation. The theme will need to be refined in order to produce a testable hypothesis. This can be explored through class discussion or group discussion. You will then have to explore the theme independently, closely following the data handling cycle.

Discuss the following themes in groups, producing a testable hypothesis for each one:

1. Boys are better than girls
2. Commonly used letters in written English
3. Reaction times
4. Height and weight
5. Weather
6. How do you travel to school?

Take each of these six hypotheses and explore them using the data-handling cycle. You should state how you would collect the data, whether it would be a survey or an investigation, and indicate any problems you might encounter in performing the investigation. As your knowledge of statistics increases throughout this course you may be able to revisit this task and complete it in greater depth.

2 Collection of data

Tallies have been used for centuries: to count livestock, to mark time passing, to record debts, etc. The tally marks were easily etched into wood, clay, bone, pebbles and so on.

Tallies are a simple way of recording numbers of things quickly and you probably first encountered them when you were in primary school. This should not detract from their usefulness (you were taught to read at primary school and that is still a useful skill!). The tally provides visual as well as numerical information, and many years ago this would have been useful for people who couldn't read or write.

A 'split' tally was used in Medieval Europe, where the stick was split lengthwise down the middle once the tallies had been recorded, providing both parties with a record or receipt of the transaction.

By the early nineteenth century, tally sticks were no longer in vogue and a decision was taken in Parliament to destroy all of their existing tally sticks. A further decision was taken to burn all of the tally sticks privately, and there were so many of them that they overloaded the furnaces and caused the House of Lords to go up in smoke, literally!

You will not need your calculator for anything in this chapter. You can put it away and not have to fear any number crunching!

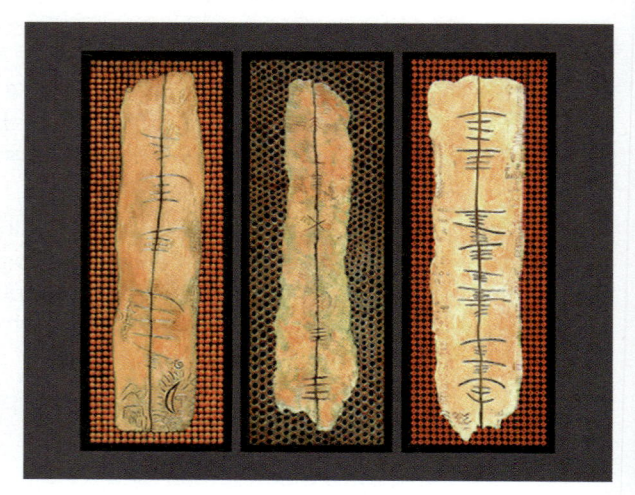

2.1 Types of data

2.2 Grouping data

2.3 Data sources

This chapter will show you how to:
- create and read a tally chart
- create a frequency table
- classify data
- distinguish between primary and secondary data
- identify mistakes in frequency tables
- group data
- determine the best method of data collection.

The exercise questions in this chapter are given individual target grades as a guide.

Visual overview

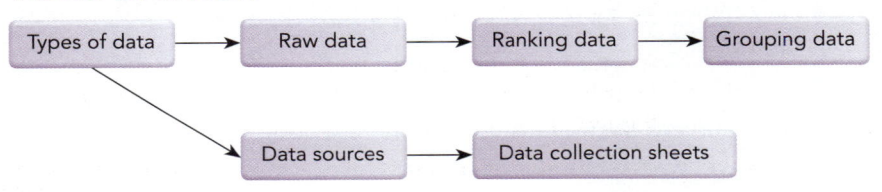

Types of data → Raw data → Ranking data → Grouping data

Types of data → Data sources → Data collection sheets

What you should already know

- **E** How to ask questions. This will help you to decide how to design data collection sheets (KS3, level 5).
- **E** How to plan your work. You need to be organized when working with statistics, so that your experiments provide you with the information you require (KS3, level 5).

Quick check

1. List the data in numerical order, starting with the smallest.
   a 53, 86, 31, 69, 42, 18, 101, 76
   b 0.85, 0.58, 8.5, 0.805, 50.8, 5.08
   c −7, 16, 42, −21, −0.3, 14.2

2. Think about how you would arrange the clothing in a charity shop if you were in charge. Would you sort by colour, size, style, gender? Why would you choose to do it this way?

2.1 Types of data

This section will show you how to:
- understand the different types of data so that you will be able to work with the data effectively.

KEY WORDS
Bivariate data
Categorical data
Continuous
Data
Discrete data
Qualitative data
Quantitative data
Variable

When you are faced with **data**, either that you have collected or that you have sourced from elsewhere, you need to know what sort of data you will be dealing with so that you can process it and present it in the most appropriate manner.

If you were to conduct an experiment to see how many times people blink in one minute, the number of blinks would vary from person to person. The number of blinks is called the **variable**, because its value will vary. You usually give each variable a letter that we can refer back to.

Example 1

State the variable in each of these situations.

a Lily measures the volume of water (in ml) that each of 10 dogs in the boarding kennel drinks each day.

b Colin records how long he spends (in minutes) browsing the Internet each day for six weeks.

c Rob surveys each of his friends on Facebook to see how many friends each of them has.

Solution

(Included is the letter we would be likely to assign to each variable although you may have chosen a different letter, which is fine!)

a Volume of water w

b Length of time t

c Number of friends f

Qualitative data describes the quality of the variable. This could be colour, texture, smell, taste or emotions (one person's opinion may be different to another's: for example, purple and lilac may be both valid descriptions of the colour of a flower).

Quantitative data is data made up of numerical values (it will involve a quantity or amount). These can be measurements or counted data. Within quantitative data we encounter both discrete data and continuous data.

Discrete data is data that can be thought of as 'stepped' data, where there are specific (and valid) values and you *cannot* have in-between values. Often we use shoe size to be a good example of discrete data. English shoe sizes can be 4, $4\frac{1}{2}$ 5, $5\frac{1}{2}$, 6, etc. but there is no size 4.7 or $5\frac{3}{4}$. The only values available to use are 'stepped' in halves.

Categorical data is the name give to data that has been put into categories or classified in some way. Even if the categories involve numbers, this is different to quantitative data. In science, we may look at the state of a substance and determine whether it is solid, liquid or gas. As opposed to qualitative data, this is not open to interpretation. It is not possible for one person to judge a substance to be a gas whilst another person judges it to be a solid.

Bivariate data is the name given to a data set which uses two variables. This may be the heights *and* weights of the people asked, it may be the ages of the mother *and* child being studied, or any other combination of variables. These variables will tend to be quantitative at this level, since they will then be easier to work with. They will often be set in a scatter plot that you will look at in more depth in Chapter 11.

Example 2

Cheryl is checking entry forms at a horse and pony show. The form asks for the gender of the horse, its age, and its colour.

State whether each of the variables on the form is qualitative, quantitative, discrete or continuous.

Solution

Gender: categorical because gender fits neatly into one of two categories, either male or female, there are no other options.

Age: quantitative and continuous because age is numerical and measured data and is never accurate; even though we give our age in discrete steps (we say we are 15 or 16) our actual age is changing all the time.

Colour: qualitative because we are describing the hair.

Example 3

Miguel is a car salesman. He keeps records on each car he sells. As part of each record, he notes

- year of manufacture
- manufacturer (e.g. Citroen, Ford, Hyundai, etc)
- model (C3, Fiesta, i20, etc)
- insurance group (these are numbered from 1 to 50)
- cost price
- colour.

From the records that Miguel keeps, give an example of

a categorical data

b discrete data

c qualitative data.

Data collection: Chapter 2 Collection of data

> **Solution**
> a Manufacturer, model and insurance group are all categories that each car will fit into one of (the car can only be one make and model and will only fit into one insurance group).
> b Cost price is numerical data with distinct steps; the car could cost £13 457.23 or £13 457.24 but there are no values possible in between.
> c Colour describes a quality of something.

Exercise 2A

1 Emma works in a charity shop. She sorts the clothes by colour and size. Are these variables qualitative, quantitative, discrete or continuous? **AO3**

2 Within the animal kingdom, vertebrates (animals who have a backbone) can be classified as mammals, reptiles, amphibians, fish or birds. What type of data is this? **AO3**

3 A recipe states that the oven should be set to 200°C, 400°F or Gas Mark 6. The dish then needs to be cooked for 25 mins. Which of these would be continuous data? **AO3**

4 Henri buys dog food online. He has to select the pack he wants from the table below. **AO3**

Weight / Type	2 kg	5 kg	10 kg	25 kg
Puppy	£10.80	£20.33	£38.31	£72.43
Adult	£9.13	£18.31	£30.69	£69.69
Senior	£10.04	£19.45	£37.75	£78.65

Which of the variables is

a discrete?

b continuous?

c categorical?

5 State whether each of the following is qualitative data or quantitative data? For the quantitative data, state whether it is continuous or discrete. **AO3**

a The price of a packet of crisps.

b The number of seagulls on a beach.

c The time taken to run a marathon.

d The distance in km between two stops that a train makes.

e The score you get on your next exam.

f The average speed that a cyclist travels at on his way to work.

g The weight of a bag of sugar.

h The colour of a jumper.

6 Sanu works for an estate agent. He keeps records of the houses for sale. Details of what is shown on each record are given below. Identify categorical, quantitative, discrete and continuous data from these variables:

- number of bedrooms
- parking available – yes/no
- number of bathrooms
- council tax band
- town
- age of property
- post code
- preferred date of moving
- price.

AO3

7 When Dee checks her mobile phone bill, she notices that it lists the number she called, the time spent on the call and the cost of the call. Which of these variables are

a discrete?

b continuous?

c Would you describe the time and cost of the call when put together as categorical, bivariate or quantitative?

AO3

8 Sachin works in a computer shop and keeps records of all computers sold. Give examples of qualitative, quantitative, discrete, continuous and categorical data that may be stored as part of those records.

AO3

Data collection: Chapter 2 Collection of data

2.2 Grouping data

This section will show you how to:
- begin to group and process your data.

KEY WORDS
Class intervals
Frequency distribution table
Frequency table
Ranked data
Raw data
Ungrouped data

Raw data is the term used for data that has been collected but is unorganized and unprocessed. The data may be in a long list rather than in neat groups. When we carry out a survey (see Chapter 4) we end up with large amounts of data.
When we process the raw data, we often choose groups that are easy to work with or that represent the data in a meaningful way. You will see in Chapter 5 how choosing different groupings can produce vastly different interpretations of data.

Here is the data for the amount of rainfall each day at Heathrow Airport during October 2010.

Date	Rain – Daily (0900–0900) mm	Date	Rain – Daily (0900–0900) mm	Date	Rain – Daily (0900–0900) mm
01/10/2010	10.4	12/10/2010	0.0	23/10/2010	0.2
02/10/2010	21.8	13/10/2010	0.0	24/10/2010	0.0
03/10/2010	3.8	14/10/2010	0.0	25/10/2010	0.2
04/10/2010	0.2	15/10/2010	0.8	26/10/2010	4.0
05/10/2010	12.8	16/10/2010	0.8	27/10/2010	0.2
06/10/2010	0.0	17/10/2010	0.0	28/10/2010	0.0
07/10/2010	0.0	18/10/2010	1.0	29/10/2010	2.6
08/10/2010	0.0	19/10/2010	4.0	30/10/2010	2.4
09/10/2010	0.0	20/10/2010	0.2	31/10/2010	3.4
10/10/2010	0.0	21/10/2010	0.0		
11/10/2010	0.0	22/10/2010	6.0		

As you can see, this **ungrouped data** is just a long list of numbers that needs processing. The first part of the processing may be to rank the data. This means sorting the data into order (numerical order in this case).

Here is the **ranked data** for the daily rainfall.

0.0	0.0	2.6
0.0	0.0	3.4
0.0	0.2	3.8
0.0	0.2	4.0
0.0	0.2	4.0
0.0	0.2	6.0
0.0	0.2	10.4
0.0	0.8	12.8
0.0	0.8	21.8
0.0	1.0	
0.0	2.4	

From this sorted data, we can produce a **frequency distribution table** where each item of data is listed alongside the number of times it occurs. This can help to highlight natural groupings for the data which otherwise may not be so easy to spot.

Here is the frequency distribution table for the rainfall data.

Rainfall (mm)	Frequency
0	13
0.2	5
0.8	2
1.0	1
2.4	1
2.6	1
3.4	1
3.8	1
4.0	2
6.0	1
10.4	1
12.8	1
21.8	1

Data collection: Chapter 2 Collection of data

From the frequency distribution table, we can now decide how to group the data in a **frequency table**. There are many possibilities, which will all give a slightly different picture of the data.

One grouping could give us:

Rainfall, R (mm)	Frequency
$0 \leq R < 5$	27
$5 \leq R < 10$	1
$10 \leq R < 15$	2
$15 \leq R < 20$	0
$20 \leq R < 25$	1

The intervals for the groups are called the **class intervals**. Using this grouping, you can see that we lose all the detail about the group $0 \leq R < 5$.

Notice here that the 5 mm can appear only in one group. It is not included in the first group, but is included in the second group. If the class intervals had been $0 \leq R \leq 5$ and $5 \leq R < 10$, then theoretically, a value of exactly 5 mm would belong in both the first and second groups. If it is placed in both groups, we would then have too many entries in the frequency table. If it is not placed in both groups, how would you decide which group it ought to go in? You must be very careful when writing out your class intervals to ensure that every value appears in one and only one interval (i.e. nothing is repeated and nothing is missed).

We do not need to have the class intervals being of equal width, so instead, we may choose:

Rainfall, R (mm)	Frequency
$0 \leq R < 1$	20
$1 \leq R < 2$	1
$2 \leq R < 3$	2
$3 \leq R < 4$	2
$4 \leq R < 5$	2
$5 \leq R < 10$	1
$10 \leq R < 20$	2
$20 \leq R < 30$	1

This gives us more detail, i.e. that the majority of readings are in the $0 \leq R < 1$ interval rather than in the much wider $0 \leq R < 5$ interval.

The class intervals that you choose may be dependent upon how you wish to present the data.

Another way to sort the data initially is to create a tally chart before putting the data into a frequency table.

Data collection: Chapter 2 Collection of data

Example 4

Here are the shoe sizes of the 25 children in Year 5 at Woodburd Primary School.

1	1	$1\frac{1}{2}$	3	4
3	3	$3\frac{1}{2}$	$2\frac{1}{2}$	2
2	2	3	4	$1\frac{1}{2}$
$2\frac{1}{2}$	$3\frac{1}{2}$	$4\frac{1}{2}$	3	$2\frac{1}{2}$
$3\frac{1}{2}$	2	2	2	2

Create a tally chart and hence a frequency table for this data.

Solution

The tally can help us to create the frequency table.

Shoe Size	Tally	Frequency
1	II	2
$1\frac{1}{2}$	II	2
2	IIII II	7
$2\frac{1}{2}$	III	3
3	IIII	5
$3\frac{1}{2}$	III	3
4	II	2
$4\frac{1}{2}$	I	1

Each occurrence of the shoe size is marked by a vertical line. When we reach the fifth item, the line goes diagonally across the other four. This is makes it easier to add up for the frequency column.

The total of each tally is transferred into the frequency column.

Exercise 2B

1 Lita is a judge at a dog show. Here are the breeds of the 40 dogs in the 'working' group that she has to judge.

AO3

Boxer	Bullmastiff	Great Dane	Boxer	Mastiff
Boxer	Boxer	Dobermann	Mastiff	Newfoundland
Great Dane	Newfoundland	Bullmastiff	Newfoundland	Bullmastiff
Dobermann	Boxer	Boxer	Great Dane	Bullmastiff
Bullmastiff	Bullmastiff	Mastiff	Great Dane	Boxer
Newfoundland	Great Dane	Newfoundland	Newfoundland	Newfoundland
Boxer	Mastiff	Boxer	Bullmastiff	Newfoundland
Bullmastiff	Boxer	Boxer	Boxer	Mastiff

23

Data collection: Chapter 2 Collection of data

Copy and complete the frequency table to show the breeds of dog.

Breed	Tally	Frequency
Boxer		
Bullmastiff		
Dobermann		
Great Dane		
Mastiff		
Newfoundland		

2 Shaun has 20 CDs that are his favourites. They are each by one of five groups. He writes down the group for each one.

AO3

Kings of Leon	Radiohead	Muse	Kings of Leon
Radiohead	Arcade Fire	Radiohead	Kings of Leon
Muse	Radiohead	Radiohead	Muse
Radiohead	Kasabian	Kings of Leon	Muse
Radiohead	Kings of Leon	Arcade Fire	Radiohead

Design and complete a frequency table to show the number of CDs he owns by each group.

3 Lou works in a library. She records the items that people return one morning. Here is her record.

AO3

Novel	CD	Non-fiction	Children's	Teenage	Children's	Teenage	Novel
Novel	CD	Non-fiction	Novel	Non-fiction	CD	Novel	CD
Novel	Novel	Non-fiction	Teenage	Non-fiction	Teenage	Teenage	Non-fiction
Children's	Teenage	CD	Children's	Children's	Teenage	Novel	CD
Teenage	CD	CD	CD	Novel	Non-fiction	Teenage	Non-fiction
Children's	Non-fiction	CD	Teenage	Non-fiction	Children's	Teenage	Children's
Novel	Teenage	Novel	Teenage	Children's	Teenage	Novel	Teenage

Design and complete a frequency table to show the number of each item returned that morning.

Data collection: Chapter 2 Collection of data

4 Jeff is conducting a survey to find out the destinations of people catching trains from London Victoria station. Here are the results from the first 50 people asked: **AO3**

Bromley South	Swanley	Chatham	Longfield	Chatham	Dover	Deal	Bromley South	Faversham	Chatham
Bromley South	Swanley	Longfield	Swanley	Dover	Dover	Deal	Meopham	Deal	Dover
Swanley	Chatham	Bromley South	Bromley South	Bromley South	Faversham	Deal	Chatham	Deal	Chatham
Swanley	Longfield	Swanley	Bromley South	Longfield	Faversham	Swanley	Meopham	Sole Street	Dover
Chatham	Swanley	Chatham	Longfield	Chatham	Deal	Bromley South	Swanley	Faversham	Longfield

Design and complete a frequency table to display this information.

5 Scott is taking bookings at a travel agency. He has to keep a record of how much each booking costs (in £) so that he can calculate his commission. This is his record for Friday: **AO3**

2139	4076	1012	670	479
10078	3452	1173	769	6969
3034	2156	5412	3213	898
4135	5367	1209	2134	526
1008	1264	876	1285	3241

a Copy and complete the frequency table.

Amount (£)	Tally	Frequency
0–999		
1000–1999		
2000–2999		
3000–3999		
4000–4999		
5000 and over		

b Now change the class intervals so that they are unequal and complete the new frequency table. What effect does this change have on the appearance of the data in the table?

6 The dogs from Question 1 all have to be weighed at the show. Brenda records their weights (in kg). Use the information she recorded below to create a frequency table. (You do not have to have equal class intervals of equal width; use the data to help you to determine sensible class intervals.) **AO3**

60	80	34	88	50	50.7	62.1	61.5	50	28.4
38	81.4	46	45	66	87.3	63.2	77	80	81
27	39	37	60.7	57	59	65	48.5	75.3	30.2
101	49	40.6	42	95	49.3	61	69	70	93

25

2.3 Data sources

This section will show you how to:
- understand the importance of knowing where your data comes from
- understand how you can begin to process your data.

KEY WORDS

Data collection sheet
Data logging
Experiments
Observation
Observation sheet
Primary data
Questionnaires
Secondary data
Spreadsheets
Surveys

You may have noticed that there are many ways we can obtain data. It is important that you know the strengths and weaknesses of each different data collection method so that you will be able to pick the best method for the data you require. In order to be an efficient statistician, you will need to know different ways to record your data.

Primary data is data collected directly by or on behalf of the researchers. The methods of collecting primary data can be expensive and time-consuming, but the researcher can obtain exactly the right data for their purposes. The data will be trustworthy since the researcher knows who has collected it and that there was no bias. It is important when carrying out research which is costing both time and money that the data collected is accurate and reliable.

Researchers collect primary data by conducting experiments, posing questionnaires and surveys, holding focus groups, having a dedicated panel to interview as well as by observation. Even within these different methods there are different ways of communicating with people. For example, questionnaires can be submitted electronically, completed over the telephone or by using the postal system. Each collection method comes with its own advantages and disadvantages.

Secondary data is data that is not collected specifically by or for the researcher. Instead, the researcher takes information that is already available (i.e. someone else has collected it) and makes use of it. This is much cheaper to obtain and takes less research time, but may not be as reliable as primary data. The statistician using the secondary data may not have access to the original questions, the age of the data or the data collection method. Often, secondary data will have already been partly processed and this means that some of the original details will have been lost.

Sources of secondary data include commercial databases that are publicly available, newspapers, journals and various government agencies. Nowadays, instead of trawling through back issues of journals, many researchers are able to locate secondary data online. A good place to start is with online libraries; they often list national statistics websites and can also show sites for the local area.

You may like to investigate these websites when you need secondary data.

Data source	Website address
The Met Office – statistics on Weather and Climate Change	www.metoffice.gov.uk
Office for National Statistics	www.statistics.gov.uk
Census – population statistics	www.ons.gov.uk/census
Eurostat – statistics on the EU and candidate countries	http://epp.eurostat.ec.europa.eu/portal/page/portal/eurostat/home/

Example 5

Kate is investigating whether boys or girls have larger feet. Should she use primary or secondary data?

Solution

Kate could use primary data by asking pupils in her year group to complete a simple questionnaire involving questions about their sex and shoe size. With only a small number of questions to answer, the data would not take long to collect. She may also be able to take secondary data from a local or government health website to use instead of, or as well as, her own data.

Experiments are an important source of data. These were discussed in Chapter 1. Remember to design the experiment so that there is no possibility of bias.

Questionnaires and **surveys** are discussed in detail in Chapter 5.

Data logging is a mechanical process of collecting primary data and as such would not be affected by human error as other methods may be. It is usually just counting or storing numbers in a system to build up a history of data. The rainfall collection from Section 2.2 could be logged mechanically with the data stored on a computer system. The daily totals could then be used to give a monthly average that can be compared to other places in the UK. When you are setting up a data logging system, you need to think carefully about how often the data is sampled. If results are recorded hourly, the results can be totalled to give the daily amount, but if only the daily amounts are recorded in the first place, they cannot be broken down to give hourly totals. Usually too much information can be processed to give the required data, but this is not the case with too little information and the experiment may have to be conducted again.

Example 6

Imagine you have been asked to count the number of people who use a particular footpath over a week. Why would a data logging machine be useful?

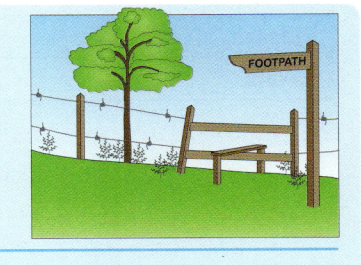

Solution

It would take several people a significant amount of time to sit and physically count everyone who uses the path. They may miscount or miss some people by chatting to others etc. A data logging machine could be set part-way along the footpath and each time a person walked past it, they would be 'counted'. You could then collect the data logged at the end of the week and it would contain the data ready to be uploaded to a computer for processing.

Data collection: Chapter 2 Collection of data

When designing experiments, it is worth giving extra thought to the additional uses that the collected data may be put to. In the above example, it could be useful to know whether or not the 'counted' people walked individually or in groups. It would have been a simple addition to the original system to log the time at which people were 'counted'. This would enable groups of people to be identified and distinguished from lone walkers.

Observation is probably the most basic method of primary data collection available to us. We are simply recording things that we see on an **observation sheet** (also known as a **data collection sheet**). The observation sheet must be structured in a way that allows the data to be collected without losing too much detail or having too many options (which can be overwhelming for the observer to complete).

Example 7

Georgia is a television repair engineer and is recording the sizes of television screens at the houses she visits to see which size is most popular (television screens are measured and sold in discrete sizes).

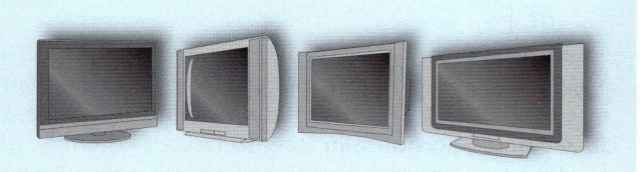

She looked in an electrical store and noted down the common sizes and produced the following observation sheet:

	Under 32"	32"–41"	42"–44"	45"–50"	Over 50"
Televisions					

When she had visited a few houses, she noticed that there were different types of television: LCD, Plasma, CRT and LED. How could she adapt her observation sheet to include this information?

Solution

She could add incorporate the additional rows so that she could distinguish between the different types of television and extend her observation sheet thus:

	Under 32"	32"–41"	42"–44"	45"–50"	Over 50"	Totals
CRT						
LCD						
LED						
Plasma						
Totals						

Data collection: Chapter 2 Collection of data

When designing the observation sheet, you must also consider *how* different people will see things. Earlier, we thought about how two different people may describe a flower as purple or lilac. These differences need to be considered when designing the observation sheet, so that two different observers would not return two different results following an observation of the same event. In some cases, observers will need training to avoid problems of inter-observer bias.

On different days of observations being carried out, there can be external factors that affect the data. An ice-cream vendor is likely to have more business at the beach on a sunny day in August, than on a rainy day. He may be there on the same day of the week and at the same time, but the outside influence of bad weather will affect his trade. This would affect any observations being made about the ice creams and ice lollies sold.

Using **spreadsheets** is another way of recording data. Often this can be done automatically by a computer system as soon as the data is collected, without the need for a person to manually enter the information into the program.

Example 8

Liz is a nurse and is going to perform basic health checks and offer healthy living advice to the employees of a department store. She needs to record each person's gender, weight and height and from that, calculate their Body Mass Index (BMI). She will offer the healthy living advice based on the BMI. Discuss how she could carry out this task efficiently.

Solution

Liz could manually enter in the height and weight information and have a formula set up within the spreadsheet which would calculate the BMI for her. She could also include a graph for each person, showing whereabouts on the BMI graphs they lie. Once the data was entered into the spreadsheet, it could be used in a variety of ways: to find the average height, weight or BMI for the employees, to create graphs and charts displaying the data (grouped or individually), to compare male and female workers, etc.

Exercise 2C

1 Here is a data collection sheet to be used for a survey about the cost of new cars. Give two criticisms of the data collection sheet.

Cost, £ / Manufacturer	Ford	Vauxhall	Citroen	Porsche	BMW
0–4000					
4000–9000					
10 000–14 000					
15 000–20 000					

2 List two advantages and two disadvantages of primary data.

3 List two advantages and two disadvantages of secondary data.

Data collection: Chapter 2 Collection of data

4 Helmsfield Town Council want to survey the amount of traffic using the main road. Give a full explanation of the best data collection method for them to use, with reasons.

5 Design a data collection sheet to be used in a survey of shop workers about their hourly wage.

6 Elliott has been asked to determine whether or not the pupils at his school would use a tuck-shop. Would he be better using primary or secondary data for this? Give reasons for your answer.

7 Hashim is investigating whether children are taller now than they were 50 years ago. Would you advise him to use primary or secondary data for this task? Explain your answer.

8 Marcus is researching his family history and takes some statistics from the previous censuses. Is he using primary or secondary data?

9 Helmsfield Town Council now would like to know about the different types of vehicle which use the main road (e.g. cars, buses, lorries, etc). If their original survey used data logging equipment, will this provide them with the information they now require? If it will not, suggest an alternative data collection method for them to use.

GRADE BOOSTER

What you need to do to get this grade

E	You can create frequency tables and identify errors in those given to you.
D	You can distinguish different types of data.
C	You can explain why you have grouped your data in the way you have. You can now make a decision on how best to collect your data.

What you should now know

- When to use primary and secondary data.
- How to create and read frequency tables.
- Different methods of data collection will suit different purposes; you should be able to choose the best collection method for your data.

EXAMINATION Questions

1 At an activities day, Simon asked each of his friends what their favourite activity was. Their replies were:

Quad biking	Quad biking	Paintballing	Archery	Climbing
Climbing	Quad biking	Archery	Climbing	Climbing
Paintballing	Quad biking	Archery	Quad biking	Quad biking

Copy and complete the table.

Activity	Tally	Frequency
Archery (A)		
Climbing (C)		
Paintballing (P)		
Quad biking (Q)		

(2 marks)

2 Here are some examples of different types of data connected with a racing game:

a time spent playing

b number of cars

c colour of the cars.

Which one of these is:

i qualitative data?

ii discrete data? *(2 marks)*

3 Alan works for the home delivery service of a large supermarket chain. He has been asked by his manager to find out how long it takes to select and pack a sample of customer orders. The tables show the results based on a sample of 75 orders.

Table 1

Time, t (minutes)	Number of orders
$0 \leqslant t < 3$	1
$3 \leqslant t < 6$	5
$6 \leqslant t < 9$	7
$9 \leqslant t < 12$	24
$12 \leqslant t < 15$	24
$15 \leqslant t < 18$	8
$18 \leqslant t < 21$	6

Table 2

Time, t (minutes)	Number of orders
$0 \leqslant t < 6$	6
$6 \leqslant t < 10$	8
$10 \leqslant t < 11$	22
$11 \leqslant t < 14$	18
$14 \leqslant t < 21$	21

Give two reasons why the first table is a better form of grouping than the second. *(2 marks)*

4 A machine has an automatic counter that records the total number of tins produced every hour.

   a What form of data collection procedure is used in this case?

   b Give one advantage in using this method. *(2 marks)*

5 The data show the number of television sets in 30 homes.

2	3	1	4	2	3	2	1	1	4
2	2	2	3	1	3	2	2	3	1
2	1	4	2	1	1	2	4	3	2

Copy and complete the tally chart and the frequency column.

Number of televisions	Tally	Frequency
1		
2		
3		
4		

(4 marks)

6 State whether each of the following variables is qualitative, discrete or continuous.

   a the number of pages in a newspaper

   b the length of time spent reading a newspaper. *(2 marks)*

7 For her Statistics coursework, Mina wanted to find out how popular her local clothes shop was. She wanted to know

   a the number of females going into the shop per minute

   b the number of teenagers going into the shop per minute

   c the total number of people going into the shop per minute.

Which one of the above could be found using a data logging machine? *(1 mark)*

Data collection: Chapter 2 Examination questions

8 The frequency table shows the number of times members of a club attended monthly meetings in one year.

Number of meetings attended	Frequency
0	1
1	3
2	6
3	2
4	13
5	11
6	17
7	15
8	19
9	16
10	8
11	4
12	10

The data is put into a grouped frequency table.

Number of meetings attended	Frequency
0–3	12
4–6	
7–9	
10–12	

a Copy the second table and complete the frequency column. *(3 marks)*

b Give one advantage of using

  i the original frequency table

  ii the grouped frequency table. *(2 marks)*

9 a Sammi collects some data that is discrete. What is meant if data is described as 'discrete'?

b Which of these types of measurements are continuous data?

  frequencies   lengths   weights   shoe sizes   *(2 marks)*

10 Stephen works in a newsagent on a Saturday morning. He records the number of items bought by each customer. The results for last Saturday were as follows.

Number of items bought by each customer	Tally	Frequency
1													
2																									
3																	
4							
5					
6				

a Copy and complete the frequency column. *(2 marks)*

b How many customers were there? *(2 marks)*

c What was the total number of items bought? *(2 marks)*

Data collection: Chapter 2 Examination questions

WORKED EXAMINATION Questions

1 A sports centre keeps a daily record of the members that come for a swim. State whether each of the following variables is qualitative, discrete or continuous.

    a The number of members. *(1 mark)*

    discrete – this is a number and so cannot be qualitative and it is counted, which makes it discrete.

    b The age of the members. *(1 mark)*

    continuous – although the members will be either 14 or 15 etc, their ages are constantly changing and so are not discrete data.

2 The data sets below refer to the morning walks Tina takes during April.

    Set A   The time (rounded to the nearest second) e.g. 43 minutes 32 seconds.

    Set B   The number of other dogs met during the walk, e.g. 6.

    Set C   The route taken, e.g. down by the river.

    a Which of these data sets is

        i discrete? *(1 mark)*

        Set B – The number of other dogs met during the walk, e.g. 6

        ii qualitative? *(1 mark)*

        Set C – The route taken, e.g. down by the river

        iii continuous? *(1 mark)*

        Set A – The time (rounded to the nearest second), e.g. 43 minutes and 32 seconds

b i Matt prepares the following table to organise the data from Set A.

Time (minutes)	Tally	Frequency
30–40		
40–50		
50–60		
70–80		

Identify two mistakes he has made in preparing his table. *(2 marks)*

Mistake 1 – there are overlaps of 40 and 50 minutes, we would not know in which group to put time of 40 or 50 minutes.

Mistake 2 – there is a gap between 60 and 70 minutes. We have nowhere to put any time of those lengths in the table.

ii Correct the mistakes you have identified by writing appropriate class intervals in the left-hand column in the table below. Cover the range 30 minutes to 80 minutes using five class intervals. *(2 marks)*

Time (minutes)	Tally	Frequency
$30 \leq t < 40$		
$40 \leq t < 50$		
$50 \leq t < 60$		
$60 \leq t < 70$		
$70 \leq t \leq 80$		

1 mark for covering the correct range in five class intervals, **1 mark** for no gaps and no overlap.

3 Sampling

What do you think of if someone says 'take a sample' or 'get a sample'? How many everyday things can you think of that involve a sample?

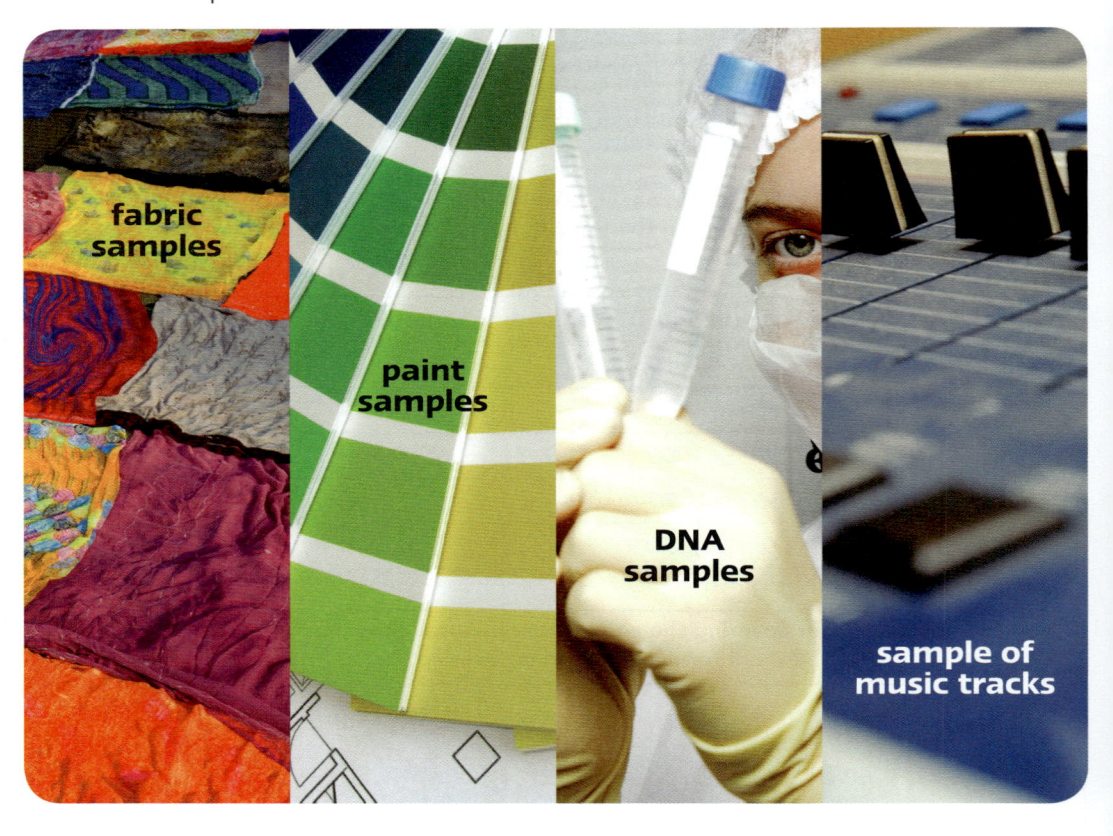

fabric samples

paint samples

DNA samples

sample of music tracks

As you can see, samples appear in all sorts of places from the medical profession to the music industry. You may have thought of alternatives to those listed above. We need to know how to take a sample in order to obtain the best possible results for our experiments and surveys.

3.1 Sampling

This chapter will show you how to:

- obtain a random sample
- obtain a stratified random sample
- obtain a cluster sample
- obtain a quota sample
- obtain a convenience sample

Higher tier only

- obtain a cluster or multistage sample
- obtain a systematic sample.

The exercise questions in this chapter are given individual target grades as a guide.

Visual overview

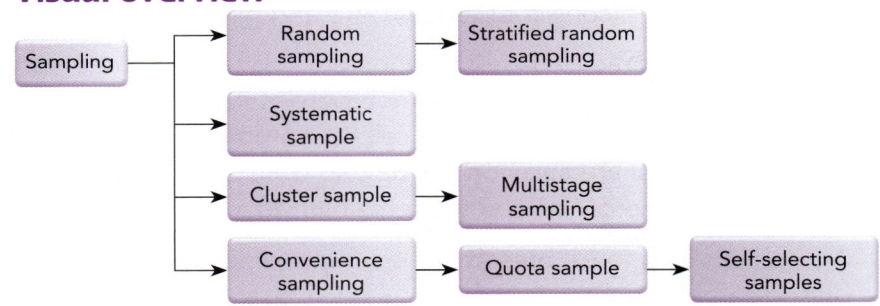

Sampling → Random sampling → Stratified random sampling
Sampling → Systematic sample
Sampling → Cluster sample → Multistage sampling
Sampling → Convenience sampling → Quota sample → Self-selecting samples

What you should already know

- **G** How to round to the nearest whole number (KS3, level 4).
- **E – C** How to multiply and divide (KS3, levels 5–7).
- **E** How to find simple percentages (KS3, level 4).
- **D – C** How to find fractions of amounts (KS3, levels 6–7).

Quick check

1. Find 10% of these amounts:
   - **a** 50
   - **b** 104
   - **c** 2379
   - **d** 1005

2. Find $\frac{2}{11}$ of 1320.

3. Round each of these to the nearest whole number:
   - **a** 25.4
   - **b** 69.9
   - **c** 421.624
   - **d** 270.7688

3.1 Sampling

> **This section will show you how to:**
> - understand the different ways of sampling from a population
> - understand the strengths and weaknesses of different sampling methods.

KEY WORDS

Biased
Cluster sampling
Convenience sampling
Multistage sampling
Population
Quota sampling
Random sample
Sample
Sample frame
Sample size
Stratified random sample
Systematic sampling

Types of survey: questionnaires and interviews

When we are conducting research, it is often not feasible to gather *all* the information possible; instead we take a **sample** and base our findings on the data collected from the sample. It would be too immense a task, when investigating the possible link between a person's final earnings and their highest level of qualification, to gather data from every retired person in the country. Instead it is sensible to take data from a sample made up of different ages and genders from all over the country. If we gather information from a non-biased sample of the population, the sample data is likely to be indicative of the population overall.

The **population** is defined as everything or everybody being considered. If your hypothesis states that 'The boys in Starfish class have larger feet than the girls in Starfish class', then your population would consist of the 30 boys and girls in Starfish class and no others.

It may be that some of the population are unavailable to be part of the sample on any given day. When we have discounted these members of the population, the list that we are left with (those available to us) make up what we call the **sample frame**. It may be that in Starfish class Holly, Tara and Michael are away on holiday, so whilst the population is the children of Starfish class, the sample frame consists of the remaining 27 children.

A sample is said to be **biased** if the sample data does not properly represent the population. A biased sample can occur from:

- an ill-defined population, which can happen if you do not correctly define the population and ask the wrong people or use the wrong items
- an unrepresentative sample, which can happen if you have failed to include a major sector of the population
- poor data collection, which can happen as a result of poorly worded, leading questions or inter-observer bias.

The **sample size** needs to be considered as part of the data collection process. A large sample will cost more time, money and effort to collect data from than a smaller sample, but may be more representative and may produce better results. For a small population, five to ten per cent is a large enough sample size and for larger populations, of size n (i.e. there are n members of the population), we take a sample of size $\sqrt{n}$. For example, for a population of size 400, we would take a sample of 20 since $\sqrt{400} = 20$. However, if you are testing food or another item, which will ultimately become useless after it has been sampled, it is acceptable to take a smaller sample (if you sampled every cake produced in a bakery, there would be no cakes left to sell!).

Data collection: Chapter 3 Sampling

When you conduct a survey or an experiment, the size of the sample will affect the variability and reliability of your results. A larger sample will give more reliable (and less variable results), but will inevitably take longer to collect data from and will therefore be more expensive.

Random samples

Random samples (also known as **simple random samples**) are created when each member of the population has an equal chance of being included in the sample. In order to generate the sample, we number each member of the population and then select members randomly until we have sufficient to make up our sample. We can find the random numbers we need by using a random number table, the random number generator function on a calculator or the random number function in a spreadsheet. As different people create the sample, they will inevitably be including different members of the population as thrown up by their random numbers, unless they all start from the same point in a random number table.

Example 1

Here are the names of the resident families in Downham Road. Create a 10% random sample of the 51 houses in Downham Road to be used in a survey about refuse collection. Use the first number (33) from the second row of the Random Number Table as your starting point.

House number	Name
1	Noakes
2	Newton
3	Whittam
4	Smith
5	Singh
6	Belmore
7	Leydon
8	Muncey
9	Simpson
10	Homden

Data collection: Chapter 3 Sampling

House number	Name
1	Noakes
2	Newton
3	Whittam
4	Smith
5	Singh
6	Belmore
7	Leyden
8	Muncey
9	Simpson
10	Homden
11	Jeffery
12	Bassam
13	Carter
14	Whately
15	Lee
16	Love
17	Green

House number	Name
18	Patrick
19	Sweeney
20	Vizard
21	Hoyle
22	Blackshaw
23	Costello
24	Sanderson
25	Woods
26	Howarth
27	Harrison
28	Zhu
29	Horackova
30	Balasz
31	Poole
32	Cant
33	Townsend
34	Foster

House number	Name
35	Trinh
36	Jones
37	Leach
38	Walsham
39	Karia
40	Grimshaw
41	Thurtle
42	Southwell
43	Topham
44	Harvey
45	Leonard
46	Cambridge
47	Robinson
48	Cox
49	McKinney
50	Cilia
51	Pearson

Random number table

62 30 61 02 87 79 12 20 67 33 72 27 42 50 20 78 67 03 19
33 18 98 91 03 18 40 62 29 49 88 88 94 92 26 82 30 29 89
81 33 30 76 87 02 05 24 72 33 76 02 21 97 87 20 16 03 26

Solution

10% of 51 = 5.1, so we need to select five of the 51 houses randomly.

From the beginning of line 2 of the random number table, and taking two digits at a time, we create our randomly generated list of houses for the survey. (There is no need to number the houses as they are already numbered. If your sample frame is not already numbered, you will need to do this first.)

We ignore the two-digit numbers greater than 51 and we ignore 00 as there are no houses with numbers greater than 51 or numbered 00. We discount any repeated two-digit numbers as we require five distinct houses to survey (in reality, if we had a repeated number, we would only have four houses on the list and would not have fulfilled the 10% needed).

The houses in our sample then are:

33 18 ~~98~~ ~~91~~ 03 ~~18~~ 40 ~~62~~ 29 → 33 18 03 40 29

33	Townsend
18	Patrick
03	Whittam
40	Grimshaw
29	Horackova

You can see that if we had used line 1 of the random number table, the houses making up our sample would have been:

~~62~~   30   ~~61~~   02   ~~87~~   ~~79~~   12   20   ~~67~~   33   →   30   02   12   20   33

30	Balasz
02	Newton
12	Bassam
20	Vizard
33	Townsend

A different method of generating the numbers (using the random number generator on a calculator or in a spreadsheet) would have generated different lists again. Remember, it is acceptable to have a different sample set from someone else performing the same task, unless you are told to start from a precise point on a specific line of a particular random number table.

Example 2

Nadine wants to choose a sample of the 500 tracks on her MP3 player. She selects every tenth track to make up the sample. Explain why this is *not* a random sample.

Solution

In a random sample, every member of the sample frame has to have an equal chance of being selected. This is not the case here; if Nadine starts her sample with track 1, then tracks 2 to 10 cannot possibly be included in the sample, but track 11 must be included. For a random sample, nothing should be certain to be either left out or included in the sample.

It is possible to obtain a random sample without using random numbers. In order to do it, you need to have enough equally sized pieces of paper to write every member of the sample frame on their own piece. You then put all the papers into a container (box, bag, hat, etc.) and mix them up before withdrawing as many pieces as the sample requires.

In the previous example, Nadine would need 500 pieces of paper (all the same size, so that a larger piece was no more likely to be picked nor more likely to fall to the bottom). She would need to write each of the numbers 1 to 500 on a piece of paper, before muddling them ready to pick out the 50 she needs for her sample. This is a valid method, but in practical terms it can take a great deal of effort. It is perfectly acceptable to offer this as a method of random sampling in the exam (often it is called the 'hat method') but you must ensure that you list *every* step.

Stratified random sample

When taking a random sample, it is possible for an entire sector of the population to be excluded from the sample, simply because of how randomness dictates the sample set. This can make the sample less representative of the population and can potentially lead to bias from the survey or experiment results.

> **Note**
>
> The word 'stratify' comes from the Latin 'strata', meaning layer or level.

Data collection: Chapter 3 Sampling

Paul wants to survey a sample of the youth group members to find out where they would like to go for their summer trip. When he takes a random sample, his sample contains only female members. Jake complains that the sample is unfair and asks Paul to come up with a different way to select a more representative sample in order to avoid bias.

Izzy suggests using a **stratified random sample** instead of a simple random sample in order to achieve a representative mix of male and female members within the sample group. The big difference between a stratified random sample and a simple random sample is that we ensure each group within the population is represented by the same **proportion** as make up the population as a whole.

The youth club has 30 female members and 20 male. If Paul is taking a 10% sample, he will need five people altogether in the sample, 3 female and 2 male (10% of 30 = 3 and 10% of 20 = 2). For each different sector of the population (male and female in this case), Paul would carry out a simple random sample to obtain the required number from within each sector.

A stratified random sample involves slightly more work than a simple random sample, but the sample set is likely to be more representative of the entire population and make any findings more valid and reliable.

Example 3

Students at Langafel College have agreed to take part in the pilot of a new maths exam. As part of the pilot, a sample of students will be asked their views about the new exam. Miss Cummings takes a stratified random sample of the students to ensure that her sample is as representative of the population as possible. Calculate the number of students from within each gender and course needed to make up a sample size of 10%. Use the table below which gives the numbers of students taking the exam from the different courses, split into gender groups.

	Course				
	Hair and beauty	Motor vehicle	Public services	Animal welfare	Languages
Male	14	44	104	97	199
Female	155	4	74	285	169

Solution

Firstly, we need to find the total number of students taking the exam:

14 + 155 + 44 + 4 + 104 + 74 + 97 + 285 + 199 + 169 = 1145

The sample size we need is 10%. 10% of 1145 is $\frac{10}{100} \times 1145 = 114.5$

We will need 115 students altogether.

We then take each type of student in turn to find out how many from each group will go into the sample.

There are 14 male students taking Health & Beauty. They make up $\frac{14}{1145}$ of the population.

We need the same proportion of that group in our sample, so we use that same fraction and multiply it by the size of the sample.

$\frac{14}{1145} \times 115 = 1.406$ (to 3 d.p.)

If we use this method on each group of students, we will have the correct number of students from within each sector making up our sample.

	Course					
	Hair and beauty	Motor vehicle	Public services	Animal welfare	Languages
Male	1.406	4.419	10.445	9.742	19.987
Female	15.568	0.402	7.432	28.624	16.974

Clearly, we cannot have 1.406 male Hair and beauty students in our sample, so we round each figure to the nearest whole number.

	Course					
	Hair and beauty	Motor vehicle	Public services	Animal welfare	Languages
Male	1	4	10	10	20
Female	16	0	7	29	17

We then need to check that we have the necessary 115 students.

1 + 16 + 4 + 0 + 10 + 7 + 10 + 29 + 20 + 17 = 114

We do not have enough students in our sample set (we have 114 and we need 115). This will be because we have rounded every value. To overcome this problem, we need to include another student. It seems sensible in this situation to add a female Motor vehicle student, as there are currently no representatives from that sector at all. In another situation, you would look for the figure which would be closest to being rounded up (without actually being so). Here, this would have been the figure 10.445, so we would have chosen to include an extra member of the male Public services course to complete our sample quota had we not had a sector with zero representation. Solving the problem in this way would get you full marks in an exam.

Data collection: Chapter 3 Sampling

Systematic sampling

In this method of sampling, we are choosing items from the sample frame at regular intervals, say every 6th or 10th item. Once you know the size of the sample required, you have to calculate the size of the interval (how many to skip each time). You then randomly choose a starting point in the first interval and count on from that starting point until you have fulfilled your quota.

Example 4

Rebecca wants to survey a sample of library users to find out about their borrowing habits. How could she choose a systematic sample?

Solution

She chooses to use a systematic sample by asking every 20th person entering the library building to complete her questionnaire.

There are problems associated with this method of sampling and we need to be very careful where we apply it. One problem is that of population availability. In the above example, Rebecca wanted to conduct a survey about library borrowing habits, so library users was an appropriate population. Had the survey asked people's opinions about raising the entrance fee at the swimming pool, library users would not have been a suitable population, since many of the swimming pool users might not also be library users.

Choosing from the wrong population could lead to biased results if some of the intended population are not involved in the sampling process.

Example 5

Pavlos has been asked to conduct a survey about the cost of heating homes. All of the houses in the area are terraced, with eight houses in each terrace.

He chooses the houses using a systematic sample. There are 240 houses in total and Pavlos wants a sample size of 30, so he will need to pick every 8th house (240 ÷ 30 = 8). How could this sample be biased?

Solution

If Pavlos' starting point is house number 8 (choosing randomly from the first interval of 1 to 8), the houses in the sample will be those numbered:

8, 16, 24, 32, 40, 48, 56, 64, 72, 80, 88, 96, etc.

This means that every house on the list to be surveyed is an end-of-terrace and therefore more exposed than a mid-terrace. These houses will naturally require more heating than a mid-terrace and so the results of the survey will be biased towards a higher heating bill and therefore be unrepresentative of the whole population of houses.

Convenience sampling

This style of sampling is very quick to organise. There is no need to number or order the sample frame before you begin; you merely work with what is available to you at the time!

In a convenience sample of 20 students, you can simply ask the first 20 students to arrive at school or the first 20 students who turn up to hockey/football practice.

This can of course lead to an enormous problem of bias. If the survey were about sport/exercise habits, then asking 20 students attending hockey/football practice is likely to give very different results to asking the first 20 students who turn up to orchestra practice. Neither sample set is likely to be representative of the entire school student body, therefore neither is a good sample to use.

Quota sampling

This type of sampling is probably the easiest to see in use in the real world. The companies who commission research may want interviews conducted within a specific sector of the population, say males aged 25 to 40, when testing out a new men's aftershave.

If you are asked to take part in a survey which is using quota sampling, you will be asked some 'screening' questions first of all to determine whether or not you are part of their target audience. You may not have to answer any more questions if you do not meet their criteria.

Cluster sampling

Cluster is simply another word for group. We use cluster sampling when the population can be put into (or falls naturally into) groups. There must be a good mixture of the different elements from the population within each cluster, so that one cluster can be selected at random and the population of that cluster used as the sample set. The numbers in each cluster need to be spread out as equally as possible.

Cluster sampling at first appears to be very similar to stratified random sampling, but it is not. In a stratified random sample, we group together the members of the population with similar characteristics (e.g. gender, age, employment status, etc.). In a cluster sample, we need a variety of characteristics in every cluster, as the cluster itself will be the sample rather than choosing some from each strata as we do in a stratified random sample.

Example 6

Tash has to survey a sample of army personnel. She has a small budget, therefore it would be better if she did not have to travel far. Suggest how Tash could obtain a representative sample of army personnel that takes these factors into consideration.

Solution

It would be sensible for Tash to take each regiment of the army as a cluster (since every regiment would consist of people from most ranks and thus ensures the overall mix of people we need) and then randomly select one cluster (i.e. one regiment) with whom to carry out the survey. She would then only have to travel to one place to conduct the survey.

Tash would number each regiment and then randomly select one using any random number sampling technique.

This sampling method can lead to bias if the clusters are not sufficiently representative of the population, but it is an excellent method for selecting samples from very large populations. If the clusters are geographical, this method can cut down the costs of travelling around the country to perform experiments or to interview people.

Just as research companies who conduct national opinion polls do, you need to ensure that each cluster contains as representative a mix as possible of:

- gender
- age groups
- social backgrounds
- economic backgrounds
- geographical areas.

If your clusters each contain a sufficient mix of these elements, it is safe to proceed with the sampling.

Multistage sampling

Multistage sampling is a more complex form of cluster sampling where the initial clusters are still too big to be considered as the sample, and so are broken down further into new, smaller clusters. This process can be repeated until the correct sample size is reached. In multistage sampling, random sampling is always used to select the cluster(s) used.

Example 7

There are adult education centres all across the county of Kent with thousands of people enrolled on various courses. The adult education system is split into five regions across the county and there are a number of districts within each region. The districts then contain the main centres and the satellite centres. Outline a method of selecting a sample of students to survey.

Solution

As the population is so large in this scenario, we would be well advised to obtain our sample by using the multistage sampling method. For the purposes of adult education, the county is split into five regions and each region is split into districts. As far as is possible, these districts will be of a similar size so that budgeting and management responsibilities are evenly spread around the county.

We would randomly choose a number between 1 and 5 to get our starting region and then number the districts within to obtain a smaller cluster. From there, we would number the centres and use random number selection to get us to one particular centre (main or satellite). From there we could continue as previously outlined to obtain a sample of students.

Data collection: Chapter 3 Sampling

Self-selecting sample

A self-selecting sample occurs when people are given the choice to participate in a survey. Often in this type of sample, people are asked their opinion about a recent purchase or experience. There could be a large negative bias, since happy customers do not always take the time to voice their opinions.

Example 8

In December 2010, Facebook hosted a survey about how many books people had read from the 100 listed. What type of a sample will be involved in this survey?

Solution

This is a perfect example of a self-selecting sample, since Facebook users themselves chose whether or not to take part in the survey. Only Facebook users made up the sample frame, excluding a large section of the country's population. Those who hosted the survey need to be aware that respondents might not cover a variety of genders, age groups, social backgrounds, economic backgrounds or geographical areas as would be desirable when drawing conclusive results.

Combining different sampling methods can sometimes be the most effective way to obtain a representative sample. You could combine multistage sampling with stratified random sampling or quota sampling to ensure that the various elements of the population are all present in the sample.

Exercise 3A

1 Rosie has to choose five friends to go out with her for her birthday. She decides to be fair to all her friends and choose the five at random. She numbers each of her thirty friends and uses the random number table below to make her selection.

42	41	04	37	99	20
40	60	89	18	14	41
20	25	43	69	89	82

  a Starting at 42 on the first row, write down the number of each friend Rosie selects.

  b Explain why Rosie could not have obtained her sample by starting with the 40 on the second row.

2 Describe how you would take a systematic sample of the 1350 cars in a car park if you needed a sample of 50.

3 Shannon works in a factory that produces clothing. She has to test a sample of the clothing made each day. Each worker puts their completed items into their own box, because their wage is dependent upon how much they have produced. Each day, Shannon takes her sample by picking 20 items out of Alfie's box just before lunchtime.

  a What type of sampling is this?

  b Explain why this sample may be biased.

Data collection: Chapter 3 Sampling

4 Nat wants to find out how far people travel to get to work. She asked the first ten teachers that she met at her school.

  a Which sampling method has she used?

  b Give reasons why this sample may be biased.

5 Give one advantage and one disadvantage of cluster sampling.

6 Rachel needs to sample the bacteria present in the water from Lake Hills. She collects water samples in 50 ml tubes. Describe how she could obtain a random sample of 25 tubes.

7 Explain why it might be preferable to use a stratified random sample instead of a simple random sample.

8 Suzy is investigating how much money people spend downloading tracks from iTunes. She is only asking people aged 25 years or under. What type of sampling is this?

9 Olivia is taking a stratified random sample of people holidaying on a cruise ship. Using the information in the table below, calculate how many guests from Flamingo Deck she ought to include in her sample of 100 passengers.

	Deck						
	Albatross	Eagle	Flamingo	Kingfisher	Nightingale	Ostrich	Peacock
Number of guests	410	285	204	401	378	145	177

10 Which of these sampling methods would give you a random sample of 100 people at a football match with 46 000 spectators? Give reasons for your answer.

  a asking every 460th person who arrives at the stadium

  b issuing each spectator with a uniquely numbered ticket upon arrival and then picking 100 of the numbers at random

  c asking 100 people all sitting in the stand nearest to the East exit.

GRADE BOOSTER

What you need to do to get this grade

E	You can obtain a random sample from a population.
D	You can identify the sample frame.
C	You can give the advantages and disadvantages of more than one sampling method.
C	You can select a sample using a variety of sampling methods.
C	You can obtain a stratified random sample.
B	You can obtain a stratified random sample involving more than one strata.

What you should now know

- Why we take samples.
- How to take a sample using a variety of sampling methods.
- The advantages and disadvantages of the different sampling methods.

Higher tier only

- That results will vary depending upon the sample taken.

EXAMINATION Questions

1 The table shows how many students are in a school.

Lower school	Upper school	Sixth form
720	480	400

Chelsey wants to survey 100 students from the school using a stratified sample.

a Work out how many students Chelsey should include in her survey from the Lower School.
(3 marks)

b Twenty-five students from the Sixth form are to be chosen. Describe a method of choosing a random sample of these Sixth-form students. *(2 marks)*

2 The table shows a factory layout divided into four different work areas. The numbers of male and female staff in each area are given.

	\multicolumn{4}{c}{Work area}
	Production	Office	Sales	Warehouse
Male	180	6	6	106
Female	53	24	10	15

The factory owner wishes to undertake a survey to find the reaction of the staff to the introduction of a new bonus payment scheme. He decides to take a systematic sample of 20 male production staff.

a Explain how the sample could be selected. *(3 marks)*

b Give **two** reasons why this sample would be unrepresentative of the whole staff. *(2 marks)*

c As an alternative the owner is advised to take a sample, stratified by sex and work area, of 50 of the 400 staff.

    i Calculate the number of sales staff to be included in this sample. *(2 marks)*

    ii Calculate the number of female office staff to be included in this sample. *(2 marks)*

3 The table shows the number of GCSE passes for 30 Year 11 students. The gender of each student is also shown.

Student	Gender	Number of passes
01	M	4
02	M	7
03	F	9
04	M	8
05	F	6
06	F	6
07	M	9
08	M	2
09	F	7
10	M	4
11	F	8
12	M	7
13	F	5
14	M	5
15	M	4
16	M	3
17	M	5
18	F	10
19	M	2
20	M	4
21	F	8
22	M	3
23	F	7
24	M	2
25	M	1
26	M	4
27	F	9
28	M	5
29	M	6
30	M	2

Here is a table of random numbers from 01 to 50.

Line 1	15	41	01	15	20	16
Line 2	32	22	33	30	19	08
Line 3	04	31	49	29	13	29
Line 4	14	23	37	11	24	29

Data collection: Chapter 3 Examination questions

a Starting with the first number on Line 1 of the random number table and reading across from left to right, select a random sample of size eight. Write your answers in a copy of the table.

Student number								
Gender								
Number of passes								

(3 marks)

b Starting with the first number on Line 3 of the random number table and reading from left to right, select a random sample of size six stratified by gender. Write your answers in a copy of the table.

Student number						
Gender						
Number of passes						

(4 marks)

4 The list gives the surnames of the 28 families living in a street.

01	Anderson	15	Joab
02	Bailey	16	Lovejoy
03	Brown	17	McKinney
04	Brownley	18	Morgan
05	Cadman	19	North
06	Cargill	20	Patel
07	Crowther	21	Paybet
08	Fenton	22	Randall
09	Fernandez	23	Shah
10	Garland	24	Singh
11	Grinling	25	Taylor
12	Halliday	26	Thorns
13	Holding	27	Wong
14	Imeson	28	Woodcock

Obtain a random sample of five different families using pairs of digits selected from the following list, starting at 23.

39 20 09 18 23 00 14 83 75 36 62
92 01 21 33 15 22 09 08 68 27

(4 marks)

54

5 The diagram shows the layout of a new housing estate in Stokeville.

Houses numbered 01 to 50 cost £450 000 each
Houses numbered 51 to 150 cost £300 000 each
Houses numbered 151 to 500 cost £190 000 each

Cost £450 000   Cost £300 000   Cost £190 000

The house builder agrees to undertake a sample survey to find out residents' views on introducing parking charges on the estate. He decides to question one female from each of the houses numbered 31 to 50 on the estate.

  a Give **two** reasons why this method of sampling is unsuitable. *(2 marks)*

  b At a later date the builder extends the survey by selecting a simple random sample of 50 houses from the 500 on the estate.

    i Explain how the sample could be chosen in this case. *(2 marks)*

    ii Why might a stratified sample be more appropriate in this case? *(1 mark)*

    iii In a stratified sample, how many houses costing £300 000 would be included in a sample of 50? *(2 marks)*

6 Boris is investigating if the distance from a polling station affects whether people usually vote in his town. He plans to ask a random sample of people some questions. Define the population for this survey. *(2 marks)*

7 Peter wishes to conduct a survey in his constituency to estimate the proportion of Labour voters in the area. The constituency is split into five wards; each ward has six polling districts. All eligible voters are registered with their local polling district. Peter needs to select his sample of voters from one polling district only. Describe how Peter could select the sample of voters using multistage sampling methods. *(3 marks)*

8 The head teacher of a school thought that fewer pupils stayed for school lunches than the previous year. He decided that a survey of the eating habits of the school should be carried out. Give **one** reason why each of the following methods would **not** give random results.

  a Standing outside the school canteen on Monday lunchtime questioning the pupils as they arrive. *(1 mark)*

  b Sending a questionnaire to every pupil on the school register whose surname begins with S. *(1 mark)*

Data collection: Chapter 3 Examination questions

WORKED EXAMINATION Questions

1 Five different machines produce lightbulbs for a company. Lou is considering these three methods for testing the bulbs produced.

A Lou takes the first 50 lightbulbs produced on Monday morning from Machine 1.

B Lou takes every 10th lightbulb produced on Monday morning from Machine 1.

C Lou takes one lightbulb at random from each machine twice each day on every day of the week.

a Name the sampling method being used in each case. *(3 marks)*

A: Convenience sampling

B: Systematic sampling

C: Random sampling

> 1 mark for each correct name.

b i Which of the three methods would you advise Lou to use? *(1 mark)*

C – Random sampling

> 1 mark, linked to your reason.

ii Give a reason for your choice *(1 mark)*

This method takes lightbulbs from every machine at different times of the day and on different days and so will give a good mix of lightbulbs to test.

> You need to give a reason why you have chosen this method. Think carefully about the strengths of the chosen method; list as many as you can but do not contradict yourself.

iii Give a different reason for not choosing each of the other two. *(1 mark)*

Method A only takes from one machine at one point of time in the week. If this machine is faulty at that time, it will give a biased sample in favour of bad lightbulbs. It does not test what the other machines are producing at all.

Method B only takes light bulbs from one machine on one day. Bulbs from other machines have not been tested at all. Lou will not know if one of the other machines is producing faulty light bulbs if her sample from Machine 1 only produces samples of good light bulbs.

> You have to remember to give a reason for dismissing each of the other methods. Don't just give a reason for dismissing one of them; you may not get the mark.

2 Helen is trying to take a sample of fish from a lake in order to estimate how many of each type of fish are in the lake. As she catches one, she notes down the species and then releases it.

a Explain why this is not a good way to take the sample. *(1 mark)*

Helen may catch the same fish several times. For example, there may be only one carp in the lake but if she catches it seven times, she may think there are at least seven carp.

> You are told in the question that this is not a good sampling technique. What the examiner wants to see from you is the reason that this is a bad way to take the sample. Try to concentrate on the real-life situation and what implications this sampling method could have, rather than trying to give a technical explanation. Your suggestion for an improved method also needs to have a reason to support it.

b Suggest a way to improve this sampling method. *(1 mark)*

Helen could catch them and then put them in a holding tank until she has done her sample and then release them all at the end of the sample collection. Alternatively she could mark the fish that she catches (or tag them) before releasing them so that she can identify previously caught fish and discount them.

4 Conducting a survey or experiment

Surveys are an important tool for finding out people's opinions. They are often used by businesses to gather feedback from people using them, so that they can improve their service and give customers what they want.

Statistical experiments, on the other hand, are used to test a theory (known as a **hypothesis** in statistics) or to find the effects of a product. You have seen the outcomes of these experiments used in TV advertisements for all sorts of goods, such as make-up, toothpaste and cat food.

The results of poorly conducted experiments are often seen in the media. For example, why is it that '9 out of 10 toothpastes and toothbrushes are recommended by dentists…' or '8 out of 10 owners said their cats preferred it…'? The main reason is that samples are often very small or, in the case of the toothpaste and the cat food, the people sampled may already be using the product.

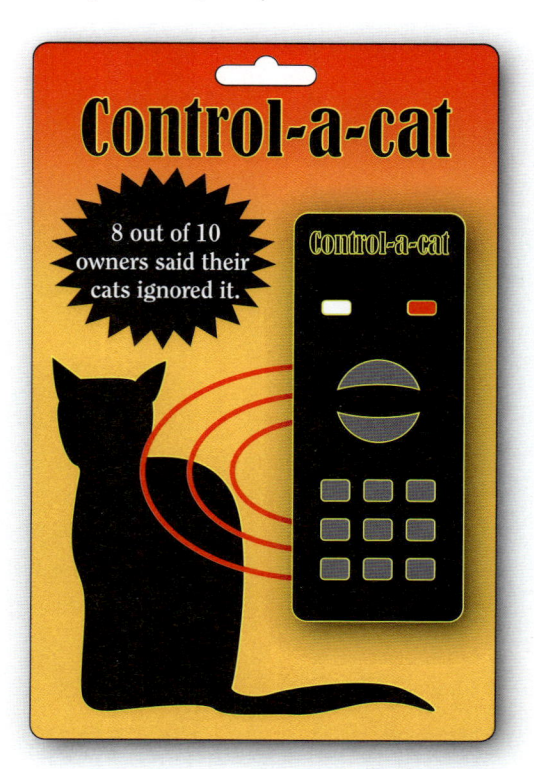

Another example is when the statistics are hidden in very small print on the advertisement. This technique is often used in advertising for make-up. Next time you look at a magazine, see if you can find an example of a poorly conducted experiment.

4.1 Surveys

4.2 Questionnaires

4.3 Experimental design

This chapter will show you how to:
- understand the different ways of conducting a survey
- design a data collection sheet
- understand the difference between a census and a sample
- understand when to use a pilot study
- understand closed and open questions
- use the two types of opinion scale
- conduct a statistical experiment correctly

Higher tier only
- use the technique of random response when collecting sensitive data.

The exercise questions in this chapter are given individual target grades as a guide.

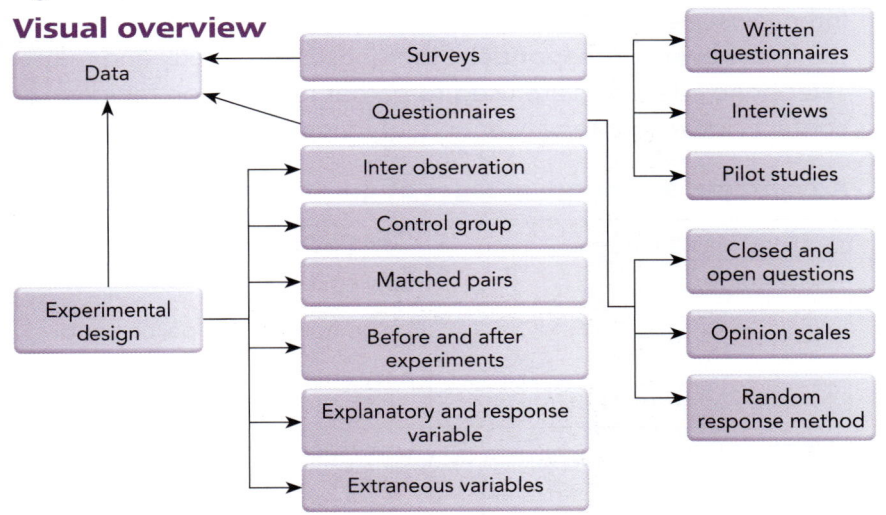

Visual overview

Data ← Surveys → Written questionnaires
Data ← Questionnaires → Interviews
                       → Pilot studies
                       → Closed and open questions
                       → Opinion scales
                       → Random response method

Experimental design → Inter observation
                   → Control group
                   → Matched pairs
                   → Before and after experiments
                   → Explanatory and response variable
                   → Extraneous variables

What you should already know

F How to extract information from tables and diagrams (KS3, level 4).

Quick check

The table shows the results when a class of students were asked if they catch a bus to school.

	Catch the bus to school	
	Yes	No
Boys	10	7
Girls	5	8

1. How many students are there in the class?
2. How many boys catch the bus?
3. How many girls are there in the class?

59

4.1 Surveys

This section will show you how to:
- conduct a survey.

KEY WORDS

Census
Data collection sheet
Hypothesis
Interview
Pilot study
Population
Respondent
Sample
Survey

Types of survey: questionnaires and interviews

A **survey** is an organised way of asking a lot of people a few, well-constructed questions, or of making a lot of observations in an experiment, in order to reach a conclusion about something.

Surveys are used to test out people's opinions or to test an idea or **hypothesis**.

Surveys can be divided into two categories, **questionnaires** and **interviews**. Questionnaires can be completed in a variety of ways including postal surveys and, more recently, online surveys. Response rates from postal and online surveys are often low so you will often see an incentive for completing the questionnaire, such as entry into a prize draw or vouchers for high-street shops.

Interviews are a more flexible form of research than questionnaires. The interviewer asks the interviewee or **respondent** the questions directly and may ask follow-up questions. Telephone interviews are used to gather information rapidly. They allow for some personal contact between interviewer and interviewee, for follow-up questions.

Advantages and disadvantages of questionnaires and interviews

	Questionnaires	Interviews
Advantages	Low cost Large numbers of participants Easy analysis	Personal contact Ability to probe and ask follow-up questions Detailed answers
Disadvantages	Low response rate from mail surveys Lack of detail	Time-consuming High cost, including training the interviewer People don't like unsolicited telephone interviews

Data collection sheets

If you want to collect data to analyse, you will need to design a **data collection sheet** that is clear and easy to fill in. For example, if you want to find out Year 10 students' preferences for the end-of-term trip from four options you could ask:

> Where do you want to go for the Year 10 trip at the end of term – Blackpool, Alton Towers, The Great Western Show or London?

Data collection: Chapter 4 Conducting a survey or experiment

You would put this question to a group of Year 10 students, on the same day, entering their answers straight onto a data collection sheet, as below.

Place	Tally	Frequency
Blackpool	┼┼┼┼ ┼┼┼┼ ┼┼┼┼ ┼┼┼┼ ///	23
Alton Towers	┼┼┼┼ ┼┼┼┼ ┼┼┼┼ ┼┼┼┼ ┼┼┼┼ ┼┼┼┼ ┼┼┼┼ ┼┼┼┼ ┼┼┼┼ /	46
The Great Western Show	┼┼┼┼ ┼┼┼┼ ////	14
London	┼┼┼┼ ┼┼┼┼ ┼┼┼┼ ┼┼┼┼ //	22

Notice that plenty of space is available for the tally marks, and how the tallies are gated in groups of five to make counting easier when the survey is complete.

This is a good, simple data collection sheet because:
- only one question (*Where do you want to go?*) has to be asked.
- all the four possible venues are listed.
- the interviewer can easily and quickly tally the answer from each interviewee, then move on to the next interviewee.

Notice, too, that since the question listed specific places, they must appear on the data collection sheet. You would lose many marks in an examination if you just asked the question: *Where do you want to go?*

Data sometimes needs to be collected to obtain responses for two different categories. In this case, the data collection sheet takes the form of a two-way table.

Example 1

The head of a school carries out a survey to find out how much time students in different year groups spend on their homework during a particular week. He asks a **sample** group of 60 students and fills in a two-way table with headings as follows.

	0–5 hours	6–10 hours	10–20 hours	More than 20 hours
Year 7				

This is not a good table as the headings overlap. For example, a student who does 10 hours' work a week could tick either of two columns. Response sections should not overlap, so that there is only one possible place to put a tick.

Solution

A better table would be like this.

	0 up to 5 hours	More than 5 and up to 10 hours	More than 10 and up to 15 hours	More than 15 hours
Year 7	┼┼┼┼ //	////		
Year 8	////	┼┼┼┼ //		
Year 9	///	┼┼┼┼ //	//	
Year 10	///	┼┼┼┼	///	/
Year 11	//	////	////	//

This gives a clearer picture of the amount of homework done in each year group.

Data collection: Chapter 4 Conducting a survey or experiment

Census data

The largest data-gathering exercise in the UK is undertaken every 10 years by the Government and is known as a **census**. This is a Latin word meaning 'registration of citizens'. The UK census gathers information from every household in the country. This is different from a sample, as this only gathers information from a sub-section of the available **population**. Note that population means a group but doesn't necessarily have to be human. It could be books in a library, or bicycles used in Scotland.

Advantages and disadvantages of surveys and censuses

	Census	Sample
Advantages	Accuracy of data Everyone participates Unbiased results	Low cost Shorter analysis time required
Disadvantages	High cost Time-consuming Analysis is slower	Possibility of biased data Some groups may be excluded

Pilot studies

A **pilot study** is used to eliminate problems in the design of an experiment or survey. It will often be part of a research strategy. Any problems that it raises can be addressed before the main study is undertaken, and this will avoid wasting time and money. A pilot study can also be used to give an indication of the type of responses and hence an idea of the final outcome of the survey.

Exercise 4A

1. 'People like the supermarket to open on Sundays.'

   a To see whether this statement is true, design a data collection sheet that will allow you to capture data while standing outside a supermarket.

   b Does it matter on which day you collect data outside the supermarket?

2. The organiser of the school tuck shop wants to know which types of chocolate it should get in to sell – plain, milk, fruit and nut, whole nut or white chocolate.

   a Design a data collection sheet that you could use to ask students in your school which of these chocolate types are their favourite.

   Hints and tips
   Include space for tallies.

   b Invent the first 30 entries on the chart.

3. When you throw two dice together, what total are you most likely to get?

   a Design a data collection sheet on which you can record the data from an experiment in which two dice are thrown together and note the total of the two numbers shown on the dice.

   b Carry out this experiment for at least 100 throws.

   c Which totals are most likely to occur?

4 Who uses the buses the most in the mornings? Is it pensioners, mums, schoolchildren, the unemployed or some other group? Design a data collection sheet to be used in a survey of bus passengers.

Make sure all possible responses are covered.

5 Design a data collection sheet to show:

   a how students in different year groups travel to school in the morning.

   b the types of programme that different age groups prefer to watch on TV.

   c the favourite sports of boys and girls.

   d the amount of time students in different year groups spend on the computer in the evening. Invent about 40 entries for each one.

6 Hassan wanted to find out who eats healthy food.

He decided to investigate the hypothesis:

Boys are less likely to eat healthy food than girls are.

   a Design a data collection sheet that Hassan could use to help him do this.

   b Hassan records information from a sample of 40 boys and 25 girls. He finds that 17 boys and 15 girls eat healthy food.

   Based on this sample, is the hypothesis correct? Explain your answer.

7 What kind of tariffs do your classmates use on their mobile phones? Design a data collection sheet to help you find this out.

8 You are asked to find out what shops the parents of the students at your school like to use.

When creating a data collection sheet for this information what two things must you include on the collection sheet?

9 Becky wants to find out what snacks people eat in her school during break time.

Explain why she should do a pilot study first.

10 David thinks that there are more silver cars on the road in the UK than any other colours. Explain why David should do a sample survey rather than a census.

11 Explain the difference between a sample and a census.

12 Salma wants to find out how many people who attend her school own a smartphone. Explain whether she should take a sample or a census.

13 Give two reasons to use a pilot study.

63

Data collection: Chapter 4 Conducting a survey or experiment

4.2 Questionnaires

This section will show you how to:
- ask suitable questions to collect reliable and valid data
- put together a clear, easy-to-use questionnaire.

KEY WORDS

Closed question
Continuous
Discrete
Exhaustive response
Leading question
Open question
Opinion scale
Random response

When you are putting together a questionnaire for a survey, you must think very carefully about the sorts of question you are going to ask. Here are five rules that you should *always* follow.

- Never ask a **leading question** designed to get a particular response.
- Never ask a personal or irrelevant question.
- Keep each question as simple as possible.
- Include questions that will get a response from whomever is asked.
- Make sure the responses do not overlap and keep the number of choices to a reasonable number (six at the most).

The following questions are badly constructed and should probably not appear in any questionnaire.

What is your age?

☐ Under 15   ☐ 16–20   ☐ 21–30   ☐ 31–40   ☐ Over 40

This is personal. Many people will not want to answer.

It is always better to give a range of ages as in this example.

Slaughtering animals for food is cruel to the poor defenceless animals. Don't you agree?

This is a leading question, designed to get a 'yes' response.

Are you a vegetarian?   ☐ Yes   ☐ No

An impersonal question such as this works better.

Do you go to discos when abroad?

This can be answered only by people who have been abroad.

Have you been abroad for a holiday?   ☐ Yes   ☐ No
If yes, did you go to a disco whilst you were away?   ☐ Yes   ☐ No

A start-up question with a follow-up question works better.

Data collection: Chapter 4 Conducting a survey or experiment

When you first get up in a morning and decide to have some sort of breakfast that might be made by somebody else, do you feel obliged to eat it all or not?

> This question is too complicated. It is better to ask a series of shorter questions. For example:

What time do you get up for school? ☐ Before 7   ☐ Between 7 and 8   ☐ After 8

Do you have breakfast every day? ☐ No   ☐ Yes

If no, on how many school days do you have breakfast?
☐ 0   ☐ 1   ☐ 2   ☐ 3   ☐ 4

A questionnaire is usually a specialised data collection sheet, put together to test a hypothesis or a statement. For example, a questionnaire might be constructed to test this statement.

> People buy cheaper milk from the supermarket as they don't mind not getting it on their doorstep. They'd rather go out to buy it.

A questionnaire designed to test whether this statement is true or not should include these questions.

- Do you have milk delivered to your doorstep?
- Do you think milk is cheaper at the supermarket?
- Would you buy your milk only from the supermarket?

Once these questions have been answered, the responses can be checked to see whether the majority of people hold views that agree with the statement.

From what you have read so far, can you start to identify different types of questions?

Closed questions have specific answers that can be chosen from a list. This type of questionning gives an easy-to-analyse data set, and useful information can be gathered quickly. This type of question does not discriminate against the less talkative or less articulate respondents. The data, however, is often found to be clustered around the centre of the response sheet, which means that respondents avoid the extreme positive and negative answers and tend to answer fairly neutrally. Closed questions can be used to cover all possible answers; this is **exhaustive response**. However, they need to be constructed carefully to do this. For example, a question that asks what TV channels you watch but offers only BBC1 and ITV1 in the response section is definitely *not* exhaustive.

Open questions are those with no specific response. More complete information can be gathered in this way. Each participant in the survey, however, could give a completely different answer to a question, making the data slow to collect and very difficult to analyse. Misinterpretation of the answers is often a problem. Simple examples of this would be:

- What do you eat for breakfast?
- What do you think about technology?

Data collection: Chapter 4 Conducting a survey or experiment

Another method that is used to gather opinions from a population is an **opinion scale**. Scales may be **discrete** or **continuous**.

A discrete opinion scale looks like this.

☐ Strongly agree

☐ Agree

☐ Disagree

☐ Strongly disagree

A continuous opinion scale, where the respondent places a marker on the line, looks like this.

Strongly Disagree   Strongly Agree

|—————————————————|

Example 2

Design a question to investigate whether students' French teachers set them homework.

Solution

Do you get French homework in your lesson?

☐ Always

☐ Sometimes

☐ Never

This method will gather all possible responses and will be easy to analyse.

A useful technique for gathering information about sensitive issues, such as whether someone has a criminal record or whether they have taken drugs, is random response. Two questions are put before the respondent; one is sensitive, one is not. The respondent flips a coin. If it shows heads they answer question A, if tails question B. The interviewer has no idea which question the respondent has answered.

Example 3

200 people are asked to answer one of the following questions.

		Yes	No
A	Do you have a criminal record?	☐	☐
B	Turn to a random page in a book. Is it an odd-numbered page?	☐	☐

Before answering a question, each person secretly flips a coin. If it lands on heads they answer question A, if it lands on tails they answer question B.

The interviewer, who has no idea which of the two questions was answered each time, records 56 'yes' answers.

Estimate how many people have criminal records.

Solution

The probability of answering question A is $\frac{1}{2}$ as a coin has the probability of $\frac{1}{2}$ for heads and $\frac{1}{2}$ for tails.

Therefore, on average, 100 people answered question A and 100 answered question B.

The random page number must be either odd or even, hence the answer may be 'yes' or 'no'.

Of those who answered question B, 50 people answered 'yes' as the probability of a random page having an odd number is $\frac{1}{2}$. Therefore six people must have answered 'yes' to question A.

An estimate of the number of respondents who have criminal records must therefore be 6.

Example 4

A teacher asks 120 students in Year 9: 'Have you ever smoked cigarettes?' Before they answer, they roll a dice. If it comes up as an even number they answer 'yes', if an odd number comes up they answer truthfully.

68 pupils answered 'yes' and 52 answered 'no'.

Estimate how many people have smoked cigarettes.

Solution

The probability of an even number is $\frac{1}{2}$ so you would expect 60 'yes' answers.

68 – 60 = 8 so 8 pupils out of 60 have smoked. So you would expect about 16 of the 120 to have smoked cigarettes.

Exercise 4B

1 These are questions from a questionnaire on healthy eating.

a
Fast food is bad for you. Don't you agree?
☐ Strongly agree   ☐ Agree   ☐ Don't know

Give **two** criticisms of the question.

b
Do you eat fast food?   ☐ Yes   ☐ No
If yes, how many times on average do you eat fast food a week?
☐ Once or less   ☐ 2 or 3 times   ☐ 4 or 5 times   ☐ More than 5 times

Give **two** reasons why these are good questions.

Data collection: Chapter 4 Conducting a survey or experiment

D

2 This is a question from a survey on pocket money.

How much pocket money do you get each week?
☐ £0–£2   ☐ £0–£5   ☐ £5–£10   ☐ £10 or more

  a Give a reason why this is not a good question.

  b Rewrite the question to make it a better question.

C

3 Design a questionnaire to test this statement.

'People under 16 do not know what is meant by all the jargon used in the business news on TV, but the over-twenties do.'

4 Design a questionnaire to test this statement.

'The under-twenties feel quite at ease with computers, while the over-forties would rather not bother with them. The 20–40s are all able to use computers effectively.'

5 Design a questionnaire to test this hypothesis.

'The older you get, the less sleep you need.'

6 A head teacher wants to find out if her students think they have too much, too little or just the right amount of homework. She also wants to know the parents' views about homework.

Design a questionnaire that could be used to find the data that the head teacher needs to look at.

7 Anja and Andrew are doing a survey on the type of music people buy.

  a This is one question from Anja's survey.

Folk music is just for country people. Don't you agree?
☐ Strongly agree   ☐ Agree   ☐ Don't know

  Give **two** criticisms of Anja's question.

  b This is a question from Andrew's survey.

How many CDs do you buy each month?
☐ 2 or fewer   ☐ 3 or 4   ☐ more than 4

  Give **two** reasons why this is a good question.

  c Make up another good question with responses that could be added to this survey.

8 Design a questionnaire to test this hypothesis.

'People with back problems do not sit properly.'

Data collection: Chapter 4 Conducting a survey or experiment

9 As each customer left a store, an assistant gave them a questionnaire containing the following question.

> **Question:** How much do you normally spend in this shop?
>
> **Response:** ☐ Less than £15   ☐ More than £25
>
> ☐ Less than £25   ☐ More than £50

Explain why the response section of this questionnaire is poor.

10 Frank needs to find out the marital status of his employees. He asks the question:

> What is your marital status?
> Married ☐
> Divorced ☐

a Explain why this is not exhaustive.

b Rewrite the question to make it exhaustive.

11 David is doing a survey on the age of people who live in his village.

a Explain why he should use a closed question to gather the data.

b Some of the people he asks do not want to answer the question. Describe a method he could have used to gather the data.

12 Why do we sometimes need to use the technique of random response to gather data?

13 Karen wants to find out how many Year 11 students text during lessons. Describe a method she could use to get an estimate of the numbers who text during lessons.

14 James wants to know how many people in his workplace earn more than £50 000. He asks a sample of 40 people 'Do you earn more than £50 000?' Before answering the question, they secretly flip a coin. If it lands on heads they answer truthfully; if it lands on tails they flip the coin again and answer 'yes' if it lands on heads and 'no' if it lands on tails. James's question returned 15 'yes' answers.

AO4

How many people actually earned more than £50 000?

Data collection: Chapter 4 Conducting a survey or experiment

4.3 Experimental design

This section will show you how to:
- obtain data from a range of statistical experiments
- recognise the different variables involved
- overcome any problems that occur when conducting an experiment.

KEY WORDS
Control group
Explanatory variable
Extraneous variable
Inter-observer bias
Matched pair
Observe
Response variable
Field experiment
Laboratory experiment
Natural experiment

The simplest form of experiment is when you **observe** something and record the results. The data is often recorded using tally charts, with which you are already familiar. Now you need to consider the problems that occur when something is observed.

When two people view things in different ways, **inter-observer bias** can occur. A typical example of this might be when you are collecting data on the colour of people's eyes. Some observers may record brown eyes as hazel, or green eyes as grey. For the experiment to be successful, this problem needs to be overcome. So observers have to be trained. They may be given photographic examples of the correct response, or be encouraged to work together when making subjective decisions.

When designing an experiment to test effects of a single treatment, such as whether drinking cherry juice cures arthritis, it is always important to have a **control group**. The reason is that the symptoms of arthritis may get better or worse without the cherry juice. The control group must be matched as closely as possible to the experimental group, for example, with similar ages and symptoms. Once the two groups have been selected, one group is randomly chosen to receive the treatment. The results from the two groups can then be compared to see if the treatment is effective.

In medical trials it has been found that people's health often improves if they think they are being treated. The control group is given a placebo, which looks like the medication but is not. If the control group knew they were taking the placebo, the results would be ruined. Therefore, the tester uses a blind trial, in which neither group knows whether they are receiving the treatment or the placebo. In a double blind trial, neither the groups nor the tester knows who receives the placebo and who the treatment.

Example 5

Describe how you would test the statement:

'Eating chocolate causes you to put on weight.'

Solution

Select two groups of people of similar ages and weights, with the same number of males as females.

One group would then be randomly assigned as the control group and the other the experimental group. The members of both groups would be weighed.

The experimental group would be given the same amount of chocolate to eat each day over the period of the experiment. The control group would not eat any chocolate over the period.

Both groups would then be weighed again at the end of the experiment and the differences in weights recorded and analysed to find out if the chocolate had an effect.

Matched pairs

This is possibly the simplest type of experiment. If you wanted to use the matched pair method to compare the effects of two types of diet pill, you would select pairs of people who are as alike as possible in age, weight, diet, gender, income and so on. Ideally, identical twins are used for this type of experiment. Each pair would be given a different pill and the results compared.

Other types of experiment

Laboratory experiments take place in an artificial environment where the researcher is in total control of all the factors that could affect the experiment. For example, if we were testing the effects of fertiliser on tomato plants using this method, all factors that could influence the result would be controlled, such as amount of light, heat, humidity, etc.

Field experiments take place in a natural environment where the researcher has control over the explanatory variable. For example, if we again tested the effects of fertiliser on tomato plants using this method, we would control only the amount of fertiliser applied to the plants; all other factors would not be considered.

Natural experiments are experiments that are not manipulated by researchers and are simply observations of outcomes. For example, a researcher might note one year that his outdoor tomato plants generated more tomotoes when he stopped watering the plants twice a day. But obviously there are many other factors, such as the weather, that could affect this outcome. Natural experiments are the most unreliable type of experiment.

Before-and-after experiments

As the name suggests, this type of experiment measures the variable to be tested before and after the experiment. It is suitable to be tested on an individual rather than a group.

Example 6

Peter wants to find out if a six-week training programme lowers his resting heart-rate. Describe a statistical experiment to determine this.

Solution

Peter must first find an average of his resting heart-rate, taken at the same time each day over a period of time. He then completes the training programme and again finds an average, taken in the same way as before the experiment. He can then compare the results.

Data collection: Chapter 4 Conducting a survey or experiment

Explanatory, response and extraneous variables

The **explanatory variable** is the variable of which the effect is going to be investigated; the **response variable** is the outcome. These are also known as independent and dependent variables. An example would be if a farmer wanted to find out if using a fertiliser increased the weight of his crops. The fertiliser would be the explanatory variable and the weight of the crops the response variable.

An **extraneous variable** is something that can influence the results of an experiment. The earlier example, testing the statement: 'Eating chocolate causes you to put on weight', has many possible extraneous variables. Someone from the control group could eat chocolate, or perhaps put on weight for a variety of other reasons. It is therefore important to eliminate all the extraneous variables. In this case you could make the diets of both groups identical except for the chocolate. They would also have to do identical forms of exercise.

Exercise 4C

1. A company produces Supasize tomato plant food. It claims that it increases the amount of tomatoes the plants produce.

   Design a simple statistical experiment to test this claim.

2. A farmer is thinking about using a new feed for his cows that is reported to increase the amount of milk they produce. The feed is expensive so he decides to perform a statistical experiment to test out the claims.

   a Why should he use a control group?

   b What extraneous variables might he need to overcome?

   c Explain what is meant by the dependent and independent variables in this case.

3. The drug company Flaxo have developed a product that cures acne.

   a Explain what is meant by a blind trial and why it should be used in this experiment.

   b Design a statistical experiment to test this claim.

4. A weed killer advert states: 'Kills all dandelions on your lawn!'

   John wants to test these claims on his lawn.

   a Design a statistical experiment to test the claim.

   b What extraneous variables might have an effect on the results?

5. Explain the term 'inter-observer bias'.

6. Gwen states that green beans grow better in a greenhouse than outside. Carol disagrees and says hers grow just as well outside.

   Design a statistical experiment to find out who is correct.

GRADE BOOSTER

What you need to do to get this grade

D	You can design a data collection sheet.
	You can design a simple statistical experiment.
C	You can design a questionnaire.
	You know the difference between a census and a sample.
	You know what a control group is.
	You understand opinion scales.
B	You can perform calculations from data collected using random response.
	You can eliminate extraneous variables from an experiment.

What you should now know

- How to conduct a survey.
- How to design a data collection sheet.
- The difference between census and samples.
- When to conduct a pilot study.
- The difference between closed and open questions.
- What opinion scales are and how to use them.
- How to correctly conduct a statistical experiment.

Higher tier only

- How to use the random response technique when collecting sensitive data.

EXAMINATION Questions

1 Jason is carrying out a survey about how much exercise pupils in his school do.

    a One of his questions is:

       'How many days a week do you exercise for 30 minutes or more?'

       Design a response section for Jason's question. *(2 marks)*

    b Give **one** reason why Jason may **not** want to ask every pupil in the school. *(1 mark)*

    c Jason asks a group of Year 11 girls.

       Give **one** disadvantage of his choice of sample. *(1 mark)*

                                     AQA, March 2009, Foundation, Statistics Paper 1, Question 10

2 Peter receives a questionnaire in the post about a new local radio station.

Three of the questions are shown below.

Give **one** criticism of each question.

Question 1:

How many hours have you listened to the radio during the past six months? *(1 mark)*

Question 2:

How much do you earn each year? Please tick one box.

☐ Less than £10 000   ☐ £10 000 up to £20 000   ☐ More than £20 000

Question 3:

If you have already heard our new radio station, give one reason why you enjoyed listening to it. *(1 mark)*

                                     AQA, June 2003, Foundation, Statistics Module, Question 2

Data collection: Chapter 4 Examination questions

3 Rodney is considering opening a small restaurant in the village where he lives.

To find out the views of local people, he delivers a questionnaire to every house in the village.

   a Included in the questionnaire is a closed question asking for people's ages.

      i Explain what is meant by a *closed question*. *(1 mark)*

      ii Give **one** advantage of using a closed question for age. *(1 mark)*

   b Only 12% of the questionnaires are returned to Rodney.

      How might Rodney have improved the success rate? *(1 mark)*

   c The returned questionnaires showed that some of his questions had been badly worded.

      What should Rodney have done before he delivered his questionnaire to avoid this problem? *(1 mark)*

   d One of Rodney's questions was:

      'How often do you eat out at a pub or restaurant?'

      Give **two** criticisms of this question. *(2 marks)*

          AQA, June 2007, Higher, Statistics Module, Question 2

4 Rob is carrying out research into the cost of vending-machine snacks in his school.

He asks people who are waiting in a queue at a vending machine this question.

'Do you agree that vending-machine snacks are good value?'

   a Give **two** criticisms of this question. *(2 marks)*

   b Explain why Rob should have carried out a pilot survey first. *(1 mark)*

5 A travel agent decides to survey all existing customers, using a postal questionnaire.

   a One question is shown below.

      'How much do you spend each year on holidays abroad?'

      Please tick one box.

      £1000–£1500 ☐

      £1500–£2000 ☐

      £2000–£3500 ☐

      £3500–£6000 ☐

      £6000 and over ☐

      Give **two** distinct criticisms of the response section of this question. *(2 marks)*

   b Of 2000 questionnaires posted out, only 93 were returned.

      Give **two** ways in which the response rate could be increased. *(2 marks)*

          AQA, June 2005, Higher Statistics Module, Question 1

Data collection: Chapter 4 Examination questions

6 One of the classification questions used in a survey was:

'How much do you pay each month on your mortgage?'

Please tick one box.

Under £200 ☐
£200–£300 ☐
£300–£700 ☐
over £700 ☐

    a Give **one** criticism of the response section. *(1 mark)*

    b Give **one** criticism of the question asked. *(2 marks)*

AQA, June 2008, Higher Statistics Module, Q2c

7 A teacher believes that his students will do better in an examination if they drink a cup of strong coffee before sitting the paper. To test his theory, half of his class are given a cup of coffee to drink before a test, the other half have nothing to drink.

    a What is the *explanatory* variable? *(1 mark)*

    b What is the *response* variable? *(1 mark)*

    c Give **two** factors the teacher should consider when placing pupils in the two groups. *(2 marks)*

WORKED EXAMINATION Questions

1 The Highways Agency proposes to build a bypass around a village.

Ben designs a questionnaire to obtain opinions on the proposals from the villagers.

One of his questions is:

Do you agree that the bypass will be a disaster for our village?

☐ Yes, definitely   ☐ No

Give **two** distinct criticisms of Ben's question.

> You will gain **1 mark** for this comment with a reason.

Criticism 1: It is a leading question, as it starts with "Do you agree…".

Criticism 2: The question implies that the bypass will either be a disaster, or it won't. There is no middle ground.

> You will gain **1 mark** for this comment with a reason.

(2 marks)

5 Tabulation

How would you feel if you saw the football results for a season like this?

Brookfield Wanderers:
10 played
Home: 2 won, 3 drawn, 0 lost, 6 goals for, 5 goals against
Away: 1 won, 3 drawn, 1 lost, 7 goals for, 5 goals against
Goal difference = 3   Points = 15

This is the information for just one team! Imagine having the information for 20 teams in a league written out like this. The tables we are used to seeing (like the one in the picture) have the same information, for all 20 teams, and it's much easier to handle. Presenting the information in this way means that a lot of data is shown in a compact, accessible and readable way. This is one example of a two-way table. The chances are you look at two-way tables more times than you realise. Nutritional information on food packets, sports results, train timetables and TV guides are all other examples.

FOOTBALL — Watch Highlights
COUNTY LEAGUE TABLE

POSITION	TEAM	P	W	D	L	F	A	GD	Pts
1	Newbury Rangers	11	8	1	2	27	5	22	25
2	East Bradstone United	11	6	5	0	24	13	11	23
3	Granston Town	11	6	2	3	22	11	11	20
4	Fullanbury United	11	6	2	3	15	10	5	20
5	Mickleton Town	11	5	2	4	20	14	6	17
6	Pitcastle	11	3	6	2	17	16	1	15
7	Gardbury Rovers	11	4	3	4	13	14	-1	15
8	Brunchester	11	3	6	2	11	12	-1	15
9	Williston Wanderers	11	4	3	4	12	14	-2	15
10	Anbury	11	4	3	4	14	19	-5	15

HOME • SPORT • HEADLINES • RESULTS • TABLES • FIXTURES • CONTACT US

Data is only useful if it makes sense. Tables present the data in an ordered, understandable way.

When you're doing your investigations and processing your data, creating tables is the first step. Taking a jumble of numbers and putting them into a table gives structure and allows the data to be analysed. When you are dealing with research involving a small number of people, there is less of a need for tables, but there are a few occasions where they are useful.

Before a new medicine can hit the shelves it will have been put through vigorous trials testing how effective it is, but also what the possible side effects are. To make sure that they are confident the medicine does its job the manufacturers need to test it out on several thousand cases. There will be several phases of clinical trials over a number of years. Without putting these thousands of numbers into tables, the information would be meaningless and difficult to read or interpret.

5.1 Tally charts and frequency tables

5.2 Grouped frequency tables

5.3 Two-way tables

This chapter will show you how to:

- record data in a tally chart
- present data in a frequency table
- use grouped class sizes
- read and interpret frequency tables
- design, use and read two-way tables

Higher tier only

- understand how the grouping of data can affect how it is interpreted.

The exercise questions in this chapter are given individual target grades as a guide.

Visual overview

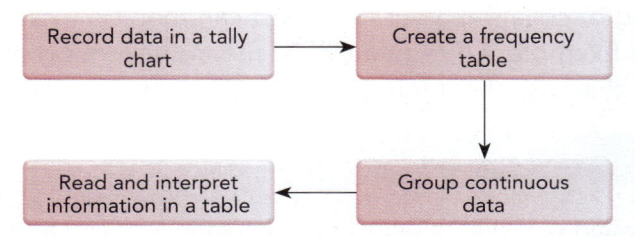

Record data in a tally chart → Create a frequency table → Group continuous data → Read and interpret information in a table

What you should already know

- **D** How to create a hypothesis (KS3, level 4).
- **D – A** How to sample (KS3, level 4–7).
- **C** How to design a questionnaire (KS3, level 5).

Quick check

1 Which of the following is the odd one out? Explain two possible answers.

Shoe size	Eye colour	Height	Number of siblings	Birth date

2 Design a question, with appropriate response boxes, to find out how much pocket money your friends get each week.

5.1 Tally charts and frequency tables

KEY WORDS
Continuous data
Discrete data
Frequency
Tally

This section will show you how to:
- create a tally chart to record data you are collecting
- create a tally chart from existing data
- turn these tally charts into frequency tables.

Putting data into tables helps in three ways: it looks better; it is easier to access; and it is easier to analyse.

Tables are good for helping to collect data and they are good for sorting it out once you've got it.

If you have one specific question, tally charts are good for helping to collect the data. For example, how many times a week do your classmates play sport?

Tables are also useful when doing an experiment. For example, if you are testing whether silver is the most popular car colour, you could do a tally to record the colours of cars in the car park.

If you've done a questionnaire to find out a variety of information, you can then use the **tally** charts to collate specific elements of it.

Whether collecting or collating, your tally chart can then be totalled up to create the 'frequency' column as seen in Example 1. **Frequency** just means how many and represents the total in that category. You can then use the information to make some initial observations about the data.

Example 1

Jessica wanted to find out what the most popular 'soap' was amongst her class mates. She created a tally chart to record her results as she went round asking each one for their opinion. Here are her results.

Soap	Tally	Frequency
Eastenders	⊪ III	8
Coronation Street	⊪ II	7
Emmerdale	III	3
Hollyoaks	⊪ IIII	9
Neighbours	II	2
Other	I	1

Once she'd asked everyone she totalled up the tallies and recorded the results in the frequency table.

a What is the most popular soap?
b How many people were asked?

Solution

a From this table you can see the most popular soap was Hollyoaks, because it has the highest frequency with nine people.

b If you add up the frequency column, you can work out the total number of people who were asked.

8 + 7 + 3 + 9 + 2 + 1 = 30

Jessica asked 30 people.

The type of data is important when designing the table. Frequency tables are only appropriate for **discrete** data, either qualitative (as in Example 1) or quantitative (as in Example 2). **Discrete data** is data that can be thought of as 'stepped' data, where there are specific (and valid) values and you cannot have in-between values. **Continuous data** can take any values in a given range, e.g. height. Qualitative data is non-numerical data, e.g. eye colour. Quantitative data is numerical data, e.g. number of rooms in a house.

Example 2

Tyler did a questionnaire to find out the amount and type of exercise his friends did each week.

One of the questions he asked was the following:

'On average, how many times a week do you play some kind of sport?

0   1   2   3   4   5 or more'

He collated the results and put them into a tally chart.

Number of times sport played	Tally	Frequency
0	IIII	4
1	IIII III	8
2	IIII IIII III	13
3	IIII	5
4	III	3
5 or more	I	1

a How many people did Tyler ask?
b Which is the most common response?

Solution

a By adding up the frequency column we can see that Tyler asked 34 people.
b The most common response is twice a week. This has the highest frequency, 13.

Tabulation: Chapter 5 Tabulation

Exercise 5A

1 Annabelle works in a ladies shoe shop and she needs to place an order for next season's stock. It is important that she orders the right quantity in each shoe size, so she looks at the sales over the last week to give her an idea. The sales are shown below.

3, 3, 3, 4, 4, 4, 4, 4, 4, 4, 5, 5, 5, 5, 5, 5, 5, 5, 5, 5, 5, 5, 6, 6, 6, 6, 6, 6, 6, 6, 6, 6, 6, 6, 6, 7, 7, 7, 7, 7, 7, 7, 7, 7, 8, 8, 8, 9

a Put the data into a tally chart.

b Complete the 'frequency' column.

c Which shoe size should she order the most of? Why?

d What was the total number of pair of shoes sold that week?

2 Tom watches Shurnhold United play their home matches over a season. He records the number of goals they score and the number of goals they concede in each game. He puts most of the information into frequency tables; however, there are some gaps.

No. scored	Tally	Frequency
0								
1		7
2												
3		3
4				

No. conceded	Tally	Frequency
0		8
1							
2									
3					
4		4

a Copy and complete the tables.

b How many more goals did they score than concede?

c 'Shurnhold United scored more goals than they conceded, which means they won more matches than they lost.' Is this hypothesis true or false?

3 The canteen at Chester High sells a new kind of drink and wants to record the sales over the first week to see how popular it is. The results are in the table below.

Day of the week	Tally	Frequency
Monday	||||| ||||| |||	
Tuesday	||||| ||||| |||||		
Wednesday	||||| ||||| ||||| |||||		
Thursday	||||| ||||| ||||| ||||| |||	
Friday	||||| ||||| ||||| ||||| ||	

a Copy and complete the table.

b On which day were the most number of cans sold?

c The total number of apple juices sold over the week was 96. Was the new drink more or less popular than apple juice?

d Why do you think the sales increased as the week went on?

4 An independent train company wanted to know what their passengers thought of the service. Passengers were asked whether they agreed with a series of statements. One of the statements was, 'The service was good value for money.' The response options and the number of people who responded in that section are listed below.

Strongly agree: 12   Agree: 30   Disagree: 31   Strongly disagree: 9

a Put the information into a tally chart and complete the frequency column.

b What was the most popular response?

c Looking at these results, what conclusion would you draw about the value for money with this particular train line?

5 A reception teacher asked her class how many brothers and sisters they had. The responses are listed below.

0, 1, 3, 4, 2, 2, 1, 0, 1, 1, 1, 2, 3, 5, 2, 3, 1, 0, 0, 1, 1, 2, 2, 2, 1, 1, 3, 4, 7

a Design and complete a tally chart to present this information. Include a frequency column.

b How many children had two brothers and sisters in total?

c How many children were in the class altogether?

d Design a tally chart that you could use to find out just how many brothers the class have. Try it out on your class.

5.2 Grouped frequency tables

KEY WORDS

Class width
Grouped frequency

This section will show you how to:
- group data as you put it into a table to help record information when there are lots of different values in the data set
- understand how changing the groups can affect the meaning and interpretation of the statistics.

So far in this chapter we have looked at discrete data where there are a small number of individual values. Sometimes, there can be a lot of different values and so it is impractical to write out every single value. In these situations, it makes more sense to group them together in a **grouped frequency** table (see Example 3). The table works in exactly the same way as the ones we have already used, except that a mark in the frequency column could represent one of a number of different values.

Tabulation: Chapter 5 Tabulation

Example 3

Andrew is the manager of a small firm and he wants to see out how intelligent his employees are. He decides to use their IQ as the measure of intelligence and so asks the 97 members of staff to do an online IQ test.

He decides to record the results in a grouped frequency table.

The smallest value recorded is 82 and the highest value is 138.

He decides the easiest way to group the information is in their 'tens' value, so all the 80s together, all the 90s together, etc.

IQ	Frequency
80–89	5
90–99	11
100–109	33
110–119	27
120–129	19
130–139	2

a If the average IQ score is 100, what can Andrew see from this table?

b How can he tell this?

Solution

a By presenting the data like this he is able see that the majority of his employees are on or above average.

b He can tell this because 33 + 27 + 19 + 2 = 81 of them have an IQ of 100 or more.

Wherever possible the groups should be evenly spread, with the same number of values in each group. However, in some circumstances this may not be possible because the values may not group evenly or the final group may be open-ended. The interpretation of the data can be significantly affected by the choice of group, especially when you move on to using the mean, median, mode and range to analyse the data. So grouping the data should be done carefully and deliberately, with appropriate choice of **class width**.

The second situation where it is appropriate to group data is when the data is continuous. In these situations a value can be anything in a given range. For example, when measuring the height (in cm), of a group of 25 people, no two people are exactly the same height. Example 4 shows such a case. Notice that the difference from Example 3 is the notation we use to describe the groups.

Example 4

Miss Hodges asked her class to estimate how long they thought a minute was. She asked them all to stand up, she started the clock, and then asked them to sit down when they thought a minute was over. The results for her class are in the table.

Time, t (seconds)	Frequency
$15 \leq t < 30$	1
$30 \leq t < 45$	6
$45 \leq t < 60$	17
$60 \leq t < 75$	4

Notice how she has grouped the values.

a What does $15 \leq t < 30$ mean?
b Why is it important to make sure that groups do not overlap?
c What was the most common estimate?
d Which group would Miss Hodges' estimate of 62 seconds fit into?

Solution

a $15 \leq t < 30$ means anyone who estimated 15, 16, 17 18, 19 ... all the way up to 29 seconds. Using the < sign means that 30 is not included; this is because it is included in the next range of values.

b No data value can be put in more than one group, so it is important to make sure the groups do not overlap.

c You can see that the majority of people estimated a minute was in the range $45 \leq t < 60$, because the frequency is the highest in this category (17).

d Her result is between 60 and 75, so it would go into the $60 \leq t < 75$ group.

Exercise 5B

1 Dan wanted to find out how much time his friends spent on a computer each week. He asked them to make a record of the number of hours they spent over one week. The results are listed below.

2, 3, 5, 5, 7, 10, 11, 11, 12, 12, 14, 14, 14, 14, 15, 15, 16, 16, 17, 18, 19, 20, 20, 20, 21, 22, 25, 28, 30, 35

a Copy and complete the table.

Number of hours	Frequency
0–6	
7–12	
13–18	
19–24	
25–30	
31–36	

b How many people were on the computer for 13–18 hours?
c How many people were on the computer for 12 hours or less?
d How many people were on for more than 24 hours.

Tabulation: Chapter 5 Tabulation

2 Jasmine measured the height of 25 people in cm. Her results are listed below.

145, 145.5, 150, 153, 154, 156.5, 157, 161.5, 163, 167, 167.5, 168, 170, 170.5, 171.5, 174, 178, 179, 179, 180, 181.5, 182, 183, 183.5, 184

a Copy and complete the grouped frequency table.

Height, h (cm)	Frequency
$145 \leq h < 155$	
$155 \leq h < 165$	
$165 \leq h < 175$	
$175 \leq h < 185$	

b How many people are 155 cm or taller?

c Which group would someone with a height of 165 cm go in?

3 Nigel needed to create an advert and decided to research how long adverts currently ran for on TV. He recorded the length of adverts over the course of an evening to the nearest second. The results are below.

5, 5, 7, 8, 10, 10, 11, 11, 11, 12, 13, 14, 14, 15, 15, 16, 17, 18, 19, 19, 20, 21, 22, 24, 24, 24, 24, 26, 27, 29, 29, 30, 31, 31, 32, 33, 34, 34

a Create a grouped frequency table to show this information.

b How many adverts did he record in total?

c If Nigel wants his advert to have the largest group, what time frame should he use for his advert?

4 A group of geographers was studying the amount of rainfall in Uganda over a number of years. The rainfall was recorded (in mm) over three years. The results are below.

88, 128, 185, 134, 71, 55, 87, 100, 119, 142, 85, 80, 72, 189, 120, 77, 54, 90, 101, 120, 140, 69, 60, 90, 90, 115, 130, 115, 65, 60, 90, 90, 120, 150, 90, 81

a Design and complete a grouped frequency table to present this data.

b Write two statements to describe the Ugandan rainfall.

5 Graham believes that the salary of his employees is evenly spread over the pay scale. He shows this using the grouped frequency table below.

Pay per year to the nearest thousand (£000s)	Frequency
11–20	8
21–30	7
31–40	9
41–50	6

The raw values (in thousands) are:

11, 12, 17, 17, 18, 19, 19, 20, 21, 21, 21, 22, 23, 26, 28, 31, 35, 36, 36, 37, 38, 39, 40, 40, 41, 41, 41, 42, 44, 50

a Present this data using class widths of five thousand.

b Does this support Graham's belief? Give a reason for your answer.

c Which table do you think is the more reliable?

5.3 Two-way tables

KEY WORDS
Two-way table

This section will show you how to:
- use two-way tables, which are a good way of presenting data where you want to look at more than one variable at a time
- read and create two-way tables.

Two-way tables show information in a clear and ordered way and allow you to interpret and process the information clearly. They also help you to work out appropriate values for a stratified sample.

Example 5

The two-way table below shows the number of boys and girls in each year group at Oaks High.

	Girls	Boys	Total
Year 7	126	154	280
Year 8	146	139	285
Year 9	132	121	253
Year 10	122	154	276
Year 11	144	132	276
Sixth Form	111	98	209
Total:	781	798	1579

a Which year group has the most girls?
b How many more boys than girls are there in the school?
c Which is the biggest year group?

Solution

a There are more girls in Year 8 than in any other year group, with 146 female students.
b There are 798 − 781 = 17 more boys than girls in the school.
c Which year group has most students?

Tabulation: Chapter 5 Tabulation

Exercise 5C

1. At Meadow School the number of students in each year group is broken down into girls and boys. Some of the results are missing.

	Girls	Boys	Total
Year 7	94	80	174
Year 8	89		190
Year 9	22		117
Year 10	100	92	
Year 11		102	201
Total:	404		

   a Copy and complete the table.
   b Which result looks out of place and why?
   c What is the total number of students in Year 10 and 11?

2. Jack decided that there were more left-handed men than there were left-handed women. He decided to ask everyone who walked past him in his local supermarket one morning. His results are shown in the two-way table below.

	Male	Female
Left-handed	8	11
Right-handed	45	81

   a Calculate the total number of men asked.
   b Calculate the total number of women asked.
   c What fraction of the people he asked were:
      i   Left-handed men?
      ii Left-handed women?
   d There were more left-handed women than there were men; this means Jack was wrong. Is this true or false? Give a reason for your answer.

3. Tom's football team were having a particularly good season. The results from the top five teams are recorded below.

		Home				Away					
	P	W	D	L	F	A	W	D	L	F	A	GD	Pts
Fallowfield	10	5	0	0	16	0	3	1	1	11	3	24	25
Chesterton United	11	5	1	0	15	5	1	4	0	9	8	11	23
Merryfield	11	4	0	2	15	6	2	2	1	7	5	11	20
Clover Town	11	3	1	1	7	5	3	1	2	8	5	5	20
Tapton Rangers	11	2	1	2	14	7	3	1	2	6	7	6	17

   a Which team had conceded the most goals while playing away?
   b Tom's team have won six games, drawn two and have scored 15 goals. Which is Tom's team?

4 A group of racing drivers wanted to improve their pit stop times. They looked at their time from their last race and split the pit stop session into 3 parts – entry into the pit lane, stationary time, and exit from the pit lane. Their results are in the table below.

	Entry (seconds, to 1 d.p.)	Stationary (seconds, to 1 d.p.)	Exit (seconds, to 1 d.p.)	Total (seconds, to 1 d.p.)
D. Wo	7.8	5.8	9.8	
G. Hinchliffe	7.9	6.9	10.1	
K. Patel	8.1	5.2	9.7	
H. Hulsenburge	8.3	5.5	10.4	
P. Terzaga	8.4	6.3	11.3	
S. King	8.6	6.2	11.3	

a The pit time is the total of all the three times.

  i Complete the total column of the table.

  ii Who was the fastest?

  iii Who was the slowest?

b Every driver wants to improve so they reach the pit in the least possible time.

  i Who had the quickest time at each stage?

  ii If one driver achieved all three of these times, what would the total pit time be?

  Each driver compares his times with the best in that section so they can see which area they need to improve first.

  iii Work out which area each driver needs to improve on.

5 This season's goal score records for the top five teams in a county football league are listed below.

Hulse City – Home: 17 goals for, 0 goals against. Away: 11 goals for, 5 goals against.

Liston Villa – Home: 15 goals for, 5 goals against. Away: 11 goals for, 10 goals against.

Starns Town – Home: 15 goals for, 6 goals against. Away: 9 goals for, 5 goals against.

Marrsfields FC – Home: 7 goals for, 5 goals against. Away: 8 goals for, 11 goals against.

Oldrige Athletic – Home: 10 goals for, 8 goals against. Away: 11 goals for, 11 goals against.

a Design and complete a two-way table to present this information.

b Which team has a total of:

  i 24 goals scored for?

  ii 11 goals scored against?

  iii 28 goals scored for?

c Which team has the:

  i largest difference between their goals scored for and their goals scored against?

  ii smallest difference between their goals scored for and their goals scored against?

d What does this tell you about their place in the table?

Activity 1

'Most people in my class have two siblings.'

Create a question to ask your class to test this hypothesis.

Design a tally chart to record the data.

Ask your class mates, fill in the table and complete the 'frequency' column.

1. How many people in your class have three or more siblings?
2. How many people have fewer than three siblings?
3. How many siblings do most people in your class have?
4. For your class, what conclusion would you draw about the hypothesis?

Activity 2

'I have a fair, unbiased six-sided dice.'

Create a tally chart to record the number thrown on a six-sided dice.

Throw your dice 30 times and record the number thrown each time in your tally chart.

Complete the frequency column.

1. How many times did you throw a multiple of 3?
2. How many times did you throw a square number?
3. Would you say your dice is a fair dice? Explain your answer.

GRADE BOOSTER

What you need to do to get this grade

G	You can design and record results in a tally chart.
	You can use and interpret a frequency table.
F	You can group data appropriately.
E	You can use two-way tables.
B	You can understand how grouping data can affect the way it is interpreted.

What you should now know

- How to create a tally chart to collect or record data.
- How to create a frequency table – both grouped and ungrouped.
- How to interpret frequency tables, including grouped frequency tables.
- How to design and read two-way tables.

Higher tier only

- How to understand how the grouping of data can affect how it is interpreted.

EXAMINATION Questions

1 Kapin recorded the number of items bought in his shop over the course of one Saturday morning. The tally of his results is shown in the table below.

Number of items	Tally	Frequency
1	IIII II	
2	IIII IIII IIII I	
3	IIII IIII IIII IIII II	
4	IIII IIII II	
5	IIII	
6	III	

a Complete the frequency column of the tables. *(2 marks)*

b How many people came into the shop in total? *(2 marks)*

c How many items were sold in total over the course of the morning? *(3 marks)*

2 An IT firm wanted to know how many times they were called out to each computer of a company they provided for. The results are listed in the table below.

Number of times	Frequency
0	5
1	6
2	8
3	8
4	9
5	10
6	12
7	15
8	11
9	8
10	6
11	1
12	2

a Copy and complete the grouped frequency table below. The first group has been done for you. *(3 marks)*

Number of times	Frequency
0–3	27
4–6	
7–9	
10–12	

b Give one advantage of using:

  i the original table

  ii the grouped frequency table. *(2 marks)*

3 Heaton Theme Park wanted to launch a 'Family Ticket'. They needed to find out what the most common combinations of adults and children coming together to the park were. One day during half term they recorded the numbers of adults and children who were admitted in groups under 10. The results are in the table below.

		\multicolumn{4}{c}{Number of adults}
		1	2	3	Total
Number of children	1	12	8	1	21
	2	21	15	2	38
	3	13	16	0	29
	4	5	2	2	9
	5	6	1	1	8
	6	1	2	0	3
	Total	58	44	6	

a Work out the total number of people admitted to the park. *(2 marks)*

b Lucy's family falls into a group with 12 other families. How many adults and children are there in her family? *(1 mark)*

c What is the largest number of people in one group? *(1 mark)*

d The park decides they are going to launch a 'family ticket' which covered groups with one or two adults and up to three children. How many people who visited on this day would have been able to use it? *(2 marks)*

Tabulation: Chapter 5 Examination questions

4 A doctor's surgery wanted to work out whether its waiting times were in line with other surgeries. It used the table below to help it decide.

Area	% under 10 minutes	% 10–20 minutes	% over 20 minutes	Number of patients
North Yorkshire	75	23	2	1258
North West	72	27	1	1354
West Midlands	65	30	5	1785
Eastern	45	49	6	1234
Trent	90	9	1	1985
South East	55	35	10	1548
South West	66	31	3	1112
London	21	62	17	2101
Wales	89	9	2	2231
Scotland	81	10	9	1983

a What was the % waiting for under 10 minutes in the West Midlands? *(1 mark)*

b Which area had the shortest waiting times? Give a reason for your answer. *(2 marks)*

c What was the total number of patients seen over the week? *(2 marks)*

d Roundtree Surgery is in the South West. It currently has 65% of its patients waiting for under 10 minutes and 5% waiting for over 20. How does this compare with the average for the area? *(2 marks)*

WORKED EXAMINATION Questions

1 A garden centre received a delivery of young trees. The height of the trees they sell needs to be within a given range. The grouped frequency table below shows the heights of all the trees in the delivery.

Tree height (h) (cm)	Frequency
$150 \leq h < 160$	16
$160 \leq h < 170$	22
$170 \leq h < 180$	14
$180 \leq h < 190$	8
$200 \leq h < 210$	7
$220 \leq h < 230$	2
$230 \leq h < 240$	1

a How many trees were delivered in total? *(1 mark)*

To work out the total number of trees in the delivery you need to add up all the numbers in the frequency column:

$16 + 22 + 14 + 8 + 7 + 2 + 1 = 70$

Answer: 70

b Any tree 2 metres or more cannot be sold and must be returned. How many trees does this apply to? *(2 marks)*

2 metres = 200 cm, so all the trees in the last 3 categories must be taken off.

$7 + 2 + 1 = 10$

Answer: 10

c The trees sell best when they are 165 cm–180 cm tall. Suggest an alternative way of grouping the data to show how many trees would be in this category more clearly. *(3 marks)*

One category would need to be $165 \leq h < 180$.

To show those trees that are 2 m or more, it is necessary to use unequal groups.

Answer:

Tree height in cm
$150 \leq h < 165$
$165 \leq h < 180$
$180 \leq h < 200$
$200 \leq h < 240$

6 Diagrammatic representation

Without the use of diagrams and charts to display it, data simply becomes a list of meaningless numbers. Diagrams bring the data to life and make it easy to interpret. You will see data presented this way in advertisements on TV and in magazines. Being able to draw and interpret graphs will help you in many other subjects, including Geography, History, Science and Business studies.

The bar graph shown below details the increase of mobile phone usage from 1987 to the present day. This is a typical graph that you might see used in the media.

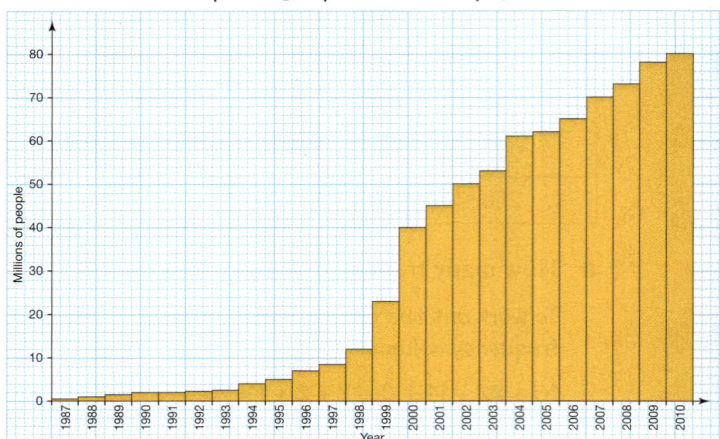

First ever graphs

The illustration on the right dates from the tenth century and is thought to be the first ever graphical representation. It shows how the planets' orbits change over time. You can just make out the words 'Mercury', 'Saturn' and 'Mars'. Note the use of the hand-drawn grid – they didn't have graph paper a thousand years ago!

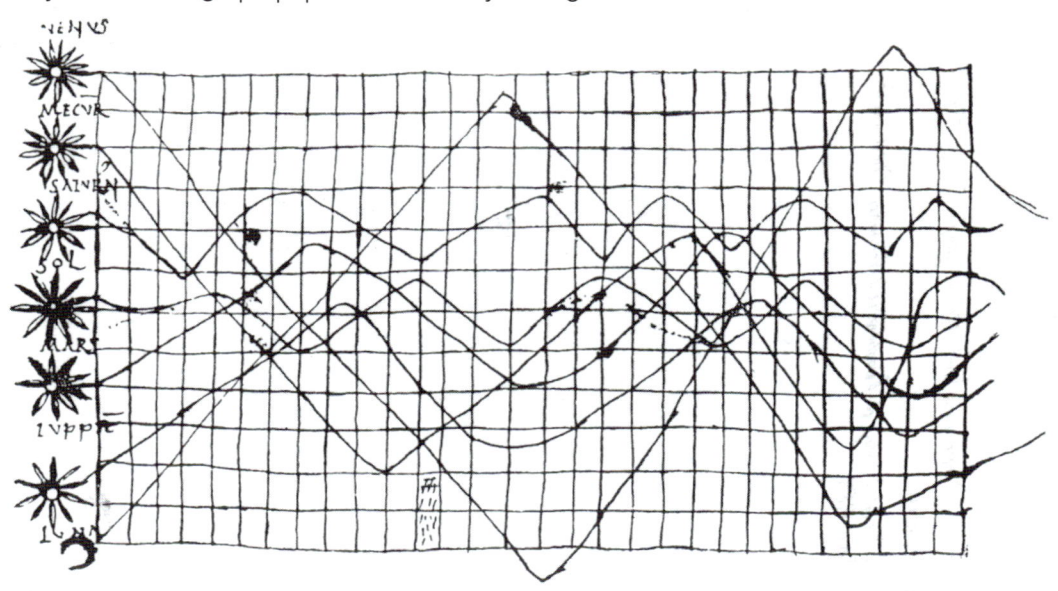

6.1 Pictograms, line graphs and bar charts

6.2 Pie charts

6.3 Misleading graphs

6.4 Choropleth maps

6.5 Stem-and-leaf diagrams

6.6 Histograms and frequency polygons

6.7 Cumulative frequency graphs

This chapter will show you how to:
- draw and interpret graphs for discrete data including pictograms, line graphs, histograms with equal class widths, bar charts, pie charts and cumulative frequency curves
- recognise a misleading graph
- draw and interpret choropleth maps

Higher tier only

- draw and interpret graphs for continuous data, including histograms with unequal class widths, frequency polygons and cumulative frequency curves
- draw and interpret cumulative frequency step polygons
- draw and interpret comparative pie charts.

The exercise questions in this chapter are given individual target grades as a guide.

Visual overview

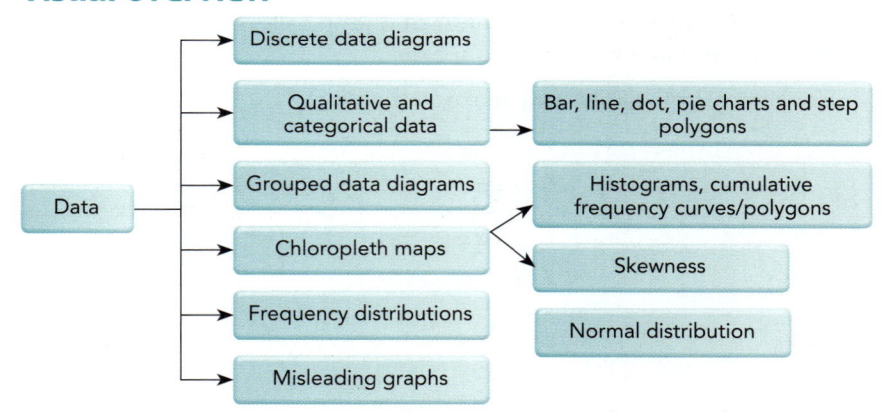

Data → Discrete data diagrams
Data → Qualitative and categorical data → Bar, line, dot, pie charts and step polygons
Data → Grouped data diagrams → Histograms, cumulative frequency curves/polygons
Data → Chloropleth maps → Skewness
Data → Frequency distributions → Normal distribution
Data → Misleading graphs

What you should already know

F How to use a tally for recording data (KS3, level 4).

F How to read information from charts and tables (KS3, level 4).

Quick check

The list below shows the sizes of shoes sold by a high-street shop over a one-week period.

7	11	6	2	6	4	10	5	12	5
2	12	6	7	7	4	12	7	10	7
2	2	11	6	12	8	10	12	9	6
11	7	6	11	12	4	6	12	9	5
2	8	4	8	8	3	2	5	5	

1 Construct a tally chart to show how many different sizes were sold in the week.
2 Which was the most popular size?

97

6.1 Pictograms, bar charts and line graphs

This section will show you how to:
- show collected data as pictograms
- draw bar charts to represent statistical data
- draw a line graph to show trends in data.

KEY WORDS
Axis
Bar chart
Bar line graph
Class interval
Dot plot
Dual bar chart
Key
Line graph
Pictogram
Population pyramid
Symbol
Trend
Vertical line graph

Data collected from a survey can be presented in pictorial or diagrammatic form to help people to understand it more quickly. You see plenty of examples of this in newspapers and magazines and on TV, where every type of visual aid is used to communicate statistical information.

Pictograms

A **pictogram** is a frequency table in which frequency is represented by a repeated **symbol**. The symbol itself usually represents a number of items, as Example 2 shows. However, sometimes it is more sensible to let a symbol represent just a single unit, as in Example 1. The **key** tells you how many items are represented by a symbol.

Example 1

The pictogram shows the number of phone calls made by Mandy from her mobile phone during a week.

How many calls did Mandy make in the week?

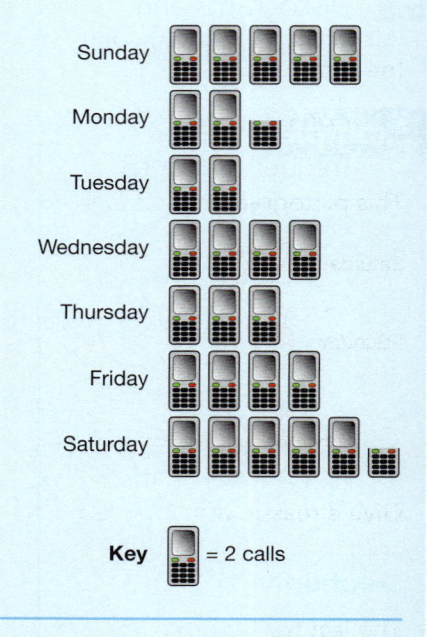

Sunday
Monday
Tuesday
Wednesday
Thursday
Friday
Saturday

Key 📱 = 2 calls

Solution
From the pictogram, you can see that Mandy made a total of 52 calls.

Although pictograms can have great visual impact (particularly as used in advertising) and are easy to understand, they have a serious drawback. Apart from a half, fractions of a symbol cannot usually be drawn accurately and so frequencies are often represented only approximately by symbols.

Examples 2 and 3 highlight this difficulty.

Example 2

The pictogram shows the number of Year 10 students who were late for school during a week.

How many students were late on:

a Monday?
b Thursday?

Monday 🚶🚶🚶🚶
Tuesday 🚶🚶
Wednesday 🚶🚶🚶
Thursday 🚶🚶🚶
Friday 🚶🚶🚶🚶🚶

Key 🚶 = 5 students

Solution

The key shows that each stick figure represents five students. If you assume that each 'limb' of each symbol represents one student, and its 'body' also represents one student, then the answers are:

a 19 students were late on Monday
b 13 were late on Thursday.

It is difficult to read the last symbol on Thursday, as the 'body' and the lower 'limb' could be seen as the same line.

Example 3

This pictogram is used to show how many trains ran late in the course of one weekend.

Saturday 🚂
Sunday 🚂🚂🚂🚂

Key 🚂 represents 4

Give a reason why the pictogram is difficult to read.

Solution

The last train symbol on Sunday is drawn as a fraction of 4. However, we cannot easily make out what this fraction is specifically.

Diagrammatic representation: Chapter 6 Diagrammatic representation

Bar charts

A **bar chart** consists of a series of bars or blocks of the same width, drawn either vertically or horizontally from an **axis**.

The heights or lengths of the bars always represent *frequencies*.

The bars are always separated by narrow gaps of equal width, to make the chart easier to read.

Example 4

The grouped frequency table below shows the marks of 24 students in a test.
Draw a bar chart for the data.

Marks	1–10	11–20	21–30	31–40	41–50
Frequency	2	3	5	8	6

Solution

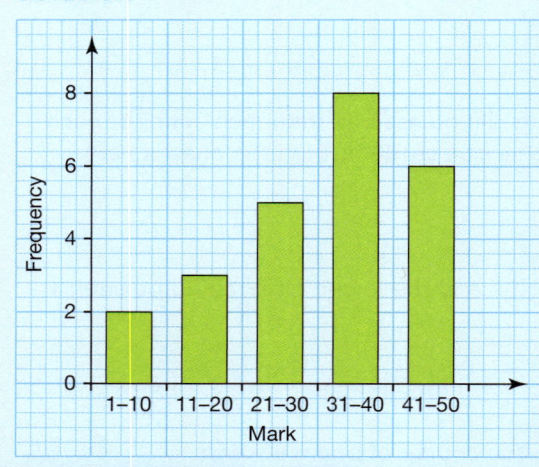

Note

- Both axes are labelled.
- The class intervals are written under the middle of each bar.
- The bars are separated by equal spaces.

You can use a dual bar chart to compare two sets of related data, as the next example shows.

Example 5

This **dual bar chart** shows the average daily maximum temperatures for England and Turkey over a five-month period.

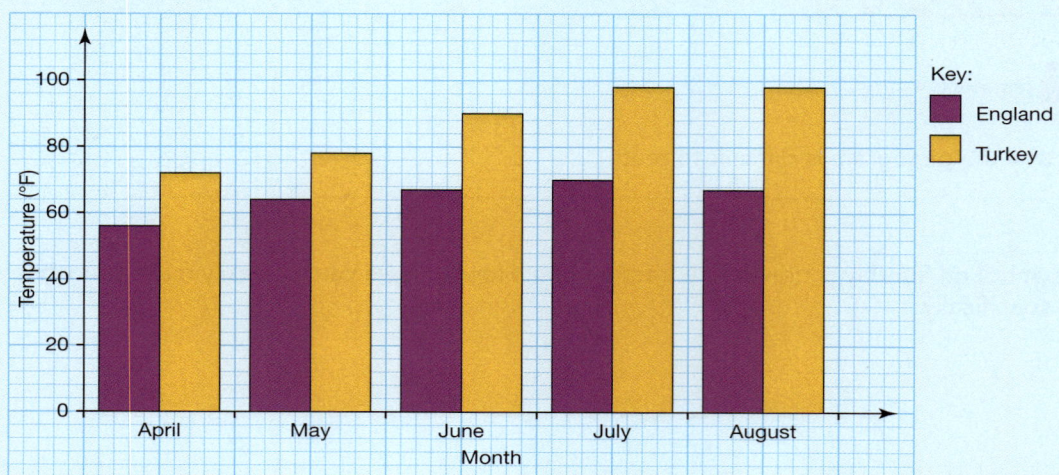

Key:
England
Turkey

In which month was the difference between temperatures in England and Turkey the greatest?

Solution

The largest difference can be seen in August.

> **Note**
> You must always include a key to identify the two different sets of data.

Line graphs

Line graphs are usually used in statistics to show how data changes over a period of time. One such use is to indicate **trends**, for example, whether the Earth's temperature is increasing as the concentration of carbon dioxide builds up in the atmosphere, or whether a firm's profit margin is falling year-on-year.

Line graphs are best drawn on graph paper.

Example 6

This line graph shows the outside temperature at a weather station, taken at hourly intervals. Estimate the temperature at 3.30 pm.

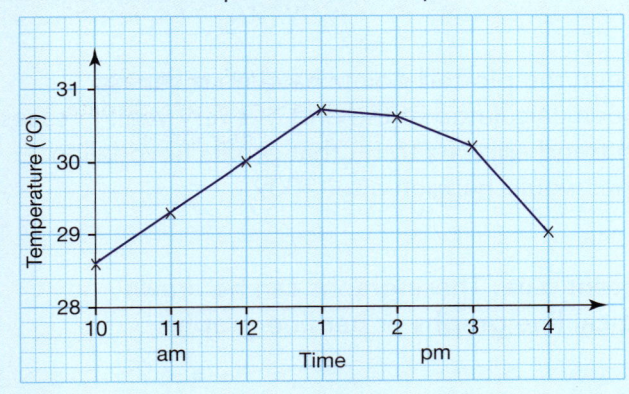

Solution

At 3.30 pm the temperature is approximately 29.6 °C.

> **Note**
> The temperature axis in the last example starts at 28 °C rather than 0 °C. This allows the use of a scale that makes it easy to plot the points and then to read the graph. The points are joined with lines so that the intermediate temperatures can be estimated for other times of the day.

Diagrammatic representation: Chapter 6 Diagrammatic representation

Example 7

This line graph shows a company's yearly profit over a six-year period. Between which years did the company have the greatest increase in profits?

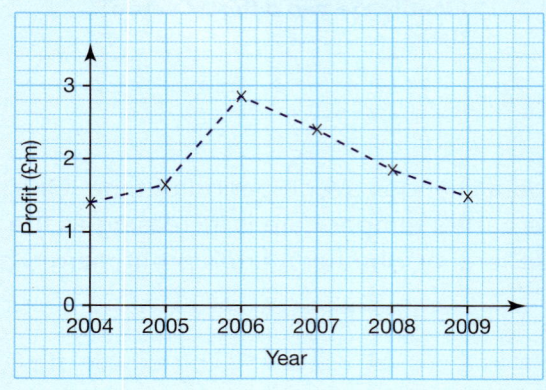

Solution

The graph shows that profits rose from £1.6m in 2005 to £2.8m in 2006. This was when the company had the greatest increase in profits.

In the graph in the last example, the values between the plotted points have no meaning because the profit of the company would have been calculated at the end of every year. In cases like this, the lines are often dashed. Although the trend appears to be that profits have fallen after 2006, it would not be sensible to predict what would happen after 2009.

Vertical or bar line graphs

You can use vertical lines instead of bars to represent data. These graphs can be drawn horizontally or vertically. These are known as **vertical line graphs** or **bar line graphs**.

Example 8

The graph shows the number of tries scored by Laugharne first XV rugby team during the first 12 matches of the season.

a How many times did the team score two tries?

b What does the frequency represent?

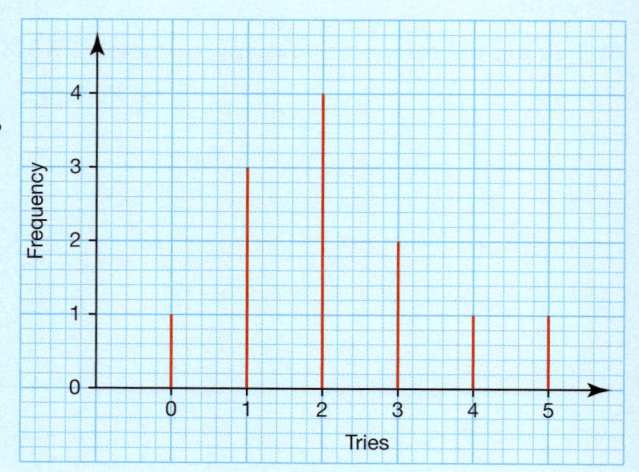

Solution

a The graph shows that the team scored two tries on four occasions.

b The frequency represents the number of games played.

Other types of graph

Some graphs are more suitable for small data sets and discrete data.

A dot plot shows each item of numerical data above a number line or horizontal axis.

Dot plots make it easy to see gaps and clusters in a data set, as well as how the data spreads along the axis.

Composite bar charts

Composite bar charts display several pieces of information from a single source in one bar. Each piece is layered on top of the previous one and shaded in different colours. This makes it easy to compare several pieces of information from similar sources. The vertical axis is often scaled out of 100%. This type of graph also requires a key.

Example 9

The table below shows the marks achieved in six tests taken by two brothers.

a Draw a composite bar chart to display this information.

b Draw another composite bar graph showing each subject score as a percentage of the total scores

Subject	John	Robert
English	50	64
Maths	64	78
Biology	72	43
Physics	38	67
Chemistry	71	57
Geography	52	62

Diagrammatic representation: Chapter 6 Diagrammatic representation

Solution

a

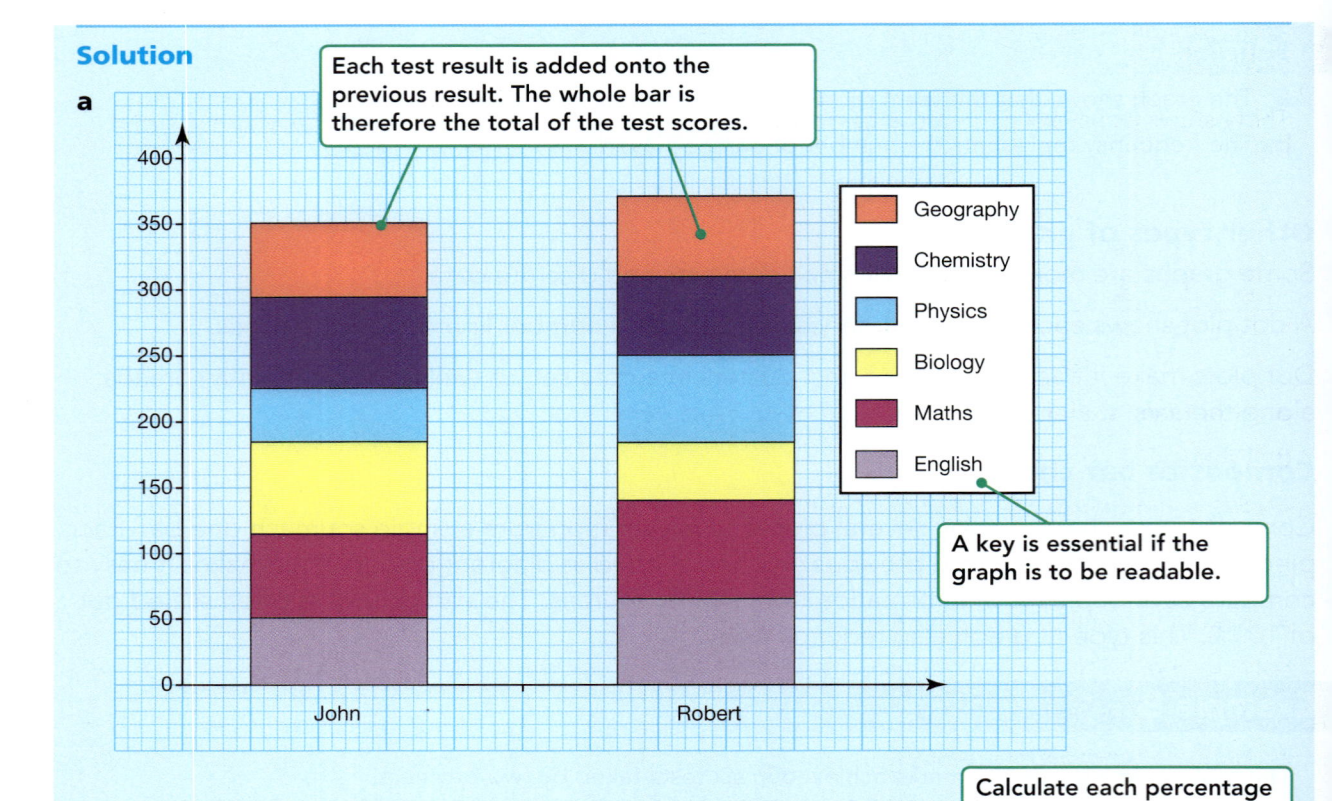

Each test result is added onto the previous result. The whole bar is therefore the total of the test scores.

A key is essential if the graph is to be readable.

Key: Geography, Chemistry, Physics, Biology, Maths, English

b First calculate the subject marks as a percentage of the total marks.

Calculate each percentage as shown.

Subject	John	%	Robert	%
English	50	$\frac{50}{347} \times 100 = 14$	64	$\frac{60}{371} \times 100 = 16$
Maths	64	18	78	21
Biology	72	21	43	12
Physics	38	11	67	18
Chemistry	71	20	57	15
Geography	52	15	62	17
Total	347	100	371	100

The blocks should now come to 100%.

Example 10

Thirty students have their heart rates measured. The data is represented in the form of the dot plot below.

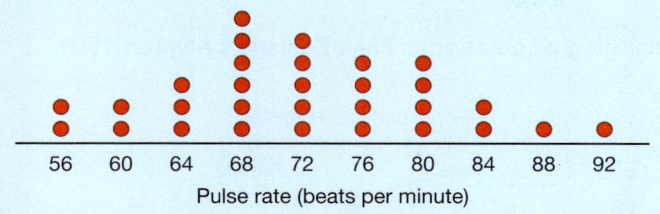

a How many students had a heart rate of 72 beats per minute (bpm)?
b What is the range of the data?
c Suggest a reason why a student has a heart rate of 92..

Solution

a Reading from the graph, five students had a heart rate of 72 bpm.
b The range of the data is the difference between the greatest and least values.
   Range = 92 − 56 = 36
c Here are two possible reasons.
   The student has been exercising, for example, having run to class or just finished a PE lesson.
   The student could have a naturally high heart rate.

Diagrammatic representation: Chapter 6 Diagrammatic representation

Population pyramids are used to compare percentages of populations by age and gender. They look like back-to-back horizontal bar graphs.

Example 11

The two population pyramids below show the changing population in New Zealand between 1901 and 2001.

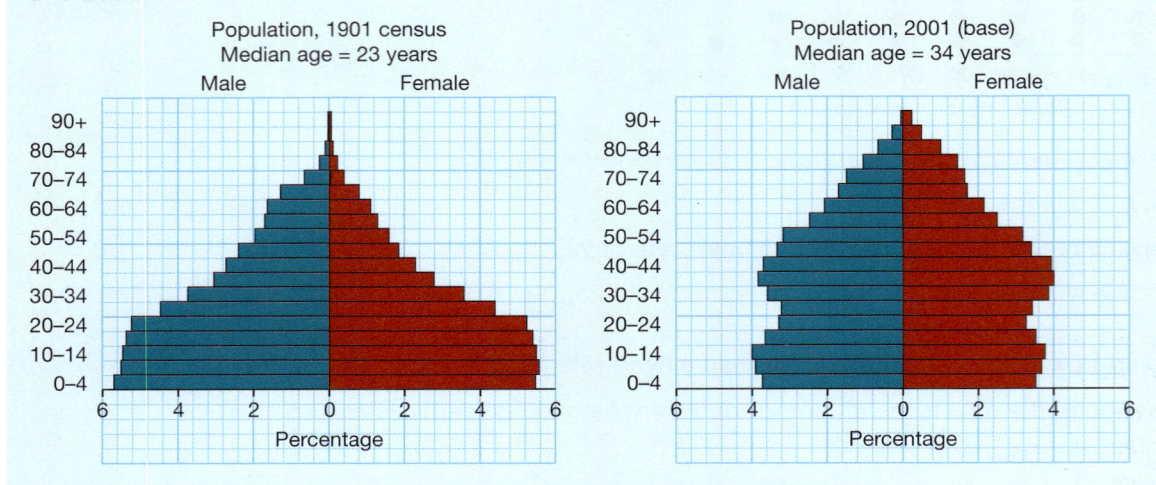

Population, 1901 census
Median age = 23 years

Population, 2001 (base)
Median age = 34 years

a What percentage of males made up the 60–64 age group in 1901?
b What percentage of females made up the 40–44 age group in 2001?
c Comment on how the population has changed.

Solution

a On the 1901 graph, males are represented by the blue bars on the left. The blue bar for the 60–64 age group represents 1.6%.

b On the 2001 graph, females are represented by the red bars on the right. The red bar for the 40–44 age group represents 4%.

c The population has become more balanced, with fewer children under 4 and more people over 40 showing a lower birth rate and longer life expectancy. The 1901 population is that of a developing country.

Exercise 6A

1 The frequency table shows the numbers of cars parked in a supermarket's car park at various times of the day. Draw a pictogram to illustrate the data. Use a key of 1 symbol to represent 5 cars. **AO3**

Time	9 am	11 am	1 pm	3 pm	5 pm
Frequency	40	50	70	65	45

2 Mr Weeks, a milkman, kept a record of how many pints of milk he delivered to 10 flats on a particular morning. Draw a pictogram for the data. Use a key of 1 symbol to represent 1 pint. **AO3**

Flat 1	Flat 2	Flat 3	Flat 4	Flat 5	Flat 6	Flat 7	Flat 8	Flat 9	Flat 10
2	3	1	2	4	3	2	1	5	1

3 The pictogram, taken from a Suntours brochure, shows the average daily hours of sunshine for five months in Tenerife.

May ☀☀☀☀⯒
June ☀☀☀☀☀⯒
July ☀☀☀☀☀☀
August ☀☀☀☀☀⯒
September ☀☀☀☀☀

Key ☀ represents 2 hours

a Write down the average daily hours of sunshine for each month.
b Which month had the most sunshine?
c Give a reason why pictograms are useful in holiday brochures.

4 The pictogram shows the amounts of money collected by six students after they had completed a sponsored walk for charity.

Anthony £££££
Ben ££££££
Emma £££££
Leanne ££££
Reena ££££££
Simon £££££££

Key £ represents £5

a Who raised the most money?
b How much money was raised altogether by the six students?
c Robert also took part in the walk and raised £32. Why would it be difficult to include him on the pictogram?

5 A newspaper showed the following pictogram about one of its team member's family and the number of emails they each received during one Sunday.

		Frequency
Dad	✉✉✉	
Mum	✉▷	
Teenage son	✉✉✉▷	
Teenage daughter		23
Young son		9

Key ✉ represents 4 emails

a How many emails were received by:
  i Dad?
  ii Mum?
  iii the teenage son?
b Copy and complete the pictogram.
c How many emails were received altogether?

Diagrammatic representation: Chapter 6 Diagrammatic representation

6 A survey was taken on the types of book read by students of a school.

Type	Frequency
Thriller	51
Romance	119
Science fiction	187
Historical	136

This data is to be put into a pictogram. Design a pictogram to show the information, using as few symbols as possible.

AO3

7 A pictogram is to be made from this frequency table, which shows the ways students travel to school.

Car	342
Bus	336
Walk	524

Explain why a key of four students to a symbol is not a good idea.

AO3

8 Draw pictograms to show the following data:

a the number of hours for which you watched TV every evening last week

b the magazines that students in your class read

c the favourite colours of students in your class.

AO3

9 For her survey on fitness, Maureen asked a sample of people, as they left a sports centre, which activity they had taken part in. She then drew a bar chart to show her data.

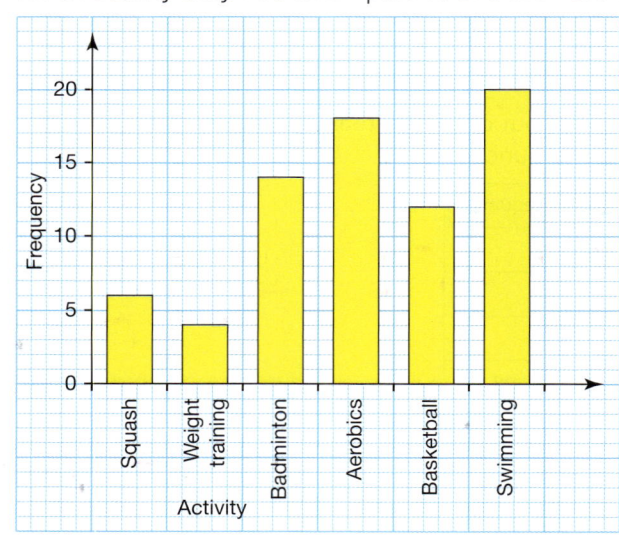

a Which was the most popular activity?

b How many people took part in Maureen's survey?

c Give a probable reason why fewer people took part in weight training than in any other activity.

d Is a sports centre a good place in which to do a survey on fitness? Explain why.

10 The frequency table below shows the grades achieved by 100 Year 10 students in their mock GCSE examinations.

AO3

Grade	F	E	D	C	B	A
Frequency	12	22	24	25	15	2

a Draw a suitable bar chart to illustrate the data.

b What fraction of the students achieved a grade C or grade B?

c Give one advantage of drawing a bar chart rather than a pictogram for this data.

11 This table shows the numbers of points Richard and Derek were each awarded in eight rounds of a general knowledge quiz.

AO3

Round	1	2	3	4	5	6	7	8
Richard	7	8	7	6	8	6	9	4
Derek	6	7	6	9	6	8	5	6

a Draw a dual bar chart to illustrate the data.

b Comment on how well each of them did in the quiz.

12 Kay did a survey on the time it took students in her form to get to school on a particular morning. She wrote down their times to the nearest minute.

AO3

15	23	36	45	8	20	34	15	27	49
10	60	5	48	30	18	21	2	12	56
49	33	17	44	50	35	46	24	11	34

a Draw a grouped frequency table for Kay's data, using class intervals 1–10, 11–20, …

b Draw a bar chart to illustrate the data.

c What conclusions can Kay draw from the bar chart?

13 This table shows the number of accidents at a dangerous crossroads over a six-year period.

AO3

Year	2000	2001	2002	2003	2004	2005
Number of accidents	6	8	7	9	6	4

a Draw a pictogram for the data.

b Draw a bar chart for the data.

c Which diagram would you use if you were going to write to your local council to suggest that traffic lights should be installed at the crossroads? Explain why.

14 The dual bar graph below shows the minimum and maximum temperature readings, in degrees Celsius, for one day in August in five cities.

AO4

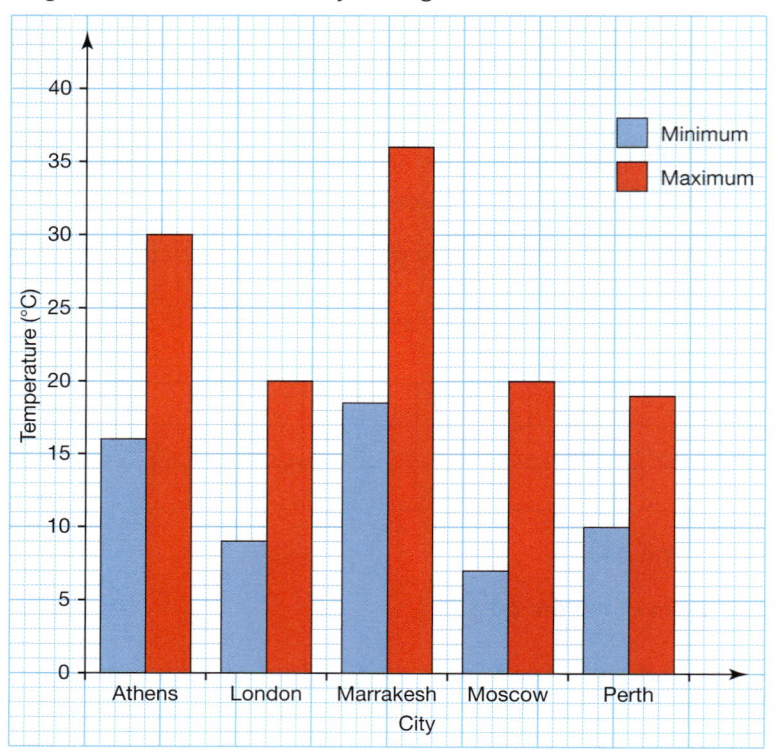

Farouk says that the minimum temperature reading is always about half the maximum temperature reading for most cities.

Is Farouk correct? Give reasons to justify your answer.

15 The dual bar graph shows the average daily temperature readings, in degrees Celsius, in England and Scotland.

AO4

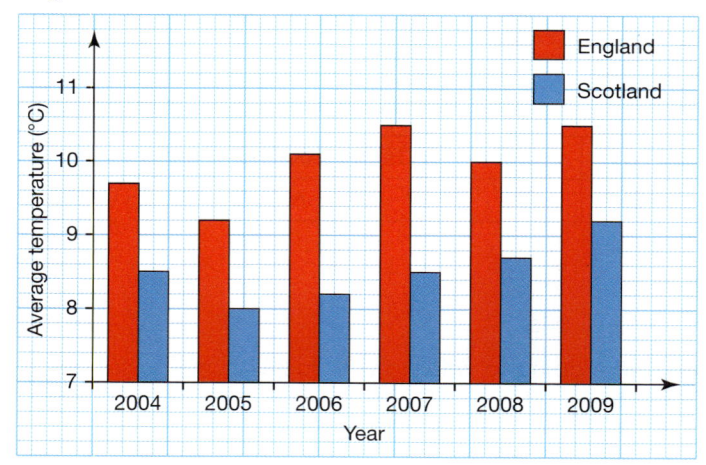

Derek says that the graph shows that the temperature reading in England is always more than double the temperature reading in Scotland.

Explain why Derek is wrong.

16 Conduct a survey to find the colours of cars that pass your school or your home.   **AO3**

   a Draw pictograms and bar charts to illustrate your data.

   b Compare your results with someone else's in your class and comment on any conclusions you can draw concerning the colours of cars in your area.

17 Choose a broadsheet newspaper, such as *The Times* or the *Guardian* and a tabloid newspaper, such as the *Sun* or the *Mirror*. Take a fairly long article from both papers, preferably on the same topic. Count the words in the first 50 sentences of each article.   **AO3**

   a For each article, draw a grouped frequency table for the number of words in each of the first 50 sentences.

   b Draw a dual bar chart for your data.

   c Do your results support the following hypothesis?

   'Sentences in broadsheet newspapers are longer than the sentences in tabloid newspapers.'

18 The vertical line graph shows the number of caterpillars Jade found on a sample of her marigold plants.   **AO3**

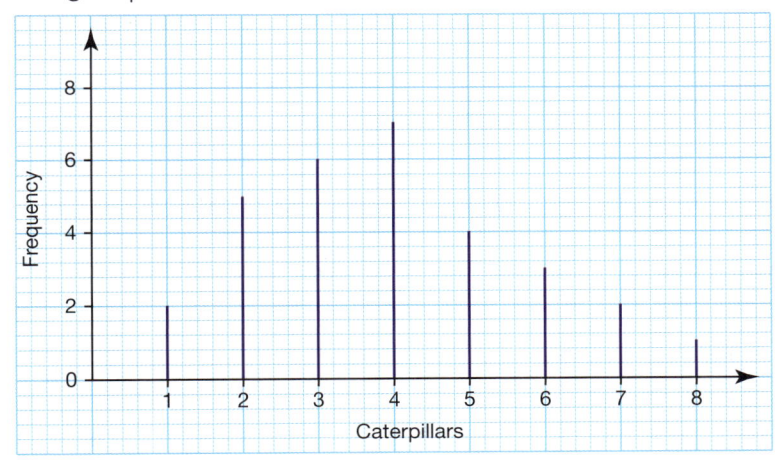

   a How many plants did Jade sample?

   b How many times did Jade find 5 caterpillars?

   c What is the range of the number of caterpillars found?

   d Represent this data as a dot plot.

19 The data below represents the shoe sizes of a class of 24 students.   **AO3**

4	10	7	7	9	4
10	6	8	7	7	9
4	10	10	7	6	9
4	9	8	8	8	7

Draw a dot plot to illustrate this data.

20 The dual bar graph shows the number of students absent from Year 10 in one week.

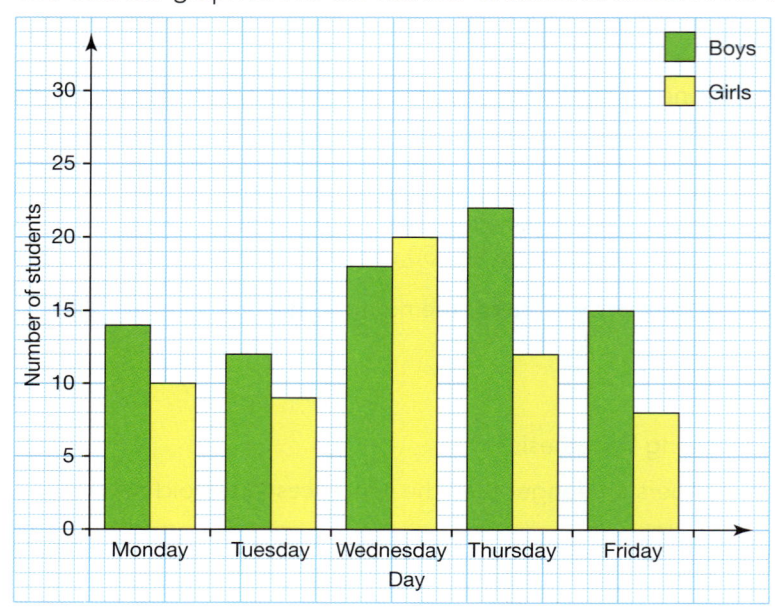

a How many boys were absent on Tuesday?

b How many girls were absent on Monday?

c How many students were absent on Friday?

d Compare how the numbers of absences change during the week, for both boys and girls.

21 This line graph shows the value of Spevadon shares on seven consecutive trading days.

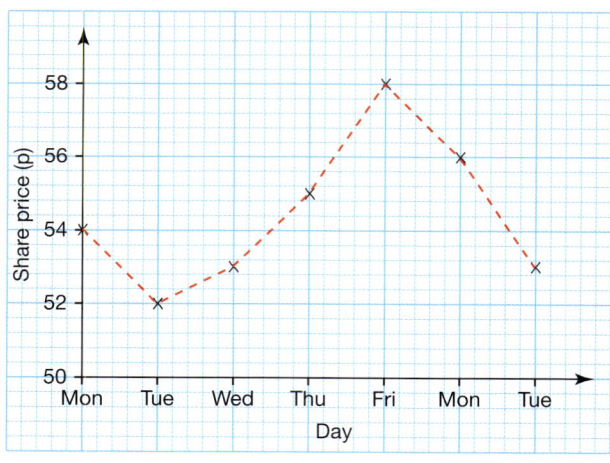

a On which day did the share price have its lowest value and what was that value?

b By how much did the share price rise from Wednesday to Thursday?

c Which day had the greatest rise in the share price from the previous day?

d Mr Hardy sold 500 shares on Friday. How much profit did he make if he originally bought the shares at 40p each?

22 The table shows the population of a town, rounded to the nearest thousand, after each census.

AO3

Year	1941	1951	1961	1971	1981	1991	2001
Population (000s)	12	14	15	18	21	25	23

  a Draw a line graph for the data.
  b From your graph, estimate the population in 1966.
  c Between which two consecutive censuses did the population increase the most?
  d Can you predict the population for 2011? Give a reason for your answer.

23 The ants in an ants' nest are counted at the end of each week.

AO3

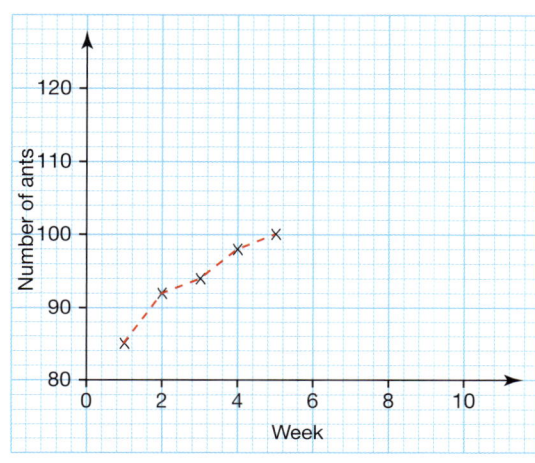

The graph shows the number of ants. At the end of week 5 the number is 100.

  a At the end of week 6 the number is 104. At the end of week 10 the number is 120.
    i Copy the graph and plot these points on the graph.
    ii Complete the graph with straight lines.
  b Use your graph to estimate the number of ants at the end of week 8.

24 The table shows the estimated number of tourists worldwide.

AO4

Year	1970	1975	1980	1985	1990	1995	2000	2005
Number of tourists (millions)	100	150	220	280	290	320	340	380

  a Draw a line graph for the data.
  b Use your graph to estimate the number of tourists in 2010.
  c Between which two consecutive years did tourism increase the most?
  d Explain the trend in tourism. What reasons can you give to explain this trend?

25 The table shows the maximum and minimum daily temperatures for London over a week.

AO3

Day	Sunday	Monday	Tuesday	Wednesday	Thursday	Friday	Saturday
Maximum (°C)	12	14	16	15	16	14	10
Minimum (°C)	4	5	7	8	7	4	3

  a Draw line graphs on the same axes to show the maximum and minimum temperatures.
  b Find the smallest and greatest differences between the maximum and minimum temperatures.

Diagrammatic representation: Chapter 6 Diagrammatic representation

26 A puppy is weighed at the end of each week, as shown in the table.

Week	1	2	3	4	5
Weight (g)	850	920	940	980	1000

Estimate how much the puppy would weigh after eight weeks.

AO3

27 When plotting a graph to show the summer midday temperatures in Spain, Abbass decided to start his graph at the temperature of 20 °C on the vertical axis.

Explain why he might have done that.

28 The table below shows the favourite colours of Year 8 students in a school.

Favourite colour	Boys	Girls
Blue	12	18
Green	16	30
Pink	32	23
Red	9	5
Black	7	18

a Draw a composite bar chart to illustrate this data

b Draw a percentage composite bar chart to illustrate this data.

29 The population pyramids below are for Kenya and the USA.

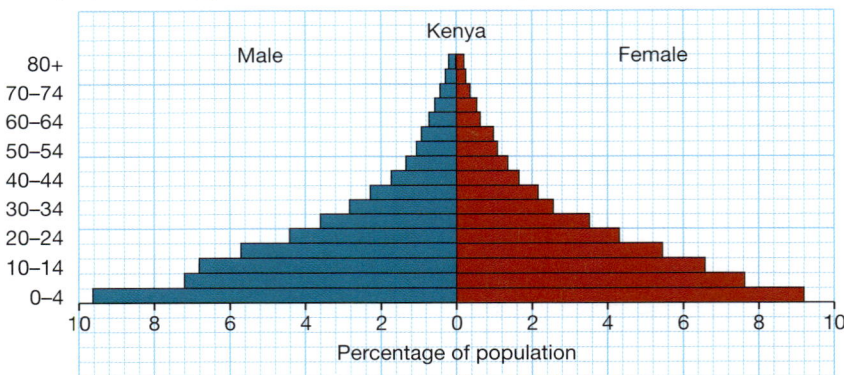

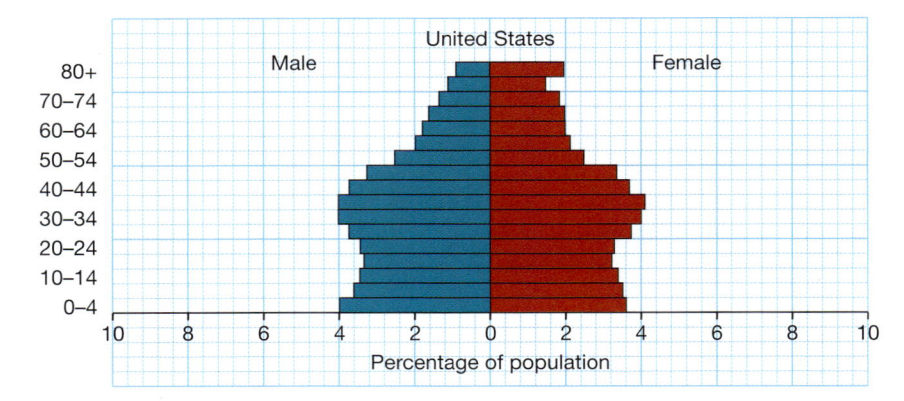

AO3

Kenya population pyramid showing Male and Female percentages by age groups from 0–4 to 80+, with axis from 10 to 10 Percentage of population.

United States population pyramid showing Male and Female percentages by age groups from 0–4 to 80+, with axis from 10 to 10 Percentage of population.

a Which age group accounts for the highest population in the USA?
b Which age group accounts for the highest population in Kenya?
c What does the USA pyramid tell you about the 80+ age group?
d Estimate the percentage of the Kenyan population that is under 10 years old.

30 The population pyramid shown is a projection of the population of Zambia for 2025.

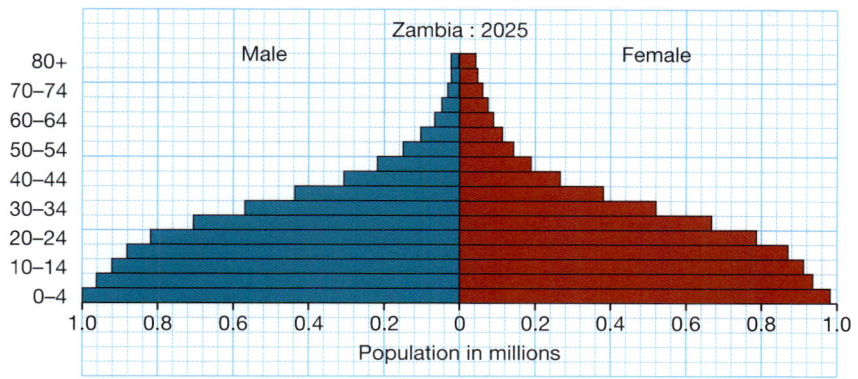

AO4

a How many millions of children are under 4?
b Which age group and gender is least represented on the pyramid?
c Why are there so few people over 50?

6.2 Pie charts

This section will show you how to:
- draw and interpret pie charts.

KEY WORDS

Angle
Comparative pie chart
Pie chart
Sector

Pictograms, bar charts and line graphs are easy to draw, but they can be difficult to interpret when there is a big difference between the frequencies or there are only a few categories. In these cases, it is often more convenient to illustrate the data on a **pie chart**.

In a pie chart, the whole of the data is represented by a circle (the 'pie'). Each category of the data is represented by a **sector** of the circle (a slice of the 'pie'). The **angle** of each sector is proportional to the frequency of the category it represents.

So, a pie chart cannot show individual frequencies, like a bar chart can, for example. It can only show proportions.

Sometimes the pie chart will be marked off in equal sections rather than angles. In these cases, the numbers are always easy to work with.

115

Diagrammatic representation: Chapter 6 Diagrammatic representation

Example 12

20 people were surveyed about their preferred drink. Their replies are shown in the table.

Drink	Tea	Coffee	Milk	Pop
Frequency	6	7	4	3

Show the results on the pie chart given.

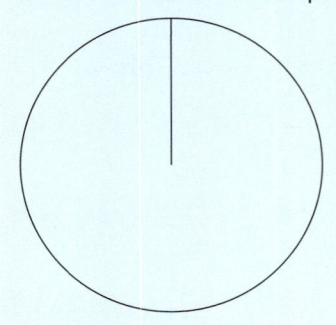

Note

In the examination you will be give a circle like this to complete.

Solution

You can see that the pie chart has 10 equally-spaced divisions.

As there are 20 people, each division is worth 2 people. So the sector for tea will have 3 of these divisions. In the same way, coffee will have $3\frac{1}{2}$ divisions, milk will have 2 divisions and pop will have $1\frac{1}{2}$ divisions.

The finished pie chart will look like this.

Preferred drinks

Note

You should always:
- label the sectors of the chart (use shading and a separate key if there is not enough space to write on the chart)
- give your chart a title.

Example 13

In a survey about holidays, 120 people were asked to state which type of transport they used on their last holiday. This table shows the results of the survey. Draw a pie chart to illustrate the data.

Type of transport	Train	Coach	Car	Ship	Plane
Frequency	24	12	59	11	14

Solution

You need to find the angle for the fraction of 360° that represents each type of transport. This is usually done in a table, as shown below.

Type of transport	Frequency	Calculation	Angle
Train	24	$\frac{24}{120} \times 360° = 72°$	72°
Coach	12	$\frac{12}{120} \times 360° = 36°$	36°
Car	59	$\frac{59}{120} \times 360° = 177°$	177°
Ship	11	$\frac{11}{120} \times 360° = 33°$	33°
Plane	14	$\frac{14}{120} \times 360° = 42°$	42°
Totals	120		360°

Draw the pie chart, using the calculated angle for each sector.

Types of transport

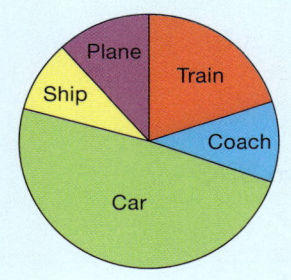

Note

- Use the frequency total (120 in this case) to calculate each fraction.
- Check that the sum of all the angles is 360°.
- Label each sector.
- The angles or frequencies do not have to be shown on the pie chart.

Diagrammatic representation: Chapter 6 Diagrammatic representation

Comparative pie charts are used to compare two sets of data. The areas of the circles must be *in proportion* to the two total frequencies.

Example 14

Mel builds two houses. She uses £40 000 of materials on the first house and £120 000 on the second. She represents this information on two pie charts. She uses a radius of 4 cm for the first house. What radius should she use for the second?

Solution

As areas of circles are in proportion:

$$\frac{\pi r^2}{\pi \times 4^2} = \frac{120\ 000}{40\ 000}$$

Cancel like terms and rearrange:

$$\frac{\cancel{\pi} r^2}{\cancel{\pi} \times 4^2} = \frac{120\ \cancel{000}}{40\ \cancel{000}}$$

$$r = \sqrt{\frac{12 \times 16}{4}}$$

$r = 6.9$ cm (to 1 d.p.)

Example 15

The two comparative pie charts shown below compare the total numbers of DVDs rented by a shop in 2007 and 2010.

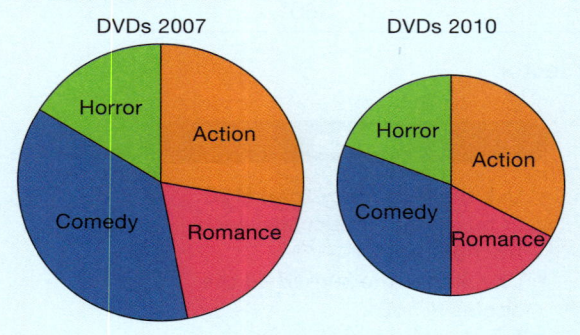

DVDs 2007 — Horror, Action, Comedy, Romance

DVDs 2010 — Horror, Action, Comedy, Romance

a What do the charts tell you about the total DVDs rented in 2007 compared to 2010?

b Give a reason for your answer to **a**.

Solution

a In a comparative pie chart the areas are proportional to the total frequency (in this case numbers of DVDs rented).

As the 2010 chart is smaller than the 2007 chart it means that fewer DVDs were rented in 2010.

b More people have started renting movies from the internet or watching them on TV service providers, hence shop rentals have declined.

Diagrammatic representation: Chapter 6 Diagrammatic representation

Exercise 6B

1 For each of the following sets of data, copy this basic pie chart and complete it.

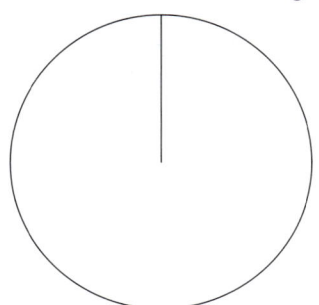

AO3

a The favourite pets of 10 children.

Pet	Dog	Cat	Rabbit
Frequency	4	5	1

b The makes of cars of 20 teachers.

Make of car	Ford	Toyota	Vauxhall	Nissan	Peugeot
Frequency	4	5	2	3	6

c The newspapers read by 40 office workers.

Newspaper	Sun	Mirror	Guardian	The Times
Frequency	14	8	6	12

2 Draw a pie chart to represent each of the following sets of data.

> **Hints and tips**
> Remember to complete a table as shown in the examples. Check that all angles add up to 360°.

AO3

a The numbers of children in 40 families.

Number of children	0	1	2	3	4
Frequency	4	10	14	9	3

b The favourite soap-opera of 60 students.

Programme	Home and Away	Neighbours	Coronation Street	Eastenders	Emmerdale
Frequency	15	18	10	13	4

c How 90 students get to school.

Journey to school	Walk	Car	Bus	Cycle
Frequency	42	13	25	10

Diagrammatic representation: Chapter 6 Diagrammatic representation

3 Mariam asked 24 of her friends which sport they preferred to play. Her data is shown in this frequency table.

Sport	Rugby	Football	Tennis	Squash	Basketball
Frequency	4	11	3	1	5

Illustrate her data on a pie chart.

4 Mandeep wrote down the number of lessons he had per week in each subject on his school timetable.

Mathematics 5   English 5   Science 8   Languages 6
Humanities 6   Arts 4   Games 2

 a How many lessons did Mandeep have on his timetable?

 b Draw a pie chart to show the data.

 c Draw a bar chart to show the data.

 d Which diagram better illustrates the data? Give a reason for your answer.

5 In the run-up to an election, 720 people were asked in a poll which political party they would vote for. The results are given in the table.

Conservative	248
Labour	264
Liberal Democrat	152
Green Party	56

 a Draw a pie chart to illustrate the data.

 b Why do you think pie charts are used to show this sort of information during elections?

6 This pie chart shows the proportions of the different shoe sizes worn by 144 students in Year 11 in a London school.

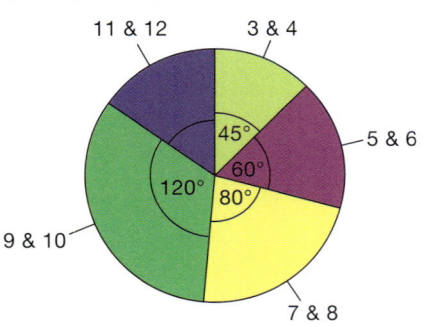

 a What is the angle of the sector representing shoe sizes 11 and 12?

 b How many students had a shoe size of 11 or 12?

 c What percentage of students wore the modal size?

Diagrammatic representation: Chapter 6 Diagrammatic representation

7 The table below shows the numbers of candidates, at each grade, taking music examinations in Strings and Brass.

AO3

	Grades					Total number of candidates
	3	4	5	6	7	
Strings	300	980	1050	600	70	3000
Brass	250	360	300	120	70	1100

a Draw a pie chart to represent each of the two examinations.

b Compare the pie charts to decide which group of candidates, Strings or Brass, did better overall. Give reasons to justify your answer.

8 In a survey, a rail company asked passengers whether their service had improved.

What is the probability that a person picked at random from this survey answered: 'Don't know'?

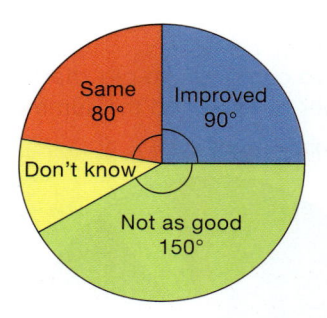

AO3

(Pie chart: Same 80°, Improved 90°, Don't know, Not as good 150°)

9 You have been asked to draw a pie chart representing the different ways in which students come to school one morning.

AO3

What data would you collect to do this?

10 Medi draws two comparative pie charts to illustrate her expenditure in December and January. She spends £3510 in December and the pie chart she draws has a radius of 3 cm. Her January pie chart has a radius of 5 cm. Calculate how much money she spends in January. **AO3**

11 A clothing company's profits increase from £205 000 in 2009 to £345 000 in 2010. Sue is asked to draw two comparative pie charts to illustrate this increase. If she chooses a radius of 5 cm for the 2010 graph, calculate the radius she should use for the 2009 graph. **AO3**

12 The table shows the average weekly household expenditure on various commodities in 1972 and 2005.

AO3

Item	Average weekly expenditure (£) in 1972	Average weekly expenditure (£) in 2005
Housing	37	120
Utilities	12	60
Food	32	75
Alcohol/tobacco	20	16
Clothing	22	49
Personal goods	22	78
Motoring	16	64
Leisure activities	25	95
Other	14	43
Total	200	600

Draw comparative pie charts to compare household expenditure in 1972 and 2005.

Use a radius of 4 cm for the 2005 chart.

Draw only the Housing, Utilities and Food sectors on your charts.

Diagrammatic representation: Chapter 6 Diagrammatic representation

A

13 This table shows the numbers of students studying languages in Years 10 and 11 at a comprehensive school.

AO3

Subject	Year 10	Year 11
French	28	50
German	16	37
Spanish	20	34
Total	64	121

Draw two comparative pie charts to illustrate the data.

Use a radius of 3 cm for Year 10.

14 The two comparative pie charts illustrate the rainfall in the nine English regions during the summer of 1976 and the summer of 2005.

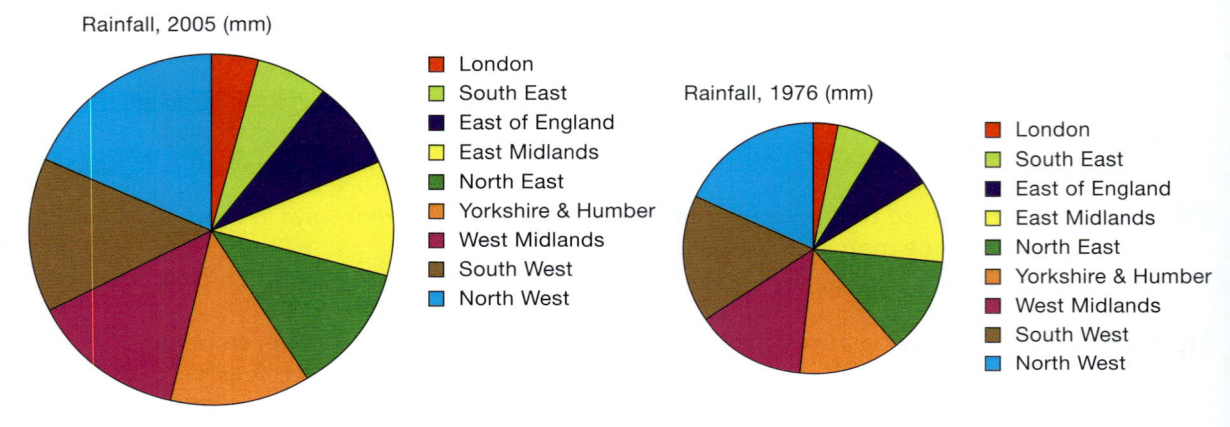

AO4

Rainfall, 2005 (mm)
- London
- South East
- East of England
- East Midlands
- North East
- Yorkshire & Humber
- West Midlands
- South West
- North West

Rainfall, 1976 (mm)
- London
- South East
- East of England
- East Midlands
- North East
- Yorkshire & Humber
- West Midlands
- South West
- North West

What do the two graphs tell you about the total rainfall during the two years?

6.3 Misleading graphs

This section will show you how to:
- identify and comment on graphs that misrepresent the data set from which they are drawn.

KEY WORDS

Misleading
Scale

Data is often misrepresented in the media, especially in advertisements. Graphs can sometimes deliberately show **misleading** data in order to gain the attention of the audience.

Diagrammatic representation: Chapter 6 Diagrammatic representation

Example 16

The graph below shows the results when 300 schoolchildren were surveyed about their favourite computer games.

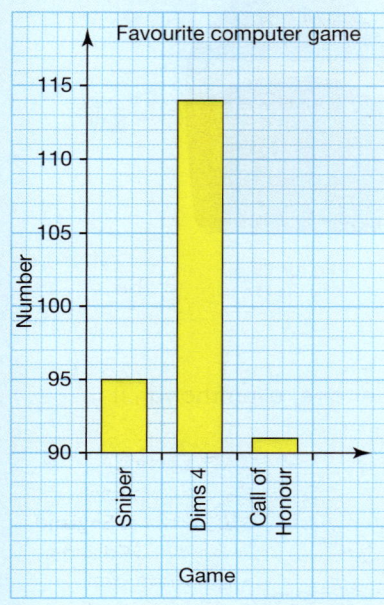

[Bar chart titled "Favourite computer game" with vertical axis "Number" starting at 90 going to 115, showing: Sniper ≈ 95, Dims 4 ≈ 114, Call of Honour ≈ 91. Horizontal axis labelled "Game".]

a Explain what is misleading about the graph.
b Redraw the graph to make it less misleading.

Solution

a The horizontal axis starts at 90 which makes it look as if the most popular game is Dims 4, by a high margin, and the least popular is Call of Honour, even though there is only a difference of 23.

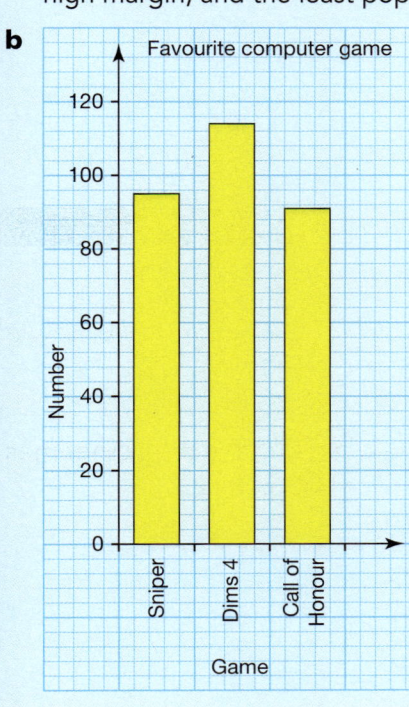

b

[Redrawn bar chart titled "Favourite computer game" with vertical axis "Number" from 0 to 120, showing: Sniper ≈ 95, Dims 4 ≈ 114, Call of Honour ≈ 91. Horizontal axis labelled "Game".]

123

Diagrammatic representation: Chapter 6 Diagrammatic representation

Example 17

a Explain why this advertisement for Kencup coffee might be misleading.

b Which jar is the better value?

750 g for £6.50   1 kg for £9.50

Solution

a The larger jar looks as if it is at least three times the size of the smaller one, even though it contains only 250 g more coffee.

b For the small jar, cost per gram = $\frac{650}{750}$ = 0.86p

For the large jar, cost per gram = $\frac{950}{1000}$ = 0.95p

The smaller of the two jars is the better value.

Example 18

The graph shows crime figures in Wales over a four-year period.

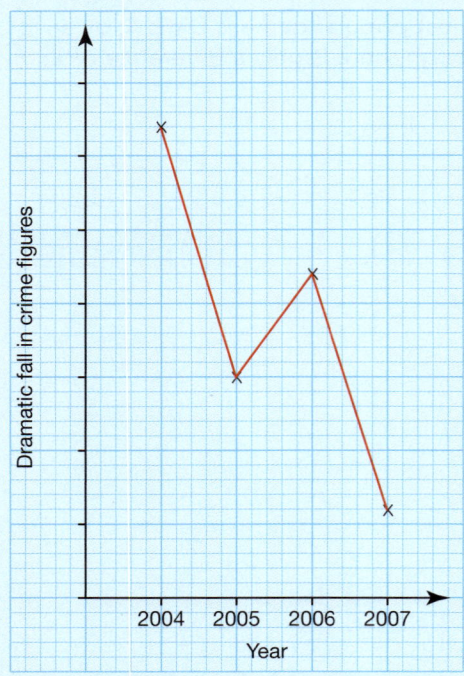

a Why is this graph misleading?

b What is wrong with the label 'Dramatic fall in crime figures'?

Solution

a There is no vertical **scale** so we don't know what the reduction in crime figures is.

b Without a scale we are unable to tell whether the fall is dramatic or not. The top of the vertical axis could be 10 000 and the bottom 9990, which is hardly a dramatic fall.

Exercise 6C

1 A children's charity produces an advert to show how much money they have raised over the last two years.

Toys 4 Tots

We have doubled our income since 2008 to 2009

2008   2009

Why is the advertisement misleading?

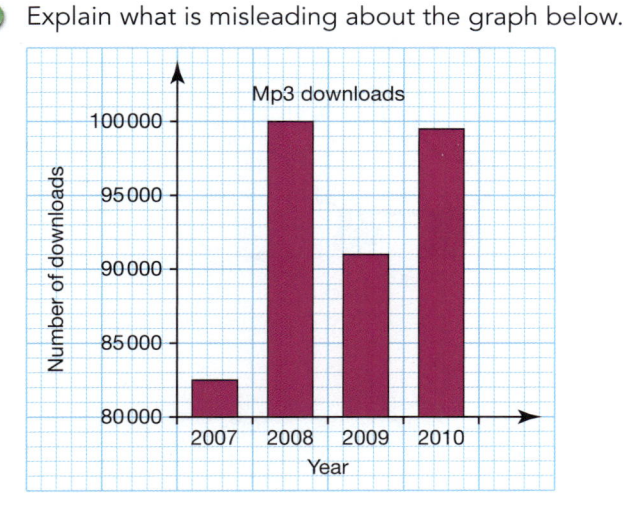

2 Explain what is misleading about the graph below.

3 The *Daily Fable* newspaper publishes the following graph to show the fall in household gas bills over a four-year period.

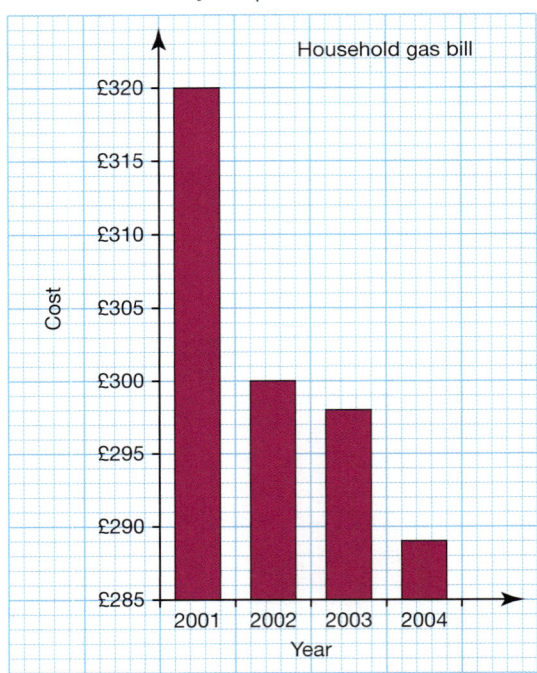

Why could the graph be misleading?

4 The graph below was produced to illustrate the enormous increase in New Zealand's sheep population during the 1990s.

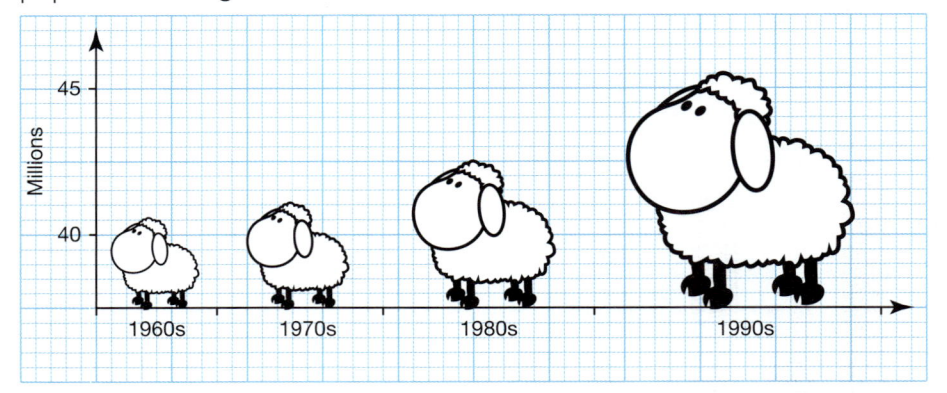

a State two ways in which this graph is misleading.

b Describe the change in the sheep population from the 1960s to the 1990s.

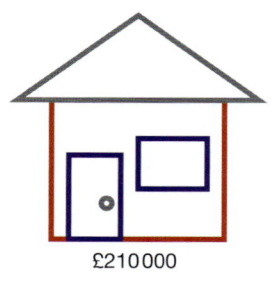

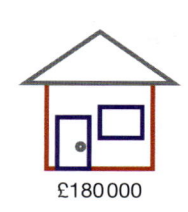

Diagrammatic representation: Chapter 6 Diagrammatic representation

5 The drawings below show the decrease in average house prices over the last two years. **AO4**

£210 000   £180 000

Explain what is misleading about the drawings.

6 A UK magazine wants to illustrate the huge increase in inflation over the past four years. **AO3**

Use the table below to draw a misleading graph to show this. It should have two misleading features.

Year	Average inflation
2007	1.9%
2008	2.1%
2009	2.3%
2010	2.5%

7 Give a reason why the graph shown below is misleading. **AO4**

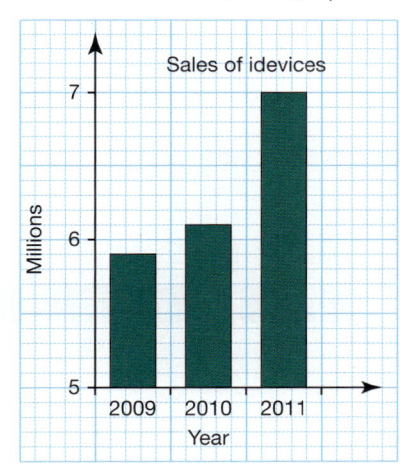

127

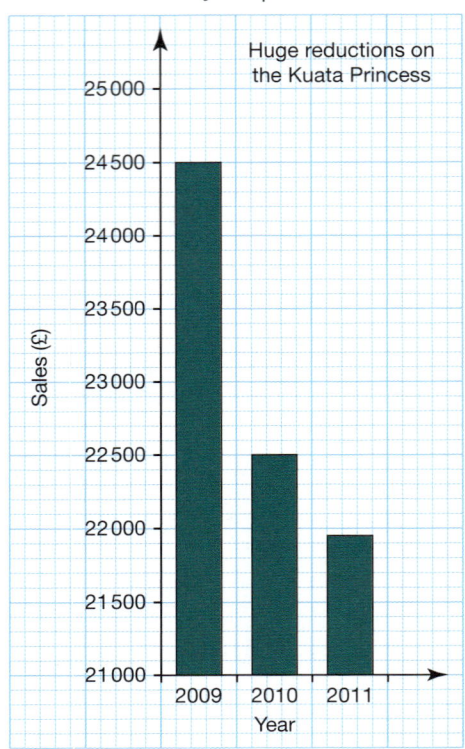

Diagrammatic representation: Chapter 6 Diagrammatic representation

8 A garage uses the graph below to show the 'massive drop' in the price of their best-selling car over a three-year period.

AO4

Explain why this graph is misleading.

6.4 Choropleth maps

This section will show you how to:
- recognise a choropleth map
- draw and interpret a choropleth map.

KEY WORDS

Choropleth map

Choropleth maps are maps in which areas are shaded differently, to illustrate a distribution. The coloured map of the UK used on TV programmes on election night, to show the political distribution, is a good example of this type of map. Choropleth maps are used in geography, for example, to show population distributions.

Diagrammatic representation: Chapter 6 Diagrammatic representation

The map below shows the population density of London. This is a typical example of a choropleth map, as used by the media. You can see from the map that central London has the greatest population density, with eight regions having more than 10 000 people per square kilometre (km^2).

Population density, 2008
(people per square km)

- 10 000 or over
- 7500–9999
- 5000–7499
- 2500–4999
- 2499 or under

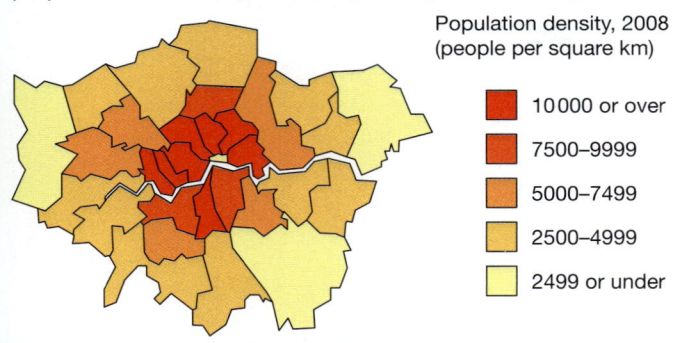

Example 19

The choropleth map shows the population density for Wales.

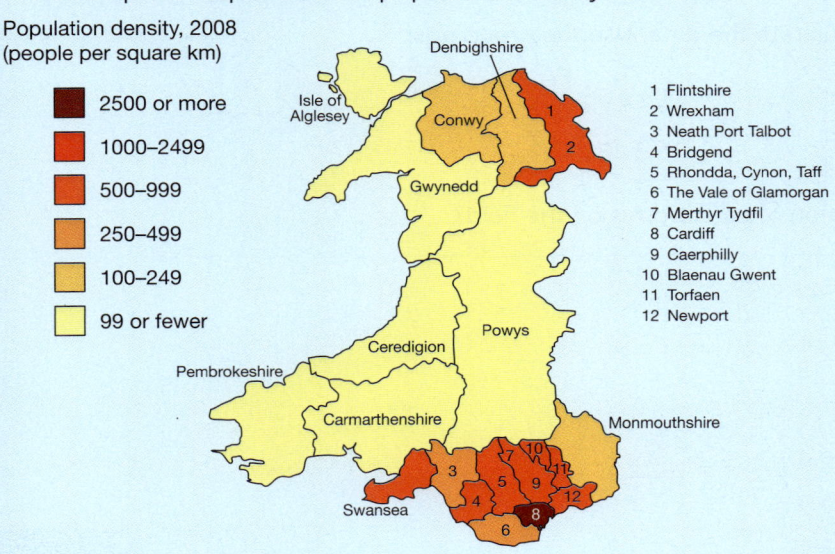

Population density, 2008
(people per square km)

- 2500 or more
- 1000–2499
- 500–999
- 250–499
- 100–249
- 99 or fewer

1 Flintshire
2 Wrexham
3 Neath Port Talbot
4 Bridgend
5 Rhondda, Cynon, Taff
6 The Vale of Glamorgan
7 Merthyr Tydfil
8 Cardiff
9 Caerphilly
10 Blaenau Gwent
11 Torfaen
12 Newport

a Which region has the highest population density?
b Give a reason for your answer to part **a**.
c What is the population density of Carmarthenshire?
d How could you improve the way the information is displayed on this map?

Solution
a Comparing the key with the colours on the map, Cardiff has the highest population density.
b The population density, at 2500 or more people per square kilometre, is shown as the darkest colour and is the highest number.
c Comparing the key with the colours on the map, Carmarthenshire has 99 or fewer people per square kilometre (km^2).
d There are six regions showing 99 or fewer people per square kilometre. It would be better to have more shades of orange to differentiate between these areas.

Diagrammatic representation: Chapter 6 Diagrammatic representation

Example 20

A class of biology students conduct a survey to find out the distribution of earthworms on the school field. They split the field up into 10 m squares. The results are shown below.

6	6	2	3
4	3	1	4
2	4	5	3
5	8	3	6
7	10	6	8
12	11	2	7
10	11	3	4

a Draw a choropleth map to illustrate the data. Use the groupings:

0 to 4

5 to 8

9 to 12

b Where is the highest distribution of earthworms on the field?

Solution

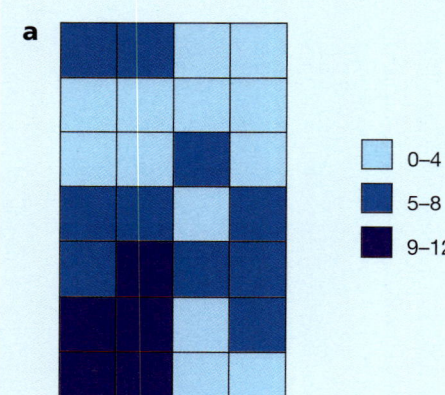

a

□ 0–4
■ 5–8
■ 9–12

b The highest concentration of earthworms appears in the bottom left-hand section of the field.

Exercise 6D

D

1 The map below shows the percentage of the English workforce at risk of losing their jobs, by area. **AO4**

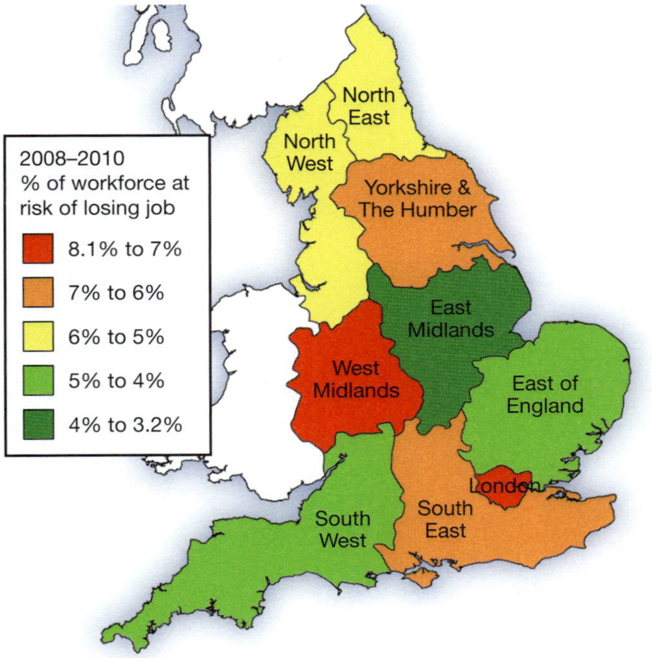
2008–2010
% of workforce at
risk of losing job
8.1% to 7%
7% to 6%
6% to 5%
5% to 4%
4% to 3.2%
North East
North West
Yorkshire & The Humber
East Midlands
West Midlands
East of England
London
South West
South East

a Name two places from the map where there is a 8.1% to 7% risk of job loss.

b Why are major cities at the centres of greatest risk?

c What is the risk of a person living in the North West of England losing their job?

Diagrammatic representation: Chapter 6 Diagrammatic representation

2 A forest is subdivided into square sections.
The number of trees in each square is shown.

A04

5	6	3	2
3	6	5	8
11	13	14	10
15	12	12	13
5	9	4	8
10	5	8	2

a Use the key to copy and complete this diagram, to produce a choropleth map to illustrate the data.

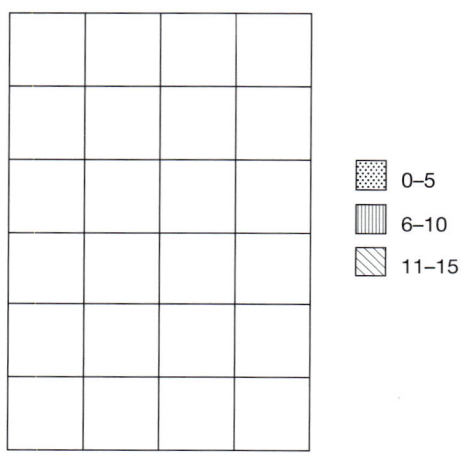

Key:
- 0–5
- 6–10
- 11–15

b Trees gather nutrients from water, allowing them to grow and flourish. A stream runs in a straight line through the forest. On your map, indicate its path with a straight line.

c Explain your answer to part **b**.

3 The table shows average rainfall in England during the month of January.

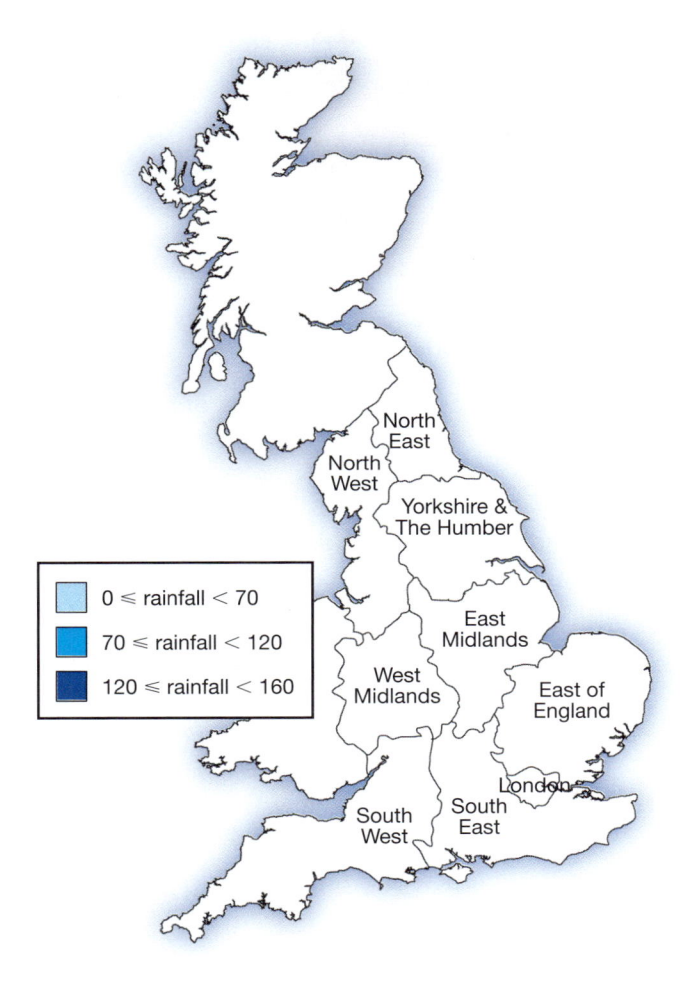

AO4

Region	Rainfall (mm)
London	26
South East	54
East of England	68
East Midlands	93
North East	110
Yorkshire and Humber	114
West Midlands	123
South West	142
North West	158

Key:
- 0 ≤ rainfall < 70
- 70 ≤ rainfall < 120
- 120 ≤ rainfall < 160

a Use the map and key to illustrate this data on a choropleth map.

b Which area of the country receives the most rainfall?

c Give a reason why you chose the area in part **b**.

Diagrammatic representation: Chapter 6 Diagrammatic representation

4 The diagram below is taken from an article about the risks of coronary heart disease. It was published in a journal of the Royal Statistical Society, in 2003.

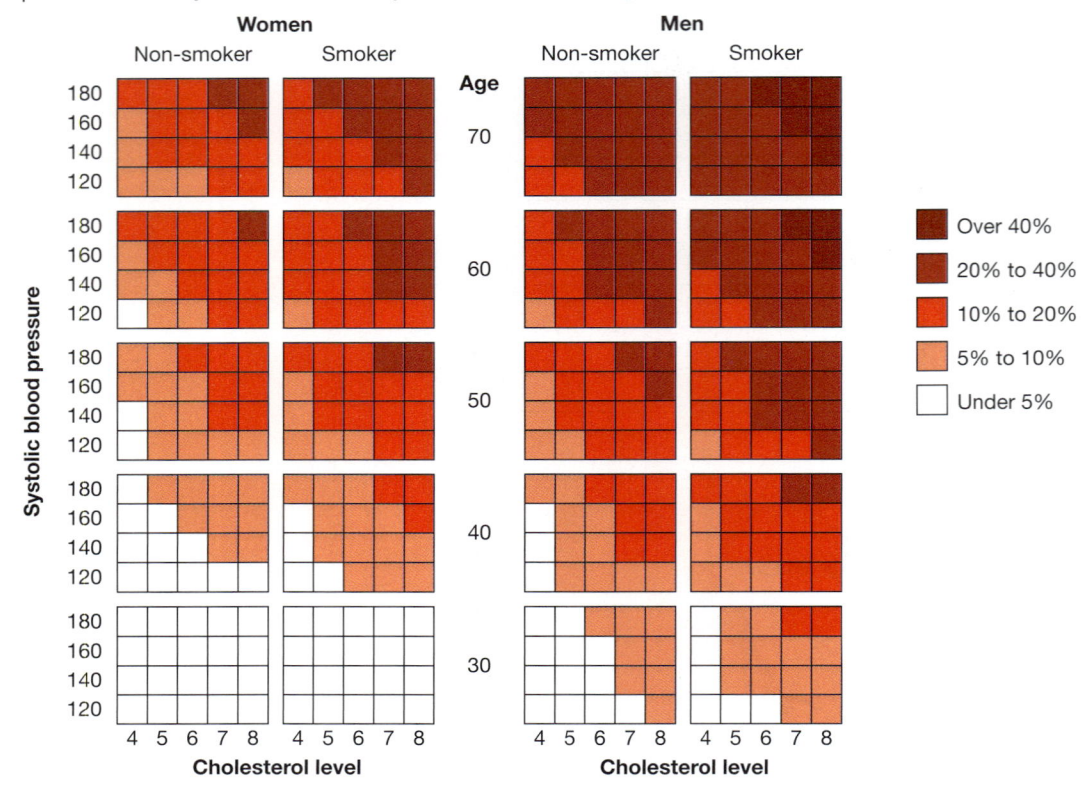

AO4

Legend:
- Over 40%
- 20% to 40%
- 10% to 20%
- 5% to 10%
- Under 5%

a What is the risk of a man aged 60, who smokes and has a cholesterol level of 8 and a blood pressure of 180, developing heart disease?

b What is the risk of a 30-year-old woman developing heart disease?

c List four factors that increase a person's risk of developing heart disease.

5 The map below shows the crime rates in England and Wales.

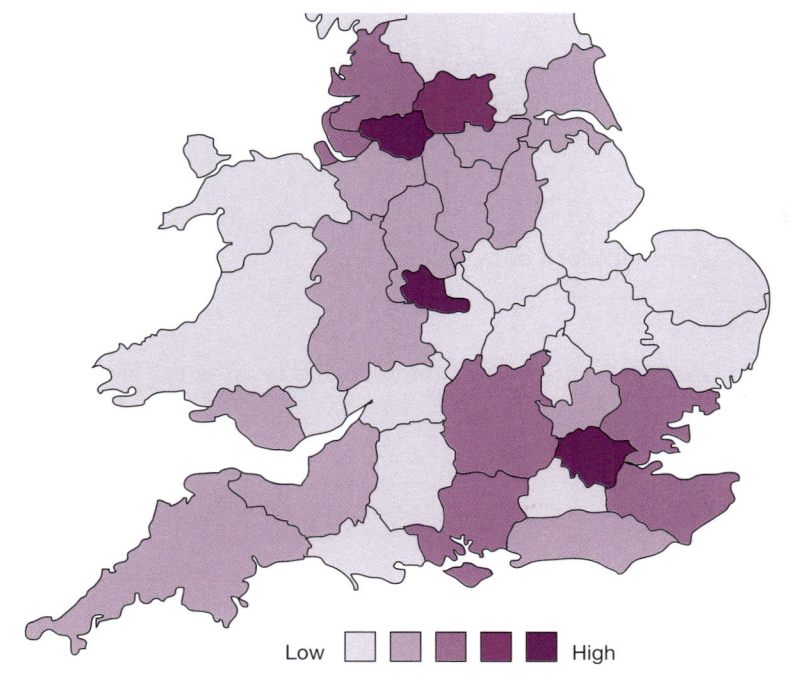

AO4

C

Low ▢ ▢ ▢ ▢ ▢ High

a What is the name of this type of shaded map?

b What do you think the three areas that show the highest crime rate on the map represent?

6.5 Stem-and-leaf diagrams

This section will show you how to:
- draw and interpret a stem-and-leaf diagram.

KEY WORDS
Key
Median
Ordered
Range
Stem-and-leaf

Stem-and-leaf diagrams are a simple way of displaying a set of data values. The distribution of the data looks very similar to a horizontal bar graph, with the lists of numbers forming the bars. These numbers may be left in the order they are given, but it is usual to rearrange them, to give an **ordered** stem-and-leaf diagram. The diagrams can be used to find measures such as the **range** and the **median** easily.

Diagrammatic representation: Chapter 6 Diagrammatic representation

Example 21

A nurse at a health centre measured the heights (to the nearest centimetre) of 21 men. She produced the list below.

172	153	166	171	147	151	152
189	153	153	148	155	158	167
189	159	165	164	166	178	188

Construct a stem-and-leaf diagram to represent these data values.

Solution

All of the heights have three digits, so take the first two (the hundreds and tens) as the stem. Then treat the units digits as leaves.

Without reordering:

Stem	Leaves
14	7 8
15	3 1 2 3 3 5 8 9
16	6 7 5 4 6
17	2 1 8
18	9 9 8

The stem contains the tens and the leaves are the units.

Usually, the leaf section is reordered to give the final plot.

After reordering:

Stem	Leaves
14	7 8
15	1 2 3 3 3 5 8 9
16	4 5 6 6 7
17	1 2 8
18	8 9 9

You must also show a key, to explain how to use the diagram.

Key 14 | 7 represents 147 cm.

Example 22

A farmer weighed 40 potatoes. The results, in grams, are shown below.

21	20	22	57	22	43	39	51
27	29	65	34	44	18	21	52
50	21	32	43	43	45	20	55
35	36	22	32	31	42	30	44
55	52	54	63	57	39	50	47

a Draw an ordered stem-and-leaf diagram to represent the data.

b Use your diagram to find:

  i the range

  ii the median mass.

Diagrammatic representation: Chapter 6 Diagrammatic representation

Solution

a From the table:

Stem	Leaves
1	8
2	1 0 2 2 7 9 1 1 0 2
3	9 4 2 5 6 2 1 0 9
4	3 4 3 3 5 2 4 7
5	7 1 2 0 5 5 2 4 7 0
6	5 3

After reordering:

Stem	Leaves
1	8
2	0 0 1 1 1 2 2 2 7 9
3	0 1 2 2 4 5 6 9 9
4	2 3 3 3 4 4 5 7
5	0 0 1 2 2 4 5 5 7 7
6	3 5

Key 1 | 8 means 18 grams

b i The range is (greatest − smallest) so is 65 − 18 = 47.

 ii The median value is the middle value of the ordered data.

As there are 40 values, this must be halfway between the 20th and 21st terms.

20th = 39

21st = 42

Median = $\frac{1}{2}$(39 + 42) = 40.5

Exercise 6E

1 A class of 25 students obtain the following marks in a French test.

   68   59   65   54   98
   43   62   64   81   62
   75   37   74   69   93
   92   72   38   46   57
   66   81   85   67   35

Draw a stem-and-leaf diagram to illustrate the data.

AO3

2 An athlete runs 21 100 m races in a season. His times are shown below.

   10.5   11.3   10.8   11.4   11.7   11.1   11.5
   10.9   11.1   11.6   11.5   12.1   11.9   10.6
   10.8   12.0   12.3   10.9   11.5   11.3   10.6

a Construct a stem-and-leaf diagram to illustrate the data.

b Find the range.

c Write down the median value.

AO3

Diagrammatic representation: Chapter 6 Diagrammatic representation

3 The ages of 30 people in a group are shown below.

Stem	Leaves
1	6 9
2	1 7 5 6
3	3 4 6 7 7 0 1 5 5 6
4	3 1 5 1 6 2 7 8
5	5 8 0 2
6	9 2

a Construct an ordered stem-and-leaf diagram.

b Write down a key.

c How old is the youngest person?

d How old is the oldest person?

e What is the range of the ages?

f Use your stem-and-leaf diagram to work out the median age.

4 The fuel consumptions of 15 cars, in miles per gallon, are shown below.

33	50	48	35	40
28	49	26	34	27
29	31	40	29	49

a Construct a stem-and-leaf diagram.

b Work out the range of the data.

c Find the median value.

5 The weights, in grams, of 27 strawberries are shown below.

5.1	5.8	6.3	7.2	4.8	5.7	8.3	4.2	5.9
6.8	6.5	6.3	7.5	7.2	7.8	4.3	8.1	8.4
8.0	5	5.1	7.3	6.8	3.9	9.0	5.9	5.7

Draw a stem-and-leaf diagram to illustrate this information.

6 The back-to-back stem-and-leaf diagram below shows the marks obtained by two different classes in a mathematics test.

```
            Class X    | Class Y
                  9 | 2 | 0 1
                6 4 | 3 | 3 4 6
              6 5 2 | 4 | 2 6 7 8 8 8 9
            7 4 4 3 | 5 | 3 4 7 7 8
      9 7 7 5 3 1 | 6 | 0 2 4 5
          7 6 6 5 4 | 7 | 3 6
            5 4 3 2 | 8 | 2 3
              4 3 2 | 9 | 1
```

Key   For Class X, 9 | 2 means 29 marks
          For Class Y, 2 | 0 means 20 marks

a What was the highest mark scored in Class Y?

b What was the highest mark scored in Class X?

c Write down the median value of each of the data sets.

d Comment on the results of both classes.

7 The amounts of time (to the nearest hour) that 25 boys and 25 girls spent playing computer games during a week are displayed below.

```
          Boys         |        Girls
  4  17  27   6   9    | 22   8   1  12  13
 27  33  34  24  26    |  3   2  11  15  20
 20  22  13  26  27    | 21  19   5  17  20
 19   8  35  29  33    |  2   1  12  12  24
  8  12  34  26  31    |  2  13  12   9  14
```

a Draw a back-to-back stem and leaf diagram.

b Calculate the range, median and modal value of each data set.

c Use your diagram and calculations to comment on the amount of time spent by both groups playing games.

Diagrammatic representation: Chapter 6 Diagrammatic representation

6.6 Histograms and frequency polygons

This section will show you how to:
- draw and interpret histograms and frequency polygons with both equal and unequal class intervals
- calculate frequency density.

KEY WORDS
Class width
Frequency density
Frequency diagram
Frequency polygon
Histogram
Modal class

Histograms are used to represent data from grouped frequency distributions. They look similar to bar graphs but there are no gaps between the bars. Histograms are represented in two formats: equal **class-width** intervals and unequal class-width intervals.

Frequency polygons are often used instead of histograms to compare two sets of data. Each point is plotted in the centre of the group and the points are joined up using a straight line.

Histograms with equal class-width intervals

Example 23

The frequency table shows the heights of trees in a small wood. Draw a histogram and a frequency polygon to illustrate the data.

'12–' means 'greater than or equal to 12 but less than 13'.

Height (m)	12–	13–	14–	15–	16–	17–18
Frequency	2	4	7	5	3	1

140

Solution

Histogram:

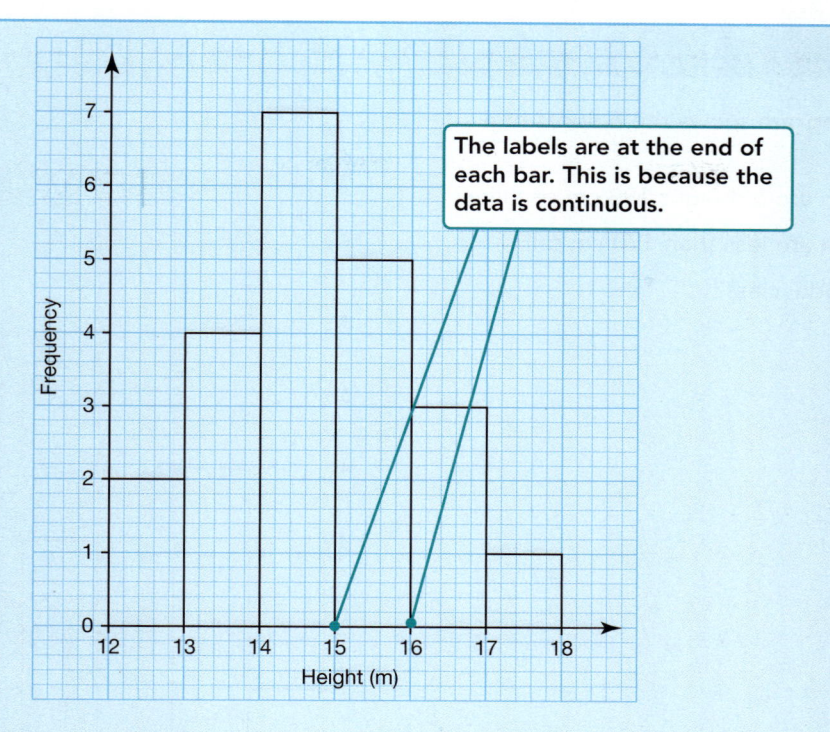

The labels are at the end of each bar. This is because the data is continuous.

Frequency polygon:

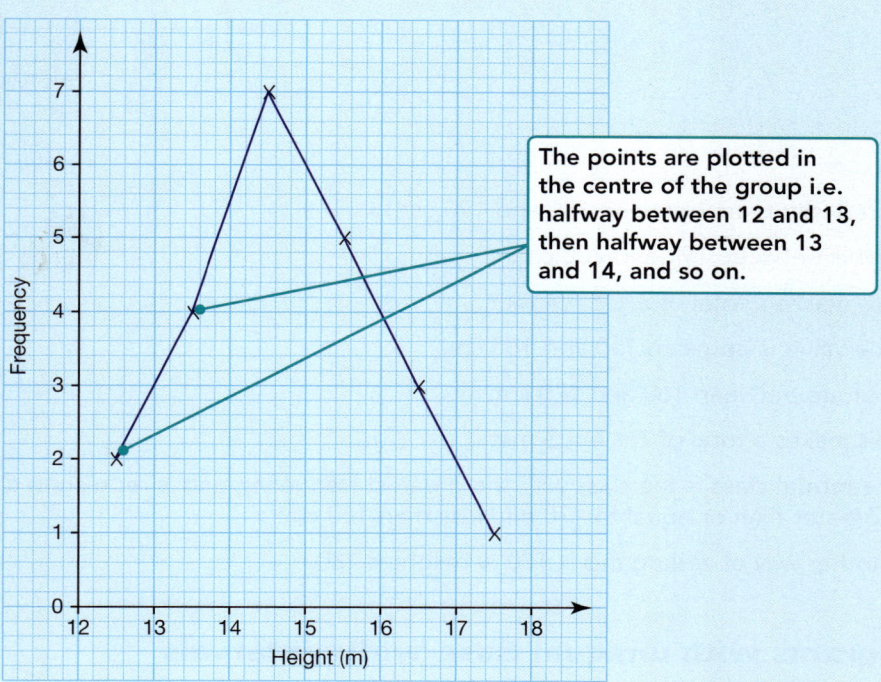

The points are plotted in the centre of the group i.e. halfway between 12 and 13, then halfway between 13 and 14, and so on.

Diagrammatic representation: Chapter 6 Diagrammatic representation

Example 24

The **frequency diagram** shows the heights of a group of men.

a How many men are of height 180 cm or taller?

b How many men are less than 170 cm tall?

c What is the modal class?

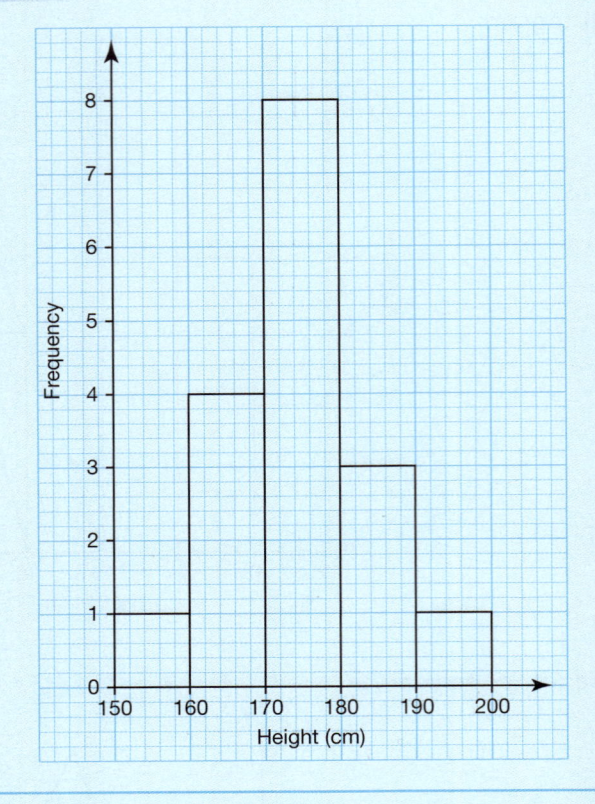

Solution

a Three values are between 180 and 190 cm.

One is between 190 and 200 cm.

This makes a total of 3 + 1 = 4 men.

b One value is between 150 and 160 cm.

Four are between 160 and 170 cm.

This makes a total of 1 + 4 = 5 men.

c The **modal class** is the class with the greatest frequency, and is represented by the tallest bar. This is greater than or equal to 170 and less than 180 cm.

Another way of writing this is 170 ⩽ height < 180.

Histograms with unequal class-width intervals

For unequal class widths, you will need to use **frequency density** instead of frequency on the vertical axis. Frequency density is related to class width and frequency by this formula:

$$\text{frequency density} = \frac{\text{frequency}}{\text{class width}}$$

This means that the area of each bar is equal to the frequency of the group it represents.

Example 25

The annual mileages driven by a group of sales representatives are as shown in this table.

Distance, D (1000 km)	Frequency
$0 \leqslant D < 6$	3
$6 \leqslant D < 12$	12
$12 \leqslant D < 16$	24
$16 \leqslant D < 20$	16
$20 \leqslant D < 30$	7

Draw a histogram to illustrate the data.

Solution

As the class widths are unequal, add a column labelled 'frequency density'.

Distance, D (1000 km)	Class width	Frequency	Frequency density
$0 \leqslant D < 6$	6	3	$3 \div 6 = 0.5$
$6 \leqslant D < 12$	6	12	$12 \div 6 = 2$
$12 \leqslant D < 16$	4	24	$24 \div 4 = 6$
$16 \leqslant D < 20$	4	16	$16 \div 4 = 4$
$20 \leqslant D < 30$	10	2	$2 \div 10 = 0.2$

Calculate the class width by subtracting the lower from the upper boundary.

Class width = 16 − 12 = 4

Frequency density = frequency ÷ class width

Frequency density = $\frac{3}{6}$ = 0.5

Now draw the histogram.

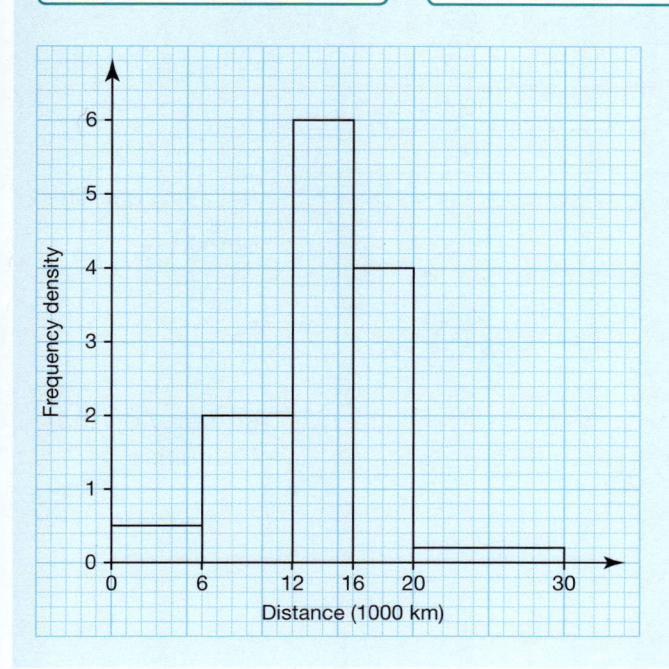

Diagrammatic representation: Chapter 6 Diagrammatic representation

Example 26

As part of her survey into potato disease, Kate weighs 129 potatoes. She produces the table shown below.

a Copy and complete the table.
b Draw a histogram to illustrate the results.
c Estimate how many potatoes weighed between 190 g and 280 g.

Weight, W (grams)	Frequency	Frequency density
$30 \leqslant W < 80$	15	0.3
$80 \leqslant W < 120$	20	
$120 \leqslant W < 160$	28	
$160 \leqslant W < 180$	44	
$180 \leqslant W < 220$		0.4
$220 \leqslant W < 300$		0.75

Solution

a Frequency density = frequency ÷ class width

Frequency density = 15 ÷ 50 = 0.3

Frequency = frequency density × class width

Frequency = 0.3 × 50 = 15

Weight, W (grams)	Frequency	Frequency density
$30 \leqslant W < 80$	15	0.3
$80 \leqslant W < 120$	20	0.5
$120 \leqslant W < 160$	28	0.7
$160 \leqslant W < 180$	44	2.2
$180 \leqslant W < 220$	16	0.4
$220 \leqslant W < 300$	6	0.75

Diagrammatic representation: Chapter 6 Diagrammatic representation

b Draw the histogram.

[Histogram with Frequency density on y-axis (0 to 2.5) and Weight (grams) on x-axis with markings at 30, 80, 120, 160, 180, 220, 300]

Find the area between the two dotted lines to give an estimate of the number of potatoes between 190 g and 280 g.

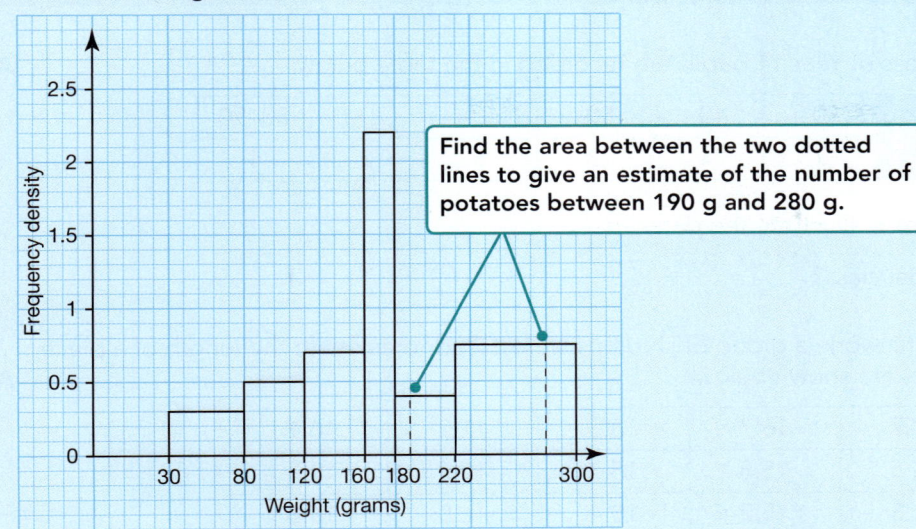

0.4 is the bar height.

30 is the difference between 220 and 190.

c To estimate how many potatoes weighed between 190 g and 280 g, use the areas of the bars.

Area for weights between 190 and 220 = 0.4 × 30 = 12

Area for weights between 220 and 280 = 0.75 × 60 = 45

Estimate of the number of potatoes weighing between 190 g and 280 g is 12 + 45 = 57.

Diagrammatic representation: Chapter 6 Diagrammatic representation

Exercise 6F

1 The weights of a class of Year 11 pupils are recorded in the table below.

Weight, K (kg)	30–	40–	50–	60–	70–	80–90
Frequency	1	4	8	6	2	1

a Draw a histogram to illustrate the data.

b What is the modal class?

2 As part of their coursework, a group of students were asked to estimate the length of a piece of string. The results are shown below.

16.0	11.7	16.7	16.3	12.2	16.1
10.2	15.5	15.8	15.3	15.2	13.3
12.7	12.8	15.2	10.4	16.0	16.0
19.1	16.7	15.1	14.0	14.8	16.0
10.1	18.3	11.6	15.3	11.2	12.6
17.6	11.6	15.3	13.3	10.3	19.3
19.2	15.1	18.4	14.5	17.0	15.1

a Copy and complete the frequency table.

Length, l (cm)	Tally	Frequency
$10 \leqslant l < 12$		
$12 \leqslant l < 14$		
$14 \leqslant l < 16$		
$16 \leqslant l < 18$		
$18 \leqslant l < 20$		

b Draw a histogram to illustrate the data.

c Write down the modal class.

d In which group is the median length?

3 The table shows a grouped frequency distribution of the science examination marks of a class of students.

Science result (%)	30–35	36–40	41–45	46–50	51–55	56–60
Number of students	2	4	8	6	4	1

a Draw a frequency diagram to illustrate the results.

b On a separate diagram, draw a frequency polygon.

4 The weights, in grams, of apples from an orchard are shown in the table below.

Weight, g (grams)	65 ⩽ g < 75	75 ⩽ g < 85	85 ⩽ g < 95	95 ⩽ g < 105	105 ⩽ g < 115
Frequency	34	56	60	45	23

Draw a histogram to illustrate the data.

5 A nurse recorded the weights of a group of women. The results are shown in the table.

Weight, W (kg)	50 ⩽ W < 60	60 ⩽ W < 70	70 ⩽ W < 80	80 ⩽ W < 90	90 ⩽ W < 100
Frequency	2	9	15	25	10

a Draw a frequency polygon to illustrate the data.

b Write down the modal group.

c In which group does the median weight lie?

6 A group of biology students recorded the lengths of a number of worms. The results are shown in the histogram below.

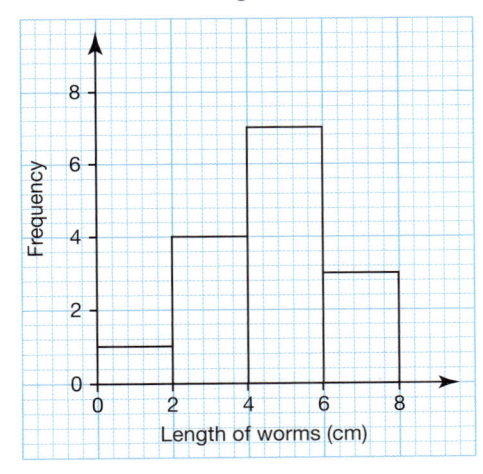

a Use the graph to draw a frequency table.

b How many worms were measured?

7 The table below shows the 'bleep test' results of a group of adults before and after a six-week training programme.

Level, L	Before	After
$0 \leqslant L < 3$	4	1
$3 \leqslant L < 6$	8	4
$6 \leqslant L < 9$	5	7
$9 \leqslant L < 12$	2	6
$12 \leqslant L < 15$	1	2

a On the same set of axes, draw two frequency polygons to illustrate the results.

b Do you think the training programme has had an effect?

c Give a reason for your answer to part **b**.

8 The weights of nails are measured in a factory as part of the quality control process. The results are recorded in the table below.

Weight, w (grams)	Frequency
$0 \leqslant w < 2$	5
$2 \leqslant w < 5$	6
$5 \leqslant w < 11$	14
$11 \leqslant w < 14$	4
$14 \leqslant w < 17$	3

Draw a histogram to illustrate this data.

9 Some students' results in a French examination are shown in the table.

Examination result	0–20	21–30	31–45	46–60	61–70
Number of students	2	12	28	6	4

Draw a histogram to illustrate the data.

> **Hints and tips**
>
> The class widths are: 0 to 20.5, 20.5 to 30.5, and so on. We use these figures because there are gaps in the data, so we use the centre of each gap as the boundary.

10 The masses of tap washers, measured to the nearest gram, are shown in the table below.

Mass, m (g)	0 to 2	3 to 5	6 to 12	13 to 16
Frequency	3	7	15	10

Draw a histogram to illustrate the data.

11 Monty measured the height of his tomato plants. The table and histogram he drew are both incomplete.

Height, h (cm)	Frequency
$8 \leq h < 12$	8
$12 \leq h < 14$	10
$14 \leq h < 18$	
$18 \leq h < 24$	
$24 \leq h < 30$	3

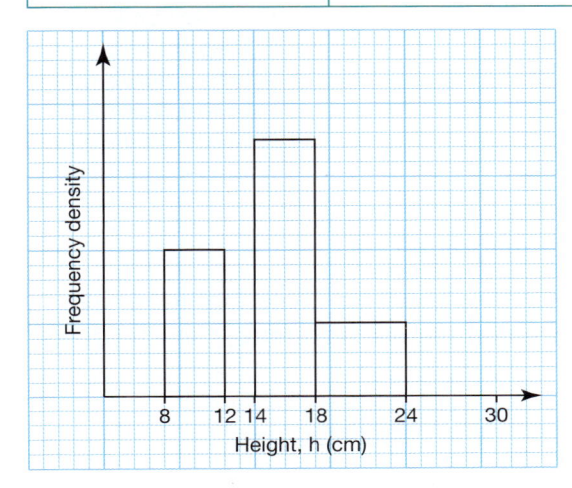

a Copy and complete the table, adding a column for frequency density.

b Copy and complete the histogram. Work out the scale on the vertical axis first.

12 The ages of the members of a gym were recorded in the table below.

Age, x (years)	Frequency
$0 < x \leq 15$	5
$15 < x \leq 20$	28
$20 < x \leq 25$	60
$25 < x \leq 35$	44
$35 < x \leq 50$	10

a Draw a histogram to represent this data.

b Members under the age of 18 receive a discount. Use your graph to make an estimate of how many members receive a discount.

Diagrammatic representation: Chapter 6 Diagrammatic representation

6.7 Cumulative frequency graphs

This section will show you how to:

- use a graph to find a measure of dispersion (the interquartile range) and a measure of location (the median).

KEY WORDS

Cumulative frequency
Cumulative frequency diagram
Cumulative frequency step polygon
Dispersion
Interquartile range
Lower quartile
Median quartile
Upper quartile

The **interquartile range** is a measure of the **dispersion** of a set of data. The advantage of the interquartile range is that it eliminates extreme values, and bases the measure of spread on the middle 50% of the data. This section will show how to find the interquartile range and the median of a set of data by drawing a **cumulative frequency diagram**.

The table shows the marks of the 50 students in a mathematics test. Note that they have been put into a grouped table. It includes a column for the **cumulative frequency**, which you can find by adding each frequency to the sum of all preceding frequencies.

Mark	Number of students	Cumulative frequency
20 to 30	1	1
31 to 40	6	7
41 to 50	6	13
51 to 60	8	21
61 to 70	8	29
71 to 80	6	35
81 to 90	7	42
91 to 100	6	48
101 to 110	1	49
111 to 120	1	50

Diagrammatic representation: Chapter 6 Diagrammatic representation

This data can then be used to plot a graph of the top value of each group against its cumulative frequency. The points to be plotted are (30, 1), (40, 7), (50, 13), (60, 21), etc., which will give the graph shown below. Note that the cumulative frequency is *always* the vertical (*y*) axis.

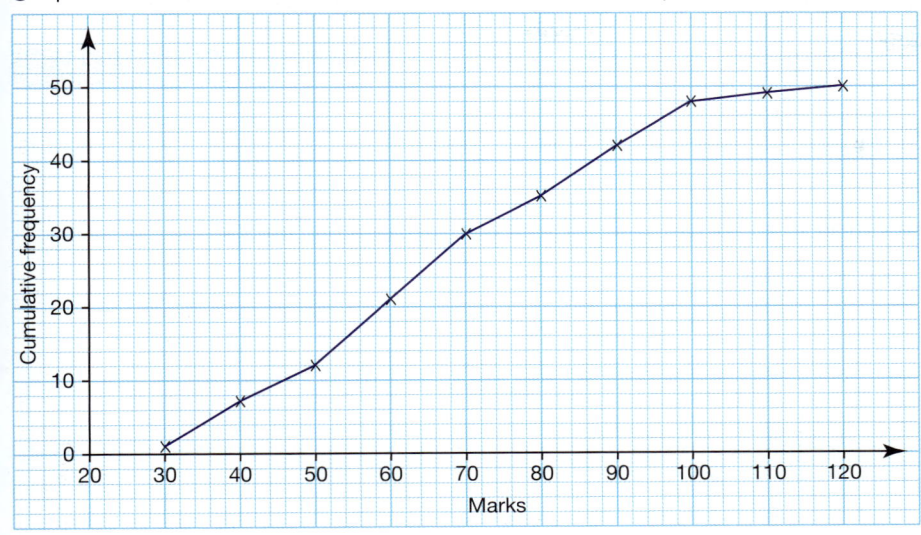

Also note that the scales on both axes are labelled at each graduation mark, in the usual way. **Do not** label the scales as shown here. It is *wrong*.

21–30 31–40 41–50

The plotted points can be joined in two different ways:
- by straight lines, to give a cumulative frequency polygon
- by a freehand curve, to give a cumulative frequency curve or ogive.

They are both called cumulative frequency diagrams.

In an examination you are most likely to be asked to draw a cumulative frequency diagram, and the type (polygon or curve) is up to you. Both will give similar results. The cumulative frequency diagram can be used in several ways, as you will now see.

The median

The **median** is the middle item of data, once all the items have been put in order of size, from lowest to highest. So, if you have n items of data plotted as a cumulative frequency diagram, you can find the median from the middle value of the cumulative frequency, that is the $\frac{1}{2}n$th value.

But remember, if you want to find the median from a simple list of discrete data, you *must* use the $\frac{1}{2}(n + 1)$th value. The reason for the difference is that the cumulative frequency diagram treats the data as continuous, even when using data such as examination marks, which are discrete.

The reason you can use the $\frac{1}{2}n$th value when working with cumulative frequency diagrams is that you are only looking for an estimate of the median.

There are 50 values in the table on the previous page. The middle value will be the 25th value. Draw a horizontal line from the 25th value to meet the graph, then go down to the horizontal axis. This will give an estimate of the median. In this example, the median is about 65 marks.

Diagrammatic representation: Chapter 6 Diagrammatic representation

The interquartile range

By dividing the cumulative frequency into four parts, you can obtain **quartiles** and the **interquartile range**.

The **lower quartile** is the item one-quarter of the way up the cumulative frequency axis and is given by the $\frac{1}{4}n$th value.

The **upper quartile** is the item three-quarters of the way up the cumulative frequency axis and is given by the $\frac{3}{4}n$th value.

The interquartile range is the difference between the lower and upper quartiles.

These are illustrated on the graph below.

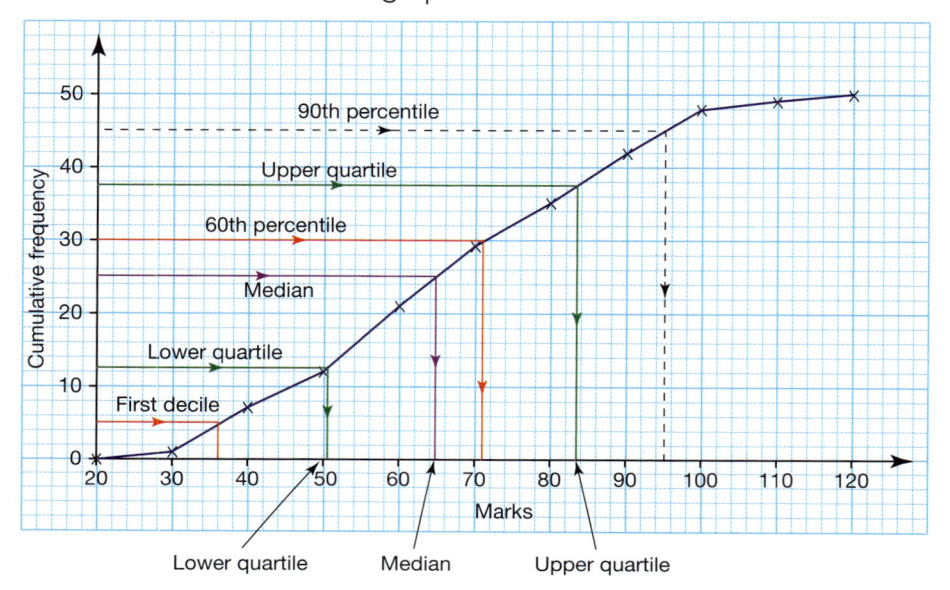

The quarter and three-quarter values out of 50 values are the 12.5th value and the 37.5th value. Draw lines across to the cumulative frequency curve from these values and down to the horizontal axis. These give the lower and upper quartiles. In this example, the lower quartile is 50.5 marks, the upper quartile is 83 marks and the interquartile range is 83 − 49 = 34 marks.

Note that problems like these are often followed up with an extra question such as: *The head of mathematics decides to give a special award to the top 10% of students. What would the cut-off mark be?*

The top 10% would be the top five students (10% of 50 is 5). Draw a line across from the 45th student to the graph and down to the horizontal axis. This gives a cut-off mark of 95.

7.1 The mode

7.2 The median

7.3 The mean

7.4 Which average to use

7.5 Grouped data

7.6 The geometric mean

This chapter will show you how to:

- calculate the mode, median and mean of small sets of data
- solve problems involving the mean, median and mode
- decide which is the best average for different types of data
- calculate the mode, median and mean from frequency tables of discrete data
- use and recognise the modal class and calculate an estimate of the mean from frequency tables of grouped data

Higher tier only

- solve problems using the mean and frequency tables
- use the weighted mean
- decide when to use the weighted mean.

The exercise questions in this chapter are given individual target grades as a guide.

Visual overview

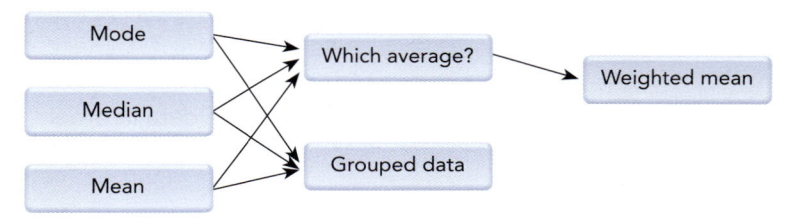

Mode, Median, Mean → Which average? → Weighted mean
Mode, Median, Mean → Grouped data

What you should already know

F How to extract information from tables and diagrams (KS3, level 7).

Quick check

1 The table below shows the number of pets of 10 children.

Number of pets	Frequency
0	2
1	3
2	4
3	1

  a How many children did not have any pets?

  b How many children had more than 1 pet?

  c How many pets did the 10 children have altogether?

7.1 The mode

This section will show you how to:
- find the mode from lists of data
- find the mode from frequency tables.

KEY WORDS
Frequency
Mode
Modal

When you take a maths test, there are usually a few people who do very well, a few who don't score very highly, and a large group in the middle with similar or the same marks.

A quick way to find a score that is a typical score (or average) is to find the most common score, or the **mode**. The mode is the score with the highest **frequency.**

It is possible that there will be more than one mode; the data set 2, 2, 3, 4, 4 has two modes, 2 and 4.

It is also possible that there will be no mode; the data set 1, 2, 4, 6, 9 has no mode as all the numbers are different.

Example 1

A group of friends counted the number of letters in their first names.
Here are the results.

6   8   7   6   4   8   6   9   7   5   6   9

What is the **modal** number of letters in their names?

Solution

Sometimes it is easier to find the mode if you put the data in order:

4   5   6   6   6   6   7   7   8   8   9   9

The mode is 6, because it appears the most often.

Example 2

Here are the marks of class 10M in a table.

Mark	2	3	4	5	6	7	8	9	10
Frequency	1	0	2	2	4	8	5	4	2

What is the modal mark?

8 people score 7 in the test

Solution

The mode is 7, because more people score 7 than any other score.

174

Data analysis: Chapter 7 Measures of location

Exercise 7A

1. A dice was thrown 12 times and the scores were 2, 4, 1, 3, 4, 1, 5, 6, 6, 4, 2, 5.
   What was the modal score?

2. Eleven cars have the following colours: Blue, black, red, white, silver, blue, red, grey, black, blue, green. What is the modal colour?

3. The numbers of cars per hour on a country road during the hours of daylight were:
   11, 13, 15, 11, 17, 12, 18, 14, 7, 9, 14, 16, 7, 11.
   What is the modal number of cars?

4. The price of a loaf of bread (in pence) at 10 shops was:
   94, 99, 101, 118, 94, 119, 101, 94, 97.
   What was the modal price?

5. The cost of a ski lift pass in seven popular resorts is:
   £112, £120, £134, £100, £88, £112, £120.
   What is the modal cost?

6. The table below shows the number of matches in a sample of 50 boxes.

Number of matches	33	34	35	36	37	38	39	40
Frequency	3	5	8	12	9	8	1	4

   What is the modal number of matches in a box?

7. The bar chart below shows the number of peas in a pod.

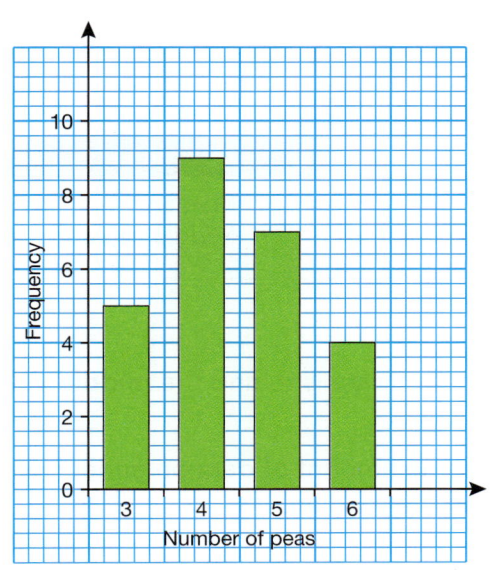

   What is the modal number of peas in a pod?

Data analysis: Chapter 7 Measures of location

8 Three numbers add up to 20.

The mode is 7.

What are the three numbers?

9 Five numbers have a sum of 30. There are two modes, one of which is 6.

What might the other three numbers be? Write down at least three different combinations.

10 The table below shows the ages of members of the school cross-country club.

Age	11	12	13	14	15	16
Male frequency	2	3	8	8	9	7
Female frequency	0	7	5	6	4	3

a What is the modal age of the male members?

b What is the modal age of the female members?

c What is the modal age of the whole club?

d A new member joins the club.

There are now two modal ages for the club and two modal ages for the males.

Which of these statements is true?

- The new member is a 15-year-old male
- The new member is a 15-year-old female
- The new member is a 13-year-old male
- The new member is a 13-year-old female

7.2 The median

This section will show you how to:
- find the median from a list of data, a table of data and a stem-and-leaf diagram.

KEY WORDS
Median
Middle value

One way of finding a number that is representative of a set of data is to find the **middle value**, or **median**.

The median can be a useful average because it has the same amount of data on either side; there are equal quantities of data bigger and smaller than the median.

To find the median, you must put the data in order.

To find the position of the middle number, add one to the number of pieces of data and halve the result.

176

Data analysis: Chapter 7 Measures of location

The position of the median, m, is given by $m = \frac{n+1}{2}$, where n is the size of the data set.

If there is an even number in the data set, then there will be a middle pair. The median is found by adding the middle pair and halving the answer.

Example 3

Find the median of these numbers:

2 9 7 6 7 3 11 2 12 4 7

Solution

First, put the data in order:

2 2 3 4 6 7 7 7 9 11 12

There are 11 numbers in the data set, so the median is in position $\frac{11+1}{2} = 6$.

The median is 7 because it is sixth in the list.

Example 4

The stem-and-leaf diagram shows the speed of 20 cars passing the school this morning.

Stem	Leaf
1	8 9
2	3 4 7 9 9 9
3	0 2 5 6 7 7 0
4	0 1 2 3
5	6

Key: 2 | 3 represents a speed of 23 mph.

What was the median speed?

Solution

With 20 speeds, the median is in position $\frac{20+1}{2} = 10.5$, or halfway between 10 and 11.

Stem	Leaf
1	8_1 9_2
2	3_3 4_4 7_5 9_6 9_7 9_8
3	0_9 2_{10} 5_{11} 6 7 7 8
4	0 1 2 3
5	6

The tenth and eleventh speeds are 32 and 35 mph.

The median is $\frac{32+35}{2} = 33.5$ mph.

177

Data analysis: Chapter 7 Measures of location

Example 5

The table below shows the number of pieces of homework received by members of 10G in a week.

Number of pieces of homework	2	3	4	5	6	7
Frequency (number of students)	1	3	5	6	7	5

What is the median value?

Solution

The total number of students can be found by adding the frequencies:

$1 + 3 + 5 + 6 + 7 + 5 = 27$, so there are 27 students in 10G.

The middle position is $\frac{27 + 1}{2} = 14$. So we need to find the tally of the fourteenth person.

Number of pieces of homework	2	3	4	5	6	7
Frequency (number of students)	1	3	5	6	7	5
Cumulative frequency	1	4	9	15	22	27

The cumulative frequency shows that if the students were put in line, the first student had 2 pieces of homework, the second to fourth students had 3 pieces, the fifth to ninth students had 4 pieces, and so on.

So the tenth to fifteenth students all had 5 pieces.

So the median (the fourteenth person's tally) is 5.

Exercise 7B

1 Find the median for each of these sets of data.

   a 5, 8, 2, 4, 6, 9, 2, 1, 7

   b 17, 23, 34, 12, 45, 64, 14, 14, 35, 33, 61

   c 20, 22, 42, 33, 10, 33, 25, 31

   d 7.1, 4.4, 11.3, 5.0, 2.8, 3.9

   e 102, 107, 104, 105, 111, 110, 110, 114

2 The prices of seven console games that Matt wants to buy are:

   £32, £39, £34, £42, £34, £38, £29

   a What is the modal cost?

   b What is the median cost?

3 The weights of parcels (in kg) delivered to the library were:

   7.4, 8.2, 11.1, 7.8, 2.5, 5.6, 7.1, 8.9, 2.3, 2.7, 2.9, 4.1

   What is the median weight?

4 The number of missing parts in packs of kitchen units was recorded for a sample of ten packs as:

4, 3, 5, 4, 1, 0, 1, 2, 0, 4

a What is the modal number of missing parts?

b What is the median number of missing parts?

c Which do you think is the better average? Explain why.

5 For these numbers:

4, 6, 3, 7, 4, 7, 5, 6, 78, 100

a Find

  i the median.

  ii the mode.

b If you add 2 to each number in part (a):

6, 8, 5, 9, 6, 9, 7, 8, 80, 102

What is

  i the median?

  ii the mode?

c If you double each number in part (a):

8, 12, 6, 14, 8, 14, 10, 12, 156, 200

What is

  i the median?

  ii the mode?

6 Here are the number of emails sent by 35 people in 1 hour.

Number of emails sent	0	1	2	3	4	5	6	7
Frequency	2	5	4	3	4	6	9	2

a Find the median number of emails sent.

b Find the modal number of emails sent.

Data analysis: Chapter 7 Measures of location

E 7 The bar chart shows the number of courgettes on the plants in a vegetable patch.

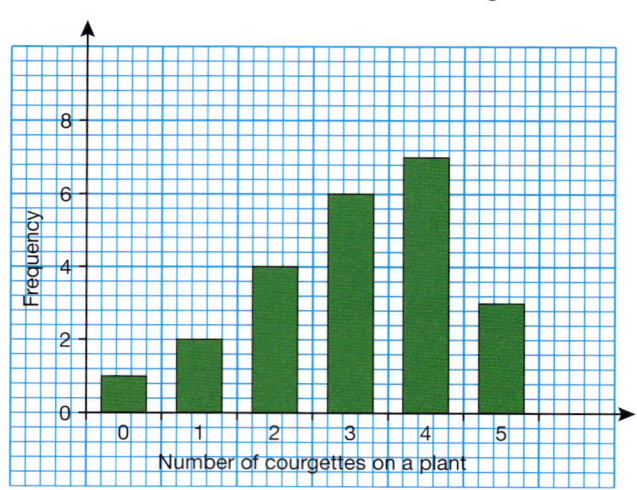

[Bar chart: Frequency on y-axis, Number of courgettes on a plant on x-axis. Bars: 0→1, 1→2, 2→4, 3→6, 4→7, 5→3]

a What is the modal number of courgettes on a plant?

b What is the median number of courgettes on a plant?

D 8 The stem-and-leaf diagram below shows the number of text messages sent in one day by a group of friends.

```
0 | 1 4 7 7
1 | 1 2 3 5 8 9
2 | 0 2 3 6 7 9 9
3 | 1 2 5 9
4 | 2 5 6
5 | 7
6 | 2
```

Key: 4 | 2 represents 42 texts.

a Find the median number of texts sent.

b Find the modal number of texts sent.

c Which is the more useful average, the median or the mode? Give a reason for your choice.

9 Seven friends compared their weights.

They were: 56 kg, 74 kg, 66 kg, 56 kg, 53 kg, 61 kg, 57 kg.

a Find the median weight.

b Find the modal weight.

c When an eighth friend joined, the mode was unchanged, but the median changed to 58 kg. What was the weight of the eighth friend?

AO3

10 Four numbers have a mode of 8 and a median of 10.

Write down the value of three of the numbers, and explain why you cannot tell the value of the fourth number.

AO3

Data analysis: Chapter 7 Measures of location

7.3 The mean

This section will show you how to:
- calculate the mean of a set of data.

KEY WORDS
Average
Mean

The median and the mode are both types of **average**, but the most commonly used average is called the **mean**.

The mean is a way of calculating how much each value would be if they were shared out equally.

To find the mean, you add all the values together, and then share them out equally by dividing.

Mean = $\dfrac{\text{sum of all the values}}{\text{total number of values}}$

This average takes into account all the values in the set of data.

Example 6

Find the mean of these numbers:

8, 7, 5, 9, 11, 14, 16, 6

Solution

Mean = $\dfrac{\text{sum of all the values}}{\text{total number of values}}$

= $\dfrac{8 + 7 + 5 + 9 + 11 + 14 + 16 + 6}{8}$

= $\dfrac{76}{8}$ = 9.5

There are 8 pieces of data in the set

Example 7

The mean age of 9 people on a bus is 37.

One person gets off. The mean age is now 33.

What is the age of the person who got off the bus?

Solution

The ages of the 9 people add up to 9 × 37 = 333.
The ages of the 8 remaining people is 8 × 33 = 264.
The person who got off is aged 333 − 264 = 69.

Data analysis: Chapter 7 Measures of location

Example 8

The table shows the number of players at football training every week this season.

Number of players at training	Frequency
10	1
11	3
12	6
13	8
14	9
15	5
16	4

Calculate the mean number of players at training each week.

Solution

Use a third column and a total row.

Number of players at training, x	Frequency, f	fx
10	1	10
11	3	33
12	6	72
13	8	104
14	9	126
15	5	75
16	4	64
TOTAL	36	484

In this column, multiply x (number of players at training) by f (frequency).

Mean = $\frac{484}{36}$ = 13.4 (to 1 decimal place)

There were 36 training sessions and a total of 484 people attending.

Exercise 7C

1 Find the mean for each set of data.

  a 4, 7, 2, 5, 8, 11, 5

  b 23, 61, 80, 52, 19, 100, 11, 50

  c 4.2, 5.1, 3.6, 9, 11.2, 4.4

  d 1, 0, 3, 2, 0, 2, 1, 0, 3, 3, 1, 2

Data analysis: Chapter 7 Measures of location

2 Here are the ages, weights and heights of the members of a mixed hockey team.

	Males					Females						
	Bill	Charlie	Dave	George	Pete	Alice	Cat	Di	Fiona	Hilary	Sue	Tina
Age (years)	18	21	24	28	19	23	19	30	24	26	19	22
Weight (kg)	72	68	74	81	59	72	59	61	68	71	65	70
Height (cm)	183	179	185	189	174	179	172	174	177	181	175	179

Find

a the mean height of the team

b the mean weight of the team

c the mean age of the team

d the mean age, weight and height of the males

e the mean age, weight and height of the females.

3 a Calculate the mean, median and mode of

6, 9, 15, 12, 10, 16, 9

b Here, each number from the original list has been doubled.

12, 18, 30, 24, 20, 32, 18

What are the mean, median and mode for this data set?

c Here, each number from the original list has been increased by 3.

9, 12, 18, 15, 13, 19, 12

What are the mean, median and mode for this data set?

4 Eight children count up their toy cars. The mean number of cars is 7. AO3

a How many cars do they have between them?

b If another child joins the group, and he has 16 cars, how many cars do they have now altogether?

c What is the mean number of cars now?

5 Six children find out that the mean amount of money they have is £3. AO3

One of them, Mick, takes his money and goes home. The mean amount of money is now £2.40.

How much money does Mick have?

6 Bill, Phil, Jill and Will work out that their mean number of CDs is 17. AO3

a Bill has got 12 CDs. What is the mean number of CDs for Phil, Jill and Will?

b Will buys 4 more CDs. What is the mean for all 4 of them now?

183

Data analysis: Chapter 7 Measures of location

7 Five whole numbers have a mode of 5, a median of 6 and a mean of 6.2.
What are the five numbers?

8 In a test, the mean mark of 12 girls was 17.5.
The mean mark for the class of 22 children was 17.6.
Calculate the mean mark of the 10 boys.

AO3

9 Chelsea F.C. won the premier League in the 2009–10 season.
The table below shows the number of goals scored per game.

Number of goals scored	Frequency
0	1
1	10
2	12
3	6
4	3
5	2
6	0
7	3
8	1

Find

a the modal score

b the median score

c the mean number of goals per game.

10 The manufacturer of packets of pins claims:
AVERAGE CONTENTS: 36 PINS
Connie tests the claim by counting the number of pins in 30 packets.
Here are her results for the first 29 packets.

AO3

Number of pins	Frequency
33	1
34	4
35	7
36	6
37	6
38	5

If the manufacturer's claim is to be proved true, how many pins should Connie find in the thirtieth packet?

11 One hundred children were asked how many days' absence they had had from school in the last month. Here are the results.

Number of days absence	Frequency
0	25
1	33
2	34
3	5
4	3

Work out the mean, median and mode for this data.

12 Maisie watched some cars go past the school.

She recorded the number of people in each car.

She has forgotten to complete two of the cells.

Number of people	1	2	3	4	5	6
Frequency	43	34	13		2	

The frequency for four people was the same as the frequency for six people, and the mean was exactly two people per car.

What are the missing frequencies?

7.4 Which average to use

This section will show you how to:
- understand the advantages and disadvantages of each type of average and decide which one to use in different situations.

KEY WORDS

Appropriate
Representative
Extreme values

Sometimes the mean, median and mode can give quite different results.

We need to know which one is most **appropriate**.

An average is supposed to be **representative** of the data as a whole.

Data analysis: Chapter 7 Measures of location

The table shows some of the advantages and disadvantages of each average.

	Mean	Median	Mode
Advantages	Allows us to work out the sum. Takes account of all the values.	Always central, so **extreme values** do not affect it.	Can be used for non-numeric data. Is always one of the data set.
Disadvantages	Affected by extreme values. Has to be calculated.	Does not take all values into account.	Can be an extreme value or not representative. Does not take all values into account. Might be more than one, or none.

Example 9

Sportex is a new company which manufactures trainers.

It carries out some market research. Each person was asked their shoe size and preferred colour.

The responses are shown below.

Shoe size	3	4	5	6	7	8	9	10	11
Frequency	7	16	25	35	61	72	81	44	9
Preferred colour	White	Black	Blue	Red	Green	Yellow			
Frequency	89	65	26	53	63	54			

a How many people took part in the survey?
b What is the mean shoe size?
c What is the median shoe size?
d What is the modal shoe size?
e Which is the best average, and why?
f What is the modal colour?

Data analysis: Chapter 7 Measures of location

Solution

a 7 + 16 + 25 + 35 + 61 + 72 + 81 + 44 + 9 = 350

b The mean is $\dfrac{7 \times 3 + 16 \times 4 + 25 \times 5 + 35 \times 6 + 61 \times 7 + 72 \times 8 + 81 \times 9 + 44 \times 10 + 9 \times 11}{350} = 7.69$

(to 2 decimal places)

c The median is in position $\dfrac{350 + 1}{2} = 175.5$

Find the median by adding the frequencies.

Shoe size	3	4	5	6	7	8	9	10	11
Frequency	7	16	25	35	61	72	81	44	9
Cumulative frequency	7	23	48	83	144	216	297	341	350

The middle pair are the 175th and 176th, both of which are size 8.

d The mode is 9, as there were most of those (81 people).

e The mode is too high to be representative, although it gives the company a guide about which size to make the most trainers.

The mean and median are very close; the median is possibly more useful as it is an integer, which is an actual shoe size.

f The modal colour is white as the most people (89) liked this.

Exercise 7D

1 a For each set of data, find the mean, the median and the mode.

  i 5, 4, 10, 3, 7, 4, 5, 4, 11, 7

  ii 16, 12, 20, 12, 18, 12, 20, 12, 16, 12

  iii 5, 2, 3, 1, 26, 6, 0, 2, 8, 7

b For each set of data, say which average is best, giving a reason for your answer.

2 Decide which average you would use for the following, giving a reason for your answer.

  a The average shoe size for the boys in your class.

  b The average height of the girls in your class.

  c The average hair colour of the students in your class.

  d The average mark in a maths exam for the students in your class.

3 Grace keeps in touch with her friends by text.

Here are the number of texts she sends in a week.

Monday	Tuesday	Wednesday	Thursday	Friday	Saturday	Sunday
11	14	12	16	12	55	62

a Calculate the mean, median and mode.

b Which do you think is the best average? Give a reason for your answer.

Data analysis: Chapter 7 Measures of location

D

4 On a box of paper clips was printed 'Average contents 100'.

A secretary had 60 boxes of these paper clips and decided to count the number of clips in each box.

Her results are shown below.

Number of clips in box	Frequency (number of boxes)
97	4
98	3
99	14
100	18
101	11
102	9
105	1
Total	60

a Calculate the mean number of paper clips per box.

b What is the median number of clips in a box?

c What is the modal number of clips in a box?

d Was the statement 'Average contents 100' accurate?

5 A company employs 30 people.

The job title, number of employees and salary are shown in the table.

AO3

Job title	Number employed	Annual salary
Chairman	1	£92 000
Managing director	1	£81 000
Supervisor	2	£35 000
Skilled worker	12	£27 000
Non-skilled worker	14	£20 000

The shop floor workers asked for a pay rise, claiming the average salary was £20 000.

The management said the average salary was £28 233.

The story went to the press, who quoted the average salary as £27 000.

a Which average were the shop floor workers using?

b Which average were the management using?

c Which average were the press using?

d Which do you think is the best average? Give a reason for your answer.

188

6 George scored 56% in a science test.

He asked his teacher for the class average.

The teacher said, 'The mean was 58%, the median was 54% and the mode was 46%.'

Decide whether these statements are true or false.

  a George is not doing quite as well as the class as a whole.

  b George is in the bottom half of the class.

  c George is scoring 10% more than most students.

  d Half the class scored 54% or more.

7 Andrew, Ed, Rob and Steve play cricket for the same club.

Here are their scores in their last six innings.

Andrew	45	48	23	8	23	109
Ed	23	43	56	74	23	12
Rob	33	56	23	127	6	11
Steve	22	55	65	11	44	24

  a Which two cricketers have the same mode?

  b Which two cricketers have the same median?

  c Which two cricketers have the same mean?

  d Who do you think is the best batsman?

8 The largest number from a set of 10 numbers is increased by 3.

Which of the mean, median and mode

  a will change?

  b will not change?

  c might change?

9 A set of numbers has a mean of 5, a median of 6 and a mode of 6.

Match the changes on the left with the effects on the right.

CHANGE	EFFECT
(A) Adding 10 to the largest number	(X) The median is unchanged, but the mean and mode might change.
(B) Adding 2 to each number	(Y) The mean increases, but the mode and median are unchanged.
(C) Removing the highest and lowest numbers from the set	(Z) The mean, median and mode all increase.

Data analysis: Chapter 7 Measures of location

10 Sue and Claire both want to represent the school in the 100 metres.

Here are their times in the last six races.

| Sue | 12.4 sec | 12.9 sec | 12.5 sec | 12.7 sec | 13.1 sec | 12.4 sec |
| Claire | 12.5 sec | 13 sec | 12.5 sec | 12.5 sec | 12.9 sec | 12.6 sec |

Who should represent the school? Give your reasons.

7.5 Grouped data

KEY WORDS
Estimated mean
Grouped data
Modal class

This section will show you how to:
- identify the modal class
- calculate an estimate of the mean from a grouped table.

Sometimes information is given to us as **grouped data**.

In these cases, we do not have the raw data, so we cannot calculate an average.

Instead, we can find the **modal class** (the most common group) and an **estimated mean**.

An estimate of the median can be found from a cumulative frequency graph, and you met this in chapter 6.

Example 10

The speeds of 50 motorists on the motorway are recorded in the table below.

Speed, s (mph)	Frequency, f
$50 < s \leq 55$	2
$55 < s \leq 60$	3
$60 < s \leq 65$	6
$65 < s \leq 70$	18
$70 < s \leq 75$	12
$75 < s \leq 80$	9

a What is the **modal class**?
b Calculate an estimate of the mean speed.

Solution

a The modal class is the one with the largest frequency: $65 < s \leq 70$ mph

b To estimate the mean, we assume that everyone in each group drives at the midway speed. Then the calculation is just the same as you used in section 7.3.

Speed, s (mph)	Frequency, f	Midway value (m)	$f \times m$
$50 < s \leq 55$	2	52.5	105
$55 < s \leq 60$	3	57.5	172.5
$60 < s \leq 65$	6	62.5	375
$65 < s \leq 70$	18	67.5	1215
$70 < s \leq 75$	12	72.5	870
$75 < s \leq 80$	9	77.5	697.5
TOTAL	50		3435

The estimated mean = $\frac{3435}{50}$ = 68.7 mph.

Note that $60 < s \leq 65$ means a speed that is greater than 60 mph and no more than 65 mph.

Exercise 7E

1 Sheraz conducted a survey at the seaside for his science coursework.

He measured the lengths of 55 pieces of seaweed.

The results of the survey are shown in the table.

Length of seaweed, l (cm)	Frequency (f)
$0 < l \leq 20$	2
$20 < l \leq 40$	17
$40 < l \leq 60$	13
$60 < l \leq 80$	11
$80 < l \leq 100$	8
$100 < l \leq 120$	3
$120 < l \leq 140$	1

Sheraz needs to calculate an estimate for the mean length of the pieces of seaweed.

a Work out an estimate for the mean length of a piece of seaweed. Give your answer correct to 1 decimal place.

b Write down the modal class.

Data analysis: Chapter 7 Measures of location

2 Mr Jackson carried out a survey to find how much time was needed by a group of pupils to complete their homework on a Wednesday evening.

Here are the results.

Number of hours, h, spent on homework	Frequency, f
0	2
$0 < h \leq 1$	11
$1 < h \leq 2$	6
$2 < h \leq 3$	3
$3 < h \leq 4$	1

Calculate an estimate for the mean time spent on homework by the pupils in the group.

3 Nicky owns a pet shop.

The table gives information about the weights of gerbils in Nicky's shop.

Weight of gerbil, w (g)	Frequency, f
$20 < w \leq 25$	2
$25 < w \leq 30$	11
$30 < w \leq 35$	7
$35 < w \leq 40$	3

Calculate an estimate for the mean weight of the gerbils in Nicky's shop.

4 Class 10R carried out a survey of their heights.

Height, h (cm)	Frequency, f
$160 < h \leq 165$	8
$165 < h \leq 170$	4
$170 < h \leq 175$	2
$175 < h \leq 180$	9
$180 < h \leq 185$	4

a Write down the modal class.

b Calculate an estimate of the mean height.

5 The results of a science exam are:

Mark, m	Frequency, f
1–10	1
11–20	0
21–30	5
31–40	16
41–50	28
51–60	45
61–70	62
71–80	25
81–90	10
91–100	2

a Estimate the mean mark.

b Write down the modal class.

c Fiona's mother had promised her a reward if she got an above average score.

Fiona scored 61. Do you think she got an above average score?

6 A computer helpline company states that 'On average we answer the telephone within 10 seconds.'

Here is the data for a particular day.

Time taken, t (sec)	$0 < t \leq 5$	$5 < t \leq 10$	$10 < t \leq 20$	$20 < t \leq 30$	$30 < t \leq 60$	$60 < t \leq 120$
Frequency, f	136	187	21	11	4	1

Is the claim justified?

Explain your answer.

7 A gardener plants two different types of tulip bulb.

He measures the heights of the tulips.

Height, h (cm)	$10 < h \leq 15$	$15 < h \leq 20$	$20 < h \leq 25$	$25 < h \leq 30$	$30 < h \leq 35$
Frequency: Type A	7	11	16	14	10
Frequency: Type B	5	8	29	12	3

Which type has the greater mean height?

8 Chris has 100 CDs.

The table below shows the lengths of them.

Length, t (minutes)	$40 < t \leq 50$	$50 < t \leq 60$	$60 < t \leq 70$	$70 < t \leq 80$
Frequency, f	11	21	54	14

Calculate an estimate for the mean length in minutes and seconds.

9 Polly's expenditure varies during the year because she sometimes has large items to pay for, such as car insurance, and Christmas presents.

She made a note of her weekly expenditure over a year:

Weekly expenditure, w (£)	$200 < w \leq 300$	$300 < w \leq 400$	$400 < w \leq 500$	$500 < w \leq 700$	$700 < w \leq 1000$
Frequency, f	16	20	11	3	2

Polly needs to know her average weekly expenditure.

Calculate an estimate of the mean.

10 Gillian helps in a charity shop.

The table below shows the takings each week.

Takings, t (£)	$0 < t \leq 400$	$400 < t \leq 800$	$800 < t \leq 1200$	$1200 < t \leq 1600$
Frequency, f	4		19	4

She cannot remember how many times the takings were between £400 and £800, but she remembers that her estimate of the mean was £774.

How many times were the takings between £400 and £800?

7.6 The geometric mean

This section will show you how to:
- understand when and how to use the geometric mean
- solve problems involving the geometric mean.

KEY WORDS

Geometric mean
Multiplier
Root

We have seen that the mean is the single number we can replace all the data with when adding.

The mean of 3, 5, 2 and 6 is 4, because 3 + 5 + 2 + 6 = 4 + 4 + 4 + 4.

The **geometric mean** is the single number we can replace all the data with when multiplying.

The geometric mean of 4, 18 and 3 is 6, because 4 × 18 × 3 = 6 × 6 × 6.

194

Data analysis: Chapter 7 Measures of location

The geometric mean of n numbers is $\sqrt[n]{\text{the product of the } n \text{ numbers}}$.
In the example, $\sqrt[3]{4 \times 18 \times 3} = 6$
We use the geometric mean when numbers have been increased (or decreased) by multiplying.

Example 11

Find the geometric mean of 2, 6, 4, 5 and 10.

Solution

The geometric mean of the five numbers is
$\sqrt[5]{2 \times 6 \times 4 \times 5 \times 10} = \sqrt[5]{400} = 4.74$ (to 2 decimal places).

We use the fifth **root** because there are five numbers.

Example 12

The table shows the average interest rate in England from 2005 to 2009.

Year	2005	2006	2007	2008	2009
Interest rate	4.8%	5.1%	5.8%	4.1%	1.3%

Calculate the mean annual interest rate over the five years

Solution

In any calculation, the original figure is 100%.

So the 2005 rate of 4.8% takes the value of any investment to 104.8% or, as a decimal, 1.048 times its original value.

In the following years, the increases of 5.1%, 5.8%, 4.1% and 1.3% take the value to 1.051, 1.058, 1.041 and 1.013 times the starting value for that year.

The overall multiplier is 1.048 × 1.051 × 1.058 × 1.041 × 1.013 = 1.228881033

Because there are five values multiplied, we take the fifth root to find the geometric mean.

The geometric mean = 1.042082177, which represents an increase of 0.042082177, or 4.2082177%

So the mean annual interest rate is 4.2% (to 1 decimal place).

Data analysis: Chapter 7 Measures of location

Exercise 7F

A

1 Find the geometric mean of

   a 5, 10 and 2

   b 2, 3 and 6

   c 2, 3, 4 and 5.

2 A credit card charges 2% compound interest per month.
What is the annual percentage rate?

3 Dave received a pay rise of 4% in 2008, 2% in 2009 and 0% in 2010.
What is his average annual pay rise? Give your answer correct to 2 decimal places.

4 Imelda and Patricia both started work on the same salary.
Imelda received pay rises over three years of 6%, 4% and 2%.
Patricia received a 4% increase on each of the three years.
Imelda thinks they will both earn the same amount as each other again, but Patricia disagrees.
Who is correct?

5 A photocopier enlarges a picture by 20% and then enlarges this enlargement by 30%.
Find the geometric mean and explain its meaning.

6 Griselda's antique vase increased in value by 20% last year, but decreased by 20% this year.
What is the annual average increase or decrease?

A*

7 A farmer grew 20 tonnes of wheat in 2008.
In 2009, he grew 23 tonnes of wheat.
In 2010, he produced 6% less than in 2009.
What is the average annual increase from 2008 to 2010?

8 Petra's horse increased in value by 3% and 4% in 2008 and 2009 respectively.
The annual average increase in 2008, 2009 and 2010 was 3.6%.
By what percentage did the horse's value increase in 2010?

9 The geometric mean of three numbers is 12.
One of the numbers is 3, and the other two numbers are equal.
What are the other two numbers?

10 The population of frogs in a pond grew by 3% every year for four years.
The following year, disease caused a 9% drop in the population.
For the next two years the population grew again, by 2% per year.
What was the average percentage growth in population over the seven years?

GRADE BOOSTER

What you need to do to get this grade

G	You can find the mode and median from a set of data.
F	You can find the mean of a small set of data.
E	You can find the median and range from a stem-and-leaf diagram.
D	You can find the mean from a frequency table of discrete data.
C	You can find an estimate of the mean from a frequency table of grouped data.
A	You can calculate the geometric mean.
A*	You can solve problems involving the geometric mean.

What you should now know

- How to calculate the mode, median and mean.
- How to solve problems involving the mean, median and mode.
- How to decide which is the best average for different types of data.
- How to calculate the mode, median and mean from frequency tables of discrete data.
- How to use and recognise the modal class and calculate an estimate of the mean from frequency tables of grouped data.

Higher tier only

- How to solve problems using the mean and frequency tables.
- How to use the geometric mean.
- How and when to use the geometric mean.

EXAMINATION Questions

1 The amount of money spent by seven customers in a DIY shop was recorded.

The values were

£5   £12   £8   £225   £20   £14   £10

   a Find the median of these values. *(2 marks)*

   b Will the mean be higher or lower than the median?

      Tick the correct box.

      Higher ☐   Lower ☐

      Give a reason for your answer. *(2 marks)*

AQA June 2007, Foundation, Question 3

2 Amber has a calculator which can generate random numbers.

She sets it to generate random numbers from the list 1, 2, 3, 4 and 5.

   a Write down the mean of 1, 2, 3, 4 and 5. *(1 mark)*

   b She now uses her calculator to generate a sample of 100 of these random numbers as shown in the table.

Number	Frequency
1	27
2	20
3	17
4	16
5	20

      Calculate the mean of the sample of random numbers. *(3 marks)*

   c Comment on your answers to part **a** and part **b**. *(1 mark)*

AQA June 2007, Foundation, Question 7

3 Some of the teachers at Faye's school arrive by car.

Faye counts the number of people in each of the first 11 cars to arrive one day.

Here are her results.

1   3   1   1   1   2   4   1   1   1   1

   a Explain why the mode is equal to 1. *(1 mark)*

   b Explain why the median is equal to 1. *(2 marks)*

   c The mean number of people in each of these cars is 1.5454 …

      In this context, why might the mean be considered the least appropriate to use of the mean, mode and median? *(1 mark)*

AQA June 2009, Foundation, Question 2

4 The table shows the time, in minutes, for which a sample of cars were parked in a short-stay city car park.

Time, t (minutes)	Frequency, f
$0 < t \leq 20$	6
$20 < t \leq 60$	18
$60 < t \leq 80$	30
$80 < t \leq 100$	9
$100 < t \leq 160$	12

Calculate an estimate of the mean time. *(2 marks)*

AQA June 2007, Higher, Question 6

5 The table shows the number of days on which it rained each week in Dryville during the 52 complete weeks of 2008.

Number of days on which it rained	Frequency	
0	21	
1	17	
2	8	
3	3	
4	2	
5	1	
6	0	
7	0	

a In how many weeks were there **exactly** 4 days on which it rained? *(1 mark)*

b In how many weeks were there **at least** 3 days on which it rained? *(1 mark)*

c Use the table to show that there were 55 days on which it rained in Dryville. *(2 marks)*

d Use part **c** to calculate the mean number of days per week on which it rained in Dryville in 2008. *(2 marks)*

AQA June 2009, Foundation, Question 5

Data analysis: Chapter 7 Examination questions

6 Joan is a Road Safety Officer for a City Council.

Part of her work involves recording the number of vehicles exceeding the speed limit as they pass local schools.

The following table gives the data recorded over a 120-day period e.g. on 42 days two vehicles per day exceeded the speed limit.

Number of vehicles per day exceeding speed limit	2	5	6	10	14	15	20
Number of days	42	28	18	14	10	5	3

a Calculate the mean number of vehicles per day exceeding the speed limit.

Give your answer to two decimal places. *(2 marks)*

b Due to a fault on the recording equipment, Joan's records did not show a further two vehicles **each** day which were exceeding the speed limit.

What effect will this error have on the values for the mean? *(1 mark)*

AQA June 2006, Higher, Question 11

7 The frequency table shows the number of times members of a club attended monthly meetings in one year.

Number of meetings attended	Frequency
0	1
1	3
2	6
3	2
4	13
5	11
6	17
7	15
8	19
9	16
10	8
11	4
12	10

a What is the modal number of meetings attended by the members? *(1 mark)*

b How many members does the club have? *(2 marks)*

c The total attendance for the year was 875.

Use this fact and your answer to part **b** to work out the mean number of meetings attended by each member. *(2 marks)*

AQA June 2008, Foundation, Question 5

WORKED EXAMINATION Questions

1 In a skating competition, twelve judges award marks for Sue's performance.

The marks, out of 10, are shown below.

3   6   7   8   9   9   10   10   10   10   10   10

a For these scores work out

  i the mode

  10 as there are more 10s than any other number (1 mark)

  ii the median

  The middle pair are the sixth and seventh numbers, which are 9 and 10

  9.5 (halfway between 9 and 10) (1 mark)

  iii the mean

  $3 + 6 + 7 + 8 + 9 + 10 + 10 + 10 + 10 + 10 + 10 = \frac{102}{12}$

  8.5 (2 marks)

b Sue is unhappy because the judges use the mean as her overall score.

Give a disadvantage of using the mean in this case.

The very low value (3) influences the mean (1 mark)

2 The table shows the time, in minutes, that a sample of customers spent in a supermarket on a Wednesday morning.

Time, t (minutes)	Frequency, f
$0 < t \leq 30$	5
$20 < t \leq 60$	14
$60 < t \leq 80$	23
$80 < t \leq 100$	11
$100 < t \leq 130$	7
Total	60

Middle value, m	$f \times m$
15	75
40	560
70	1610
90	990
115	805
Total	4040

Calculate an estimate of the mean time.

Estimate of mean = $\frac{4040}{60}$ = 67.3 minutes (2 marks)

> You will gain **1** mark for giving the sum and dividing by 60

> You will gain **1** mark for the correct answer.

> You will gain **1** mark for using midpoints consistently with fm.

8 Measures of spread

Measures of spread are important because they tell you how close, overall, the data is to an average value. These measures are very important in the retail industry as they help to calculate how many items of each size a retail outlet should keep in stock, for example.

Measures of spread include the range, interquartile range and standard deviation. You will also learn about the normal distribution and how to compare scores by standardising them.

Being familiar with measures of spread also enables us to differentiate between data sets with the same or similar average. For example, imagine two companies A and B employing five people each. Company A pays all its workers the same salary of £15 000 per annum. The mean average wage of company A is therefore £15 000. Company B pays one person £35 000, one £15 000, one £10 000 and the other two £7 500 each. The mean average wage is still £15 000 per annum. If we look only at the mean averages, the companies appear to pay their workers very similar amounts. Using the different measures of spread that you will learn in this chapter will enable you to differentiate between the two companies.

8.1 Box-and-whisker plots

8.2 Variance and standard deviation

8.3 Using a calculator to work out standard deviation

8.4 Properties of frequency distributions

This chapter will show you how to:
- draw and interpret a box plot
- calculate outliers

Higher tier only

- relate a normal distribution to the mean and standard deviation
- calculate variance and standard deviation of discrete data, with and without a calculator
- calculate variance and standard deviation of grouped data, with and without a calculator
- standardise scores and interpret the results.

The exercise questions in this chapter are given individual target grades as a guide.

Visual overview

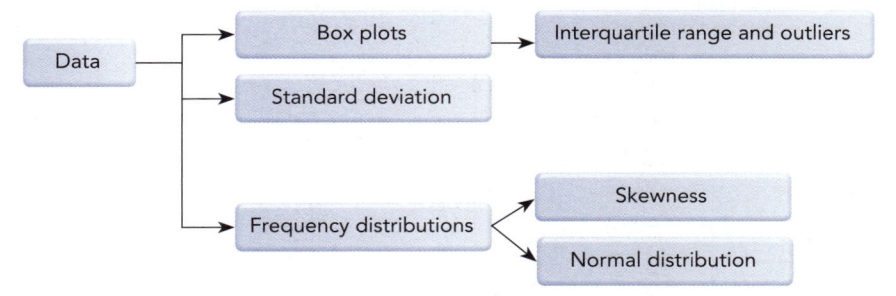

Data → Box plots → Interquartile range and outliers

Data → Standard deviation

Data → Frequency distributions → Skewness

Frequency distributions → Normal distribution

What you should already know

F How to calculate mean, median, mode and range (KS3, level 4).

Quick check

Find the mean, median, mode and range of the following data set.

3, 6, 5, 8, 9, 2, 2

8.1 Box-and-whisker plots

This section will show you how to:
- draw and read box plots.

KEY WORDS

Box-and-whisker plot
Box plot
Highest value
Lower quartile
Lowest value
Median
Outlier
Skewness
Upper quartile

A useful way of displaying data for comparison is by means of a **box-and-whisker plot** (or just **box plot**). This requires five pieces of data. These are the **lowest value**, the **lower quartile** ($Q1$), the **median** ($Q2$), the **upper quartile** ($Q3$) and the **highest value**. They are drawn in the following way.

Lowest value | Lower quartile, Q_1 | Median, Q_2 | Upper quartile, Q_3 | Highest value

These data values are always placed against a scale so that they are plotted accurately.

The following diagrams show how the cumulative frequency curve, the frequency curve and the box plot are connected for three common types of distribution.

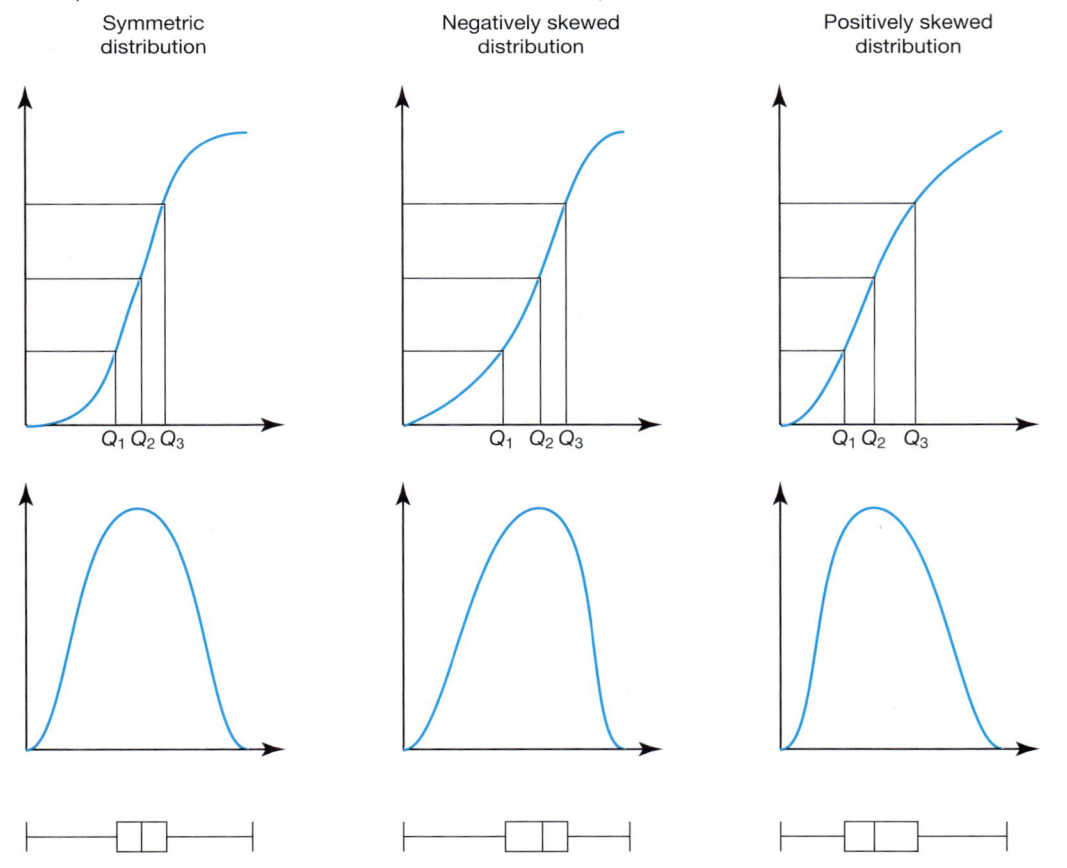

Symmetric distribution | Negatively skewed distribution | Positively skewed distribution

$Q_1 Q_2 Q_3$ | $Q_1 \; Q_2 Q_3$ | $Q_1 Q_2 \; Q_3$

Data analysis: Chapter 8 Measures of spread

Calculating skewness from a box plot

In symmetrical distributions the median value is exactly halfway between the upper quartile ($Q3$) and the lower quartile ($Q1$). In distributions that are *positively* skewed, the median value is closer to the lower quartile than the upper quartile. In distributions that are *negatively* skewed, the median is closer to the upper quartile than the lower.

- Symmetrical distributions: $Q2 - Q1 = Q3 - Q2$
- Negatively skewed distribution: $Q2 - Q1 > Q3 - Q2$
- Positively skewed distributions: $Q2 - Q1 < Q3 - Q2$

Outliers

An **outlier** is defined as an observation that is:

- less than $Q1 - 1.5(Q3 - Q1)$
- greater than $Q3 + 1.5(Q3 - Q1)$.

From these definitions, it is clear that outliers can be calculated from quartiles.

Example 1

The box plot for the girls' marks in last year's examination is shown below.

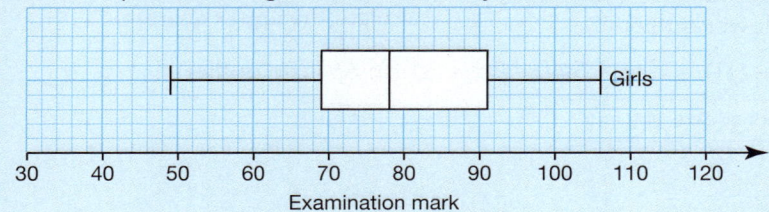

The boys' results for the same examination are: lowest mark 39, lower quartile 65, median 78, upper quartile 87, highest mark 112.

a On the same grid, draw the box plot for the boys' marks.

b Comment on the differences between the two distributions of marks.

Solution

a The data for boys and girls is plotted on the grid below.

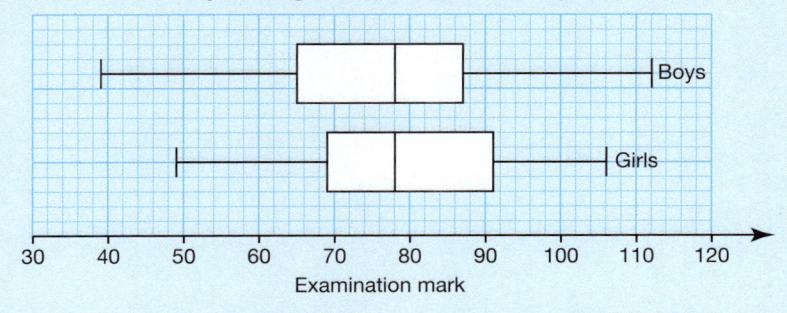

b The girls and boys have the same median mark but both the lower and upper quartiles for the girls are higher than those for the boys, and the girls' range is slightly smaller than the boys'.

This suggests that the girls did better than the boys overall, even though a boy got the highest mark.

205

Data analysis: Chapter 8 Measures of spread

Example 2

The weights, to the nearest kilogram, of 19 children are shown below.

19	37	66	21	22
35	31	41	31	27
40	34	26	30	20
36	49	48	32	

Draw a box plot to illustrate the data. Indicate any outliers on your plot.

Solution

Put the data in order:

19, 20, 21, 22, 26, 27, 30, 31, 31, 32, 34, 35, 36, 37, 40, 41, 48, 49, 66

Lower quartile ($Q1$) = $\frac{1}{4}(n + 1)$th value = $\frac{1}{4}(19 + 1)$th value
= 5th value = 26 kg

Median ($Q2$) = $\frac{1}{2}(n + 1)$th value = $\frac{1}{2}(19 + 1)$th value
= 10th value = 32 kg

Upper quartile ($Q3$) = $\frac{3}{4}(n + 1)$th value = $\frac{3}{4}(19 + 1)$th value
= 15th value = 40 kg

Outliers are less than $Q1 - 1.5(Q3 - Q1) = 26 - 1.5(40 - 26)$
= 5 (lowest value is 19 so there are no lower outliers).

Outliers are greater than $Q3 + 1.5(Q3 - Q1) = 40 + 1.5(40 - 26) = 61$ (so 66 is an outlier).

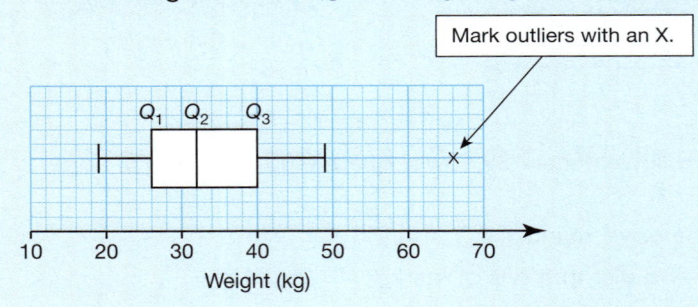

Notes
- Use the $\frac{1}{4}(n + 1)$th value to calculate the lower quartile.
- Use the $\frac{1}{2}(n + 1)$th value to calculate the median.
- Use the $\frac{3}{4}(n + 1)$th value to calculate the upper quartile.

Mark outliers with an X.

Weight (kg)

Exercise 8A

1 The box plot shows the times taken for a group of pensioners to do a set of 10 long-division calculations.

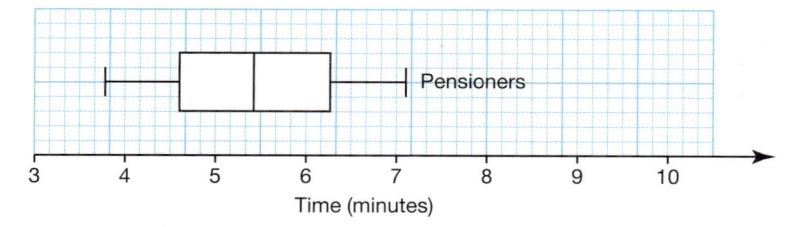

The same set of calculations was given to some students in Year 11. Their results are: shortest time 3 minutes 20 seconds, lower quartile 6 minutes 10 seconds, median 7 minutes, upper quartile 7 minutes 50 seconds and longest time 9 minutes 40 seconds.

a Copy the diagram and draw a box plot for the students' times.

b Comment on the differences between the two distributions.

2 The box plot shows the sizes of secondary schools in Dorset.

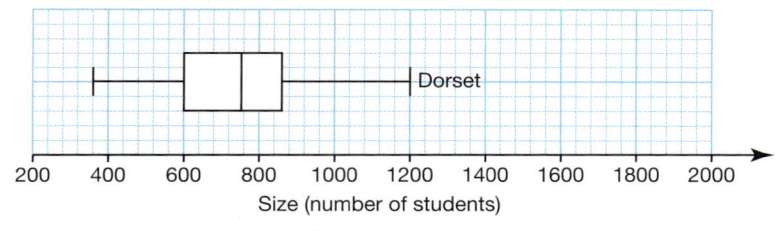

The data for schools in Rotherham is: smallest 280 students, lower quartile 1100 students, median 1400 students, upper quartile 1600 students, largest 1820 students.

a Copy the diagram and draw a box plot for the sizes of schools in Rotherham.

b Compare the two distributions.

3 The box plots for the noon temperature at two resorts, recorded over a year, are shown on the grid below.

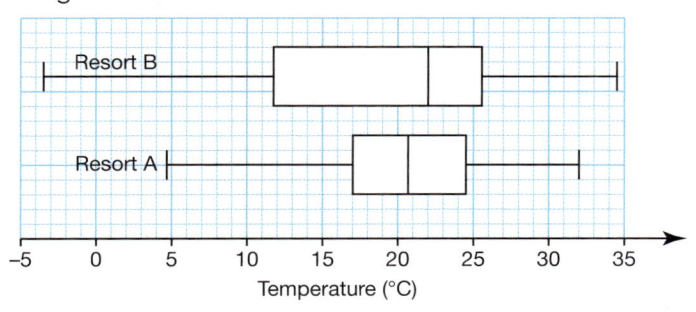

a Comment on the differences in the two distributions.

b Mary wants to go on holiday in July. Which resort would you recommend? Why?

Data analysis: Chapter 8 Measures of spread

4 The following table shows some data about the annual salaries for 100 men and 100 women. **AO4**

	Lowest salary (£)	Lower quartile (£)	Median salary (£)	Upper quartile (£)	Highest salary (£)
Men	6500	16 000	20 000	22 000	44 500
Women	7000	14 000	16 000	21 500	33 500

  a Draw box plots to compare both sets of data.
  b Compare the distributions.

5 The table shows the monthly salaries of 100 families. **AO3**

Monthly salary (£)	Number of families
1451–1500	8
1501–1550	14
1551–1600	25
1601–1650	35
1651–1700	14
1701–1750	4

  a Draw a cumulative frequency diagram to show the data.
  b Estimate the median monthly salary and the interquartile range.
  c The lowest monthly salary was £1480 and the highest was £1740.
    i Draw a box plot to show the distribution of salaries.
    ii Is the distribution symmetric, negatively skewed or positively skewed?

6 A health practice had two doctors, Dr Excel and Dr Collins. **AO3**
The following box plots were created to illustrate the waiting times for their patients during October.

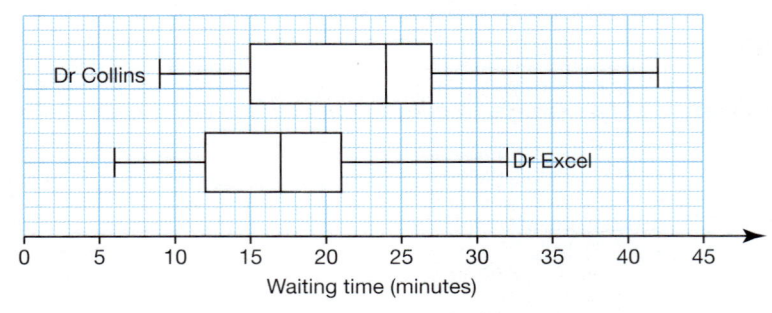

  a For Dr Collins, what is:
    i the median waiting time?
    ii the interquartile range for his waiting time?
    iii the longest time a patient had to wait in October?
  b For Dr Excel, what is:
    i the shortest waiting time for any patient in October?
    ii the median waiting time?
    iii the interquartile range for his waiting time?
  c Anwar was deciding which doctor to try to see. Which one would you advise he sees? Why?

7 The box plots for a school's end-of-year mathematics tests are shown below.

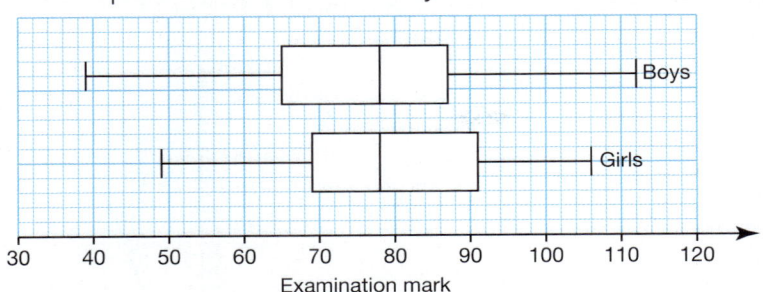

Comment on any differences that will exist between the means of the boys' and the girls' test results?

8 Rodrigo was given a diagram showing box plots for the amount of daily sunshine in the resorts of Bude and Torquay for August but no scale was shown. He was told to write a report about the differences between the amounts of sunshine in both resorts.

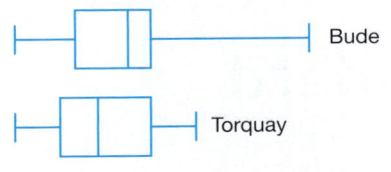

Invent a report that could be possible for him to make from these box plots with no scales shown.

9 Indicate whether the following sets of data are likely to be symmetric, negatively skewed or positively skewed.

  a Heights of adult males.
  b Annual salaries of adult males.
  c Shoe sizes of adult males.
  d Weights of babies born in Britain.
  e Speeds of cars on a motorway in the middle of the night.
  f Speeds of cars on a motorway in the rush hour.
  g Shopping bills in a supermarket the week before Christmas.
  h Number of letters in the words in a teenage magazine.
  i Time taken for students to get to school in the morning.
  j Time taken for students to run 1 mile.

Data analysis: Chapter 8 Measures of spread

10 Below are four cumulative frequency diagrams and four box plots.

Match each cumulative frequency diagram with a box plot.

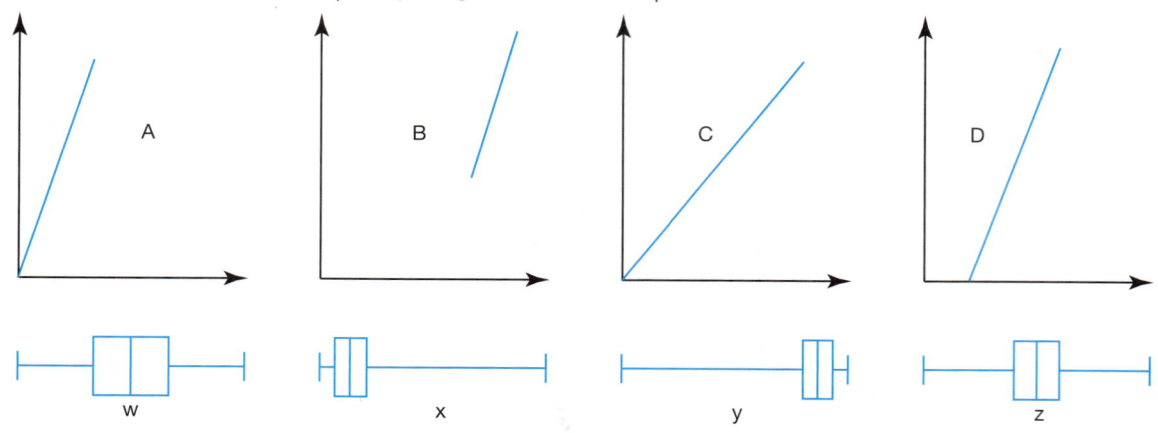

A B C D

w x y z

8.2 Variance and standard deviation

This section will show you how to:

- calculate the standard deviation and variance for grouped and discrete frequency distributions.

KEY WORDS

Standard deviation
Variance

Standard deviation indicates how tightly the values of a data set are clustered about the mean. The greater the standard deviation, the more spread out the data is. The actual value of standard deviation is the average distance the data values are away from the mean.

Variance is simply the standard deviation squared.

In normal distributions, the region that is one standard deviation away from the mean in any direction accounts for 68% of the data. The region that is two standard deviations from the mean accounts for roughly 95% and the interval of three standard deviations either side of the mean accounts for 99.8 %. These values will be explored in more detail in the next section.

The formula for standard deviation is:

$$\sqrt{\frac{\Sigma(x - \bar{x})^2}{n}} \text{ or } \sqrt{\frac{\Sigma x^2}{n} - \bar{x}^2}$$

The formula for variance is:

$$\frac{\Sigma(x - \bar{x})^2}{n} \text{ or } \frac{\Sigma x^2}{n} - \bar{x}^2$$

where $\bar{x}$ is the mean, n is the number of values and Σx^2 is the sum of the squares of the values.

Data analysis: Chapter 8 Measures of spread

Example 3

When Kate made 12 profiteroles she weighed each one to the nearest gram. Her results are shown below.

12, 10, 15, 13, 24, 16, 9, 12, 13, 15, 19, 12

Calculate the mean, variance and standard deviation of the weights of the profiteroles.

Solution

Mean = $\bar{x}$ = $\dfrac{12 + 10 + 15 + 13 + 24 + 16 + 9 + 12 + 13 + 15 + 19 + 12}{12}$ = $\dfrac{170}{12}$ = 14.17

$\Sigma x^2 = 12^2 + 10^2 + 15^2 + 13^2 + 24^2 + 16^2 + 9^2 + 12^2 + 13^2 + 15^2 + 19^2 + 12^2 = 2594$

Variance = $\dfrac{\Sigma x^2}{n} - \bar{x}^2 = \dfrac{2594}{12} - 14.17^2 = 15.38$ (2 d.p.)

Standard deviation = $\sqrt{\dfrac{\Sigma x^2}{n} - \bar{x}^2} = \sqrt{15.38} = 3.92$ ← This is the number of values.

To calculate the standard deviation from a grouped frequency table, use this formula.

Standard deviation = $\sqrt{\dfrac{\Sigma f x^2}{\Sigma f} - \left(\dfrac{\Sigma f x}{\Sigma f}\right)^2}$ ← This calculation gives an estimate of the mean. Square this.

Example 4

The data in the table below shows the results when Jasmine weighs a sample of potatoes grown on her farm.

Weight, w (g)	65 ≤ w < 75	75 ≤ w < 85	85 ≤ w < 95	95 ≤ w < 105	105 ≤ w < 115
Frequency	30	70	63	44	23

a Calculate the standard deviation for the weight of the potatoes.

A local supermarket will buy her potatoes if 68% of them weigh between 70 and 105 grams.

b Will the supermarket buy Jasmine's potatoes?

Data analysis: Chapter 8 Measures of spread

Solution

a Redraw the table.

Weight, w (g)	Frequency, f	Midpoint, x	fx	fx²
65 ⩽ w < 75	30	(65 + 75) ÷ 2 = 70	2100	147 000
75 ⩽ w < 85	70	80	5600	448 000
85 ⩽ w < 95	63	90	5670	510 300
95 ⩽ w < 105	44	100	4400	440 000
105 ⩽ w < 115	23	110	2530	278300
	Σf = 230		Σfx = 20 300	Σfx² = 1 823 600

a Standard deviation = $\sqrt{\frac{\Sigma fx^2}{\Sigma f} - \left(\frac{\Sigma fx}{\Sigma f}\right)^2} = \sqrt{\frac{1\,823\,600}{230} - \left(\frac{20\,300}{230}\right)^2} = 11.8$

68% of the data lies within ± one standard deviation of the mean.

Mean = $\frac{\Sigma fx}{\Sigma f} = \frac{20\,300}{230} = 88.26$

Assuming a normal distribution:

Mean + 1 standard deviation = 88.26 + 11.8 = 100.1

Mean − 1 standard deviation = 88.26 − 11.8 = 76.46

The supermarket will therefore accept Jasmine's potatoes.

Exercise 8B

1 Calculate the standard deviation of the following data sets.

   a 2, 5, 6, 8, 9, 11, 15, 9, 10

   b 3, 4, 7, 12, 4, 7, 12, 3, 7, 8

   c 34.1, 45.2, 52.1, 46.1, 32.9, 42.6, 23.7, 54.1, 12.1

2 A runner's times for the 200 m sprint, over a season, are shown below.

22.2, 23.3, 22.1, 22.0, 21.9, 22.1, 21.7, 21.4, 20.9, 20.8

Calculate the mean and standard deviation of his times.

3 The table shows the number of goals scored by Wayne's team in each match.

Number of goals	0	1	2	3	4	5
Frequency	10	23	35	28	12	9

Calculate the mean, variance and standard deviation of this data.

4 The table shows the number of children per family, in a primary class.

Number of children	0	1	2	3	4	5
Frequency	3	9	24	6	3	1

Calculate the standard deviation for this data.

5 The scores of each member of a golf club, in one round of golf, are shown in the table. AO3

Score	Frequency
68	2
69	3
70	6
71	10
72	12
73	6
74	4

Calculate the mean and standard deviation of the scores.

6 The lengths of 44 oak leaves were measured and recorded, to the nearest millimetre (mm). The results are shown in the table below. AO3

Length of leaf (mm)	41–45	46–50	51–55	56–60	61–65
Frequency	2	10	21	8	3

Calculate the standard deviation for these lengths.

7 The scores for an IQ test taken by the employees of a company are shown in the table. AO3

Score	Frequency
96–100	1
101–105	7
106–110	11
111–115	15
116–120	8
121–125	3
126–130	2

Calculate the mean score and the standard deviation.

8 For a set of observations, $\Sigma f = 22$, $\Sigma fx^2 = 15\,234$, $\Sigma fx = 550$. AO3

Find the mean and standard deviation.

9 Bill weighs a sample of the pears he has grown on his farm. He has used a new variety of fertiliser, hoping to win a contract with Barrows, an upmarket grocery store. The store will buy his pears if 95% of them weigh between 500 and 600 grams. He hopes that the new fertiliser he has used will help him win the contract. AO3

Weight, w (g)	$400 \leq w < 450$	$450 \leq w < 500$	$500 \leq w < 550$	$550 \leq w < 600$	$600 \leq w < 650$
Frequency	24	35	63	44	12

Does the sample Bill has measured suggest he will win the contract?

Data analysis: Chapter 8 Measures of spread

8.3 Using a calculator to work out standard deviation

This section will show you how to:

- use the statistics functions on a calculator to work out the standard deviation for grouped and discrete frequency distributions.

KEY WORDS

Mean
Standard deviation
Variance

You will need to be able to find the **standard deviation** from a list of numbers or a frequency table. Using a calculator to do this is the most efficient way.

Press the mode/setup button [MODE SETUP] to give the screen below.

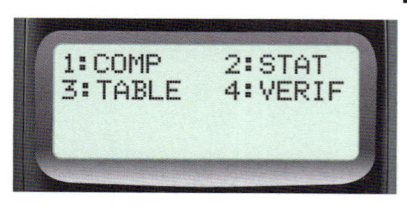

```
1: COMP     2: STAT
3: TABLE    4: VERIF
```

Press [VERIFY] 2 to enter the stats mode shown below.

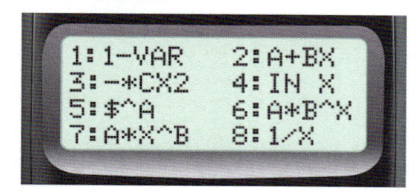

```
1: 1-VAR    2: A+BX
3: _*CX2    4: IN X
5: $^A      6: A*B^X
7: A*X^B    8: 1/X
```

Press [STAT] 1 which will display the data entry table.

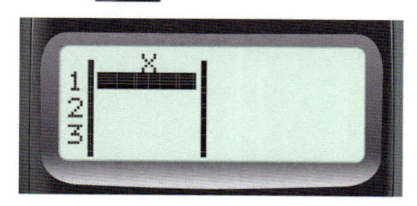

Enter the data, pressing = after each entry.

Once all the numbers have been entered press the AC button, [AC].

To find the standard deviation press [SHIFT] and [STAT] 1 to bring up the screen below.

```
1: Type     2: Data
3: Sum      4: Var
5: MinMax
```

Press `4` to bring up the next screen.

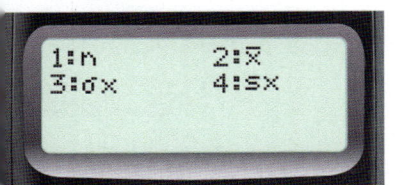

```
1: n       2: x̄
3: σx      4: sx
```

Press `3` to bring up the standard deviation.

Press `[STAT] 1` to check n = number of values you believe you have entered.

Press `[VERIFY] 2` to get the mean.

Example 5

Use your calculator to find the standard deviation of this data.

3, 6, 8, 12, 8, 9, 0, 24, 3, 1, 18

Solution
You should get an answer of 6.997 (3 d.p.).

You can also use the calculator to find the standard deviation of a frequency and grouped frequency table.

To do this we must first turn the frequency table on in the calculator.

Press `SHIFT`, `MODE SETUP` and `REPLAY` down on the replay button.

This brings up the screen below.

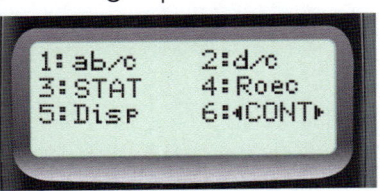

```
1: ab/c    2: d/c
3: STAT    4: Roec
5: Disp    6: ◄CONT►
```

Press `3` to show this screen.

```
Frequency?
1: ON      2: OFF
```

Press `[STAT] 1` to turn frequency on.

215

Data analysis: Chapter 8 Measures of spread

Press the mode/setup button [MODE SETUP] to give the screen below.

```
1: COMP      2: STAT
3: TABLE     4: VERIF
```

Press [VERIFY] 2 to enter the stats mode shown below.

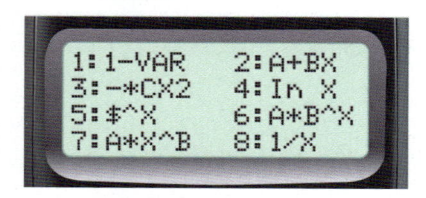

```
1: 1-VAR     2: A+BX
3: _*CX2     4: In X
5: $^X       6: A*B^X
7: A*X^B     8: 1/X
```

Press [STAT] 1, which will display the data entry table with frequency column.

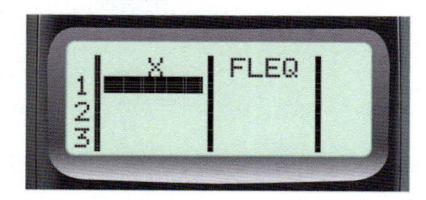

```
    X     | FLEQ
1
2
3
```

Enter the data into the x column, pressing = after each entry, then enter the frequency in the frequency column, again pressing = after each entry.

If the data is grouped enter the midpoint of each group into the x column.

Once all the numbers have been entered press the AC button, [AC].

To find the standard deviation press [SHIFT] and [STAT] 1 to bring up the screen below.

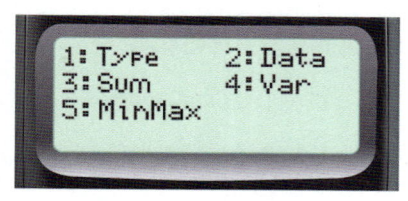

```
1: Type      2: Data
3: Sum       4: Var
5: MinMax
```

Press 4 to bring up the next screen.

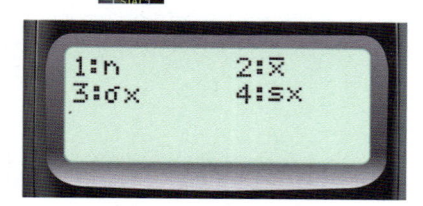

```
1: n         2: x̄
3: σx        4: sx
```

Pressing 3 will give you the standard deviation. Press [STAT] 1 to check n = number of values you believe you have entered. Press [VERIFY] 2 to get the mean.

216

Enter the data from the table below into your calculator to find the standard deviation.
Don't forget to enter the midpoints for weight, which are 55, 65 and so on.

Weight, W (kg)	50 ⩽ W < 60	60 ⩽ W < 70	70 ⩽ W < 80	80 ⩽ W < 90	90 ⩽ W < 100
Frequency	2	9	15	25	10

You should get a standard deviation of 10.34 (2 d.p.).

Exercise 8C

Try the questions from the previous section, using the statistics functions you have learned.

8.4 Properties of frequency distributions

This section will show you how to:
- recognise the shape of frequency distributions
- interpret frequency distributions
- make calculations based on the properties of a normal distribution.

KEY WORDS
Mean
Negatively skewed
Normal distribution
Positively skewed
Standardised score

The normal distribution

The diagram shows two **normal distribution** curves. The wider curve has a greater spread of data.

If we collected the heights of a large population and drew a histogram of them, they would form a bell shaped curve. This is known as a normal distribution. This type of curve occurs frequently in nature when we analyse large data sets. Two examples of a normal distribution are shown in the diagram on the right. Note that the curves are symmetrical about the mean of the data. The extreme right-hand side of the curve would show the numbers of very tall people, and the extreme left-hand side the numbers of very short people. Also in the diagram, the wider curve indicates a greater spread of data.

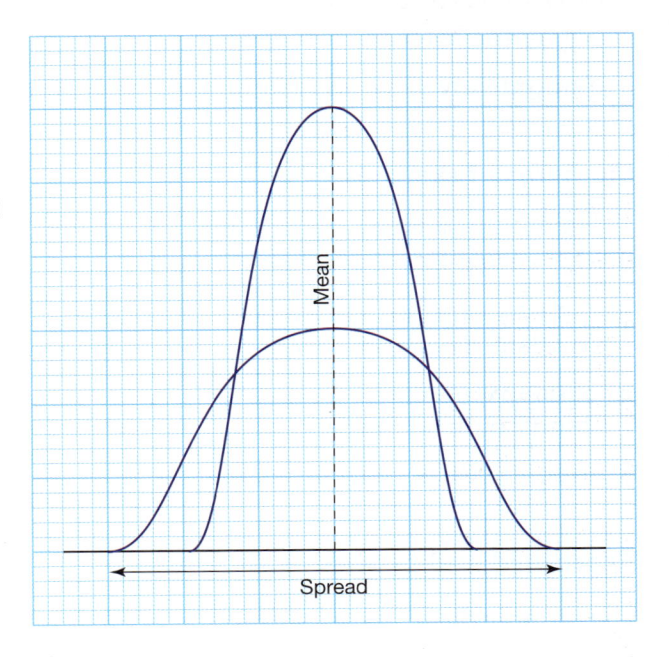

Data analysis: Chapter 8 Measures of spread

Note how the curve is symmetrical about the **mean**

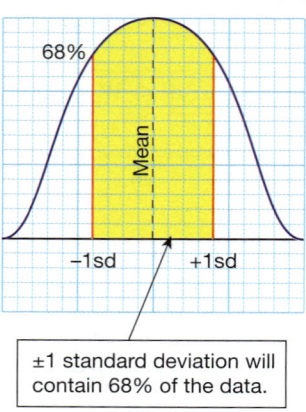

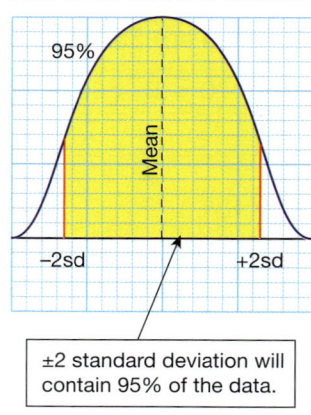

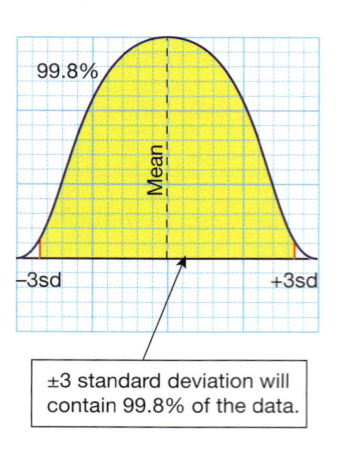

±1 standard deviation will contain 68% of the data.

±2 standard deviation will contain 95% of the data.

±3 standard deviation will contain 99.8% of the data.

Skewness

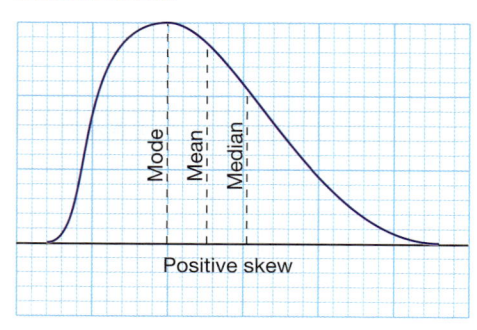

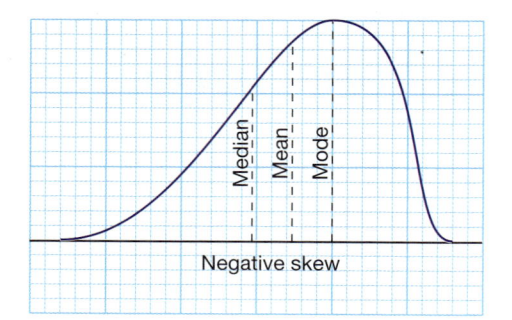

Positive skew

Negative skew

If there are extreme values towards the positive end of a distribution, the distribution is **positively skewed**. In a positively skewed distribution, the mean is greater than the mode but less than the median.

In a **negatively skewed** distribution, the mean is greater than the median but less than the mode because of the presence of extreme values at the negative end of the distribution.

Measures of skewness

There are three measures of skew. The first two are known as *Pearson's measures of skew*. The third is known as the *quartile method*.

1. $\dfrac{\text{mean} - \text{mode}}{\text{standard deviation}}$

2. $\dfrac{3(\text{mean} - \text{median})}{\text{standard deviation}}$

3. $\text{upper quartile} + \text{lower quartile} - \dfrac{2 \times \text{median}}{\text{upper quartile} - \text{lower quartile}}$

Standardised scores

The **standardised score** is used to compare results from different data sets. The standardised score shows how far the actual score is from the mean. For example, how do you compare your score in a physics examination to your score in an English examination?

In order to do this you can standardise both scores, using the formula:

$$\text{standardised score} = \dfrac{\text{score} - \text{mean}}{\text{standard deviation}}$$

Data analysis: Chapter 8 Measures of spread

The higher standardised score indicates the better performance. However, if you were to compare two rounds of golf, where a lower score is better, you would be looking for the lower of the two standardised scores.

Example 6

Describe the skewness of the three frequency diagrams.

a

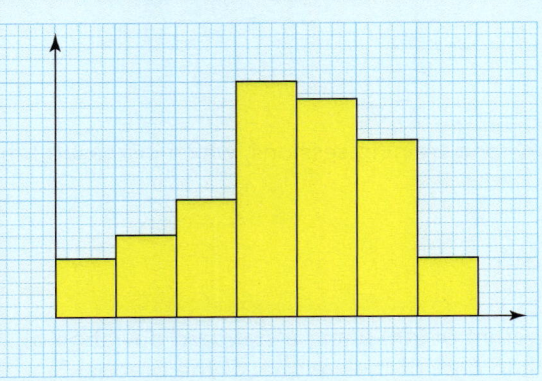

b

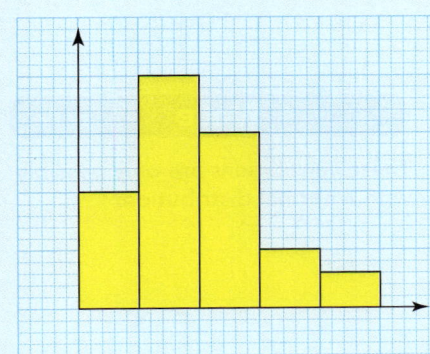

c

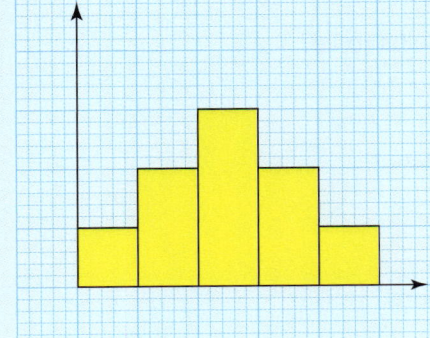

Solution

a Negative skew – most data on the right-hand side of the graph.
b Positive skew – most data on the left-hand side of the graph.
c Symmetrical – line of symmetry down the centre of the graph.

Data analysis: Chapter 8 Measures of spread

Example 7

A cyclist analysed his training over a season. The mean distance he travelled in a training session was 58 miles. The median was 51 miles and the standard deviation was 20 miles.

Use Pearson's measure of skewness ({3(mean – median)\standard deviation}) to comment on this distribution.

Solution

$$\frac{3(58 - 51)}{20} = 1.05$$

A positive skew of 1.05 suggests that he did a few very long training sessions, which increased the mean.

Example 8

A normally distributed batch of oranges has a mean weight of 200 g and a standard deviation of 15 g. Within what weight range would you expect to find 68% of the weights of the oranges?

Solution

68% of the data is found within mean ±1 standard deviation.

68% of oranges weigh between 200 – 15 = 185 g and 200 + 15 = 215 g.

Note

These calculations are only possible with a normal distribution.

Example 9

The lifetime of Osprey 100W light bulbs last is found to be a normal distribution with a mean of 500 hours and a standard deviation of 55 hours.

Between what time limits would you expect 99.8% of the light bulbs to lie?

Solution

99.8 % of data lies between ±3 standard deviations from the mean.

$500 - (3 \times 55) = 335$ hours

$500 + (3 \times 55) = 665$ hours

99.8 % of the light bulbs will last between 335 hours and 665 hours.

Example 10

Simon's scores in his physics and chemistry examinations, along with the mean and standard deviation of his class's marks, are shown below.

In which subject did he perform better?

Subject	Simon's marks	Class mean	Standard deviation
Physics	62	68	10
Chemistry	49	52	8

Solution

Standardised score for physics = $\dfrac{\text{score} - \text{mean}}{\text{standard deviation}}$

$= \dfrac{62 - 68}{10}$

$= -0.6$

Standardised score for chemistry = $\dfrac{\text{score} - \text{mean}}{\text{standard deviation}}$

$= \dfrac{49 - 52}{8}$

$= -0.375$

Simon did better in chemistry because the standardised score is greater.

Advantages and disadvantages of measures of spread

Measure	Advantages	Disadvantages
Range	Easy to calculate	Uses only two values Distorted by outliers
Interquartile range Interdecile range Interpercentile range	Unaffected by outliers Appropriate for skewed data	Cannot be calculated for small samples Uses only two values
Standard deviation	Uses every value Algebraically calculated Easily interpreted	Sensitive to outliers Inappropriate for skewed data

Data analysis: Chapter 8 Measures of spread

Exercise 8D

1 The frequency distribution shows the wages of doctors in a large hospital.

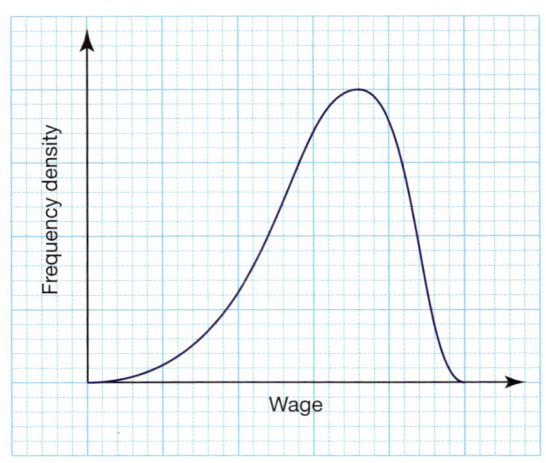

[Graph: Frequency density vs Wage, showing a distribution with a peak and a longer tail to the left]

a Copy the distribution and indicate where the mean, median and mode would lie.

b Comment on the skewness of this distribution.

c It is found that the mean is £68 000, the mode is £75 000 and the standard deviation is £5000.

Use Pearson's measure of skewness ({mean – mode\standard deviation}) to confirm your answer to part **b**.

2 A frequency distribution has a mean of 23 and a median of 15.

a Comment on the skewness of the distribution.

b Sketch the distribution. Show the position of the mean and median on your sketch.

3 A class of students sit examinations in physics and chemistry. The results are normally distributed. The mean and standard deviation of each examination are shown in the table.

	Mean	Standard deviation
Physics	65	10
Chemistry	58	5

a Sketch the two frequency distributions on the same set of axes.

b Make two comments about the distributions.

4 A sample of fish caught at a fish farm in Scotland is found to be normally distributed. The sample has a mean of 2.5 kg and a standard deviation of 400 g.

Between what limits would you expect 95% of the samples to lie?

5 Kate takes a sample of weights of newborn babies at a hospital. She finds that the weights are normally distributed, with a mean of 3.4 kg and a standard deviation of 500 g.

What percentage of the sample would you expect to have a weight of less than 2.4 kg?

6 Phil's head of year calculates the mean and standard deviation of all examinations taken by Year 11 students. The table gives the mean and standard deviation of three of the examinations sat by Phil.

Subject	Mean score	Standard deviation
French	45	10
Welsh	53	15
Spanish	62	23

Phil scored 55 in French, 59 in Welsh and 67 in Spanish.

By standardising each of Phil's scores, find out in which examination he performed best.

7 Mohammed's teacher told him he had a standardised score of 1.2 in his statistics examination. He also told him that the class mean was 62 and the standard deviation 10. What was Mohammed's actual mark?

8 The two normal frequency distributions shown are the marks gained by two different classes in the same geography examination.

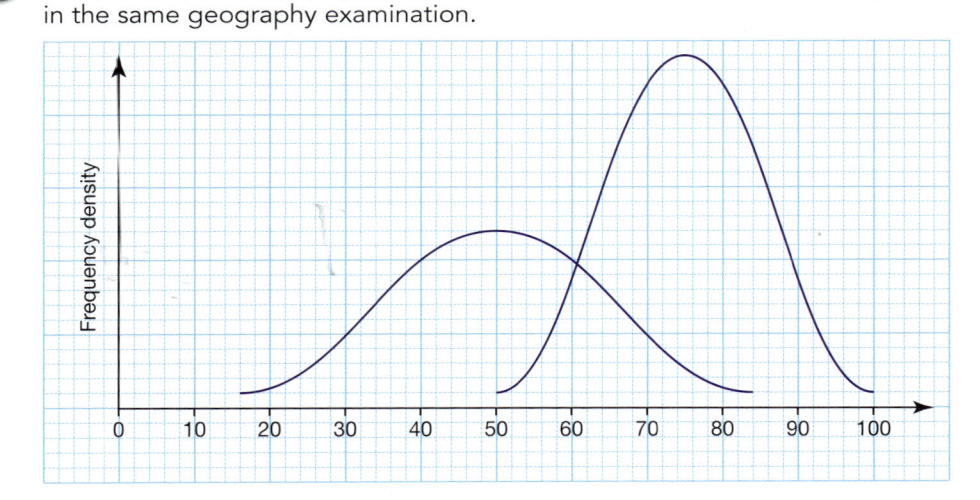

The first distribution has a mean of 50 and a standard deviation of 12.

a Between what limits does 95% of the data lie in the first distribution?

0.1% of the students in the second sample have a mark greater than 101.

b Calculate the standard deviation of the second distribution.

c Comment on the abilities of students in both classes.

Data analysis: Chapter 8 Measures of spread

A*

9 In the 1976 Montreal Olympics, Alberto Juantorena won both the 400 m and 800 m gold medals.

AO4

The tables below show the times for all the athletes in both events.

		400 M MENS FINAL RESULTS	
G	CUB	Alberto JUANTORENA	44.26
S	USA	Frederick NEWHOUSE	44.40
B	USA	Herman FRAZIER	44.95
4	BEL	Alfons BRIJDENBACH	45.04
5	USA	Maxie PARKS	45.24
6	AUS	Richard MITCHELL	45.40
7	GBR	David JENKINS	45.57
8	POL	Jan WERNER	45.63

		800 M MENS FINAL RESULTS	
G	CUB	Alberto JUANTORENA	WR 1:43.50
S	BEL	Ivo van DAMME	1:43.86
B	USA	Richard WOLHUTER	1:44.12
4	GER	Willi WULBECK	1:45.26
5	GBR	Steve OVETT	1:45.44
6	YUG	Luciana SUSANJ	1:45.75
7	IND	Sriram SINGH	1:45.77
8	ITA	Carlo GRIPPO	1:48.39

a Calculate the mean time and standard deviation for each event.

b Standardise Alberto's times in both events to find the event in which he performed better.

GRADE BOOSTER

What you need to do to get this grade

C	You can draw and interpret box-and-whisker plots.
C–B	You can calculate and draw outliers on a box-and-whisker plot.
B	You can calculate variance and standard deviation of discrete data, and interpret box-and-whisker plots.
	You can understand skewness from box-and-whisker plots.
	You know that, for normal distribution, 65% of data is within ±1 standard deviations, 95% within ±2 standard deviations and 99.8% within ± 3 standard deviations.
A–A*	You can calculate variance and standard deviation of grouped data.
	You can standardise scores and interpret the results.

What you should now know

- The advantages and disadvantages of measures of spread.
- How to draw and interpret a box-and-whisker plot.

Higher tier only

- How to calculate outliers.
- What a normal distribution is and how it relates to the mean and standard deviation.
- How to calculate variance and standard deviation of discrete data with and without a calculator.
- How to calculate variance and standard deviation of grouped data, with and without a calculator.
- How to standardise scores and interpret the results.

EXAMINATION Questions

1 The table shows the traffic using the Channel Tunnel during the period 1994–2000.

Channel Tunnel traffic (thousands)								
Year	1994	1995	1996	1997	1998	1999	2000
Passenger vehicles	82	1246	2135	2383	2864	3448	3342
Passengers on trains	315	7018	12 749	14 613	18 496	17 424	17 152
Freight vehicles	65	391	519	268	705	1133	939

Source: Adapted from monthly Digest of Statistics 2004

a Give one similarity and one difference between the annual numbers of passenger vehicles and freight vehicles over the seven-year period. *(2 marks)*

b The times taken, in minutes, by a sample of passenger trains to travel from London to Paris over a period of one month are summarised in the box-and-whisker diagram.

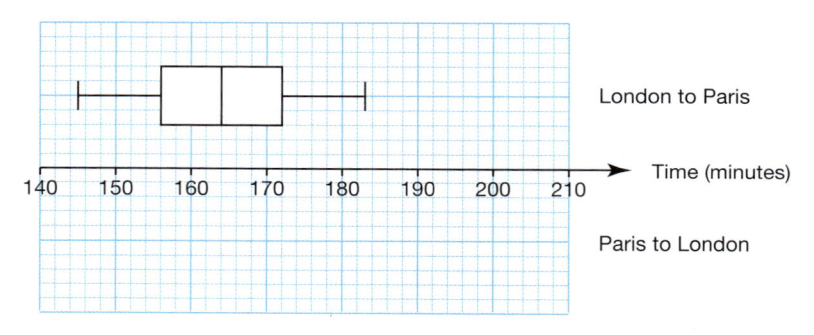

London to Paris

Time (minutes)

Paris to London

The times taken, in minutes, by a sample of passenger trains to travel from Paris to London over the same period of one month are summarised in the table.

Minumum	Lower quartile	Median	Upper quartile	Maximum
148	150	155	195	202

i Use these values to draw a box-and-whisker diagram. *(3 marks)*

ii Describe the shape of the two distributions (London to Paris and Paris to London). *(2 marks)*

iii State the least journey time beyond which any **large** outliers could occur for the Paris to London distribution. *(1 mark)*

AQA June 2007, Higher Statistics Paper, Question 9

2 Sunita is an unemployed IT consultant.

She is planning to move to the North East, North West or West Midlands of the UK to find work.

She downloads from the internet details of 25 vacancies for IT staff in each region.

A summary of the salaries in the North East and North West regions is illustrated in the box plots below.

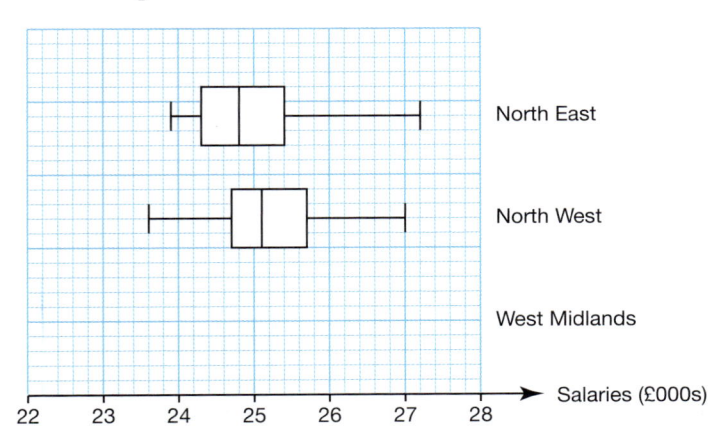

a What is the range of salaries in the North East region? *(1 mark)*

b Find the interquartile range of salaries in the North West region. *(2 marks)*

c Sunita summarises her results from the West Midlands region.

The median salary on offer was £25 000, the lower quartile salary was £23 400 and the interquartile range was £3100.

The highest salary was £26 900 and the lowest £22 300.

Use these results to draw a box plot on a grid. *(3 marks)*

d Sunita does not want to move to a region where the range in salaries exceeds £4500 or where the median salary is below £25 000.

  i State which region she should choose. *(1 mark)*

  ii Explain why the other two regions would not be selected. *(2 marks)*

AQA June 2008, Higher Statistics Paper, Question 3

Data analysis: Chapter 8 Examination questions

3 a A bank kept a daily record of the number of cheques with errors that were presented for payment.

The results from a random sample of 150 days are shown in the table.

Number of cheques with errors	Number of days
0	4
1	21
2	38
3	38
4	22
5	15
6	8
7	4

Calculate the mean, variance and standard deviation of the number of cheques each day with errors. *(5 marks)*

b Another bank recorded the times taken to process an equal number of cheque errors at two of its branches, A and B.

The times taken, in minutes, at each of the two branches were normally distributed with mean and standard deviation as shown in the table.

	Mean (minutes)	Standard deviation (minutes)
Branch A	16.5	2.8
Branch B	14	4.5

To compare the performance of both branches, it was agreed to standardise the times taken at each branch.

  i What would be the standard time for a cheque from Branch A taking 21 minutes to process? *(2 marks)*

  ii A cheque processed at Branch B had a standardised time of 2.4 minutes.

  What was the actual processing time? *(3 marks)*

  iii Between what limits would you expect approximately 99.9% of the cheque processing times for Branch A to lie? *(3 marks)*

  AQA June 2007, Higher Statistics Paper, Question 10

4 Jim and Shaun are members of a fishing club and regularly fish in a lake together.

On each occasion they record how long it takes for one of them to catch the first fish.

The times taken (in minutes) are normally distributed with mean and standard deviation as shown.

	Mean time (minutes)	Standard deviation of times (minutes)
Jim	35	6
Shaun	40	10

Records show that on Friday of last week the first fish was caught after 25 minutes.

Which of the two fishermen is more likely to have caught this particular fish?

Explain your answer fully. *(4 marks)*

AQA June 2008, Higher Statistics Paper, Question 8b

5 The mean and standard deviation of the marks in a mathematics exam and in a statistics exam are shown.

	Mean	Standard deviation
Mathematics	63	6
Statistics	73	8

The marks in both exams are normally distributed.

a John scored 54 marks in the mathematics exam and 57 marks in the statistics exam.

John claimed he was better at mathematics.

By standardising his marks, decide if the data supports his claim. *(5 marks)*

b Sketch the distributions for both mathematics and statistics on a grid like this. *(4 marks)*

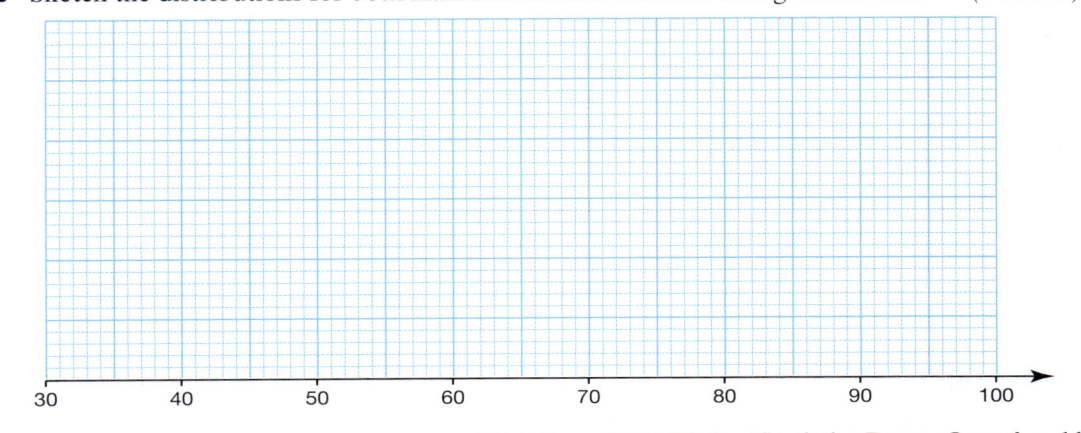

AQA June 2004, Higher Statistics Paper, Question 11

Data analysis: Chapter 8 Examination questions

6 Joan is a Road Safety Officer for a City Council.

Part of her work involves recording the number of vehicles exceeding the speed limit as they pass local schools.

The following table gives the data recorded over a 120-day period, e.g. on 42 days two vehicles per day exceeded the speed limit.

Number of vehicles per day exceeding speed limit	2	5	6	10	14	15	20
Number of days	42	28	18	14	10	5	3

a Calculate the mean and standard deviation of the number of vehicles per day that exceeded the speed limit.

Give your answers to two decimal places. *(2 marks)*

b Due to a fault on the recording equipment, Joan's records did not show a further two vehicles **each** day that exceeded the speed limit.

What effect will this error have on the values for:

i the mean?

ii the standard deviation? *(2 marks)*

c During the same period two other Road Safety Officers recorded equal numbers of actual traffic speeds at different locations in the city.

The speeds recorded by the first Road Safety Officer are normally distributed.

i Copy the grid below and complete the diagram for this distribution. *(2 marks)*

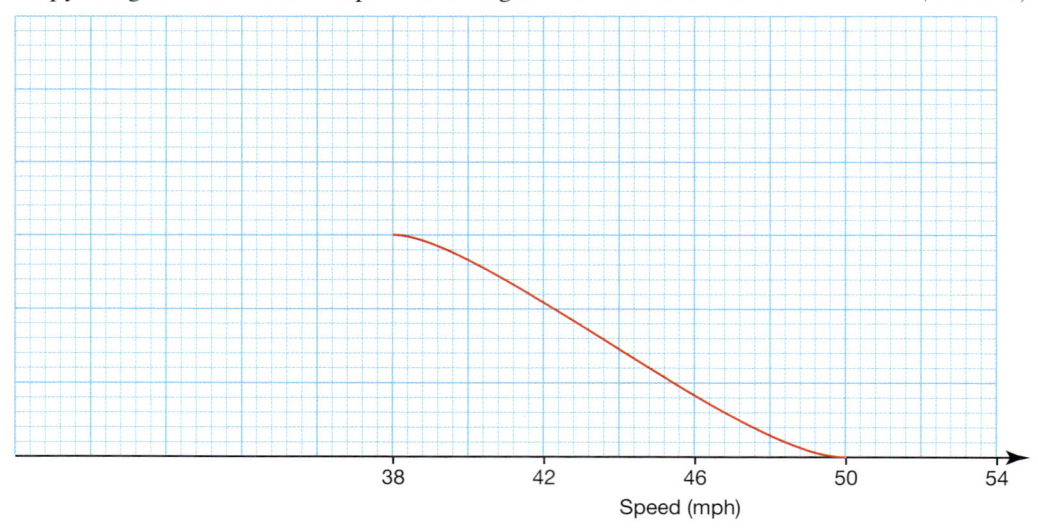

[Graph with x-axis labelled "Speed (mph)" showing values 38, 42, 46, 50, 54]

ii The speeds recorded by the second Road Safety Officer were also normally distributed.

They had a mean of 44 mph and standard deviation of 2 mph.

On the same grid draw a diagram to represent this distribution. *(3 marks)*

AQA June 2006, Higher Statistics Paper, Question 11

WORKED EXAMINATION Questions

1 The table gives the mean and standard deviation of the men's 100 m and 200 m finals at the 2008 Beijing Olympics. Usain Bolt won both races in world record times. His winning times are also shown.

Race (m)	Usain's time (s)	Mean (s)	Standard deviation (s)
100	9.69	9.9225	0.098 456
200	19.30	20.075	0.411 248

a Standardise Usain's times for both events. *(2 marks)*

b In which event did Usain perform better? Give a reason for your answer. *(2 marks)*

Standardised score = $\dfrac{\text{mean} - \text{score}}{\text{standard deviation}}$

For the 100 m = $\dfrac{9.69 - 9.9225}{0.098\ 456} = -2.36$

For the 200 m = $\dfrac{19.30 - 20.075}{0.411\ 248} = -1.88$

Usain performed better in the 100 m as it is further from the mean.

Use the formula for standardising scores to calculate each value, gaining 1 mark for each.

Usain's times were well below the mean in both races, as you would expect. The further away from the mean, which is the most negative, is therefore his best performance.

You will gain 1 mark for 100 m and 1 mark for explaining why.

(Total: 4 marks)

9 Statistics used in everyday life

Statistics are used by the Government to plan the services it provides; for example, if the birth rate were to rise, then in four years' time more primary school places would be needed and in eleven years' time more secondary schools places would be required.

Index numbers are a helpful way of looking at the way in which data is changing. Common ones are the **Retail price index** (RPI) and the **Consumer price index** (CPI). These indices are used to monitor inflation and to determine wages and pensions.

The RPI includes data on food and drink, tobacco, housing, household goods and services, personal goods and services, transport fares, motoring costs, clothing and leisure goods and services.

Recently, the CPI, which is also known as the **general index of consumer prices**, has been used more often. Although the CPI is similar to the RPI, there are significant differences. An important one is that the CPI does not include mortgage interest payments, whereas the RPI does.

GOVERNMENT SWITCHES FROM RPI TO CPI

By Sophie Baker

The Government's decision to alter private sector pension indexation from the retail price index (RPI) to the consumer price index (CPI) will reduce the value of occupational pensions, warns the Trade Union Congress (TUC).

It is not clear whether, in future, the UK will use the CPI instead of the RPI. Currently, the Government and statisticians use both. Eventually, the decision will be a political one.

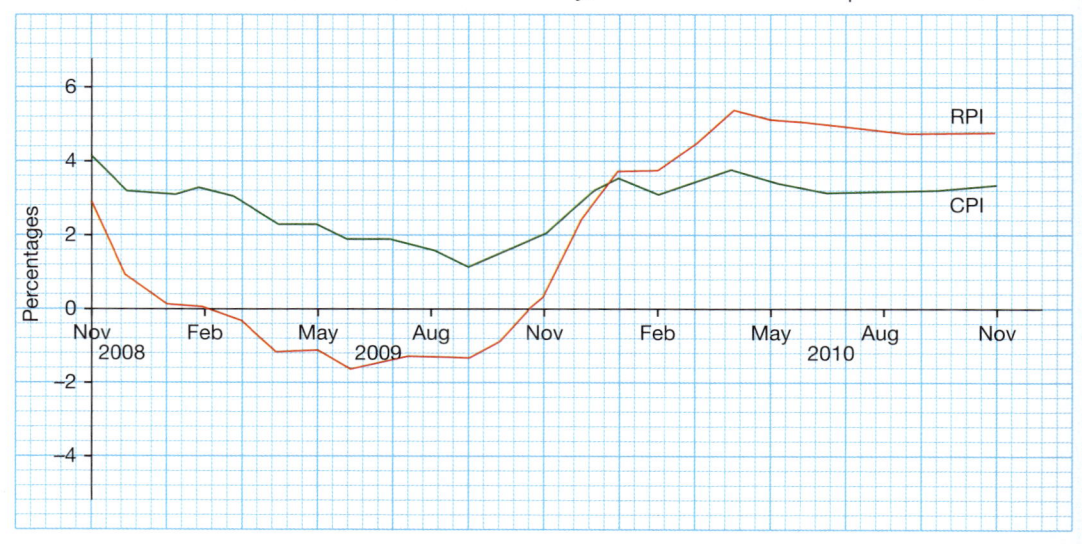

9.1 Statistics used in everyday life

This chapter will show you how to:

- calculate and use index numbers

Higher tier only

- calculate weighted index numbers
- calculate chain base numbers
- interpret the retail price index (RPI) and the consumer price index (CPI)
- interpret how statistics are used by the Government to plan services.

The exercise questions in this chapter are given individual target grades as a guide.

Visual overview

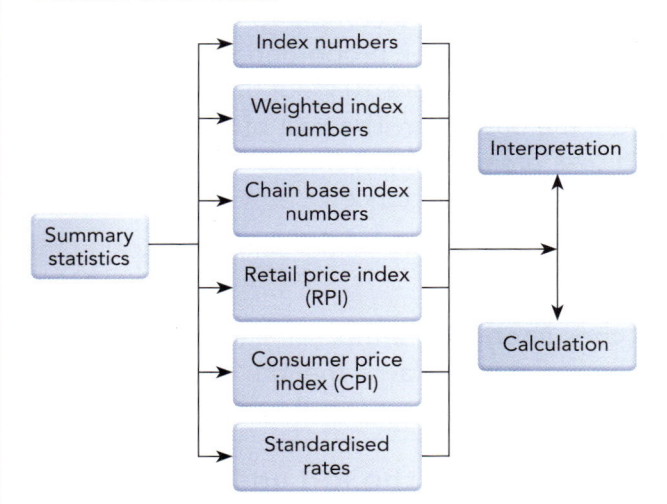

Summary statistics →
- Index numbers
- Weighted index numbers
- Chain base index numbers
- Retail price index (RPI)
- Consumer price index (CPI)
- Standardised rates

↔ Interpretation / Calculation

What you should already know

- **D** How to work out a percentage increase or decrease (KS3, level 6).
- **D** How to use a multiplying factor to work out a percentage increase or decrease (KS3, level 6).

Quick check

1. What is the multiplying factor needed to increase a quantity by 20%?
2. What is the multiplying factor needed to decrease a quantity by 20%?
3. Increase £54 by 20%.

9.1 Statistics used in everyday life

This section will show you:
- how statistics are used in everyday life and statistical information is used by the Government
- how to apply statistics in everyday situations
- how to calculate index numbers.

KEY WORDS

Chain base method
Consumer price index
Retail price index
Weighted index numbers
Standardised rates

In daily life, many situations occur in which statistical techniques are used to produce data. The results of surveys appear in newspapers every day. People are frequently given the chance to vote, there are many on-line polls and phone-ins such as reality TV shows.

The Government uses statistics to plan its services; for example, an ageing population has implications for the NHS.

General indexes of retail prices

The **retail price index** (RPI) measures how much the daily cost of living increases (or decreases). One year is taken as the base year and given an index number, usually 100. Costs of goods and services in subsequent years are compared to those in the base year. Then each of these subsequent years is given a number, proportional to the base year, such as 103. An index of 103 means that the prices in that year are 103% of the prices in the base year, or that prices have increased by 3% from the base year. The cost of the 'basket of goods bought by an average family' is compared over time. Different weightings are given to the different goods bought by the family, according to their importance.

Note: The numbers do not represent actual values but just compare current prices to those in the base year.

More recently, the **consumer price index** (CPI) has been used. This is also known as the general index of consumer prices. It is similar to the RPI. The CPI is used more commonly in other EU countries than the RPI and allows comparison of inflation rates across European countries.

Main differences between the RPI and the CPI

- The CPI does not include mortgage interest payments, so if interest rates rise the RPI will be affected but the CPI will not.
- The RPI includes council tax and other housing costs; these are not included in the CPI.
- The CPI includes some financial services not found in the RPI.
- The CPI process for working out weights is based on a wider sample of the population than is used for the RPI.

The annual percentage change in the RPI or CPI is used as a measure of inflation.

Data analysis: Chapter 9 Statistics used in everyday life

Example 1

The table shows the annual salary of a bus driver from 2000 to 2009.

Year	2000	2003	2006	2009
Annual salary (£)	18 500	20 000	22 500	24 000

a Using 2000 as the base year, calculate a salary index for 2003, 2006 and 2009, to 3 significant figures.
b What is the percentage increase in salary from 2000 to 2009?
c If the index number for 2010 is 135, what would the weekly wage have been then?

Solution

a If 2000 is the base year then the salary index for 2000 is 100.

Index for 2003 = $\frac{20\,000}{18\,500} \times 100 = 108$ (to 3 s.f.)

Index for 2006 = $\frac{22\,500}{18\,500} \times 100 = 122$ (to 3 s.f.)

Index for 2009 = $\frac{24\,000}{18\,500} \times 100 = 130$ (to 3 s.f.)

b The salary index in 2000 is 100, the index in 2009 is 130 so the salary has increased by 30%.

c The weekly wage in 2010 = $\frac{135}{100} \times 18\,500 = £24\,975$.

Example 2

A manufacturer uses weighted index numbers to monitor the costs of a manufacturing process.

Food	Weight	Index (2000 = 100)
Raw materials	125	199.8
Labour	85	226.3
Machinery and plant	110	164.3
Administration costs	68	112.6

Weights are given to the components, depending on how important they are to the process. The price index for each of the components in 2010 is known. The base year for the price index is 2000.

Calculate the weighted index for the cost of the manufacturing process in 2010. Give your answer correct to 1 d.p.

Solution

Food	Weight	Index (2000 = 100)	Weight × index
Raw materials	125	199.8	24 975.0
Labour	85	226.3	19 235.5
Machinery and plant	110	164.3	18 073.0
Administration costs	68	112.6	7656.8
Total	388		69 940.3

Weighted index = $\frac{60\,940.3}{388} = 180.3$ (1 d.p.)

Data analysis: Chapter 9 Statistics used in everyday life

The **chain base method** compares current prices to those of the previous year rather than the base year. This is demonstrated in the next example.

Example 3

The table shows the annual cost of Tariq's house insurance for the past three years.

Year	2008	2009	2010
Annual cost	302	288	280

a Use the chain base method to calculate index numbers for the years 2008 to 2010. Give your answers to one decimal place.

b What do these index numbers tell you about the percentage rise or fall in the cost of house insurance from 2008 to 2010?

Solution

a 2009 chain base index number = $\frac{288}{302} \times 100 = 95.4$

2010 chain base index number = $\frac{280}{288} \times 100 = 97.2$

b The cost of house insurance fell by 4.6% from 2008 to 2009 and fell by 2.8% from 2009 to 2010.

Note
The rate of fall in the cost of house insurance is decreasing.

The term price relative is sometimes used in economics to show today's price as a percentage of the base year price.

price relative = $\frac{\text{price}}{\text{price in base year}} \times 100$

Example 4

The price of a bale of cotton in January 2011 was $156.94. The price of a bale of cotton in its base year of 1970 was $25.33.

Find the price relative of a bale of cotton for January 2011 compared to its base year of 1970.

Solution

price relative = $\frac{156.94}{25.33} \times 100$

= 619.58% (to 2 decimal places)

Data analysis: Chapter 9 Statistics used in everyday life

The **standardised rate** is a weighted average that takes into account the national standard population per 1000 people. This allows two different populations to be compared even though they may be of a different size with a different percentage make-up of age groups. This is demonstrated in the next example

Example 5

The standardised unemployment rate of town A is 12.75

The standardised unemployment rate of town B is 28.4

a Explain what a standardised unemployment rate of 28.4 means.

b Alice is deciding whether to move to town A or to town B to look for a job. Which town would you advise her to move to? Explain your answer.

c Give a possible reason for the different standardised unemployment rates of towns A and B.

Solution

a 28.4 people per 1000 are unemployed when weighted according to the national standard population.

b Town A. It has a lower unemployment rate, so she should get a job more easily.

c Town A could be better because: it has lots of large factories; it may be near a city; it may have lots of skilled workers; it might be an expensive place to buy a house.

Town B could be worse because: a big company has closed; it might be a long way from a motorway; it may have lots of unskilled workers; it could be a deprived area.

Exercise 9A

1 In 2004 the cost of a loaf of bread was 80p. Using 2004 as a base year, the price index of bread for each of the next five years is shown in this table. AO3

Year	2004	2005	2006	2007	2008	2009
Index	100	102.5	107.5	108.7	112.5	120
Price (p)	80					

Work out the price of a loaf of bread in each subsequent year. Give your answers to 1 decimal place.

2 The general index of retail prices started in January 1987, when it was given a base number of 100. In January 2008 the index number was 198.7. AO3, AO4

If the standard shopping basket cost £42.30 in January 1987, how much would it have cost in January 2008?

Data analysis: Chapter 9 Statistics used in everyday life

3 The graph shows the exchange rate for the US dollar against the pound for each month in one year.

AO3, AO4

Exchange rate of the dollar to the pound

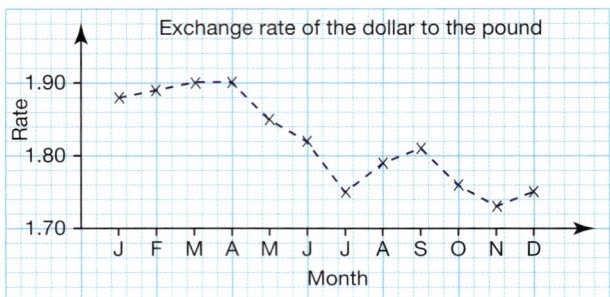

a What was the exchange rate in January?

b Between which two months did the exchange rate fall the most?

c Explain why you could not use the graph to predict the exchange rate in January of the next year.

4 Nasreen wants to compare the cost of buying some basic groceries so she devises a typical 'shopping basket'. She gives weights to the goods in the basket, depending on how important they are to her weekly shop. She also knows the price index for each of her goods in 2010. The base year for the price index is 2000.

AO3, AO4

Nasreen's shopping basket		
Food	Weight	Index (2000 = 100)
Bread	130	201.4
Fruit and vegetables	110	198.5
Meat and fish	110	164.3
Dairy products	75	199.5
Sweets, cake and biscuits	48	154.7

a Calculate the weighted index for Nasreen's shopping basket in 2010. Give your answer correct to 1 decimal place.

b Which foods does Nasreen view as:
  i the least important?
  ii the most important?

5 The retail price index measures how much the daily cost of living increases or decreases.

AO4

If 2009 is given a base number of 100, then 2010 is given 97. What does this mean?

6 The table shows the annual cost of Jess's car insurance for the past four years.

AO3

Year	2007	2008	2009	2010
Annual cost (£)	180	170	200	220

a Use the chain base method to calculate index numbers for the years 2008 to 2010 inclusive. Give your answers to one decimal place.

b What do your index numbers tell you?

7 This time series shows aeroplane parts production in Britain from November 2004 to November 2005.

AO3, AO4

Aeroplane parts production in Britain November 2004 to November 2005

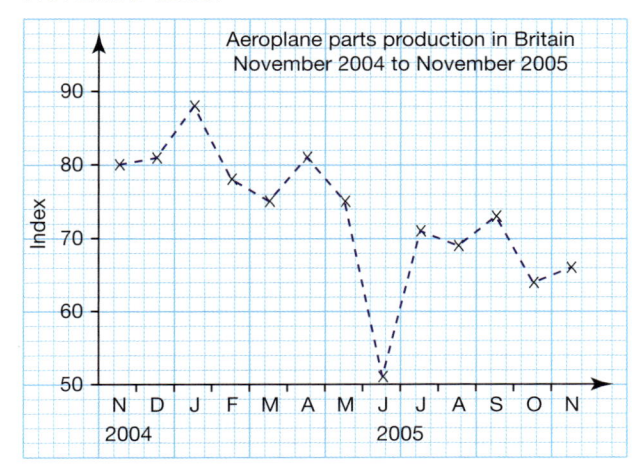

a You can see from the graph that there was a sharp drop in production in June. Think of some reasons why this might have happened.

b The average production over the first three months shown was 172 thousand parts.

  i Work out an approximate number for the average production over the last three months shown.

  ii The base month for the index is January 2000 when the index was 100. What was the approximate production in January 2000?

8 A new maternity hospital is to be built in one of two towns.

The two towns under consideration are Avem and Kidlyss.

Avem has a standardised birth rate of 12.6

Kidlyss has a standardised birth rate of 3.9

a Explain what a standardised birth rate of 12.6 means.

b On the basis of standardised birth rates, in which town should the new maternity hospital be built?

c What information might be useful in changing this decision?

GRADE BOOSTER

What you need to do to get this grade

D	You can find any percentage of a quantity.
	You can find a new quantity after an increase or decrease by a percentage.
C	You can calculate and use index numbers.
	You can calculate and interpret weighted index numbers.
B	You can **interpret** the retail price index (RPI) and the consumer price index (CPI).
	You can interpret standardised rates.

What you should now know

- How to calculate and use index numbers.

Higher tier only

- How to calculate weighted index numbers.
- How to calculate chain base numbers.
- How to interpret the retail price index (RPI) and the consumer price index (CPI).
- How to interpret standardised rates.
- How statistics are used by the Government to plan services.

EXAMINATION Questions

1 The following is taken from the UK government statistics website.

In mid-2004 the UK was home to 59.8 million people, of which 50.1 million lived in England. The average age was 38.6 years, an increase on 1971 when it was 34.1 years. In mid-2004 approximately one in five people in the UK were aged under 16 and one in six people were aged 65 or over.

Use this extract to answer the following questions about the UK in 2004.

    a How many of the population of the UK did not live in England? *(1 mark)*

    b By how much had the average age increased since 1971? *(1 mark)*

    c Approximately how many of the population were aged under 16? *(1 mark)*

    d Approximately how many of the population were aged over 65? *(1 mark)*

2 On one day in 2009 Alex spent £51 in a supermarket. She knew that the price index over the last three years was:

2007	2008	2009
100	103	102

How much would she have paid in the supermarket for the same goods in 2008? *(2 marks)*

3 Reya knew that the cost of living price index was set at 100 for 2007, 104 for 2008 and 105 for 2009. She bought some sausages for £2.10 in 2009. How much would you have expected them to cost a year earlier? *(2 marks)*

4 The house price index for a flat in Leeds was 190 in August 2006, compared with a base of 100 in April 2000.

    a Write down the percentage increase in the price of flats in Leeds in that period. *(1 mark)*

    b A flat cost £80 000 in April 2000. What was its likely value in August 2006? *(2 marks)*

AQA, May 2008, Paper 1 Higher, Question 12

Data analysis: Chapter 9 Examination questions

5 The table shows the breakdown of the Retail Price Index at July 2004.

	Group	Weight	Index (1987 = 100)
1	Food	111	152.9
2	Catering	49	231.8
3	Leisure goods	46	99.1
4	Leisure services	70	251.3
5	Housing	209	263.8
6	Fuel and light	28	139.4
7	Household goods	71	145.3
8	Household services	59	180.4
9	Clothing and footwear	51	99.0
10	Personal goods and services	42	200.0
11	Motoring expenditure	146	184.5
12	Fares and other travel costs	21	215.6
13	Alcoholic drink	68	204.3
14	Tobacco	29	313.7

(Based on the Retail Price Index, Monthly Digest of Statistics, July 2004)

The 'All groups' index for July 2004 is 198.4.

a i Calculate an 'All groups' index, **excluding** expenditure on both Alcoholic drink and Tobacco.

Give your answer to one decimal place. *(4 marks)*

ii Explain why the 'All groups' index has decreased. *(2 marks)*

b The table shows the annual cost of Rashid's car insurance for the past five years.

Year	2002	2003	2004	2005	2006
Annual cost (£)	500	546	670	640	625

i Use the chain base method to calculate index numbers for the years 2003 to 2006 inclusive.

Give your answers to one decimal place. *(4 marks)*

ii Describe what these chain base index numbers show. *(2 marks)*

AQA June 2007, Higher Paper, Question 12

6 The table shows information collected from the wages department of an engineering company.

Type of work	2003		2006
	Number of employees	Weekly wage (£)	Weekly wage (£)
Management	10	525	615
Clerical	18	210	255
Skilled	48	410	528
Semi-skilled	15	190	330

a The total weekly wage bill for 2003 is £31 560.

Using 2003 as the base year, calculate the index for the total weekly wage bill in 2006.
(5 marks)

b i Calculate the percentage increase in the weekly wage for semi-skilled workers from 2003 to 2006. *(2 marks)*

ii Explain why this value shows a higher percentage increase than the index calculated in part **a**. *(1 mark)*

AQA June 2008, Higher Paper, Question 7

7 Sliddon Ceramics use three materials in the manufacture of a product. The ratio by weight of the three materials X, Y and Z to manufacture one of these products is 3 : 5 : 12.

Three kilograms of material X are used in the manufacture of each one of these products. The costs per kilo of these materials in the years 2004–2006 were as follows.

Raw materials	Costs per kilo (£)		
	2004	2005	2006
X	3.50	3.50	5.20
Y	1.50	1.70	2.10
Z	6.00	6.80	7.40

a The total cost of materials used to manufacture one of these products in 2004 was £90.00.

Calculate the total cost of materials used to manufacture the same product in 2006.
(2 marks)

b Use the answer from part **a** to calculate, to 1 d.p, a materials cost index for 2006, with 2004 as base year. *(2 marks)*

c From 2004 to 2006 the company increased the selling price of each one of these products by 38%.

Compare this increase with the change in the cost of materials over the same period.
(1 mark)

AQA June 2009, Higher Paper, Question 10

Data analysis: Chapter 9 Examination questions

WORKED EXAMINATION Questions

1 The graph shows the average weekly household expenditure on groceries in the UK.

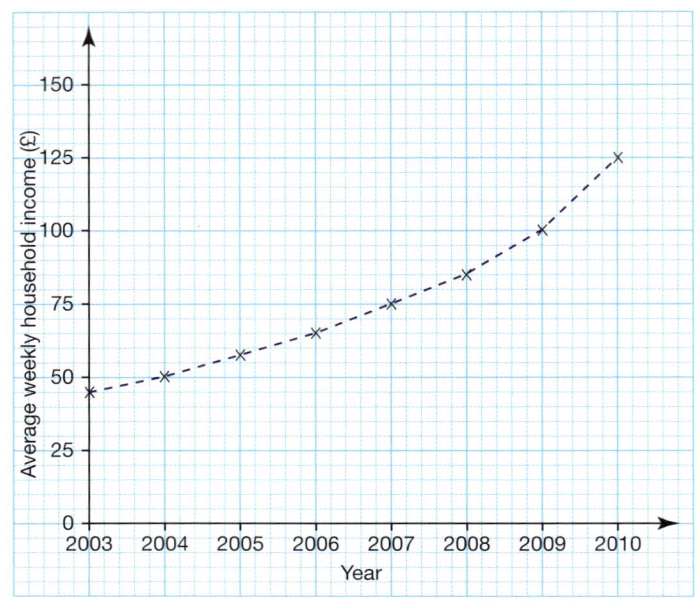

a By how much did the average weekly household expenditure on groceries increase from 2008 to 2009?

Expenditure in 2009 = 100

Expenditure in 2008 = 85

Rise = 100 − 85 = £15

> Read the values from the graph and then subtract them to find the increase, for **1 mark**.

b Between which two years was there the largest annual increase in average weekly household expenditure on groceries?

2009 and 2010, where the slope is steepest.

> Reading the graph and identifying where it has the steepest slope gives these two years, for **1 mark**.

(Total: 2 marks)

2 The table shows the annual cost of heating for the average household over the last five years.

Year	2006	2007	2008	2009	2010
Annual cost (£)	1050	1176	1198	1265	1440

a Use the chain base method to calculate index numbers for the years 2007 to 2010 inclusive.
Give your answers correct to one decimal place. *(4 marks)*

2007 $\frac{1176}{1050} \times 100 = 112.0$

2008 $\frac{1198}{1176} \times 100 = 102.0$

2009 $\frac{1265}{1198} \times 100 = 105.6$

2010 $\frac{1440}{1265} \times 100 = 113.8$

You will gain **2 marks** for showing your method (**1 mark** for multiplying by 100). And you will get another **2 marks** if all your answers are correct, or **1 mark** if only two or three are correct.

b Between which two years did **fuel** prices increase the most and by how much? *(2 marks)*

The prices increased the most from 2009 to 2010, by about 13.8%.

You get **1 mark** for identifying the years correctly.

You will gain **1 mark** for identifying the years correctly, and **1 mark** for stating 13.8% or 14%.

(Total: 6 marks)

3 The table shows the breakdown of the retail price index at January 2010.

	Group	Weight	Index (2000 = 100)
1	Food	112	187
2	Leisure goods and services	63	154
3	Housing	252	123
4	Heating and lighting	34	175
5	Household goods	68	151
6	Household services	62	192
7	Clothing and footwear	55	95
8	Personal goods and services	40	150
9	Motoring expenditure	150	220
10	Fares and other travel costs	27	213
11	Alcoholic drink	53	134
12	Tobacco	25	314

Data analysis: Chapter 9 Examination questions

a i Calculate the All Groups Index for January 2010, giving your answer correct to one decimal place. *(4 marks)*

	Group	Weight	Index (2000 = 100)	Weight × index
1	Food	112	187	20944
2	Leisure goods and services	63	154	9702
3	Housing	252	123	30 996
4	Heating and lighting	34	175	5950
5	Household goods	68	151	10 268
6	Household services	62	192	11 904
7	Clothing and footwear	55	95	5225
8	Personal goods and services	40	150	6000
9	Motoring expenditure	150	220	33 000
10	Fares and other travel costs	27	213	5751
11	Alcoholic drink	53	134	7102
12	Tobacco	25	314	7850
	Total	941		154 962

For 2010, All groups index = $\frac{154\,962}{941}$ = 164.4

You will gain **1 mark** for knowing that you need to work out weight × index, whether you work it out correctly or not.

You will gain **1 mark** for knowing that you need to divide the total of weight × index by the total of the weights and another **1 mark** for the answer.

You will gain **1 mark** for knowing that you need to add all the products of weight × index together.

246

ii Calculate the All Groups Index if tobacco is removed. *(2 marks)*

If tobacco is removed:

sum of indices = 916

sum of weight × index = 147 112

So All groups index = $\frac{147\ 112}{916}$ = 160.6

> You will gain **1 mark** subtracting 25 from your 941 calculated in part a, and subtracting 7850 from your 154 962 in part a, and dividing the new values.

> **Note**
> Follow-through marks are given here, so even if you have worked out the wrong answers earlier you will still get the marks if you show your working.

b The All Groups Index has decreased. Explain why this has happened. *(1 mark)*

Tobacco had a high index value, 314. (Its cost had increased more than 3 times since 2000.)

> You will gain **1 mark** for any reference to tobacco's high value compared to the others.

(Total: 7 marks)

10 Time series and quality assurance

UK RETAIL SALES FALL IN SEPTEMBER

By Sophie Baker

More and more high-street retailers are complaining of tough trading conditions.
According to official data, UK retail sales fell in September, the second successive month this has happened.
A spokesperson for the retail

CONSTRUCTION SECTOR BOOSTS GDP GROWTH FIGURES

It has been a remarkable year for the construction sector. In the first three months, hit by adverse weather, it contracted by 0.8%. Then, in the second quarter, it underwent a marked recovery, growing by an amazing 9.5%.
It grew another 4% in the third quarter. Overall, in the year since the recession ended, construction has grown by 11%.

Time series

A time series is a set of values of the same variable at different times, normally at uniform intervals. Time series analysis is an important tool, used by government and businesses to understand changes over time. Here are some possible questions that may arise.

- Have sales risen or fallen and how quickly are they rising or falling?
- Is seasonal variation affecting sales, for example, has consumption of heating oil fallen because it is summer?

Domestic fuel bills also vary over the year. An electricity bill can rise for many reasons, including:

- an increase in the price of electricity
- a rise in the amount of electricity used because a new garden lighting system has been installed
- the season: more electricity is used in the winter because it is colder.

Time series data can be analysed to help answer these questions.

Quality assurance

The purpose of quality assurance (QA) is to ensure that the product or service a business provides is fit for purpose and meets legal requirements and customer expectations. Decisions about whether there is a problem in the production process are made by taking samples and analysing the mean, median and range.

10.1 Moving averages

10.2 Time series

10.3 Quality assurance

This chapter will show you how to:
- draw a line graph to show trends in data over time
- use sample means, medians and ranges to ensure consistency and accuracy for quality assurance

Higher tier only
- calculate and use moving averages
- plot moving averages and draw a line of best fit to produce a trend line
- interpret questions involving these line graphs
- use trends in line graphs to predict subsequent results and justify your answers
- identify and take account of seasonal effect at a given data point
- draw and interpret Z charts.

The exercise questions in this chapter are given individual target grades as a guide.

Visual overview

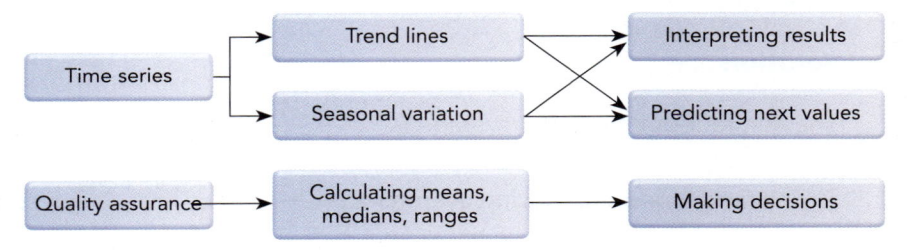

Time series → Trend lines → Interpreting results
Time series → Seasonal variation → Predicting next values

Quality assurance → Calculating means, medians, ranges → Making decisions

What you should already know

- **G** How to draw axes and plot points (KS3, level 3).
- **F** How to draw line graphs (KS3, level 4).
- **F** How to extract information from tables and diagrams (KS3, level 4).
- **F** How to calculate the mean, median, mode and range for small sets of data (KS3, level 4).

Quick check

These are the marks for 12 students in a maths test.

2, 2, 3, 4, 4, 5, 6, 6, 7, 7, 7, 7

a What is the median mark?

b What is the range of the marks?

c What is the mean mark?

10.1 Moving averages

KEY WORDS
Average
Line of best fit
Mean
Moving average
Trend
Variation

This section will show you how to:
- calculate moving averages.

A useful tool in using past data to predict future values is the construction of **moving averages**. These smooth out **variations** in data, for example, caused by changing buying patterns, and can be used to show **trends**.

A moving average is calculated by grouping the data, in sequence, depending upon the type of moving average that is required. For example, a three-point moving average would be obtained from the mean of the first three items of data, then the second to fourth items, and so on. A four-point moving average is based on the data, taken in fours.

Example 1

The table below shows monthly production figures.

Calculate the four-point moving averages from the data.

Month	Jan	Feb	Mar	April	May	June	July	Aug	Sept	Oct	Nov	Dec
Production (unit made)	290	210	320	330	240	316	325	270	380	250	370	256

Solution

The first four-point moving average is $\dfrac{290 + 210 + 320 + 330}{4} = 287.5$

The second four-point moving average is $\dfrac{210 + 320 + 330 + 240}{4} = 275$

The third four-point moving average is $\dfrac{320 + 330 + 240 + 316}{4} = 301.5$

The fourth four-point moving average is $\dfrac{330 + 240 + 316 + 325}{4} = 302.75$

The fifth four-point moving average is $\dfrac{240 + 316 + 325 + 270}{4} = 287.75$

The sixth four-point moving average is $\dfrac{316 + 325 + 270 + 380}{4} = 322.75$

The seventh four-point moving average is $\dfrac{325 + 270 + 380 + 250}{4} = 322.75$

The eighth four-point moving average is $\dfrac{270 + 380 + 250 + 370}{4} = 317.5$

The ninth four-point moving average is $\dfrac{380 + 250 + 370 + 256}{4} = 314$

Data analysis: Chapter 10 Time series and quality assurance

The data can be plotted on a graph, then the moving averages can be added. It is useful to draw a line through the moving averages, passing through as many as possible and with as many above as below it. This line can be used to show trends.

The line through the moving averages is a **line of best fit**, and is called the **trend line**. This can be used to estimate values that are not included in the data. There is more about this in Lesson 10.2, but the next examples should give the general idea.

Example 2

The numbers of visitors to a theme park during the month of August, every year from 2005 to 2010, are shown in the table below.

Year	2005	2006	2007	2008	2009	2010
Number of visitors (thousands)	37	45	42	49	47	56

a Plot these values on a graph.
b Calculate the three-point moving averages and plot them on the same axes.
c Use your graph to predict the number of visitors to the park in 2011.

Solution

a Plot the graph.

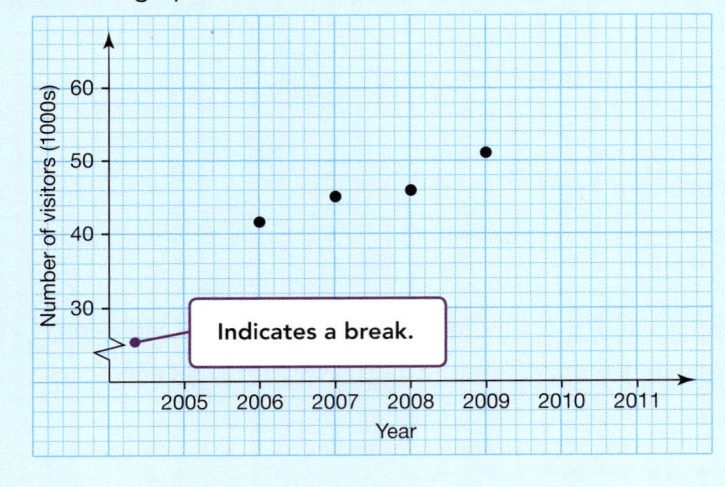

Indicates a break.

Data analysis: Chapter 10 Time series and quality assurance

b The first three-point moving average is $\dfrac{37 + 45 + 42}{3} = 41.3$

The second three-point moving average is $\dfrac{45 + 42 + 49}{3} = 45.3$

The third three-point moving average is $\dfrac{42 + 49 + 47}{3} = 46$

The third three-point moving average is $\dfrac{49 + 47 + 56}{3} = 51$

Plot each moving-average point at the centre of the three points from which it was derived. The first moving average is plotted at 2006.

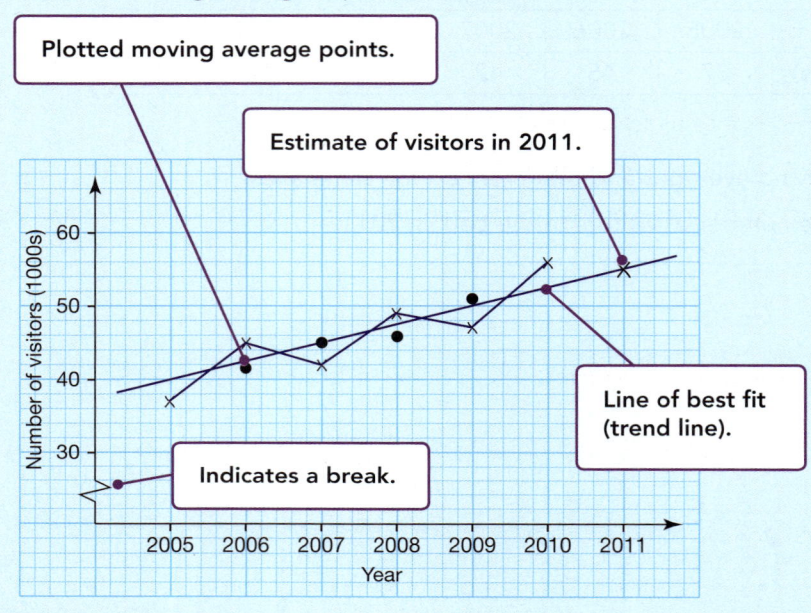

[Graph: Number of visitors (1000s) vs Year (2005–2011), showing plotted moving average points, line of best fit (trend line), estimate of visitors in 2011, and a break indicator on the y-axis.]

Draw the line of best fit.

These averages smooth out the fluctuations and give a more accurate estimation of the trend.

c Reading from the line of best fit, an estimate for the number of visitors in 2011 is 55 000.

Example 3

The table shows quarterly electricity bills paid by a household over three years.

		Year		
		2007	2008	2009
Quarter	1st	£710	£750	£770
	2nd	£410	£426	£452
	3rd	£350	£363	£382
	4th	£680	£707	£730

a Calculate the four-point moving averages for the data.
b Why is a four-point moving average used?
c Give a reason for the quarterly variations shown in the bills.
d Plot the points from the data table and the moving averages on the same graph.
e Use your graph, in combination with seasonal variation calculations, to estimate the bill in the first quarter of 2010.

Solution

a The first four-point moving average is $\frac{710 + 410 + 350 + 680}{4} = 537.5$

The second four-point moving average is $\frac{410 + 350 + 680 + 750}{4} = 547.5$

The third four-point moving average is $\frac{350 + 680 + 750 + 426}{4} = 551.5$

The fourth four-point moving average is $\frac{680 + 750 + 426 + 363}{4} = 554.75$

The fifth four-point moving average is $\frac{750 + 426 + 363 + 707}{4} = 561.5$

The sixth four-point moving average is $\frac{426 + 363 + 707 + 770}{4} = 566.5$

The seventh four-point moving average is $\frac{363 + 707 + 770 + 452}{4} = 573$

The eighth four-point moving average is $\frac{707 + 770 + 452 + 382}{4} = 577.75$

The ninth four-point moving average is $\frac{770 + 452 + 382 + 730}{4} = 583.5$

b A four-point moving average is used because there are four bills each year.

c The variation shows that more electricity is used in the first quarter, in winter when it is cold and dark, than in the third quarter, in the summer.

Data analysis: Chapter 10 Time series and quality assurance

d

> The first quarter seasonal variation is given by the difference between the trend line and the first quarter bill.

> The trend line value for first quarter of 2010.

> Note that the points are plotted in the centre of the four averaged points. i.e. between quarters 2 and 3.

e The average first quarter seasonal variation taken from the difference between the trend line and the first quarter in each year is:

2007   710 − 530 = 180

2008   750 − 555 = 195

2009   770 − 575 = 195

The average first quarter seasonal variation is $\dfrac{180 + 195 + 195}{3} = 190$

So an estimate for the first quarter of 2010 is given by:

trend line value + average seasonal variation = 597 + 190 = 787

Tabulating moving averages

It is quite common to add extra rows or columns to tables, to display moving averages more clearly.

In Example 1, above, the table would have looked like this.

Month	Jan	Feb	Mar	April	May	June	July	Aug	Sept	Oct	Nov	Dec
Production (unit made)	290	210	320	330	240	316	325	270	380	250	370	256
Four-point moving average			287.5	275	301.5	302.75	287.75	322.75	322.75	317.5	314	

This is the first four-point moving average, which is $\frac{290 + 210 + 320 + 330}{4}$ = 287.5. Note that it is centred on the four values from which it is derived.

You can see that the first four-point moving average 'spans' the first four values, although it appears to be centred on the second and third values. It is very important always to identify the type of moving average that is being used.

In Example 2, the table would have looked like this.

Year	2005	2006	2007	2008	2009	2010
Number of visitors (thousands)	37	45	42	49	47	56
Three-point moving average		41.3	45.3	46	51	

This time, the row is not offset because the first moving average is centred on values 1, 2 and 3, and therefore aligns with value 2.

The tables may be set out horizontally, as here, or vertically, as in the next lesson.

Exercise 10A

1 The number of visitors to a botanical garden each year is shown in the table below.

Year	2003	2004	2005	2006	2007	2008	2009	2010
Number of visitors (1000s)	12.2	15.3	16.8	19.4	22	26.1	29.7	30.4

Calculate a three-point moving average of the data.

Data analysis: Chapter 10 Time series and quality assurance

2 The table below shows the number of new cars sold each month by a garage.

Month	Jan	Feb	Mar	April	May	June	July	Aug	Sept	Oct	Nov	Dec
Number of new cars	9	5	30	25	20	10	12	6	28	24	15	7

a Plot these values on a graph.

b Explain the jump in sales figures during March and September.

c Calculate the four-point moving averages.

3 The table shows a household's gas bills over a three-year period.

Month	2005	2006	2007	2008
August (£)	60	63	68	72
November (£)	93	98	106	110
February (£)	155	161	168	174
May (£)	115	118	126	132

a Explain why a four-point moving average is used for this data set.

b Explain the variation in the bills received in August and February.

c Show that the first value of the four-point moving average is £105.75.

d Calculate the second value of the four-point moving average for this data set.

4 The table below shows the number of pupil absences over a 15-day period.

Day	1	2	3	4	5	6	7	8	9	10	11	12	13	14	15
Number of absences	25	30	23	40	32	25	38	22	41	21	36	26	32	43	24

a Plot the values on a set of axes.

b Calculate the four-point moving averages and plot them on the same axes.

c Draw a trend line on your graph.

d Use your trend line to predict the number of absences on day 16.

5 The table below shows the 10-mile time trial times of a cyclist over 10 races.

Race	1	2	3	4	5	6	7	8	9	10
Time (minutes)	26.1	25.2	27.4	24.6	23.5	24.2	22.9	21.7	22.8	21.1

a Plot the values on a set of axes.

b Calculate the three-point moving averages.

c Plot the moving averages on the same set of axes.

d Use a trend line to predict the cyclist's time in the 11th race.

e Why wouldn't it be sensible to use your trend line to predict the cyclist's time in the 30th race?

6 The table below shows the quarterly production figures for a small factory over a three-year period. Figures are units produced.

		Year		
		2008	2009	2010
Quarter	1	2017	3305	4002
	2	2530	3620	4135
	3	2610	3860	4245
	4	2850	3950	4376

a Calculate the four-point moving averages.

b Explain why four-point moving averages are used.

7 The table below shows how an athlete's heart rate increases over the first 10 miles of a marathon (rate taken at the end of each mile).

Mile	1	2	3	4	5	6	7	8	9	10
Heart rate (beats per minute)	135	142	149	160	154	158	163	164	168	163

a Plot the values on a suitable set of axes.

b Calculate the three-point moving averages.

c Plot the moving averages on the same set of axes.

d Estimate the athlete's heart rate at the end of mile 12.

e Why is it not sensible to use your trend line to estimate the athlete's heart rate at the end of the marathon?

Data analysis: Chapter 10 Time series and quality assurance

10.2 Time series

KEY WORDS
Cumulative
Moving average
Seasonal variation
Time series
Trend
Trend line

This section will show you how to:
- draw a line graph to show trends in time series data
- evaluate and plot moving averages
- identify seasonal variation
- predict future values
- plot and use Z charts.

Businesses and the government need to analyse data that has been gathered over time, to find out what has been happening. A **time series** is a set of values of the same variable at different times, normally at uniform intervals. These values can be plotted on a graph, to show patterns or **trends**.

Questions that may need to be answered include:

- Are sales rising or falling?
- Is unemployment rising or falling?

Often there are patterns in the data that are caused by what is called **seasonal variation**. Think how sales of ice cream might vary over the year. Businesses need to be able to find out if sales are rising or falling in the long term, despite this seasonal variation. It is also helpful for households to know if their fuel consumption is rising or falling in the long term or if the changes are due to seasonal variation.

Time series analysis shows how the values of the data are changing over time and can be used to identify patterns in the data. It can be also used to show underlying trends and seasonal variation. **Moving averages** are used to smooth out seasonal variation.

Example 4

This line graph shows the profit made each year by a company over a six-year period. Between which years did the company have the greatest increase in profits?

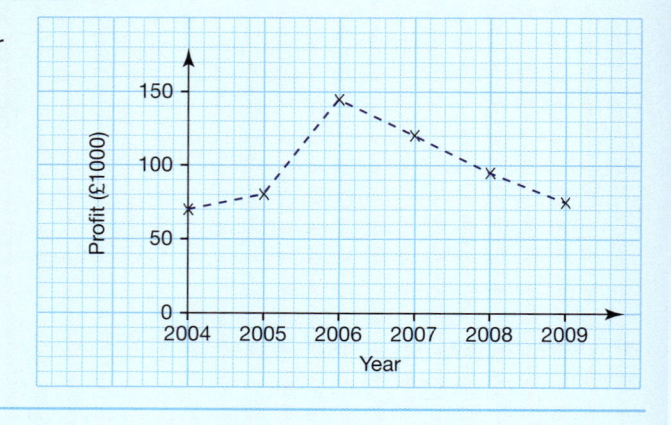

Solution

The greatest increase in profits was between 2005 and 2006 because the line is steepest.

258

Data analysis: Chapter 10 Time series and quality assurance

Example 5

The table shows a DIY store's sales of barbecues in the UK each quarter from 2005 to 2007.

Year	Quarter	Sales of barbecues (£)
2007	Q1	500
	Q2	1000
	Q3	1200
	Q4	100
2008	Q1	600
	Q2	1300
	Q3	1500
	Q4	100
2009	Q1	500
	Q2	1600
	Q3	1800
	Q4	200

a Plot this data on a graph and identify any patterns.
b Calculate four-point moving averages for this data.
c Plot these moving averages on the graph and draw in the **trend line**.
d Calculate the average seasonal effect for the first quarter (Q1).
e Work out an estimate for the value of sales in January 2010, taking into account the seasonal effect.

Solution

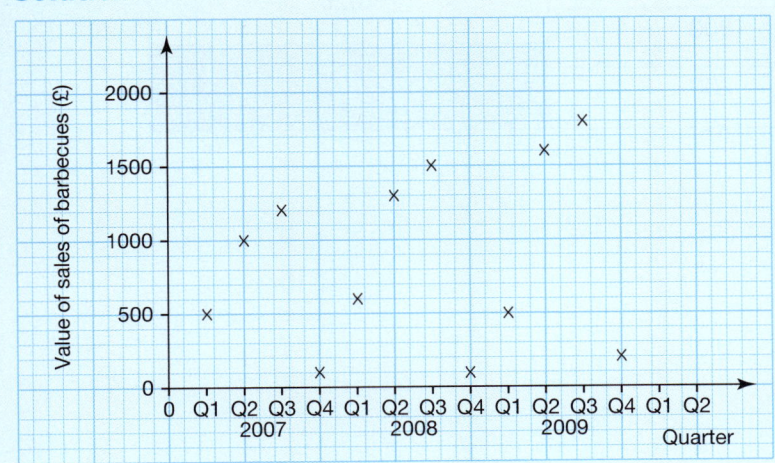

a From the graph it is clear that there is an underlying upward trend, with some seasonal variation.

Not unexpectedly, sales rise in the summer months and fall in the winter months. Sales have been higher in the first quarter of the year than the last quarter of the previous year, possibly because of New Year sales promotions to clear the previous season's stock before the start of the new season.

259

Data analysis: Chapter 10 Time series and quality assurance

b Four-point moving averages are used to smooth out this seasonal variation and because the data varies over four quarters.

The first four-point moving average is the mean of the first four values. The next four-point moving average is the mean of the second to fifth values, and so on.

The first four-point moving average is calculated as $\dfrac{500 + 1000 + 1200 + 100}{4} = 700$.

The second is $\dfrac{1000 + 1200 + 100 + 600}{4} = 725$

and so on. They are shown in this table. Note the position of the averages in the table in the centre of the period they represent.

Year	Quarter	Sales of barbecues (£)	Four-point moving average
2007	Q1	500	
	Q2	1000	
			700
	Q3	1200	
			725
	Q4	100	
			800
2008	Q1	600	
			875
	Q2	1300	
			875
	Q3	1500	
			850
	Q4	100	
			975
2009	Q1	500	
			1000
	Q2	1600	
			1025
	Q3	1800	
	Q4	200	

c The trend line shows the underlying pattern in the data. It is a line of best fit, drawn by 'eye'.

The graph of the moving averages smoothes out the seasonal variation.

The trend line shows that sales are increasing over time. It can be used to calculate the average seasonal effect.

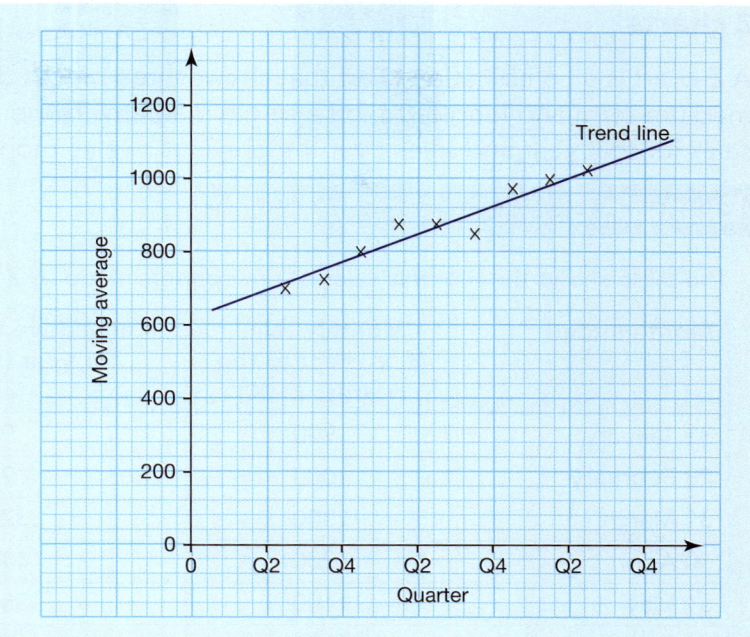

d To calculate the average seasonal effect, first read the values from the trend line and find the difference between this and the actual value. Then calculate the average of these differences.

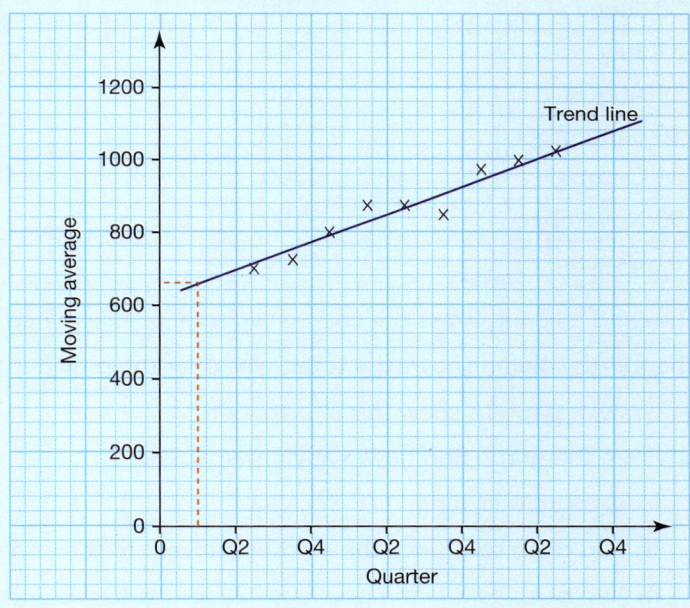

In 2007:   660 (value from trend line) − 500 (2007 Q1) = 160

In 2008:   870 − 600 = 270

In 2009:   1030 − 500 = 530

The average effect is $\dfrac{160 + 270 + 530}{3}$ = 320

e In January 2010 we can expect the sales in Q1 to be approximately:

the value from the trend line − average seasonal effect = 1070 − 320 = £750.

Data analysis: Chapter 10 Time series and quality assurance

Z charts

A Z-chart is a combination chart that shows three pieces of information, usually short-term, medium-term and long-term, on a single diagram. These could be monthly sales, **cumulative** sales for that year and sales over the previous twelve months.

Example 6

The table shows the monthly sales of newspapers made by a chain of newsagents.

Month ended	Monthly sales (£, correct to the nearest £100)	Cumulative total for year (£)	Sales over previous 12 months (£)
31 January	900	900	12 100
28 February	1000	1900	12 300
31 March	1300	3200	12 400
30 April	1200	4400	12 100
31 May	1100	5500	12 200
30 June	1100	6600	12 100
31 July	900	7500	12 000
31 August	1200	8700	12 500
30 September	1100	9800	12 200
31 October	1300	11 100	12 400
30 November	1100	12 200	12 600
31 December	1000	13 200	13 200

The third column shows the cumulative total of sales since the start of the year.

The fourth column shows the total sales over the previous twelve months.

a Draw a graph to show this information.

b From the graph find how many newspapers:

  i were sold in June.

  ii had been sold since the start of the year to the end of June.

  iii had been sold in the previous 12 months to the end of June.

Data analysis: Chapter 10 Time series and quality assurance

Solution

a

[Graph showing Unit sales (to nearest £1000) vs Month (Jan–Dec), with three lines: "Sales over previous 12 months" (around 12–13), "Cumulative total for year" (rising linearly from 0 to ~13), and "Monthly sales" (around 1). Points marked: A (Jun, ~1), B (Jun, ~6.6), C (May/Jun, ~12).]

b From the table, take the data for 30 June.

i At point A: in June £1100 worth of newspapers were sold.

ii At point B: £6600 worth of newspapers had been sold since the start of the year.

iii At point C: £12 100 of newspapers had been sold in the last 12 months.

Data analysis: Chapter 10 Time series and quality assurance

Exercise 10B

1 This line graph shows the value of the closing FTSE world index on seven consecutive trading days.

AO4

a On which day did the FTSE world index have its lowest value? What was that value?

b By how much did the FTSE world index rise, from Wednesday to Thursday?

c Which day shows the greatest rise in the FTSE world index from the previous day?

2 The table shows the population of a town, rounded to the nearest thousand, after each census.

AO3, AO4

Year	1941	1951	1961	1971	1981	1991	2001
Population (000s)	60	70	75	80	105	125	115

a Draw a line graph for the data.

b From your graph, estimate the population in 1966.

c Between which two consecutive censuses did the population increase the most?

d Can you predict the population for 2011? Give a reason for your answer.

e Could you use your graph to estimate what the population would have been in 1911?

264

Data analysis: Chapter 10 Time series and quality assurance

3 The table shows the number of visitors to a top UK tourist attraction in the period from 2003 to 2010.

AO3, AO4

Year	2003	2004	2005	2006	2007	2008	2009	2010
Number of visitors (millions)	6.8	6.3	6.5	5.5	6.0	5.8	5.4	5.3

a Plot the data from the table and draw a trend line.

b Use your graph to estimate the likely number of tourists in 2011.

c Between which two years did numbers of visits decrease the most?

d Explain the trend in the number of visits to this tourist attraction. What reasons can you give to explain this trend?

e Is it possible to use this data to predict the likely number of visits in 2020?

4 The table shows the electricity consumption by a household from January 2007 to December 2010.

AO3, AO4

Year	Quarter	Electricity consumption (000 kWh)	Four-point moving average
2007	Q1	7.1	
	Q2	5.3	
	Q3	2.9	
	Q4	5.6	
2008	Q1	7.0	
	Q2	5.2	
	Q3	3.1	
	Q4	6.4	
2009	Q1	6.9	
	Q2	4.8	
	Q3	2.8	
	Q4	7.2	
2010	Q1	8.9	
	Q2	6.7	
	Q3	3.0	
	Q4	5.9	

a Calculate the four-point moving averages for this data, correct to 2 decimal points.

b Plot the four-point moving averages on a graph and draw a trend line.

c Comment on any patterns you find in the data.

265

Data analysis: Chapter 10 Time series and quality assurance

5 This table shows the daily closing price of shares for a company over a four-week period.

AO3, AO4

Week	Day	Share price (£)	Five-point moving average (2 d.p.)
1	Mon	5.75	
	Tues	5.90	
	Wed	6.00	5.96
	Thurs	5.86	
	Fri	6.30	
2	Mon	5.86	
	Tues	6.12	
	Wed	6.27	
	Thurs	6.89	
	Fri	6.53	
3	Mon	6.25	
	Tues	6.45	
	Wed	7.04	
	Thurs	6.95	
	Fri	6.93	
4	Mon	6.34	
	Tues	6.56	
	Wed	7.12	
	Thurs	7.14	
	Fri	7.03	

a Plot the data on a suitable set of axes.

b What do you notice about the data?

c Calculate the five-point moving averages for this data. The first one has been done for you. Why do you think that this data uses a five-point moving average rather than four-point?

d Plot the five-point moving averages on the same graph as the original data.

e From the trend line, read the 'seasonal' effect on each Monday.

f Find the average seasonal effect or the average 'Monday' effect.

g What would you expect the share price to be on Monday of week 5?

Data analysis: Chapter 10 Time series and quality assurance

6 This table shows the number of visits to a website during 2009.

AO3, AO4

Month	Monthly	Cumulative total for year	Visits over previous 12 months
January	158	158	1290
February	244	402	1526
March	477		1931
April	422		2293
May	390		2616
June	389		2939
July	336		3196
August	382		3483
September	426		3803
October	390		4081
November	388		4329
December	305		4307

a Copy and complete the column, including the cumulative totals.

b Draw a Z chart for this data.

c What is happening to the number of visits to this web page over time?

7 The table below gives quarterly sales figures for a gardening centre over a period of four years.

		Year			
		2006	2007	2008	2009
Quarter	1	120	125	118	115
	2	217	223	231	138
	3	255	262	268	271
	4	140	147	152	158

a Calculate the four-point moving averages for the data.

b Why are four-point moving averages used?

c Give a reason for the quarterly variations shown in the sales figures.

d Plot the values from the data table and the moving averages on the same graph.

e Use your graph in combination with seasonal variation calculations to estimate the sales figures for the first quarter of 2010.

Data analysis: Chapter 10 Time series and quality assurance

8 The sales figures of sun creams by a supermarket between 2004 and 2007 are shown in the table below. All numbers are in tens of thousands of pounds.

		Quarter			
		1	2	3	4
Year	2004	9	14	29	21
	2005	12	16	32	22
	2006	13	18	34	25
	2007	16	21	36	29

a Plot the values from the table on a graph.

b What is the reason for plotting moving averages?

c Calculate a suitable moving average. Give a reason for your choice.

d Explain the variation in the quarterly sales figures.

e Plot your moving averages on the same set of axes.

f Draw a trend line on your graph.

g Calculate the average seasonal components of the second quarter sales figures.

h Use your trend line and the average seasonal components work out an estimate of the sales figures for the second quarter of 2008.

10.3 Quality assurance

This section will show you how to:

- decide if a manufacturing process is producing goods to the required specification.

KEY WORDS

Mean
Quality control limits
Range

Quality assurance is particularly important in manufacturing. For example, suppose a company says its bars of chocolate weigh 250 g. Then if they actually weigh, on average, 245 g the company will lose customers and will probably be taken to court by trading standards.

If the bar consistently weighs more than 250 g this will cost the company money unnecessarily.

The problem for the company is that its machines cannot make each bar weigh exactly 250 g. A big company can afford to install the technology to check the weight of each bar and reject those that are under or over weight. A smaller specialist company cannot check the weight of each bar, as it would be too costly and time-consuming; it would not be able to compete with its competitors on price if it did this. The company will monitor the machine by taking samples and then decide if the machine needs to be adjusted.

Suppose a sample of 10 bars is taken and the weights are found to be:

249 g, 248.5 g, 251 g, 252 g, 250.5 g, 251.7 g, 249.6 g, 248.8 g, 249.2 g, 251.3 g

The **mean** of these numbers is calculated as

$$\frac{249 + 248.5 + 251 + 252 + 250.5 + 251.7 + 249.6 + 248.8 + 249.2 + 251.3}{10} = 250.16 \text{ g}$$

If the **quality control limit** for the machine is ±1 g, then the sample mean is within these limits (249 g to 251 g).

The variations in individual bars can be seen on this graph.

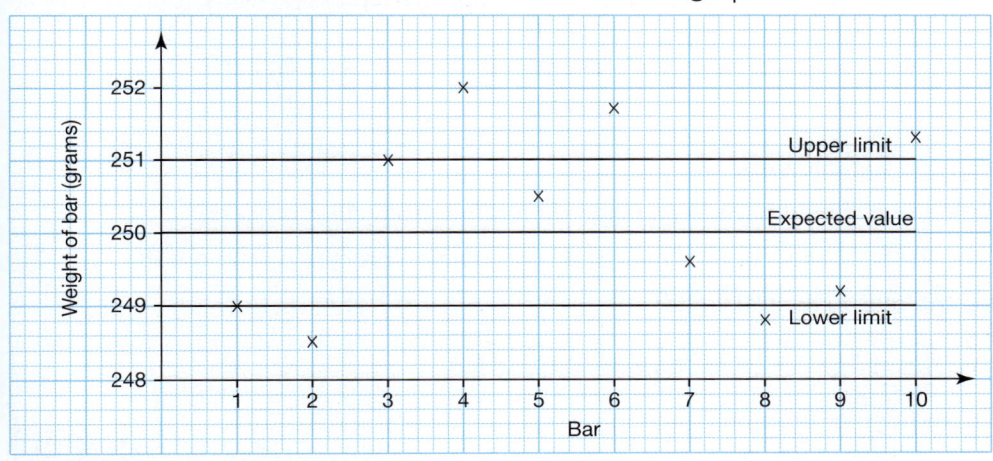

Although the sample mean is within the acceptable limits, five of the bars of chocolate were outside the quality control limits. The company must decide whether to take a further sample or reset the machine.

Often, the manufacturer will take several samples and compare the mean and **range** for the samples.

An important point is that the decisions that are made are taken in the context of the situation.

Data analysis: Chapter 10 Time series and quality assurance

Example 7

A factory uses one machine to produce bags of pasta.

The quality control staff check the process by taking samples of five bags every half hour and recording the mean weight of each sample.

The target value for the mean weight is 500 ± 0.5 g.

The table shows the results of the first 10 samples taken from the machine.

Sample number	Sample mean weight (g)
1	500.30
2	499.65
3	500.25
4	500.30
5	500.50
6	500.95
7	500.30
8	499.70
9	499.80
10	499.40

a Plot the sample means on suitable axes.

b Comment on any action that should have been taken during the production process.

c Draw in the upper and lower quality control limits of this production process on the graph.

Which values lie outside the quality control limits?

Solution

a The sample means have been plotted on this graph.

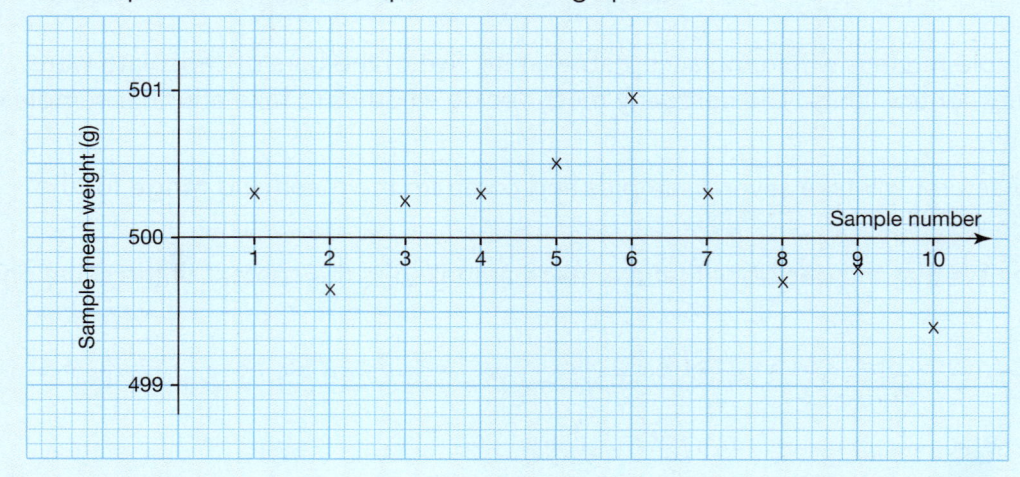

b Something must have gone wrong with the production process after sample 6 was taken, as the sample means start to decline after this sample was taken.

The machine should have been stopped after sample 8 and reset, as it was obvious then that the mean had started to decline.

c The quality control limits for the weight of the bag of pasta is 500 ± 0.5 g. The upper and lower quality control limits are added to the graph.

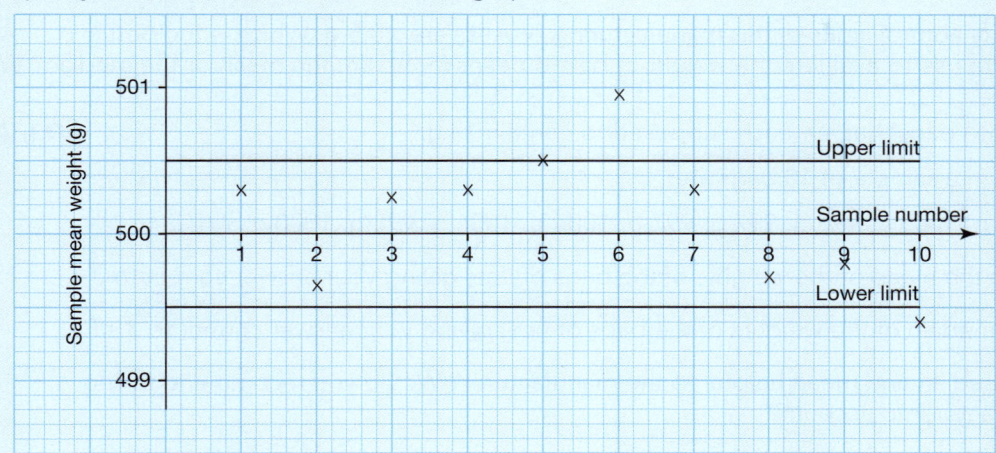

Two value (500.95 g and 499.40 g) lie outside the quality control limits.

Exercise 10C

1 A toothpaste manufacturer makes 100 ml tubes of toothpaste. **AO3, AO4**

A sample of 10 tubes is taken and the volumes are found to be:

99.8 ml, 100.1 ml, 100.1 ml, 100.2 ml, 100 ml, 99.9 ml, 99.9 ml, 100.1 ml, 100 ml, 100.3 ml

a Calculate the mean of the sample volumes.

b Do you think the machine is putting enough toothpaste into the tubes? Why?

c Might this be a problem for the manufacturer? What should the manufacturer do?

2 Tins of tuna are marked as containing 130 g of tuna. **AO3, AO4**

The weights in a sample of eight tins are:

129.5 g, 130.1 g, 129.7 g, 129.8 g, 130.4 g, 130.1 g, 129.9 g, 129.8 g

a Calculate the mean weight of tuna in the tins.

b The quality control limits for the manufacturing process are from 129.5 g to 130.5 g. Does the mean lie in this range?

c Should the manufacturer take more samples? Why?

Data analysis: Chapter 10 Time series and quality assurance

3 Baked beans are sold in tins that state the weight of the contents as 415 g. **AO3, AO4**

The weights in a sample of eight tins are:

413 g, 415 g, 413 g, 413 g, 417 g, 413 g, 418 g, 418 g

a Calculate the mean of this data.

b Calculate the median of this data.

c The quality control limits of this manufacturing process are ±0.5 g. Which is the better measure to use to evaluate the weight of baked beans in the tin, the mean or the median? Why?

4 Rice is put into bags that are each supposed to contain 1 kg. **AO3, AO4**

The weights in a sample of 10 bags are:

999 g, 1001 g, 1003 g, 995 g, 997 g, 997 g, 1004 g, 1006 g, 998 g, 1000 g, 997 g

a Calculate the mean of the weights of the bags of rice, giving your answer correct to 3 s.f.

b Find the median of the weights of the bags of rice, giving your answer correct to 3 s.f.

c Are the median and mean helpful to the manufacturer? Would you recommend taking another factor into account?

5 Bleach is put into bottles that are labelled as containing 750 ml. For this manufacturer, the quality control limits are ±1 ml. **AO3, AO4**

The manufacturer takes five samples, each of 10 bottles. The sample means are calculated as shown in the table.

Sample number	Sample mean capacity (ml)
1	748.9
2	750.7
3	749.3
4	750.4
5	749.6

a Plot these sample means on a suitable graph. (Hint: Use a scale of 2 cm for every millilitre on the vertical axis.)

b Draw in the lines that represent the expected value and the quality control limits. Label these lines as expected value, upper limit and lower limit.

c Do these samples indicate that there are problems with the manufacturing process? What advice would you give the manufacturer?

d The samples have been obtained by taking every tenth bottle off the production line. Is this a good way of doing it?

Data analysis: Chapter 10 Time series and quality assurance

6 A manufacturer puts herbs into cartons that are supposed to contain 30 g. Six samples of 10 cartons are taken and the sample means are calculated. **AO3, AO4**

The results are shown in the table below.

Sample	Sample mean (grams)
1	30.1
2	30.2
3	29.7
4	29.8
5	29.9
6	30.1

The quality control limit for the weight in the cartons is 30 g ± 1%.

a Work out the actual upper and lower quality control limits.

b Draw a graph with lines drawn on it to represent the sample mean and the quality control limits (upper and lower).

c Plot the sample means on this graph.

d Do the results indicate that there is a problem with this production process?

7 Vitamin tablets are packed into containers that should contain 200 tablets. Five samples of containers are taken and the sample mean and range are calculated. **AO3, AO4**

The results are shown in the table.

Sample number	Mean	Range
1	199	3
2	201	4
3	202	1
4	200	4
5	201	5

The acceptable range is 2 tablets.

a Copy these graphs and plot the means and ranges.

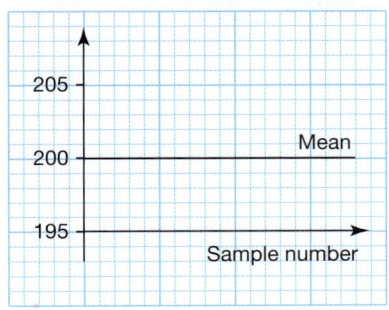

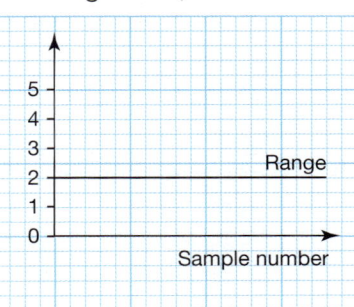

b Do your graphs indicate that there is a problem with the production process?

c What should this manufacturer do?

273

Data analysis: Chapter 10 Time series and quality assurance

8 Jam is put into jars that should contain 340 g each.

AO3, AO4

Six samples are taken and the following values are found for the sample means.

Sample	Sample mean (g)
1	339.7
2	340.2
3	338.1
4	339.8
5	340.1
6	339.9

The quality control limits for the sample mean is 340 g ± 0.5%.

a Plot these values onto a suitable graph.

b What conclusions can you draw about the manufacturing process? What advice would you give to the manufacturer?

GRADE BOOSTER

What you need to do to get this grade

G	You can draw a line graph.
F	You can work out sample means, medians and ranges.
E	You can interpret line graphs.
D	You can interpret the mean, median, mode and range obtained from a sample.
C	You can draw a trend line by eye for time series data.
B	You can work out moving averages, plot them and draw a trend line based on them.
A	You can analyse time series data to predict future values.

What you should now know

- How to draw a trend line for time series data.

Higher tier only

- How to work out moving averages and use them to identify seasonality in data.
- How to decide if a production process is manufacturing within the required specifications.

EXAMINATION Questions

1 The time series graph shows the number of students logging on to a revision website over a seven-week period.

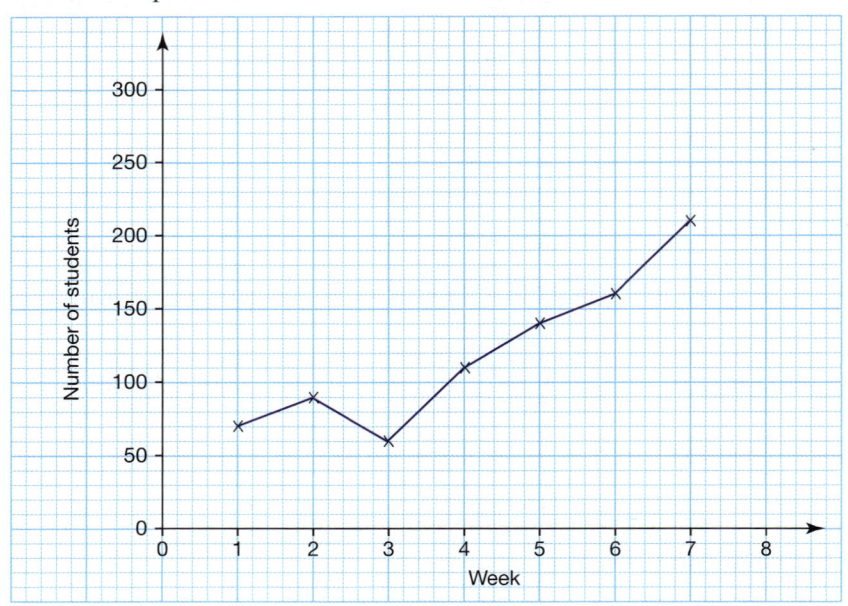

a In which week did the least number of students log on to the website? *(1 mark)*

b How many **more** students logged on in week 7 than in week 1? *(2 marks)*

c Give a possible reason why the number of students logging on peaked in week 7. *(1 mark)*

2 The graph shows the average weekly household expenditure on groceries in the UK.

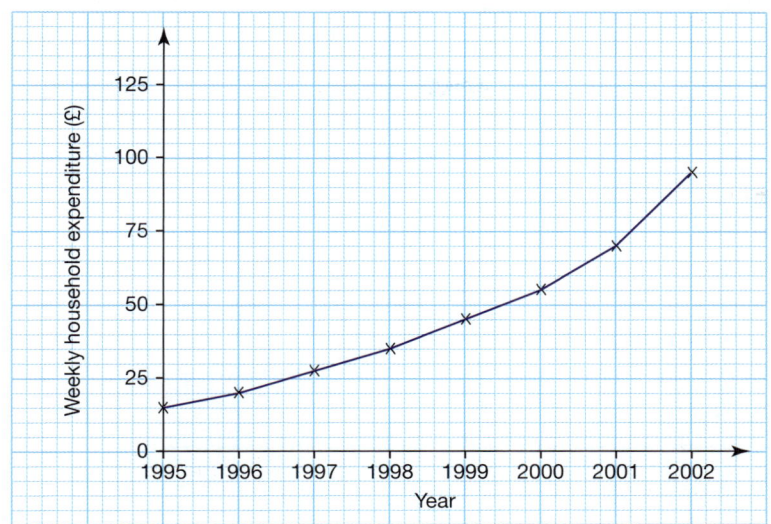

a By how much did the average weekly household expenditure on groceries increase from 2000 to 2001? *(1 mark)*

b Between which two years was there the largest annual increase in average weekly expenditure on groceries? *(1 mark)*

3 The table shows the takings (£) for lunches at a works café over a period of three weeks.

Week	Day	Takings (£)
1	Monday (M)	110
	Tuesday (Tu)	75
	Wednesday (W)	125
	Thursday (Th)	120
	Friday (F)	175
2	Monday (M)	100
	Tuesday (Tu)	70
	Wednesday (W)	115
	Thursday (Th)	120
	Friday (F)	155
3	Monday (M)	95
	Tuesday (Tu)	60
	Wednesday (W)	115
	Thursday (Th)	105
	Friday (F)	150

a Complete the time series graph below by plotting the points for week 3. *(2 marks)*

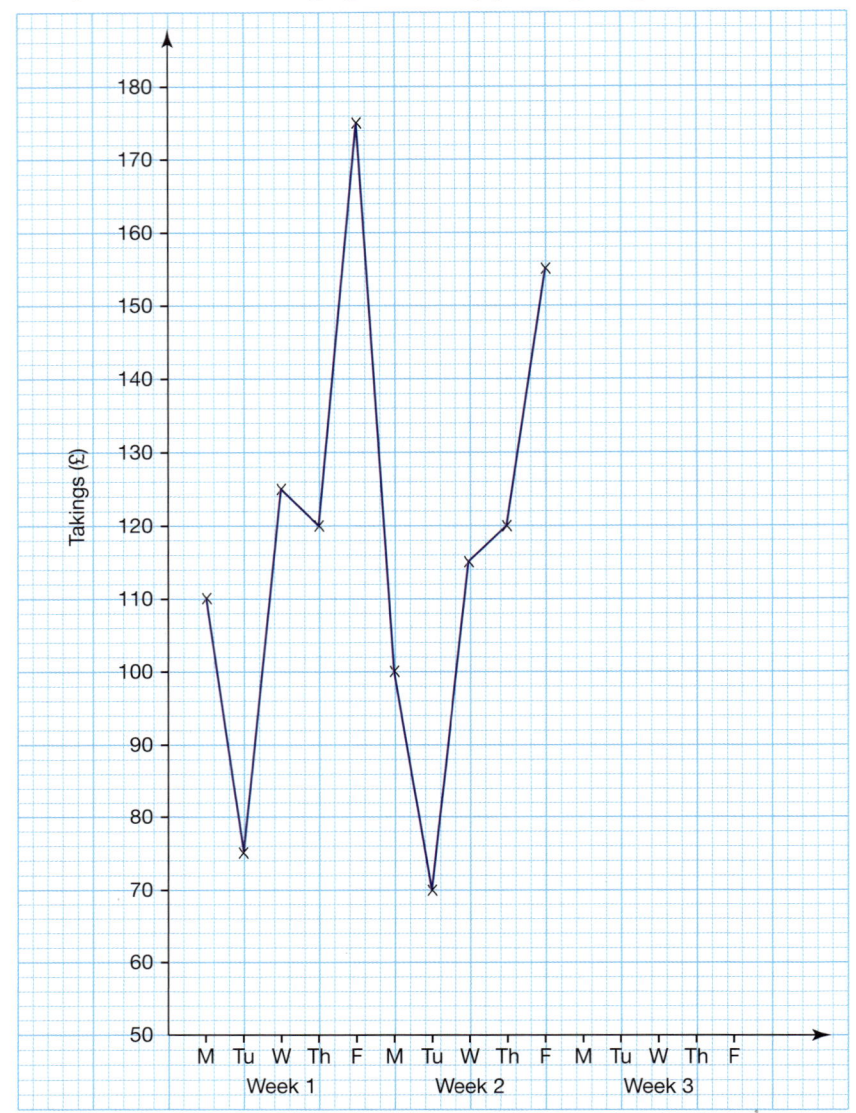

b The takings are lowest on Tuesdays. Give a possible reason for this. *(1 mark)*

c Describe **two** other patterns in the data. *(2 marks)*

(Total 5 marks)

AQA, June 2009, Foundation, Question 13

4 A factory uses one machine to produce tins of food. The Quality Control staff check the process by taking samples of 5 tins every half hour and recording the mean weight of each sample.

The target value for the mean weight is 410 g.

The table shows the results of the first 8 samples taken from the machine.

Sample number	Sample mean weight (g)
1	410.30
2	409.65
3	410.25
4	410.30
5	410.50
6	410.95
7	410.30
8	409.70

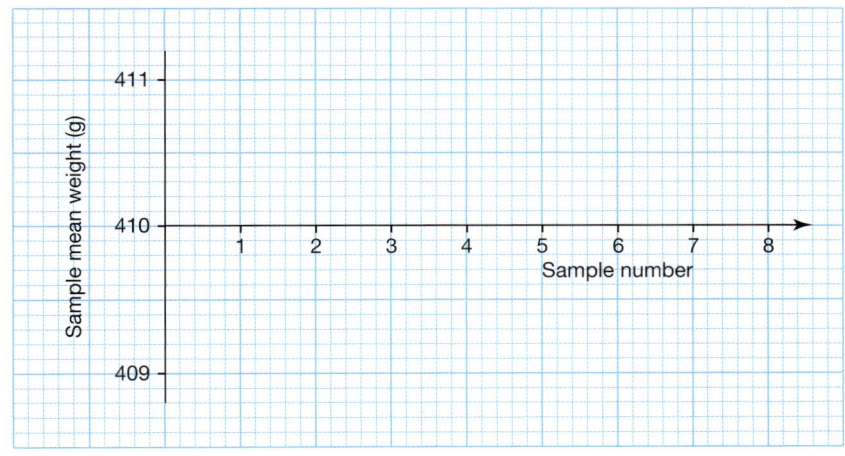

a On a copy of the grid below, draw a chart to show this data. *(2 marks)*

b At which point was the process stopped and the machine adjusted? Justify your choice.
(2 marks)

AQA, June 2006, Higher, Question 10e

Data analysis: Chapter 10 Examination questions

5 The table shows the number of visits to America by UK residents each quarter from 2002 to 2004. Some of the four-point moving averages are shown in the table.

Year	Quarter	Visits (tens of thousands)	Four-point moving average
2002	Q1	88	
	Q2	100	
			105
	Q3	118	
			107.5
	Q4	114	
			109
2003	Q1	98	
			110.5
	Q2	106	
			111.5
	Q3	124	
	Q4	118	
2004	Q1	102	
	Q2	116	
	Q3	134	
	Q4	126	

Source: *Adapted from Social Trends 2005*

a The data for number of visits each quarter has been plotted on the time series graph below.

Copy and complete the graph. *(2 marks)*

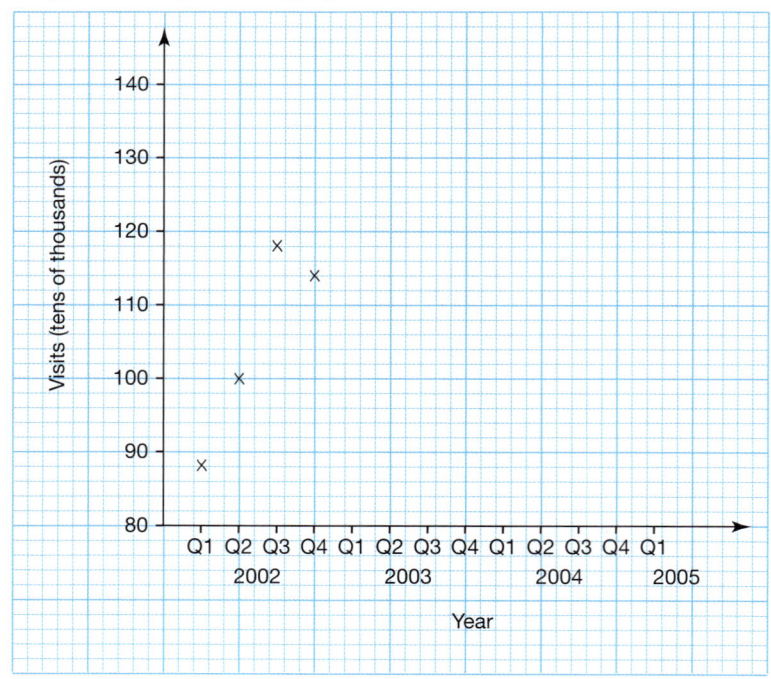

b Describe **two** different patterns in the data. *(2 marks)*

c Calculate the remaining four-point moving averages. *(4 marks)*

d i Plot the moving averages on your graph. *(2 marks)*

  ii Draw a trend line. *(1 mark)*

e Work out the value of the average seasonal effect for Q1, the first quarter. *(3 marks)*

f Use the trend line and your answer to part **e** to estimate the number of visits to America by UK residents in the first quarter of 2005. *(3 marks)*

AQA, June 2007, Higher, Question 7

WORKED EXAMINATION Questions

1 Prakash was born on 30 November and had his weight recorded regularly, as shown in the table.

Day	1	5	9	13	17
Weight (g)	4100	3800	4000	4500	4900

Estimate how much Prakash would weigh after three weeks.

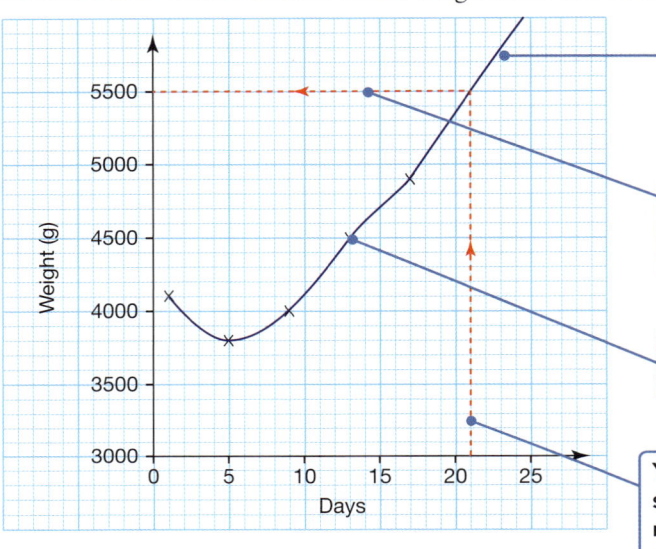

Use the table to draw the given points and plot a line graph.

*Plot the points on a graph so that you can make a prediction by extending the graph. You get **1 mark** for accuracy for this.*

*You get **1 method mark** for showing a horizontal reading from the graph to the weight.*

*You get **1 method mark** for showing 21 days (3 weeks) being read vertically to the extended graph.*

Estimated weight is 5500 g

*You get **1 mark** for accuracy for an answer close to 5500 g.*

(Total 4 marks)

Data analysis: Chapter 10 Examination questions

2 When a new bypass was opened, the volume of traffic using it was monitored three times every Monday, at 8.00 am, 1.00 pm and 6.00 pm over a four-week period. The number of vehicles passing in a 5-minute interval was recorded in the table below.

Day	Time	Volume of traffic (number of vehicles)
Monday 1	0800	199
	1300	181
	1800	217
Monday 2	0800	231
	1300	224
	1800	268
Monday 3	0800	263
	1300	248
	1800	323
Monday 4	0800	296
	1300	282
	1800	371

a Plot this data on the graph below.

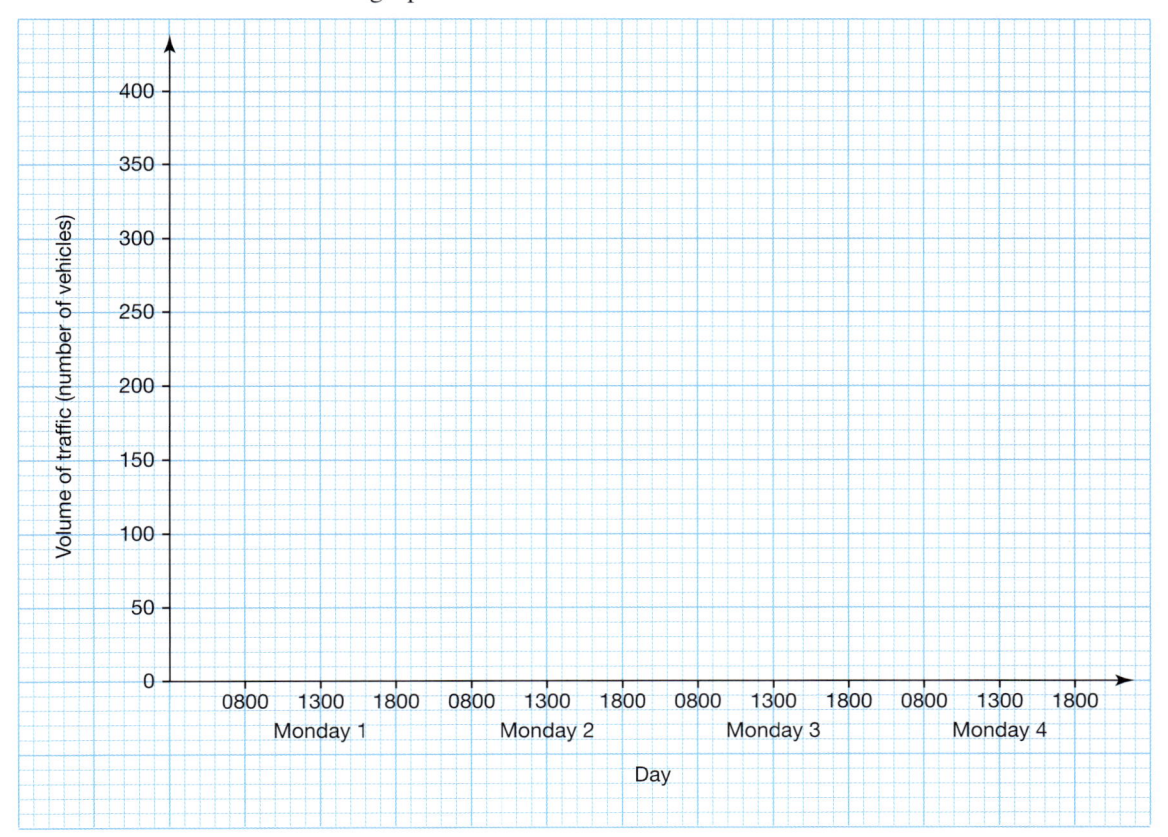

283

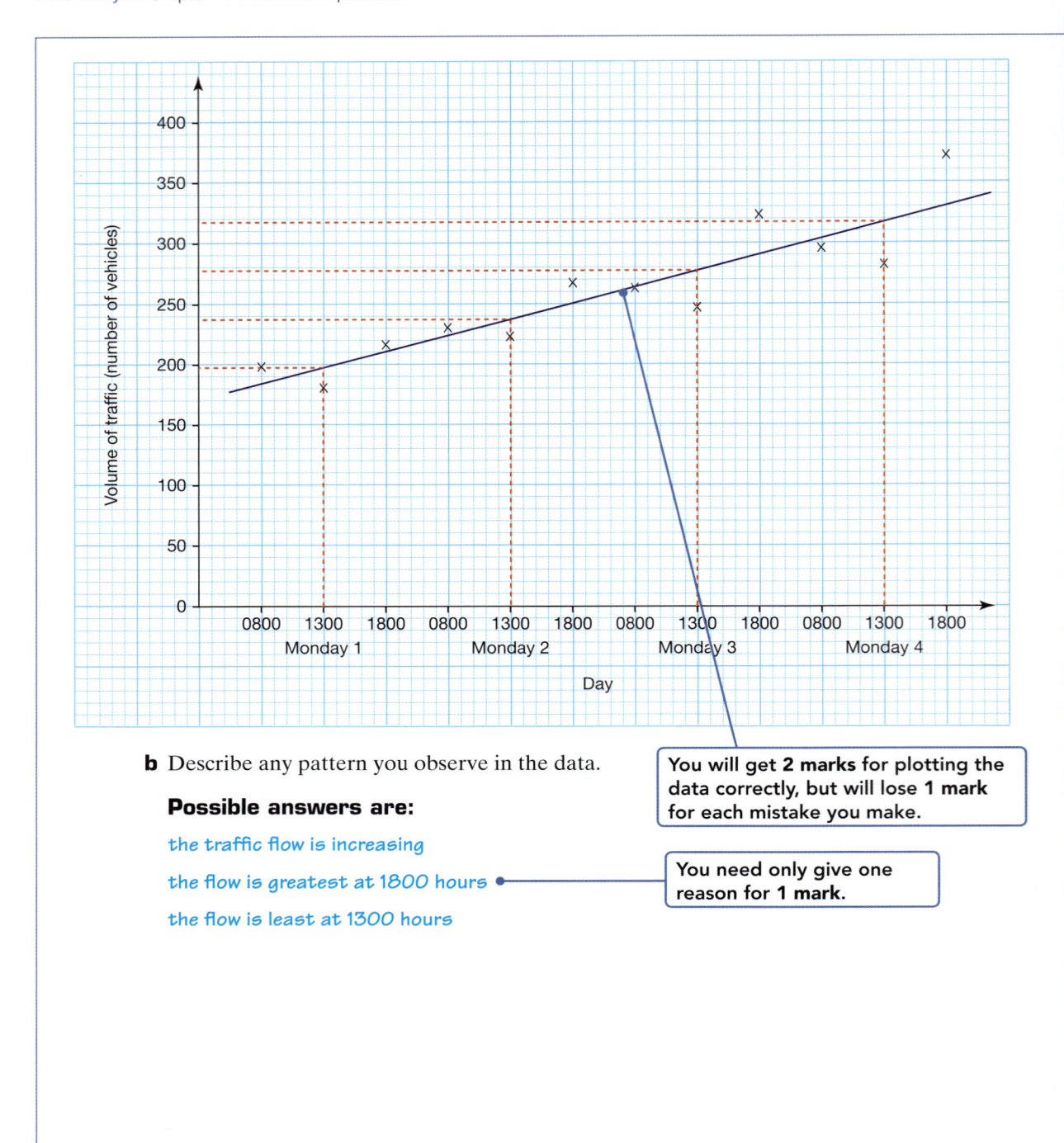

Data analysis: Chapter 10 Examination questions

[Graph: Volume of traffic (number of vehicles) vs Day, showing data points plotted across Monday 1 to Monday 4 at times 0800, 1300, 1800, with a line of best fit showing increasing trend from approximately 180 to 340 vehicles.]

b Describe any pattern you observe in the data.

> You will get **2 marks** for plotting the data correctly, but will lose **1 mark** for each mistake you make.

Possible answers are:

the traffic flow is increasing

the flow is greatest at 1800 hours

the flow is least at 1300 hours

> You need only give one reason for **1 mark**.

continued overleaf

c Complete this table by working out the three-point moving averages, giving your answers to 3 s.f. The first six have been done for you.

Day	Time	Volume of traffic (number of vehicles)	Three-point moving average
Monday 1	0800	199	
	1300	181	199
	1800	217	210
Monday 2	0800	231	224
	1300	224	241
	1800	268	252
Monday 3	0800	263	260
	1300	248	278
	1800	323	289
Monday 4	0800	296	300
	1300	282	316
	1800	371	

You get **1 mark** for each correct answer. If you show your method but your answers are wrong you will get **1 mark**.

Data analysis: Chapter 10 Examination questions

d i Plot the moving averages on the graph.

ii Draw in the trend line.

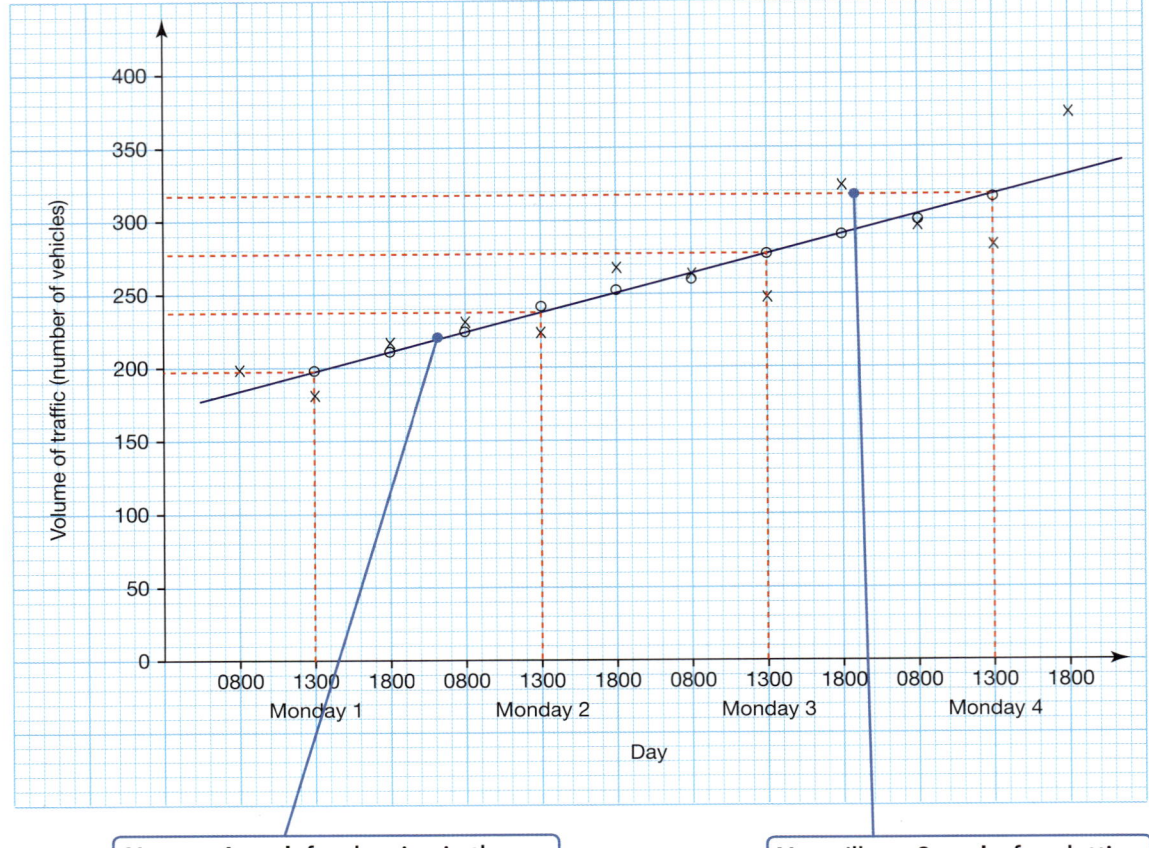

[Graph: Volume of traffic (number of vehicles) vs Day, showing readings at 0800, 1300, 1800 across Monday 1, Monday 2, Monday 3, Monday 4, with plotted points and a trend line.]

> You get **1 mark** for drawing in the trend line, but it must be between the limits, through the middle of the points

> You will get **2 marks** for plotting your answers to part c.

e Use your graph to work out the average '1300 effect'.

First Monday 1300 effect = 199 − 181 = 18

Second Monday 1300 effect = 250 − 224 = 26

Third Monday 1300 effect = 302 − 248 = 54

Fourth Monday effect = 350 − 282 = 68

Average 1300 effect = $\frac{18 + 26 + 54 + 68}{4}$ = 41.5

> You get **1 mark** for reading 199, 250, 302, 350 correctly from your trend line.
> You get **1 mark** for using your answers to work out the effect on each Monday at 1300.
> You get **1 mark** for working out the average using your answers.

(Total 13 marks)

Data analysis: Chapter 10 Examination questions

3 A small business manufactures tubs of coleslaw. Each tub is sold as containing 200 g.

To check the weights of the tubs, samples of five are collected at random from the production process. Then the mean weight of each sample is calculated.

The manufacturer requires that the sample mean weights must fall between the limits 200 g ± 0.5%. The mean weights of the first eight samples are shown below.

Sample number	1	2	3	4	5	6	7	8
Sample mean (g)	200.1	199.6	201.1	200.0	198.5	189.9	200.6	199.7

a Plot the sample means on the graph below, showing clearly the quality control limits.

1% of 200 is 2 so 0.5% of 200 is 1.

So the quality control limits are 201 g and 199 g.

You will gain **1 mark** for working out 0.5% of 200 g as 1 g. There is another **1 mark** for working out the quality control limits as 201 g and 199 g. You will get marks for the limits if you have worked them out correctly but using a wrong answer from 0.5% of 200.

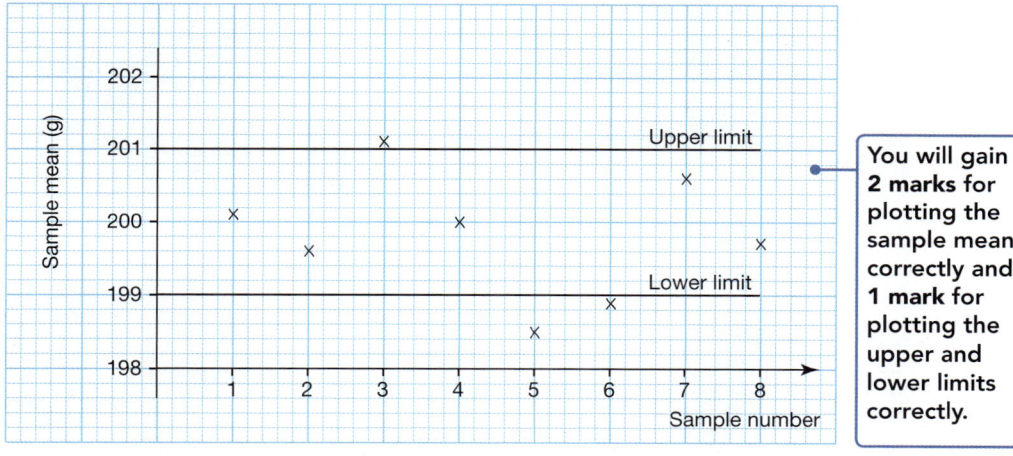

You will gain **2 marks** for plotting the sample means correctly and **1 mark** for plotting the upper and lower limits correctly.

b Comment on any action that should be taken by the manufacturer as a result of these samples.

There are three values in samples 3, 5, and 6 which are outside the quality control limits so the process needs to be stopped, the machine reset and further samples taken to check the process

You will gain **1 mark** for giving the correct action based on your graph and another **1 mark** for giving the correct evidence based on you graph, for example, samples 3, 5 and 6.

(Total 6 marks)

11 Correlation and regression

This chapter covers relationships between two sets of data, which is a very important branch of statistics. One of the most important aspects of industrial, medical or scientific research is the technique of correlation. If two variables display correlation, we can use the values of one to predict the values of the other.

We can predict the behaviour of many things in our environment such as the tides or the changes in the seasons. Many things in science, medicine and industry aren't as predictable. We can, however, discover relationships between variables and make predictions based on the results.

We may think that there is a relationship between two things, such as passive smoking and the occurrence of lung cancer, in later life. We can test this hypothesis by drawing a scatter diagram, or calculating a correlation coefficient. We can then determine if there really is a relationship between the two things.

11.1 Scatter diagrams and correlation

11.2 Spearman's rank and product moment correlation coefficients

This chapter will show you how to:
- draw and interpret a scatter diagram
- understand the different types of correlation
- draw a line of best fit through the means of the data
- understand the differences between extrapolation and interpolation
- interpret correlation coefficients

Higher tier only
- calculate the equation for a line of regression
- calculate and interpret correlation coefficients.

The exercise questions in this chapter are given individual target grades as a guide.

Visual overview

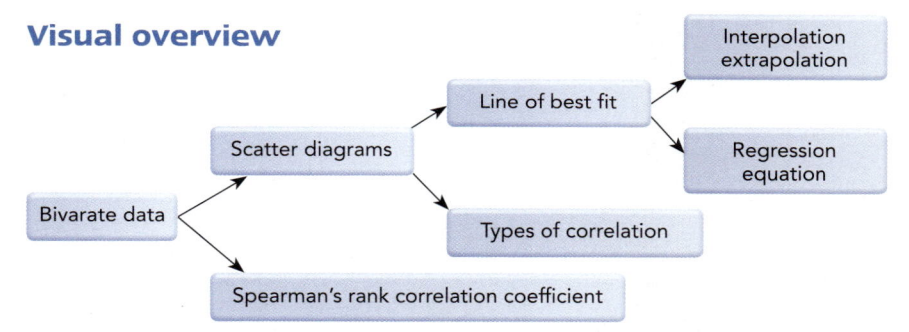

Bivarate data → Scatter diagrams → Line of best fit → Interpolation extrapolation / Regression equation
Scatter diagrams → Types of correlation
Spearman's rank correlation coefficient

What you should already know

- **F** How to plot coordinate points (KS3, level 4).
- **F** How to read information from charts and tables (KS3, level 4).
- **F** How to recognise a positive or negative gradient (KS3, level 4).

Quick check

Copy this grid and plot the pairs of points listed in the table.

x	6	8	5	7	3
y	3	9	6	4	2

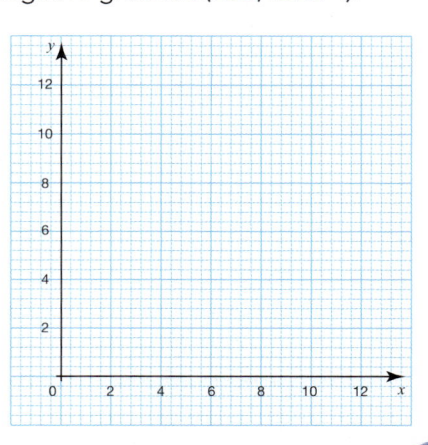

11.1 Scatter diagrams and correlation

This section will show you how to:
- draw, interpret and use scatter diagrams.

KEY WORDS
Causality
Correlation
Extrapolation
Interpolation
Line of best fit
Line of regression
Negative correlation
No correlation
Positive correlation
Scatter diagram
Variable

A **scatter diagram** (also called a scatter graph or scattergram) is a method of comparing two **variables** by plotting their corresponding values on a graph. These values are usually taken from a table.

In other words, the variables are treated just like a set of (x, y) coordinates. This is shown in the scatter diagram that follows, in which the marks scored in an English test are plotted against the marks scored in a mathematics test.

This graph shows **positive correlation**. This means that students who gain high marks in mathematics tests also tend to gain high marks in English tests.

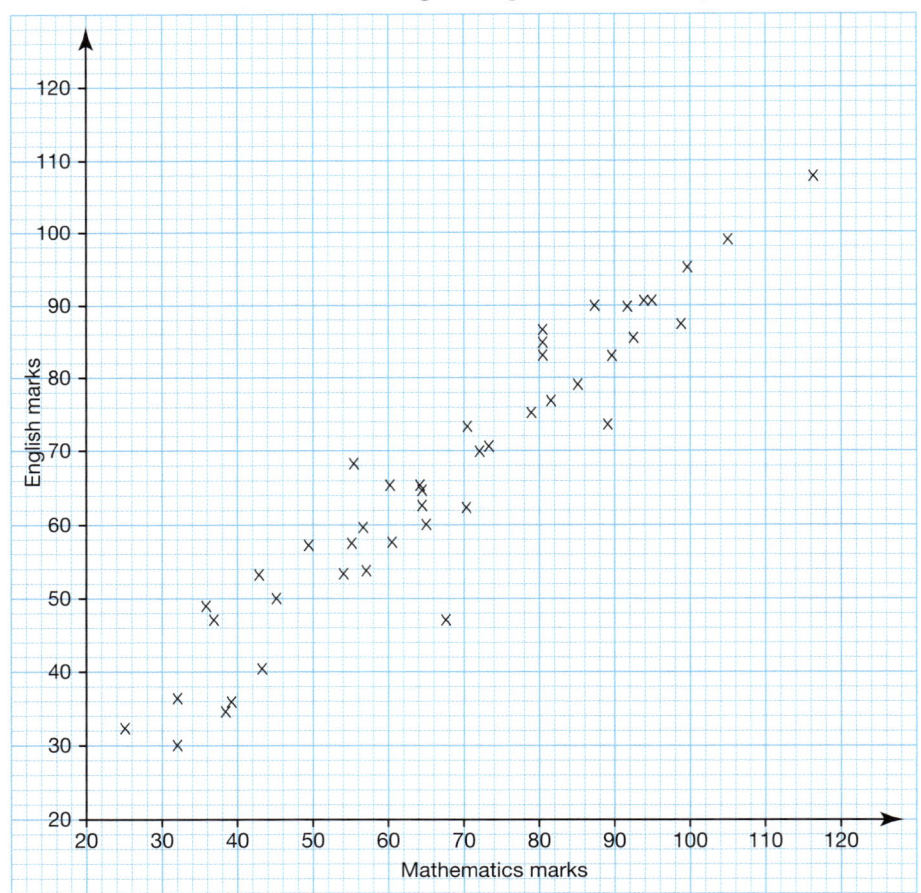

A dataset containing two variables can be described as bivariate data. This chapter will show you how to describe the relationship between two variables. For example, you may wish to describe the relationship between the heights and weights of people to investigate whether taller people weigh more.

Correlation

There are different types of **correlation**. Here are three statements that may or may not be true.

- The taller people are, the wider their arm span is.
- The older a car is, the lower its value will be.
- The distance you live from your place of work will affect how much you earn.

These relationships could be tested by collecting data and plotting the values on a scatter diagram. For example, the first statement may give a scatter diagram like the first one below.

This first diagram has **positive correlation** because, as one quantity increases, so does the other. From such a scatter diagram, you could say that the taller someone is, the wider their arm span.

Testing the second statement may give a scatter diagram like the middle one above. This has **negative correlation** because, as one quantity increases, the other quantity decreases. From such a scatter diagram, you could say that as a car gets older its value decreases.

Testing the third statement may give a scatter diagram like the one on the right, above. This scatter diagram has **no correlation**. There is no relationship between the distance a person lives from their work and how much they earn.

Correlation can sometimes be confused with **causality**. Suppose you are studying two variables X and Y. Now, if you change the value of X, then there will be a change in the value of Y if they are correlated. This does not mean that a change in X *causes* a change in Y. Correlation does not prove cause. For example, after John got married he grew gradually heavier over the first 10 years of his marriage. He said that marriage was the cause of his weight gain! If we plotted this we could probably find some correlation to support his claim. However, it is obvious that being married was not the cause of his weight gain. It was more likely to be diet and exercise. We therefore have to be careful when we claim one variable causes change in the other by showing correlation between them, as there are often many factors that can influence the result.

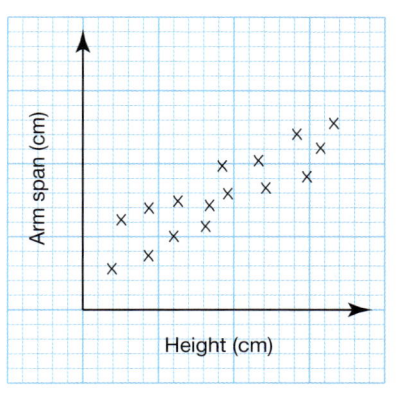

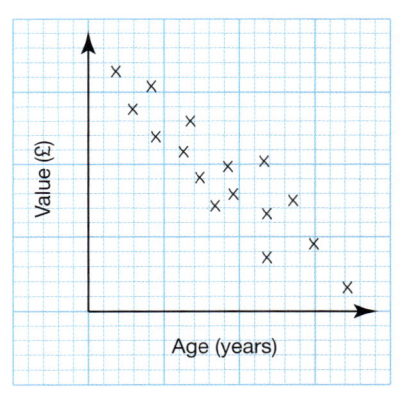

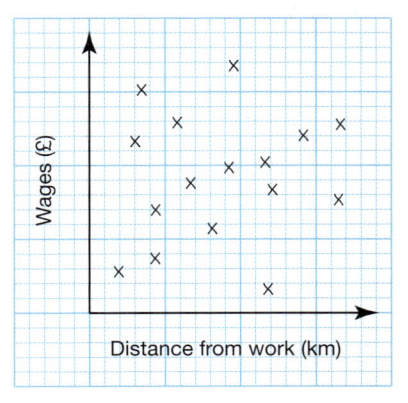

Data analysis: Chapter 11 Correlation and regression

Example 1

The graphs below show the relationship between the temperature and the amount of ice-cream sold, and that between the age of people and the amount of ice-cream they eat.

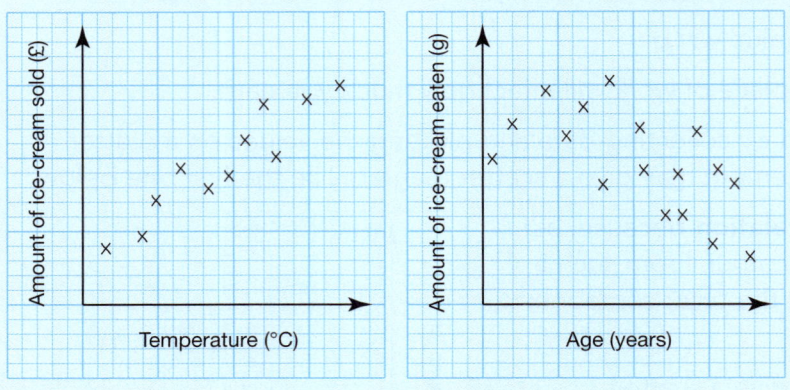

a   Comment on the correlation of each graph.
b   What does each graph tell you?

Solution

The first graph has positive correlation and tells us that, as the temperature increases, the amount of ice-cream sold increases.

The second graph has negative correlation and tells us that, as people get older, they eat less ice-cream.

Line of best fit

A line of best fit is a straight line that goes between all the points on a scatter diagram, passing as close as possible to all of them. We try to get the same number of points on each side of the line. This is often done by eye, but by far the most accurate method is to find the mean averages of both sets of data and plot these as a new point on the scatter graph. The line of best fit is then drawn through this point.

Example 2

During a mathematics lesson, a class of 30 students measured their heights and weights. The table below shows the recorded data.

Height	1.59	1.45	1.62	1.55	1.79	1.57	1.45	1.63	1.42	1.52
Weight	61	48	59	56	79	56	44	58	45	57
Height	1.51	1.68	1.79	1.51	1.65	1.53	1.63	1.61	1.55	1.64
Weight	54	63	83	56	69	53	60	62	54	61
Height	1.73	1.64	1.47	1.52	1.49	1.52	1.67	1.52	1.71	1.75
Weight	68	69	45	48	44	52	67	47	72	73

a   Draw a scatter diagram to illustrate the data.
b   Calculate the mean of both data sets and plot a line of best fit on the graph.
c   Jane is 1.5 m tall. How heavy would you expect her to be?

Solution

a

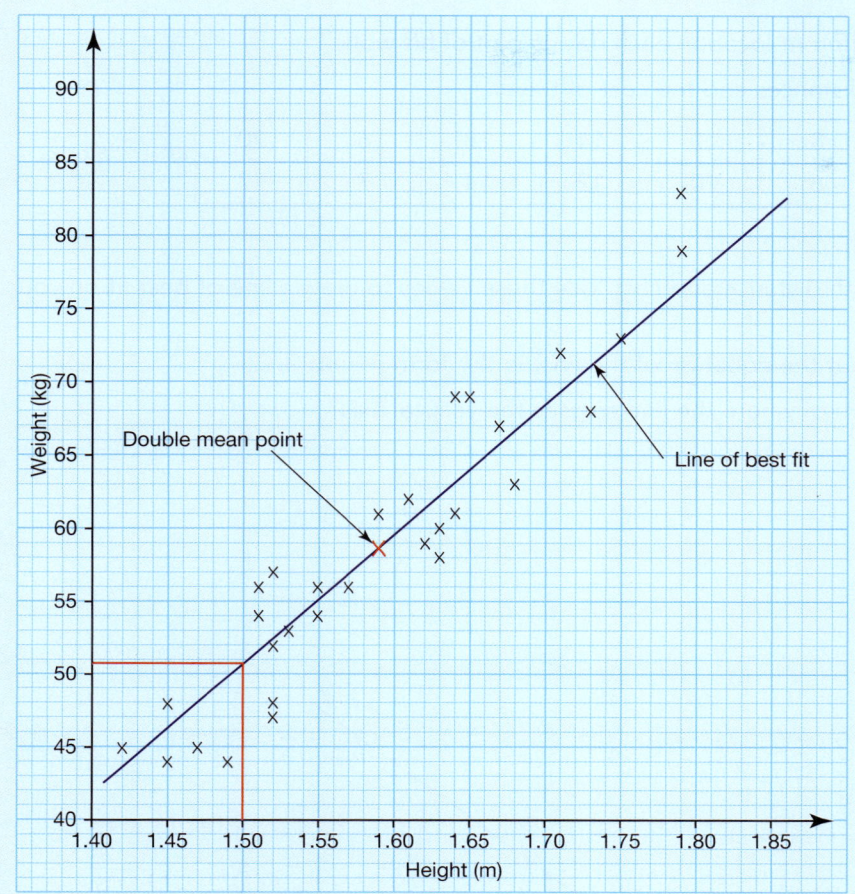

[Scatter plot showing Weight (kg) vs Height (m) with line of best fit passing through the double mean point]

b Mean height = (1.59 + 1.45 + 1.62 + 1.55 + 1.79 + 1.57 + 1.45 + 1.63 + 1.42 + 1.52 + 1.51 + 1.68 + 1.79 + 1.51 + 1.65 + 1.53 + 1.63 + 1.61 + 1.55 + 1.64 + 1.73 + 1.64 + 1.47 + 1.52 + 1.49 + 1.52 + 1.67 + 1.52 + 1.71 + 1.75) ÷ 30 = 1.59 m

Mean weight = (61 + 48 + 59 + 56 + 79 + 56 + 44 + 58 + 45 + 57 + 54 + 63 + 83 + 56 + 69 + 53 + 60 + 62 + 54 + 61 + 68 + 69 + 45 + 48 + 44 + 52 + 67 + 47 + 72 + 73) ÷ 30 = 58.8 kg

c Draw a line from 1.5m up to the line of best fit and across to the weight axis. This gives Jane's likely weight as 50.5 kg.

Lines of regression

A **line of regression** is a line that is fitted to the points on a graph; essentially a line of best fit. Hence there is very strong positive or negative correlation. Taking the horizontal axis as the x-axis, and the vertical axis as the y-axis, we can calculate the equation of a regression line in the form $y = mx + c$. Recall that m is the gradient of the line and c is the intercept on the vertical axis (i.e. where the line crosses the y-axis). This equation allows us to calculate estimates such as 'Jane's weight' in the previous example without the need to draw lines on the graph.

293

Data analysis: Chapter 11 Correlation and regression

Example 3

Rashid travels by taxi to a different location each day as part of his work.

The table below shows the distances and the cost of travel.

Distance (km)	2	8	10	14	18	6	20
Cost (£)	4	6	10	12	14	7	17

a Plot the points on a graph.
b Calculate the mean of both distance and cost. Use these values to draw a line of best fit on your graph.
c Use your graph to work out the equation of the line, in the form $y = mx + c$.
d What is your interpretation of where the line crosses the vertical axis?

Solution

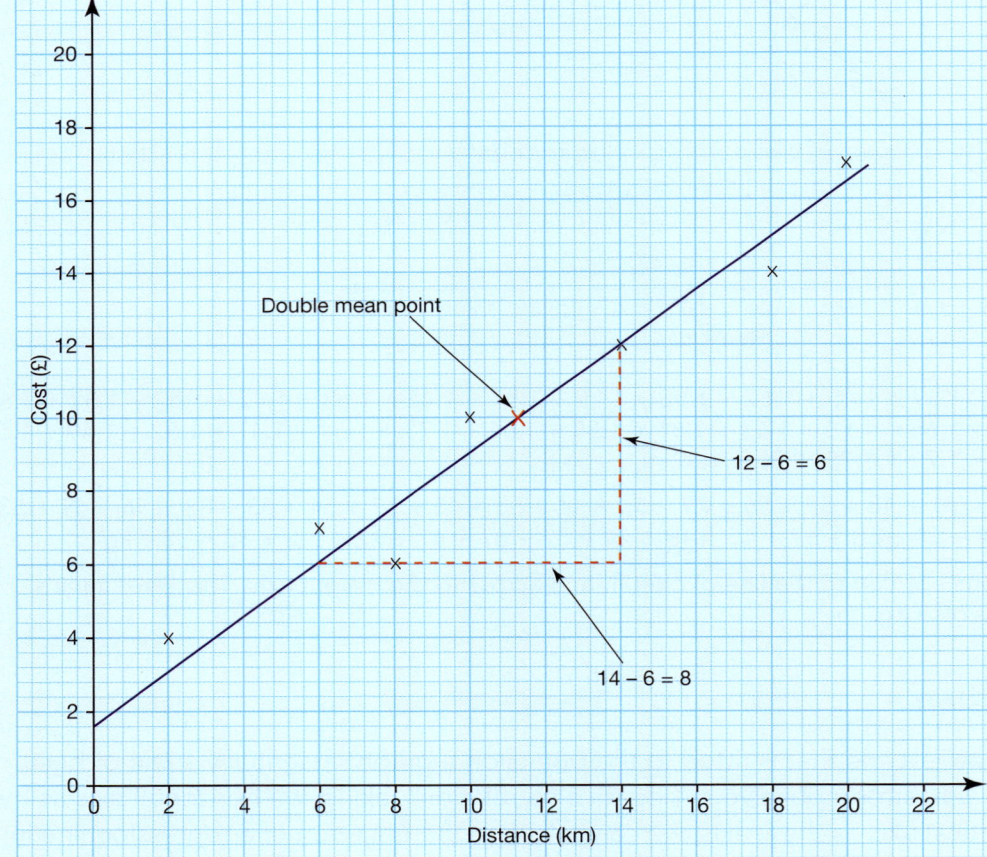

a

[Graph showing Cost (£) vs Distance (km) with plotted points, line of best fit, double mean point marked, with annotations "12 – 6 = 6" and "14 – 6 = 8"]

294

b Mean distance = (2 + 8 + 10 + 14 + 18 + 6 + 20) ÷ 7 = 78 ÷ 7 = 11.14 km.

Mean cost = (4 + 6 + 10 + 12 + 14 + 7 + 17) ÷ 7 = £10.

c To work out the equation of the line, in the form $y = mx + c$, we need to find the gradient m, and the point where the line cuts the vertical axis.

The gradient m is found by drawing a right-angled triangle on the line and working out the length of each side from the scale (as illustrated). Then divide the vertical length by the horizontal.

$$m = \frac{12-6}{14-6} = \frac{6}{8} = \frac{3}{4} \text{ or } 0.75$$

Intercept c is where the line cuts the vertical axis, where the value is 1.6.

In terms of x and y, the equation of the line is $y = \frac{3}{4}x + 1.6$.

d The point where the line cuts the vertical axis (£1.60) is the initial charge incurred before the taxi starts to move.

Interpolation and extrapolation

Interpolation is the process of obtaining a value from a scatter diagram or table for a point that is located within the data values shown. A line of best fit or a regression equation can be used to obtain the value.

Extrapolation is the process of obtaining a value that extends beyond the given data. The line of best fit is extended past the last data value. A regression equation can also be used to obtain the value. Extrapolation must be done with care as trends in data often do not continue indefinitely. The further away from the last data point you go, the less reliable is the result.

For example, a science experiment tested how far a rubber band stretched as more force was applied to it. The graph, including a line of best fit, is shown.

The line of best fit has been extended past the last data point. If we wanted to find the force required to stretch the band 17 cm (shown in red), the graph shows 34.5 newtons (N). However, the band would probably snap long before a force of 17 newtons was applied to it.

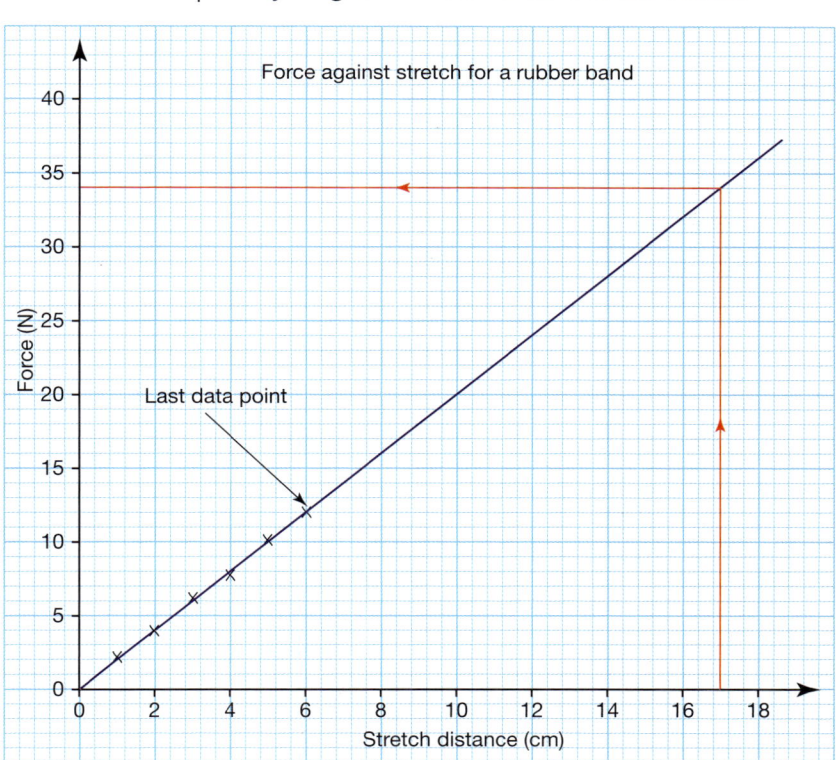

Data analysis: Chapter 11 Correlation and regression

Exercise 11A

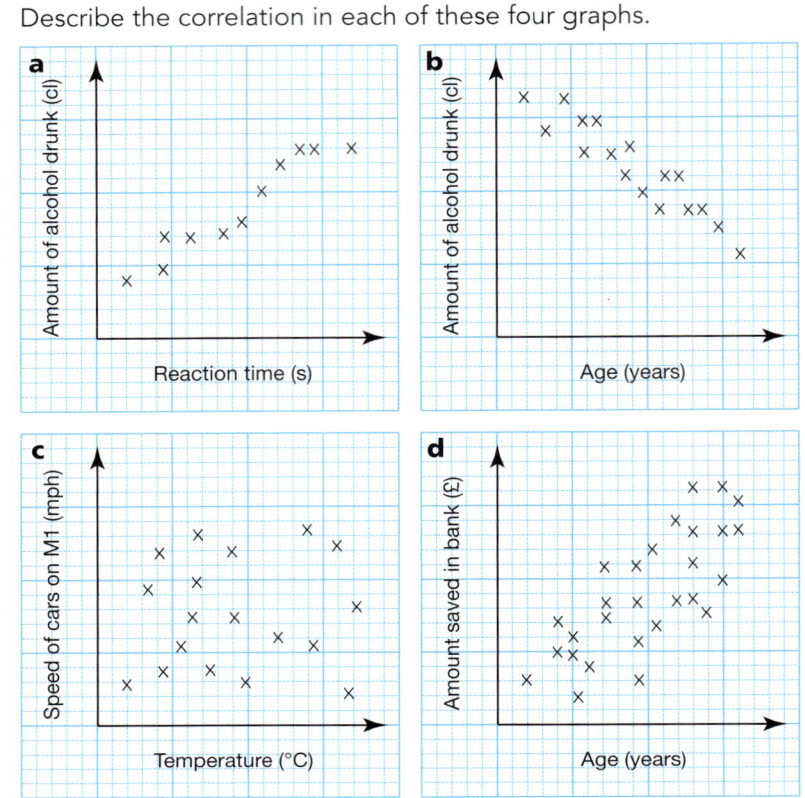

1 Describe the correlation in each of these four graphs.

a Amount of alcohol drunk (cl) vs Reaction time (s)

b Amount of alcohol drunk (cl) vs Age (years)

c Speed of cars on M1 (mph) vs Temperature (°C)

d Amount saved in bank (£) vs Age (years)

2 Write in words what each graph in question **1** tells you.

3 The table below shows the results of a science experiment in which a ball is rolled along a desk top. The speed of the ball is measured at various points.

Distance from start (cm)	10	20	30	40	50	60	70	80
Speed (cm/s)	18	16	13	10	7	5	3	0

a Plot the data on a scatter diagram.

b Calculate the mean of each data set and plot the appropriate point. Draw a line of best fit, making sure it goes through the means.

c If the ball's speed had been measured at 5 cm from the start, what is it likely to have been?

d Estimate how far from the start the ball was when its speed was 12 cm/s.

Hints and tips

In examination questions, axes are usually given and most, if not all, of the points are plotted.

Data analysis: Chapter 11 Correlation and regression

4 The heights, in centimetres, of 20 mothers and their 15-year-old daughters were measured. These are the results.

Mother	153	162	147	183	174	169	152	164	186	178
Daughter	145	155	142	167	167	151	145	152	163	168
Mother	175	173	158	168	181	173	166	162	180	156
Daughter	172	167	160	154	170	164	156	150	160	152

a Plot these results on a scatter diagram. Use the horizontal axis for the mothers' heights, labelled from 140 to 200. Use the vertical axis for the daughters' heights, labelled from 140 to 200.

b Is it true that the tall mothers have tall daughters?

5 The table below shows the marks for ten students in their mathematics and geography examinations.

AO3

Student	Anna	Becky	Cath	Dema	Emma	Fatima	Greta	Hannah	Imogen	Jasmine
Mathematics	57	65	34	87	42	35	59	61	25	35
Geography	45	61	30	78	41	36	35	57	23	34

a Plot the data on a scatter diagram. Use the horizontal axis for the mathematics scores and the vertical axis for the geography scores.

b Draw the line of best fit. (Calculate the mean of both data sets first.)

c One of the students was ill when she took the geography examination. Which student was it most likely to be?

d If another student, Kate, was absent for the geography examination but scored 75 in mathematics, what mark would you expect her to have scored in geography?

e If another student, Lina, was absent for the mathematics examination but scored 65 in geography, what mark would you expect her to have scored in mathematics?

6 A form teacher carried out a survey of 20 students from his class and asked them to say how many hours per week they spent playing sport and how many hours per week they spent watching TV. This table shows the results of the survey.

AO3

Student	1	2	3	4	5	6	7	8	9	10
Hours playing sport	12	3	5	15	11	0	9	7	6	12
Hours watching TV	18	26	24	16	19	27	12	13	17	14
Student	11	12	13	14	15	16	17	18	19	20
Hours playing sport	12	10	7	6	7	3	1	2	0	12
Hours watching TV	22	16	18	22	12	28	18	20	25	13

a Plot these results on a scatter diagram. Take the horizontal axis as the number of hours playing sport and the vertical axis as the number of hours watching TV.

b If you knew that another student from the form watched 8 hours of TV a week, would you be able to predict how long they spent playing sport? Explain why.

Data analysis: Chapter 11 Correlation and regression

7 The table shows the times taken and distances travelled by a taxi driver in 10 journeys on one day.

AO3

Distance (km)	1.6	8.3	5.2	6.6	4.8	7.2	3.9	5.8	8.8	5.4
Time (minutes)	3	17	11	13	9	15	8	11	16	10

a Draw a scatter diagram of this information, with time on the horizontal axis.

b Draw the line of best fit. (Calculate the mean of both data sets first.)

c If a taxi journey takes 5 minutes, how far, in kilometres, would you expect the journey to have been?

d How much time would you expect a journey of 4 km to take?

8 The table below shows miles per gallon in relation to the engine size for several cars.

AO3

Engine size (litres)	1	1.2	1.5	1.8	2.2	2.5	3.0	3.5
Miles per gallon (mpg)	55	50	45	41	35	30	25	20

a Plot the points on a scatter diagram, with engine size on the horizontal axis.

b Calculate the means of engine size and miles per gallon and use them to draw a line of best fit.

c Find the equation of the line of best fit, in the form $y = mx + c$.

9 A cyclist uses a heart-rate monitor to keep his heart rate between 150 and 160 beats per minute on his winter training rides.

AO4

His time trial times improve during the summer racing season. He believes that this is caused by using a heart-rate monitor during his winter training.

Is he correct to draw this conclusion?

10 The table below shows the ages and heights of 10 secondary school students.

AO4

Age (years)	11.2	11.8	12.5	13	13.4	14.2	14.8	15.3	15.8	16.3
Height (metres)	1.32	1.44	1.5	1.54	1.61	1.65	1.68	1.72	1.75	1.77

a Plot the points on a scatter diagram

b Calculate the means of the ages and heights and use these to draw a line of best fit.

c Find the equation of the line of best fit, in the form $y = mx + c$.

d Explain why it would not be sensible to extend the line of best fit so that you could determine the height of a 25-year-old adult.

11.2 Spearman's rank and product moment correlation coefficients

This section will show you how to:
- calculate and interpret the correlation between two sets of data by calculating Spearman's rank correlation coefficient
- interpret the product moment correlation coefficient and when to use it.

KEY WORDS

Spearman's rank correlation coefficient
Product moment correlation coefficient

Both **Spearman's rank correlation coefficient** (SRCC) and the **product moment correlation coefficient** (PMCC) are numerical measures of the correlation between two sets of data. They are used to find out if there is a relationship or connection between the data. For example, do students who do well in French examinations also do well in English examinations?

Both correlation coefficients range between −1 and +1, where −1 is perfect negative correlation and +1 is perfect positive correlation. They can be interpreted according to the following scale.

1	Perfect positive correlation
0.9	Very strong positive correlation
0.8	Strong positive correlation
0.7	Fairly strong positive correlation
0.6	
0.5	Moderate positive correlation
0.4	Fairly weak positive correlation
0.3	
0.2	Weak positive correlation
0.1	Very weak positive correlation
0	No correlation
−0.1	Very weak negative correlation
−0.2	Weak negative correlation
−0.3	Fairly weak negative correlation
−0.4	
−0.5	Moderate negative correlation
−0.6	Fairly strong negative correlation
−0.7	
−0.8	Strong negative correlation
−0.9	Very strong negative correlation
−1	Perfect negative correlation

Data analysis: Chapter 11 Correlation and regression

Spearman's rank correlation coefficient (SRCC) is used:
- when only rankings are given, for example, when two wine tasters each put 10 wines in order of preference
- if you think there is a non-linear relationship in the data: for example, a scatter diagram that forms a curve, such as the correlation between the number of hours an athlete trains and the improvement in the athlete's performance. You would imagine that it would increase steadily up to a point and then start to taper off into a curve when excessive training does not necessarily improve performance.

> **Hints and tips**
>
> You are expected to be able to interpret both the SRCC and the PMCC in the context of a problem. However, you will only be asked to calculate the SRCC.

The **product moment correlation coefficient** (PMCC) is used when a scatter diagram shows an approximately **linear** relationship, i.e. a straight line.

The formula to calculate Spearman's rank correlation coefficient (which will be given to you in an examination) is:

$$\text{SRCC} = 1 - \frac{6\Sigma d^2}{n(n^2 - 1)}$$

where n is the number of data values

Σd^2 is the sum of the differences between the ranks squared.

Example 4

The personal best times of 10 athletes for 100 m and 200 m are shown in the table below.

Athlete	100 m	200 m
A	10.5	21.2
B	11.1	22.3
C	10.7	21.6
D	10.1	20.4
E	11.3	22.6
F	10.9	22.4
G	10.6	21.4
H	10.3	20.2
I	11.6	22.5
J	10.4	20.9

a Calculate Spearman's rank correlation coefficient between the times for the two races.
b What does the result tell you about the athletes' times?

Data analysis: Chapter 11 Correlation and regression

Solution

a First redraw the table and rank each time for the 100 m and 200 m from fastest (rank 1) to slowest (rank 10).

Find the difference between the two ranks for each athlete, for example, for athlete B, 8 − 7 = 1.

Square the differences.

Athlete	100 m	200 m	Rank 100 m	Rank 200 m	Difference d	d^2
A	10.5	21.2	4	4	4 − 4 = 0	0
B	11.1	22.3	8	7	8 − 7 = 1	1
C	10.7	21.6	6	6	0	0
D	10.1	20.4	1	2	−1	1
E	11.3	22.6	9	10	−1	1
F	10.9	22.4	7	8	−1	1
G	10.6	21.4	5	5	0	0
H	10.3	20.2	2	1	1	1
I	11.6	22.5	10	9	1	1
J	10.4	20.9	3	3	0	0
						$\Sigma d^2 = 6$

Rank the times in order, from fastest to slowest, for example, athlete D has the fastest 100-m time (rank 1) and the second fastest 200-m time (rank 2).

This is the sum of the squares of the differences: 0 + 1 + 0 + 1 + 1 + 1 + 0 + 1 + 1 + 0 = 6

$\Sigma d^2 = 6$ $n = 10$

$$\text{SRCC} = 1 - \frac{6\Sigma d^2}{n(n^2 - 1)} = 1 - \frac{6 \times 6}{10(10^2 - 1)} = 1 - \frac{36}{990} = +0.96$$

b Look back at the correlation coefficients scale on the previous page. A coefficient of +0.96 shows very strong positive correlation and suggests that athletes who have fast 100 m times also have fast 200 m times. The reverse is also true.

The next example shows you the method to use when ranks are tied, which means that two or more values are ranked equally in the table.

Example 5

The following marks were achieved by students in geography and mathematics examinations.

Geography	Mathematics
34	44
46	57
53	62
46	65
72	89
83	62

Geography	Mathematics
68	67
29	38
75	71
63	52
66	73

a Calculate Spearman's rank correlation coefficient between the two sets of marks.
b What does the result tell you about the students' marks?

301

Solution

a Rank the marks, as in the following table.

> Note that geography has two scores at 46 which would rank at 8th and 9th, so average them to 8.5.

Geography	Mathematics	Rank geography	Rank mathematics	d	d^2
34	44	10	10	0	0
46	57	8.5	8	0.5	0.25
53	62	7	6.5	0.5	0.25
46	65	8.5	5	3.5	12.25
72	89	3	1	2	4
83	62	1	6.5	-5.5	30.25
68	67	4	4	0	0
29	38	11	11	0	0
75	71	2	3	-1	1
63	52	6	9	-3	9
66	73	5	2	3	9
					$\Sigma d^2 = 66$

> Note that mathematics has two scores at 62 which would rank at 7th and 8th, so average them to 6.5.

$\Sigma d^2 = 66 \quad n = 11$

$\text{SRCC} = 1 - \dfrac{6\Sigma d^2}{n(n^2 - 1)} = 1 - \dfrac{6 \times 66}{11(11^2 - 1)} = +0.7$

b A coefficient of +0.7 shows fairly strong positive correlation, which suggests that students who do well in mathematics generally do as well in geography, and vice versa.

> This is the sum of the squared differences: 0 + 0.25 + 0.25 + 12.25 + 4 + 30.25 + 0 + 0 + 1 + 9 + 9 = 66.

Exercise 11B

1 Peter calculates Spearman's rank correlation coefficient for three different sets of data. His results are shown in the table below.

Data sets	Spearman's rank correlation coefficient
Tyres: size against price	0.64
Age of car against resale value	−0.95
Eye colour against IQ	0.05

Comment on the relationship for each data set.

2 Eight students took an English test followed by a history test. Their results are shown in the table below.

English	History
10	9
8	7
6	6
9	8
7	5
4	4
5	3
2	1

a Calculate Spearman's rank correlation coefficient.

b What relationship exists between the two sets of data?

3 The table below shows the shoe sizes and hand-span measurements of 10 students.

Hand (cm)	Shoe size	Hand rank	Shoe rank	Difference d	d^2
12	3				
16	5				
19	10				
16	4				
23	12				
21	9				
25	11				
17	6				
18	6				
18	7				

a Copy and complete the table.

b Use the table to calculate Spearman's rank correlation coefficient.

c Comment on the relationship between the two sets of data.

Data analysis: Chapter 11 Correlation and regression

4 John states that the fewer goals a team in the Premier league concedes, the more points they will achieve by the end of the season. He produces the table below for the top 10 teams in the 2009–2010 Premier league.

AO3

Team	Total points	Goals conceded
Chelsea	86	32
Manchester United	85	28
Arsenal	75	41
Tottenham Hotspur	70	41
Manchester City	67	45
Aston Villa	64	39
Liverpool	63	35
Everton	61	49
Birmingham	50	47
Blackburn Rovers	50	55

a Use the table to calculate Spearman's rank correlation coefficient.

b Is John's statement correct? Explain your answer.

5 A TV show tested the theory that low tyre pressure in a car reduces fuel consumption. After they had performed the tests the following table was produced.

AO3

Tyre pressure (psi)	Fuel consumption (mpg)
10	38
20	38
30	41
40	43
50	46
60	44

a Calculate Spearman's correlation coefficient.

b What conclusions can be drawn from your answer to part **a**? Was the theory dismissed or confirmed?

6 Siobhan wants to test the hypothesis that:

'The more a male smokes, the lower his life expectancy.'

She produces the table below. Calculate Spearman's rank correlation coefficient and comment on her hypothesis.

AO3

Country	Percentage of males that smoke	Male life expectancy
Sweden	36	72.9
France	41	74.3
Germany	36.8	73.2
Italy	38	74.4
Norway	36.4	74
Poland	51	68.6
UK	28	73.9
USA	28.1	72.6
Brazil	39.9	57.4
China	61	66.9
India	40	58.2
Iraq	40	64.9
Japan	59	76.5
Kuwait	52	72.8
Australia	29	74.5
Nigeria	24.4	54.1
South Africa	52	62.4

7 David thinks that poorer countries have higher infant mortality rates. Calculate Spearman's rank correlation coefficient and use it to decide if he is correct.

AO3

Country	GDP per capita ($)	Infant mortality rate (number of deaths per 100 000 babies born)
United States	30 200	6.44
Singapore	24 600	3.87
Switzerland	23 800	4.92
Netherlands	22 000	5.17
Australia	21 400	5.26
UK	21 200	5.87
New Zealand	17 700	6.37
Greece	13 000	7.26
Chile	11 600	10.39
Uruguay	8900	14.11
Puerto Rico	8600	12.09
Romania	5300	18.83
Sri Lanka	3800	16.33

GRADE BOOSTER

What you need to do to get this grade

D–C	Draw and interpret a scatter diagram.
	Understand the limitations of interpolation and extrapolation.
	State the type of correlation from a scatter diagram.
C	Draw a line of best fit through the two mean points.
	Interpret a correlation coefficient.
B	Work out the equation of a line of best fit in the form $y = mx + c$.
B–A	Calculate and interpret Spearman's rank correlation coefficient.
A	Interpret product moment correlation coefficient (PMCC).

What you should now know

- How to draw and interpret a scatter diagram.
- How to work out the type of correlation from a scatter diagram.
- How to draw a line of best fit on a scatter diagram using the two means.

Higher tier only

- How to calculate the equation for a line of regression.
- How to calculate and interpret Spearman's rank correlation coefficient.

EXAMINATION Questions

1 Kelly asked 8 friends to record the number of text messages they sent and the number of calls they made on their mobile phones during one week.

The results are recorded in the table.

Number of text messages	18	22	24	25	28	32	32	35
Number of calls	36	24	26	20	13	8	10	7

a Copy the grid and draw a scatter diagram to represent the data. *(2 marks)*

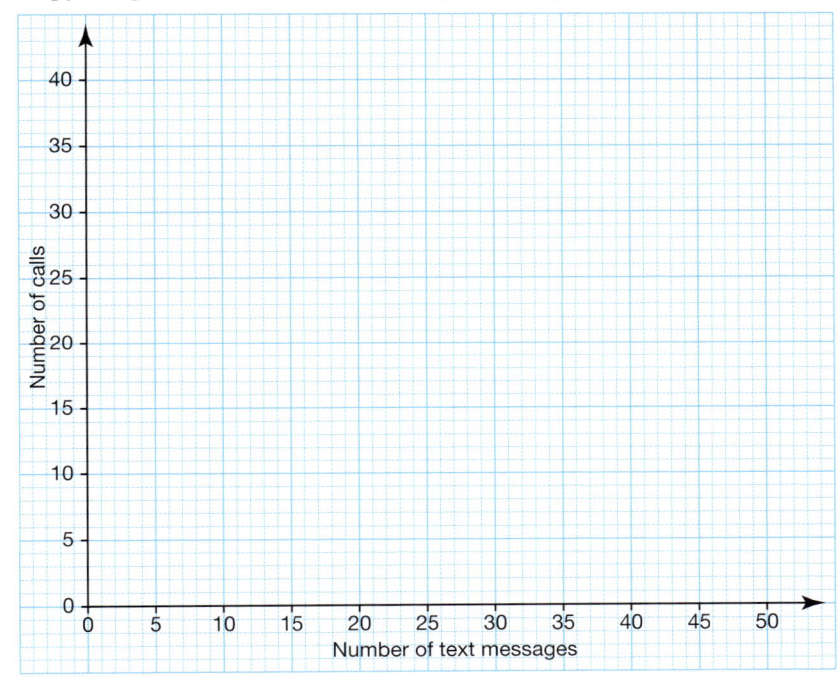

b Describe the correlation shown by the scatter diagram. *(1 mark)*

c The mean number of text messages sent is 27.

What is the mean number of calls made? *(2 marks)*

d Draw a line of best fit on your diagram. *(2 marks)*

e Susan, another of Kelly's friends, sent 30 text messages during that week.

Use your line of best fit to estimate the number of calls that she made. *(1 mark)*

f Ailsa, another of Kelly's friends, sent 45 text messages during that week.

Give **one** reason why you should not use this line of best fit to estimate the number of calls that Ailsa made. *(1 mark)*

AQA June 2006, Higher Statistics Paper, Question 3

Data analysis: Chapter 11 Examination questions

2 An expert from the local antiques club agreed to challenge a number of contestants to rank eight items of Victorian furniture correctly, according to their value.

John agreed to take part and his rankings along with those of the expert, were as follows.

Exhibit	A	B	C	D	E	F	G	H
Expert	1	3	6	7	8	3	5	4
John	8	5	2.5	4	1	6	2.5	7

a Calculate the value of Spearman's rank correlation coefficient for the two sets of data.
(4 marks)

b Interpret, in context, your answer to part **a**. *(1 mark)*

c A further eight contestants entered the competition.

The values of the correlation coefficients were:

0.35   −0.43   0.71   0.05   −0.36   −0.02   0.92   −0.81

i Which two of these values show that there is almost no correlation between the individual rankings of that contestant and those of the expert? *(2 marks)*

ii Which of these values shows the strongest correlation between the expert and contestant? *(1 mark)*

AQA June 2006, Higher Statistics Page, Question 12

3 An insurance company has eight branch offices which vary in size and number of employees.

The table shows the annual cost of running each branch office and the number of employees at each office.

Branch office	A	B	C	D	E	F	G	H
Number of employees	15	13	17	8	9	8	6	4
Annual running cost in thousands of pounds	74	87	94	41	50	53	25	32

The data is shown on the scatter graph.

For the data:

the mean number of employees is 10

the mean annual cost to run the branches is £57 000

the line of best fit passes through the point (5, 30 500).

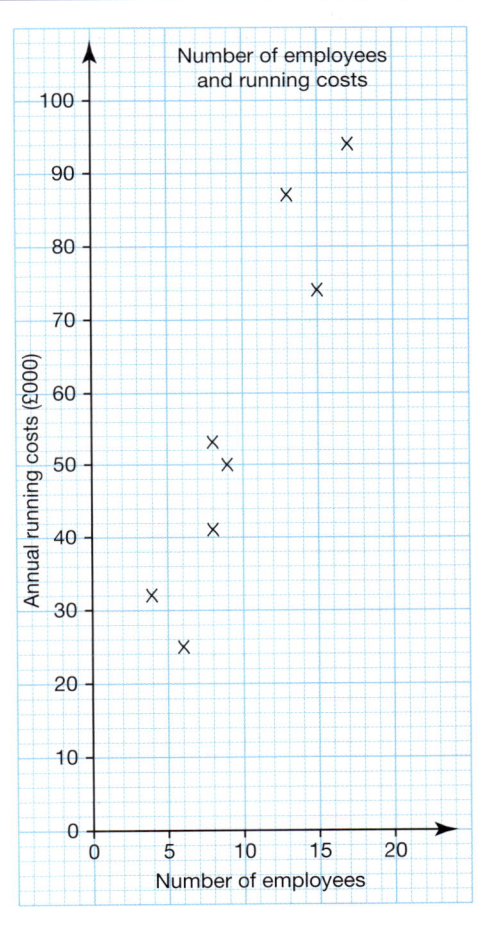

a Draw the line of best fit on the scatter diagram. *(2 marks)*

b i Calculate the gradient of the line of best fit. *(2 marks)*

 ii What does the gradient of the line represent in this context? *(1 mark)*

c Explain why office A, employing 15 staff, appears good value for money. *(1 mark)*

d Calculate Spearman's coefficient of rank correlation between the number of branch employees and branch annual running costs. *(6 marks)*

AQA June 2008, Higher Statistics Paper, Question 10

4 Sixteen different journeys made through a city centre were timed.

Eight of the journeys were made by bus.

The distance travelled and time taken for the bus journeys have been plotted on the scatter diagram below and the line of best fit has been drawn.

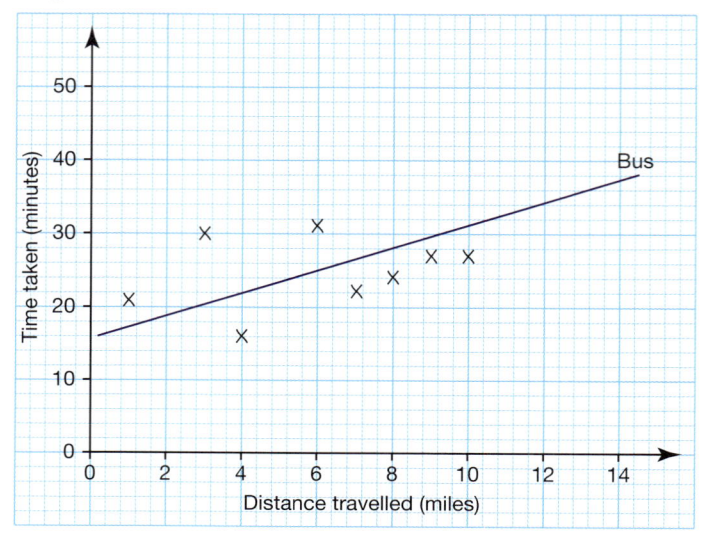

The other eight journeys were by car.

The distance travelled and time taken for the car journeys are shown in the table.

Distance travelled (miles)	6	7	2	10	5	9	1	8
Time taken (minutes)	18	23	11	36	18	31	7	32

a Plot the car journey values on a copy of the scatter diagram. *(2 marks)*

b The mean distance travelled by car was 6 miles.
Calculate the mean time taken for the car journeys. *(2 marks)*

c Draw a line of best fit for the car journeys on the scatter diagram. *(2 marks)*

d Estimate the time taken for:
  i a 12-mile car journey
  ii a 2-mile bus journey. *(2 marks)*

e Which of these estimates is likely to be more reliable?
Give a reason for your answer. *(2 marks)*

f Use the graph to find the shortest distance at which it becomes quicker to travel by bus rather than car.
Give a reason for your answer. *(2 marks)*

g Estimate the value of Spearman's rank correlation coefficient between distance travelled and time taken for the bus journeys. *(1 mark)*

h Calculate the value of Spearman's rank correlation coefficient between distance travelled and time taken for the car journeys. *(6 marks)*

i Comment on the correlation value. *(1 mark)*

AQA June 2004, Higher Statistics Paper, Question 5

5 A television football show organised a goal-of-the-month competition.

Viewers were asked to rank 10 goals scored from best to worst.

Ahmed entered the competition, giving the order as:

   H   F   D   B   I   C   J   G   A   E

His friend Peter gave the order as:

   C   I   F   D   H   B   A   E   G   J

a Copy and complete the following table and hence calculate Spearman's rank correlation coefficient between the two sets of rankings.

Goal	A	B	C	D	E	F	G	H	I	J
Ahmed's rankings										
Peter's rankings										
d										
d^2										

(6 marks)

b What does the answer suggest about the level of agreement between the two friends?

(1 mark)

c Neither Ahmed nor Peter won the competition.

The value of the correlation coefficient between Ahmed and the winner was −0.92 and between Peter and the winner was 0.03.

Give a reason why each of the entrants was not successful.

(2 marks)

AQA June 2009, Higher Statistics Paper, Question 8

Data analysis: Chapter 11 Examination questions

WORKED EXAMINATION Questions

1 A survey was carried out at eight primary schools one morning.

The table shows some information that was recorded about the number of children and the percentage of children absent.

School	A	B	C	D	E	F	G	H
Number of children	60	75	100	50	100	130	200	80
Percentage of children absent	5	8	4	2	12	10	8.5	2.5

a Calculate the value of Spearman's rank correlation coefficient for the two sets of data.

(6 marks)

> Tied rank, so take the mean of 3 and 4 (= 3.5).

> Number of children ranked from highest to lowest.

School	A	B	C	D	E	F	G	H
Number of children	60	75	100	50	100	130	200	80
Percentage of children absent	5	8	4	2	12	10	8.5	2.5
Rank P (no. of children)	7	6	3.5	8	3.5	2	1	5
Rank A (absences)	5	4	6	8	1	2	3	7
d (P − A)	2	2	−2.5	0	2.5	0	−2	−2
d^2	4	4	6.25	0	6.25	0	4	4

> Subtract A from P to find d.

> Add the d^2 values to find Σd^2. Σ means 'the sum of'.

> Absences ranked from highest to lowest.

$$\text{SRCC} = 1 - \frac{6\Sigma d^2}{n(n^2 - 1)} = 1 - \frac{6 \times 28.5}{8(8^2 - 1)} = +0.6607$$

> You will gain **2 marks** for correctly ranking both the number and percentage.
> You will gain **1 method mark** for correctly calculating d^2.
> You will gain **1 method mark** for correctly calculating Σd^2.
> You will gain **1 method mark** and **1 accuracy mark** for correctly calculating SRCC.
> Altogether, calculating SRCC is usually worth a total of **6 marks**.

b Use your answer to part **a** to comment on the statement:

'The more children there are in a school, the greater the rate of absenteeism.'

Fairly strong positive correlation, so some agreement.

> You will gain **1 mark** for stating that +0.6607 shows fairly strong positive correlation and indicating that there is some agreement with the statement. Even if you have calculated part a incorrectly, you can still get this mark by correctly interpreting your result. Answers of +0.66 or more accurate are acceptable.

c Study the graphs below and then write down the most likely value of Spearman's rank correlation coefficient for each of them.

Choose from the following list.

−0.45   0.75   −1.3   −0.98   0.98   *(2 marks)*

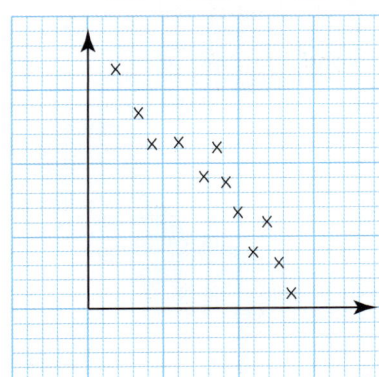

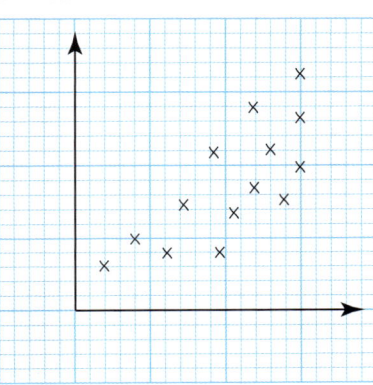

Graph 1 shows strong negative correlation, stronger than −0.45; can't be −1.3 as correlation ranges between −1 and +1, so the value is −0.98.

> Simply stating −0.98 will gain you **1 mark**, no explanation is required.

Graph 2 shows fairly strong positive correlation, not as strong as 0.96, so the value is 0.75.

> Simply stating 0.75 will gain you **1 mark**, no explanation is required.

(Total 9 marks)

12 Probability

'We have a good chance of winning the match tomorrow.' 'They say it's probably going to snow today.' 'I'm not playing that game – it's not fair!' These comments all suggest that something is uncertain. There is an element of **chance**.

Probability is the study of chance. It allows us to determine how likely something is. Then we can decide just how likely it is to snow, or whether a game really is unfair.

Probability was originally concerned with games of chance and gambling.

In 1654 Antoine Gombaud, a French nobleman with an interest in gambling questions, wanted to decide whether or not to bet on getting at least one 'double six' during 24 throws of two dice. He asked two famous mathematicians, Blaise Pascal and Pierre de Fermat, and so they created probability theory.

Probability is vital in the creation of lotteries, as the organisers have to work out how likely it is that someone wins any prize. This allows them to make the prizes the correct amount.

Games such as roulette and other casino games are arranged so that the banker wins – not by cheating, but by using probability.

Car insurance is based on probability. Inexperienced drivers are more likely to have accidents, so the cost of insurance for them is higher. Young men are statistically more likely to have an accident than young women, so males pay more for their insurance. Whether you like it or not, this is based on facts and statistics.

Now, probability theory is used in making weather forecasts, controlling the flow of traffic, and looking at patterns in the spread of infections.

- 12.1 Probability scale
- 12.2 Equally likely outcomes
- 12.3 The addition rule for events
- 12.4 Experimental probability
- 12.5 Combined events
- 12.6 Expectation
- 12.7 Two-way tables and Venn diagrams
- 12.8 Tree diagrams
- 12.9 Conditional probability

This chapter will show you how to:
- use the language of probability
- calculate the probability of events using theoretical models or experiments

Higher tier only
- predict outcomes, using theoretical models, and compare theoretical and experimental data
- calculate probabilities for combined events.

The exercise questions in this chapter are given individual target grades as a guide.

Visual overview

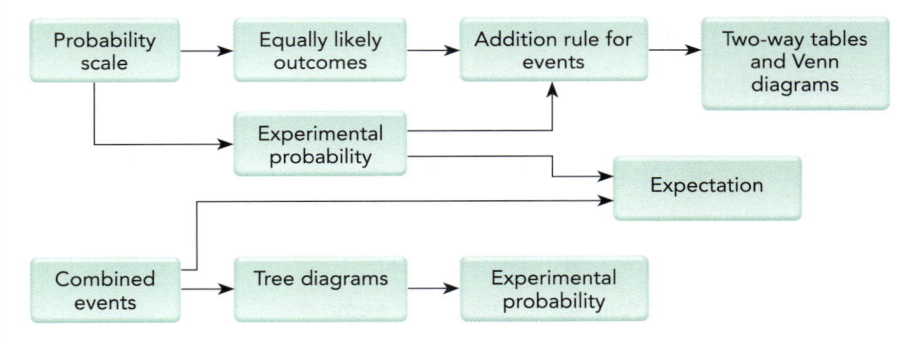

Probability scale → Equally likely outcomes → Addition rule for events → Two-way tables and Venn diagrams

Probability scale → Experimental probability → Expectation

Combined events → Tree diagrams → Experimental probability

What you should already know

- **F** That outcomes of events cannot always be predicted and that the laws of chance apply to everyday events (KS3, level 4).
- **E** How to list all the outcomes of an event in a systematic manner (KS3, level 5).
- **D** How to add, subtract and cancel fractions (KS3, level 5).

Quick check

1 Simplify these fractions

   a $\frac{9}{12}$ b $\frac{8}{12}$ c $\frac{8}{14}$ d $\frac{12}{21}$ e $\frac{14}{21}$

2 Calculate the following

   a $\frac{2}{7} + \frac{3}{7}$ b $\frac{3}{8} + \frac{5}{8}$ c $\frac{3}{8} + \frac{1}{4}$ d $\frac{1}{4} + \frac{1}{6}$ e $\frac{2}{5} + \frac{3}{15}$

3 Oliver might have bread or toast for breakfast.

   He has a choice of marmalade, strawberry jam or peanut butter.

   Write down all the possible combinations that he could have.

12.1 Probability scale

This section will show you how to:
- use the probability scale and the language of probability.

KEY WORDS
Certain
Chance
Event
Impossible
Likely
Outcome
Probability
Probability scale
Unlikely

People are always talking about probability. 'I think it's going to rain', 'I have no **chance** of passing my maths test', 'I expect I'll win the tennis match.' **Probability** is the measure of how **likely** an **outcome** is.

An **impossible event** has a probability of 0.

Something that is **certain** is given a probability of 1.

All other probabilities lie between 0 and 1.

Probabilities can be represented by marking the position on a **probability scale.**

```
Impossible      Unlikely      Even chance      Likely      Certain
   |_____|_____|_____|_____|
   0                              1/2                             1
```

Example 1

Put arrows on the probability scale to show the probability of these outcomes.

a You will get a 4 when rolling a fair dice.
b You will have two birthdays this year.
c You flip a fair coin and it lands on heads.

Solution

a This is **unlikely** as there is only one 4 and there are five other numbers on the dice, so there is only a 1 in 6 chance of this happening.
b This is impossible.
c This is an even chance, as heads and tails are equally likely.

The arrows show these on the probability scale.

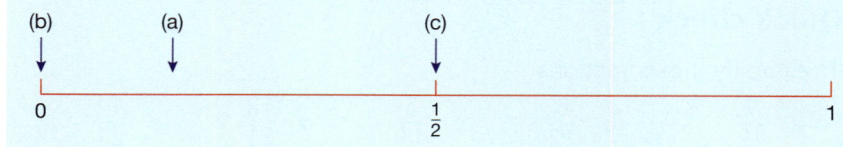

```
(b)        (a)              (c)
 ↓          ↓                ↓
 |_____|_____|_____|
 0                          1/2                1
```

Probability: Chapter 12 Probability

Exercise 12A

1 State whether each of these events are impossible, unlikely, even chance, likely or certain.

 a A new-born baby will be a boy.

 b A rolled fair dice will land on 6.

 c It will rain in Birmingham at some time during December this year.

 d The next car to drive past the school will be red.

 e You will get wet if you stand in the rain.

 f A card chosen at random from a pack will be the ace of spades.

2 For each of the following outcomes, state which of the following words best describes its probability.

 Certain   Impossible   Even chance   Likely   Unlikely

 Then mark its position on a probability scale.

 a It will rain in Bradford in the month of May.

 b You will be in school on 3 August next year.

 c I will win the lottery if I buy a ticket once.

 d I flip a fair coin and it lands heads.

3 Here are some fair spinners.

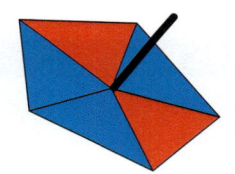

 Spinner A 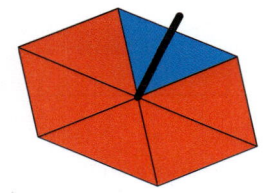   Spinner B 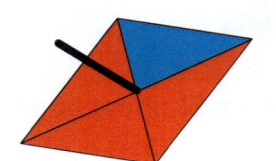   Spinner C

 a Which spinner is most likely to land on blue?

 b Which spinner is least likely to land on blue?

 c Draw a spinner which is equally likely to land on blue and red.

4 Mark these events on the probability scale.

 a The President of the USA will visit this school next week.

 b My teacher will speak in the next 30 minutes.

 c A playing card chosen at random from a pack will be red.

 d My teacher will jump up in the air 3 times in the next 30 minutes.

317

Probability: Chapter 12 Probability

G

5 Copy and complete the table below by placing a tick in the appropriate column.

Event	Impossible	Unlikely	Likely	Certain
You will toss a coin and it lands on either heads or tails				
It will snow in London in the month of June				
An athlete will run the 100 m race in less than a second				
It will rain some time in the next six months				
You will roll a dice and it lands on 7				

F

6 Write down something that is likely to happen, but is not certain.

Compare your answer with a friend's answer.

Between you, decide whose event is more likely to happen.

7 Ben goes to school by bus.

AO4

He says, 'My bus might be on time, or it might be late. So there is an even chance it will be late.'

Explain why Ben is wrong.

12.2 Equally likely outcomes

This section will show you how to:
- calculate the probability of outcomes of events using equally likely outcomes
- calculate the probability of an outcome of an event not happening, given the probability of the outcome happening.

KEY WORDS

Equally likely outcomes
Event
Random

The probability scale allows us to estimate the likelihood of **events**. Sometimes we want to be more accurate, so we can decide which of two events is more likely.

There are a number of ways of calculating probabilities. In this section we will consider results which have the same probability, known as **equally likely outcomes**.

Examples are: a fair coin landing on heads or tails.

A fair dice landing on a 1, or a 2, or a 3, or a 4, or a 5, or a 6.

Not all outcomes are equally likely. For example, when you flip a drawing pin, the pin might land point up or point down. However, they are not equally likely.

Look at these two drawing pins.

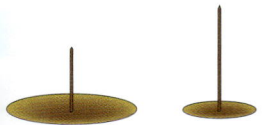

The one on the left is more likely to land point up than the one on the right because it has a larger head. The one on the right is unlikely to balance on its head because it is small. So the probability will depend on the shape.

This spinner has five equal sections.

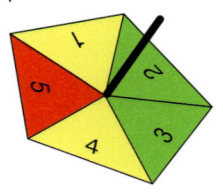

There are five sections, all the same size and equally likely:

There are two green sections out of five altogether.

The probability of it landing on a green section is $\frac{2}{5}$.

This is how you would write a score of 2 out of 5.

You can write probabilities as fractions, decimals or percentages, so you could say it is $\frac{2}{5}$, 0.4 or 40%.

The probability of an event is $\frac{\text{number of successful outcomes}}{\text{total number of possible outcomes}}$.

The probability of it landing on a prime number is $\frac{3}{5}$, because three of the five numbers are prime numbers (2, 3 and 5).

A short way of writing 'The probability of it landing on a prime number' is P(prime).

We write P(prime) = $\frac{3}{5}$.

The probability of it landing on red is $\frac{1}{5}$. This is because there is one red section out of five.

P(red) = $\frac{1}{5}$.

So we know the other four sections are not red, so the probability that it lands on 'not red' is $\frac{4}{5}$.

P(not red) = $\frac{4}{5}$.

The probability of an outcome not happening is 1 − the probability of the outcome happening.

Example 2

A bag contains 10 marbles.

Four of them are green.

Dave takes one out at **random.**

What is:

a P(green)?

b P(not green)?

Solution

a Four out of 10 are green, so the probability of it being green is $\frac{4}{10} = \frac{2}{5}$.

b P(not green) = 1 − P(green) = $1 - \frac{2}{5} = \frac{3}{5}$.

Example 3

Harry Griffiths writes his name on a set of cards, putting one letter on each:

H a r r y
G r i f f i t h s

He shuffles the cards. He chooses one at random.

What is the probability that the card he chooses is:

a a capital letter?

b a vowel?

c in the second half of the alphabet?

d in the first half of the alphabet?

Solution

a There are two cards with a capital letter out of 14, so the probability is $\frac{2}{14} = \frac{1}{7}$.

b There are three vowels; probability = $\frac{3}{14}$.

c R, R, Y, R, T, S are in the second half of the alphabet; probability = $\frac{6}{14} = \frac{3}{7}$.

d 1 − the probability of choosing a letter from the second half = $1 - \frac{3}{7} = \frac{4}{7}$.

Exercise 12B

1 A fair coin is flipped.

What is the probability it lands on tails?

2 The diagram below shows a fair square spinner.

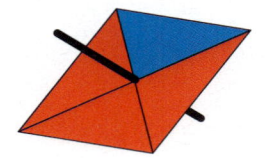

What is the probability of it landing on blue?

3 A mixed football team has five girls and six boys. The captain is chosen at random.

Write down the probability that the captain is:

a a boy

b a girl.

4 A box contains 35 pens. Eight are red, 15 are black and the rest are blue.

a How many blue pens are there in the box?

b If a pen is chosen at random what is the probability the pen is:

  i a red pen?

  ii a black pen?

  iii a blue pen?

5 A fair six-sided dice with sides numbered 1, 2, 3, 4, 5 and 6 is rolled. What is the probability of it landing on:

a a five?

b an odd number?

c a prime number?

d an even number or an odd number?

e an even number which is also a prime number?

6 Di has a set of 20 cards numbered from 1 to 20.

She picks out a card at random and then replaces it in the pack.

What is the probability that the number on the card is:

a a 4?

b even?

c bigger than 15?

Probability: Chapter 12 Probability

7 At a funfair, a dart is thrown at the board shown, and you win the amount shown on the square the dart lands in. What is the probability you win:

 a no money?

 b 25p?

 c 50p?

 d £1?

 e 33p?

25	0	0	0	25	25	0	25	0	0	25
50	0	0	25	0	0	25	0	£1	0	0	0
0	25	25	0	0	50	0	25	25	0	25	25	0
25	0	0	25	25	0	50	0	0	50	0	0	25
0	25	0	25	0	25	0	50	0	0	0	£1	0
50	0	0	0	25	25	0	0	0	25	0	0	0
0	0	0	25	0	0	0	25	25	0	25	50	0
	0	25	0	0	0	0	50	0	0	25	25

8 A card is drawn at random from a full pack of 52 playing cards. What is:

 a P(9 of clubs)?

 b P(a diamond)?

 c P(a red card)?

 d P(a king)?

 e P(not a king)?

9 In a raffle, 5000 tickets are sold. Anne buys 10 tickets, Brian buys 100 tickets, Charles buys 50 tickets and Debbie buys 40 tickets.

If there is only one winning ticket, what is the probability that:

 a Anne wins?

 b Charles wins?

 c a boy from this group wins?

 d a girl from this group wins?

 e Brian will not win?

10 The probability that my football team wins its next game is $\frac{3}{8}$. The probability that we lose is $\frac{1}{8}$. What is the probability that we draw?

11 Here is the top of a Snakes and Ladders board.

A04

100	99	98	97	96	95	94	93	92	91
81	82	83	84	85	86	87	88	89	90

Joe is on square 88.

He rolls the dice.

a What is the probability that he lands on the snake on square 94?

b What is the probability that he ends up on square 92?

c What is the probability that he does not end up on the top row of squares?

12.3 The addition rule for events

This section will show you how to:
- work out the probability of two outcomes such as P(outcome A or outcome B).

KEY WORDS
Either
Mutually exclusive event

When you flip a coin it can land **either** on heads or on tails.

These are **mutually exclusive events** – if one happens, the other one cannot.

Not all events are mutually exclusive; it might rain tomorrow, or the sun might shine, or it might do both.

Choosing an ace from a pack of cards or choosing a king are mutually exclusive.

Choosing a heart or choosing a king are not mutually exclusive; you might choose the king of hearts.

When events are mutually exclusive, you can find the probability of either of them happening by adding the separate probabilities.

Example 4

Jonathan has some cubes:

J O N A T H A N

a If he chooses a cube at random, what is the probability that it is:

  i yellow?

  ii the letter A?

  iii the letter T?

  iv the letter A or the letter T?

b Why is it wrong to add your answers to **a i** and **a ii** to find the probability of choosing a yellow cube or the letter A?

Solution

a i P(yellow) = $\frac{5}{8}$

  ii P(A) = $\frac{2}{8} = \frac{1}{4}$

  iii P(T) = $\frac{1}{8}$

  iv P(A or T) = $\frac{2}{8} + \frac{1}{8} = \frac{3}{8}$

b It would be wrong because the two outcomes are not mutually exclusive; there is a yellow cube with the letter A.

Example 5

Praveena has a bag of sweets. Some are strawberry flavoured, some are banana flavoured and the rest are lemon flavoured.

She chooses one at random.

The probability that she chooses a strawberry sweet is 0.6.

The probability that she chooses a strawberry sweet or a banana sweet is 0.85.

a What is the probability that she chooses a banana sweet?

b What is the probability that she chooses a lemon sweet?

c There are 20 sweets in the bag. How many are strawberry flavoured?

Solution

a P(strawberry or banana) = P(strawberry) + P(banana)

  0.85 = 0.6 + P(banana)

  P(banana) = 0.85 − 0.6 = 0.25

b P(lemon) = P(not strawberry or not banana) = 1 − P(strawberry or banana) = 1 − 0.85 = 0.15

c 0.6 of the sweets are strawberry. 0.6 of 20 = 0.6 × 20 = 12 strawberry sweets.

Exercise 12C

1 Pete rolls an ordinary fair dice.

What is the probability that he rolls:

a a 4?

b an odd number?

c an odd number or a 4?

2 Jo chooses a card from a pack at random.

What is the probability that she chooses:

a a queen?

b the seven of spades?

c a queen or the seven of spades?

3 Rupert has a set of stickers.

He chooses one at random.

What is the probability that he chooses:

a a car?

b a train?

c a motorbike?

d a car or a motorbike?

Probability: Chapter 12 Probability

4 A box contains 30 counters. Eleven are red, seven are black and the rest are blue or green.

   a If a counter is chosen at random, what is the probability the counter is:

   i red or black?

   ii blue or green?

   b There are twice as many blue counters as there are green counters.
   What is the probability that a blue counter is chosen?

5 Ryan is either on time for school, late or absent.
   The probability that Ryan is late for school is 0.3.
   The probability that he is absent or late for school is 0.32.

   a What is the probability that he is absent?

   b The school sends a letter home to his parents if he is late more than twice in a term.
   In a term of 10 weeks, how many times is he likely to be late?

6 Hope has a set of 25 cards numbered from 1 to 25.
   She picks out a card at random and then replaces it in the pack.
   What is the probability that the number on the card is:

   a a multiple of 5?

   b even?

   c an odd number greater than 20?

   d even or is an odd number greater than 20?

7 Holly takes a card at random from a full pack of 52 playing cards. What is:

   a P(nine of clubs)?

   b P(a diamond)?

   c P(a red card)?

   d P(a diamond or the nine of clubs)?

   e P(a red card or the nine of clubs)?

8 Mike, Alice and Debbie are playing darts.
   The probability that Mike wins is 0.4.
   The probability that Mike or Debbie wins is 0.7.
   Who is the most likely to win out of the three players?

9 Three friends, Alison, Beth and Cat, are standing for election to the School Council.
   The probability that Alison gets elected is $\frac{3}{8}$. The probability of Alison or Cat getting elected is $\frac{7}{10}$.
   Who is most likely to get elected?

326

10 A fair spinner is coloured and lettered as shown.

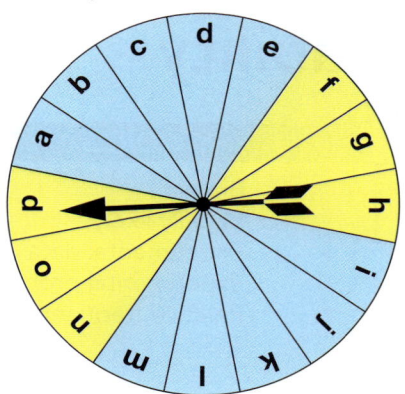

a What is the probability of it landing on the letter 'b'?

b What is the probability of it landing on yellow?

c What is the probability of it landing on a vowel?

d What is the probability of it landing on 'b' or a vowel?

e Noah says the probability of it landing on blue or a letter from his name is $\frac{5}{8} + \frac{1}{4} = \frac{7}{8}$.
Explain why he is wrong.

11 Sharon has 120 tracks on her iPod. **AO3, AO4**

She classifies them as rock, hip-hop, soul or R&B.

If she puts in on to random play, the probability of it playing a hip-hop or R&B track is $\frac{3}{5}$.

The probability of it playing a rock or hip-hop track is $\frac{1}{2}$.

The probability of it not playing an R&B track is $\frac{2}{3}$.

Use this information to complete the table below.

Type	Probability	Number of tracks
Rock		
Hip-hop		
Soul		
R&B		

Probability: Chapter 12 Probability

12.4 Experimental probability

KEY WORDS

Biased
Equally likely
Experimental data
Experimental probability
Relative frequency
Trials

This section will show you how to:
- calculate experimental probabilities and relative frequencies from experiments
- recognise different methods for estimating probabilities.

Activity

Reach the top

Put a counter in the START square.

Roll a dice.

If the number is odd, move diagonally up to the left.

If the number is even, move diagonally up to the right.

If you reach the top square, you win.

If you come off the sides, you lose.

Play the game 16 times. Keep a record of how many times you win.

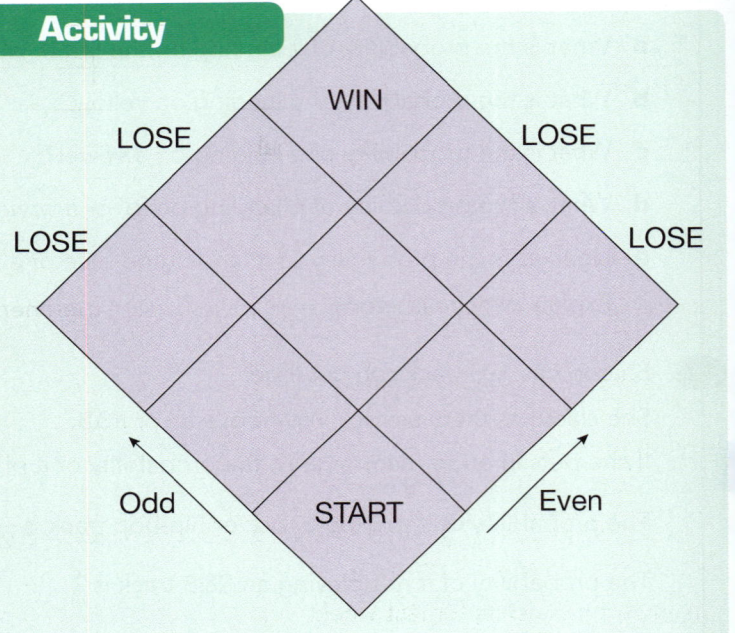

Probabilities cannot always be calculated from equally likely outcomes.

Sometimes we rely on **experimental data** by repeating **trials** a large number of times.

The fraction is similar to the one we used for equally likely outcomes. The **experimental probability** or **relative frequency** is $\frac{\text{the number of successful outcomes}}{\text{the total number of trials}}$.

Finding out whether a drawing pin lands point up or point down can only be found by experiment. A **biased** coin or dice (one which favours one side more than the other) relies on experimental data, as the outcomes are not equally likely.

Some events rely on historical data. This means looking back to similar conditions for weather forecasts, or for patterns in behaviour of a volcano.

Probability: Chapter 12 Probability

Example 6

Alison made a spinner out of card and a cocktail stick.
She did not quite get the cocktail stick through the centre.

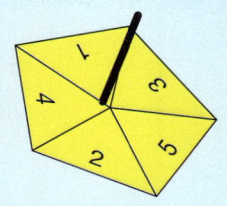

She recorded the results of 100 spins.

Score	1	2	3	4	5
Frequency	12	21	22	14	31

a Calculate the experimental probability that she scores a one.
b Calculate the experimental probability that she scores a five.

Solution

a She scored a one 12 times out of 100, so the experimental probability is $\frac{12}{100} = \frac{3}{25}$.

b She scored a five 31 times out of 100, so the experimental probability is $\frac{31}{100}$.

Example 7

Joe works in a factory making circuit boards for mobile phones. One of his jobs is to test a sample to make sure they work properly.

Here are his results for last week.

DAY	Monday	Tuesday	Wednesday	Thursday	Friday	Saturday
Number tested	210	190	95	110	260	85
Number faulty	7	6	3	5	8	3

a What is the experimental probability of a circuit board being faulty on Monday?
b What is the experimental probability of a circuit board being faulty over the whole week?
c There were 10 000 circuit boards made altogether last week. How many are likely to be faulty?

Solution

a There were 7 faulty out of 210, so P(faulty) is $\frac{7}{210} = \frac{1}{30}$.

b There were 32 faulty out of 950, so P(faulty) is $\frac{32}{950} = \frac{16}{475}$.

c We can expect $\frac{16}{475}$ of 10 000 to be faulty, or 337 to the nearest integer.

Exercise 12D

1 You can find probabilities by:

A using equally likely outcomes.

B using a survey or experiment.

C looking at historical data.

Which would you use to find the probability that:

a a dropped drawing pin will land point down?

b the next car past the school will be blue?

c a card chosen from a pack of cards will be a heart?

d you will come top in the next maths test?

2 Dave throws a dice and records how many times he gets a six.

After 20 throws, he has scored four sixes.

After 50 throws, he has scored nine sixes.

After 200 throws, he has scored 31 sixes.

After 600 throws, he has scored 96 sixes.

Dave wants to find out if his dice is fair or biased.

a What is the theoretical probability of scoring a six?

b What was his experimental probability of scoring a six after:

  i 20 throws?

  ii 50 throws?

  iii 200 throws?

  iv 600 throws?

c Do you think his dice is fair or biased? Explain your answer.

3 Joanna made an octagonal spinner.

Unfortunately, the horizontal and vertical edges were all 4 cm long but the diagonal edges were 4.25 cm long.

What effect will this have on the fairness of the spinner?

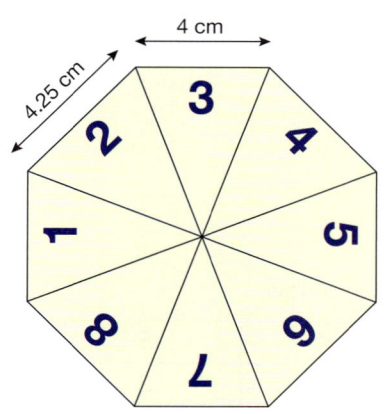

4 Pete has a bag containing some counters.

He tries an experiment where he takes a counter, makes a note of its colour and then puts it back.

He does this 100 times with these results.

Colour	Red	Blue	Black	White
Frequency	29	19	40	12

If there are 17 counters in the bag, how many of each colour are there likely to be?

5 Sally, Alice and Jack all did an experiment to find the experimental probability of a piece of buttered toast landing buttered-side down. They dropped the toast and recorded how many times it landed buttered-side up and how many times it landed buttered-side down.

Here are their results.

	Buttered-side up	Buttered-side down
Sally	78	112
Alice	113	144
Jack	49	51

a Whose results are likely to be the most accurate? Give a reason for your answer.

b Find the experimental probability of the toast landing buttered-side up based on:

  i the results of the person you chose in part **a**.

  ii all the results added together.

Probability: Chapter 12 Probability

6 Matt rolls a dice 500 times.

Here are the results.

Score	1	2	3	4	5	6
Frequency	71	102	67	99	64	97

  a Explain why the results suggest this dice is biased.

  b What is the mean score from these 500 throws?

  c What would you expect the mean score to be on a fair dice?

7 Tom, Sue and Jenny each had a dice.   **AO4**

They rolled their dice and recorded their results, which are shown below.

Score	1	2	3	4	5	6
Tom	9	8	5	10	2	6
Sue	34	36	29	41	33	41
Jenny	29	19	18	22	23	11

Do you think they are all fair dice? Use experimental probability to justify your answers.

8 Tanya flipped a fair coin 9 times and got these results.

Head   Head   Tail   Head   Head   Tail   Head   Head   Tail

Grace said, 'It keeps repeating a pattern of head, head, tail, so it will land on heads next.'

Freddy said, 'It's a fair coin, so it should have equal numbers of heads and tails. There have been more heads than tails so far, so I expect a tail next.'

Tanya said, 'There's an equal chance of head and tail next.'

Who is correct, Grace, Freddy or Tanya?

9 Which of these would suggest bias?

  a Getting a head three times when flipping a coin 10 times.

  b Getting nine threes on a five-sided spinner labelled 1 to 5, in 100 spins.

  c Getting five sixes when rolling a dice 20 times.

10 A spinner is coloured as shown.

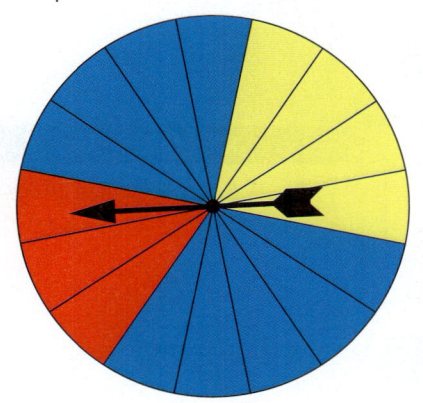

Abby spins the spinner 100 times with these results.

Colour	Blue	Red	Yellow
Frequency	53	21	26

Abby thinks the spinner is unfair as the frequency for blue is more than red and yellow combined.

a What is the theoretical probability of it landing on yellow?

b What is the experimental probability of it landing on yellow?

c What is the theoretical probability of it landing on red?

d What is the experimental probability of it landing on red?

e Do you think the spinner is biased?

Probability: Chapter 12 Probability

12.5 Combined events

This section will show you how to:
- work out the probabilities for two outcomes occurring at the same time.

KEY WORDS

Sample space diagram

Activity

Horse race

Use this board.

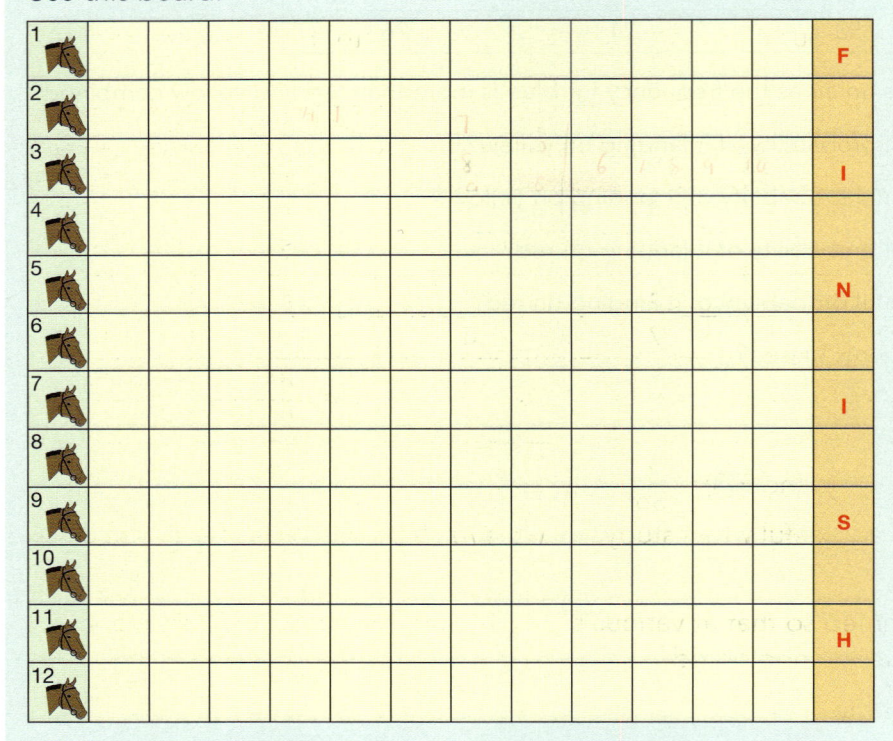

1											F
2											
3											I
4											
5											N
6											
7											I
8											
9											S
10											
11											H
12											

Put a counter on each horse.
Roll two dice and add the scores.
Move the horse with that score one square to the right.
Continue until one horse reaches the finishing line.
Play the game several times.
Which horse never moves?
Which ones win?
The activity shows that when two dice are rolled, some totals are more likely to occur than others.

Two fair dice are thrown, one red, one blue. Here is a table showing all the possible outcomes. This is called a **sample space diagram**.

		Red dice					
		1	2	3	4	5	6
Blue dice	1	(1, 1)	(2, 1)	(3, 1)	(4, 1)	(5, 1)	(6, 1)
	2	(1, 2)	(2, 2)	(3, 2)	(4, 2)	(5, 2)	(6, 2)
	3	(1, 3)	(2, 3)	(3, 3)	(4, 3)	(5, 3)	(6, 3)
	4	(1, 4)	(2, 4)	(3, 4)	(4, 4)	(5, 4)	(6, 4)
	5	(1, 5)	(2, 5)	(3, 5)	(4, 5)	(5, 5)	(6, 5)
	6	(1, 6)	(2, 6)	(3, 6)	(4, 6)	(5, 6)	(6, 6)

A score of 2 on the red dice and 3 on the blue dice is shown as (2, 3).

You can see there are 6 × 6 = 36 possible outcomes.

If we want to answer questions about the total scores, it might be better to complete the table with these totals.

		Red dice					
		1	2	3	4	5	6
Blue dice	1	2	3	4	5	6	7
	2	3	4	5	6	7	8
	3	4	5	6	7	8	9
	4	5	6	7	8	9	10
	5	6	7	8	9	10	11
	6	7	8	9	10	11	12

It is easy to see that $P(7) = \frac{6}{36} = \frac{1}{6}$, and $P(3) = \frac{2}{36} = \frac{1}{18}$.

Sample space diagrams are very useful when studying two events (in this case, the scores on two dice).

A computer game is programmed so that at various points a randomly coloured goblin appears. It might be green, yellow, blue, orange or red.

It will either be friendly or hostile.

	Colour				
	Green	Yellow	Blue	Orange	Red
Friendly	Green friendly	Yellow friendly	Blue friendly	Orange friendly	Red friendly
Hostile	Green hostile	Yellow hostile	Blue hostile	Orange hostile	Red hostile

Probability: Chapter 12 Probability

Example 8

Holly has a set of four cards numbered from 1 to 4 and a fair six-sided dice.

She picks a card at random and rolls the dice.

She says, 'The highest possible total is 10, so the probability of scoring 5 or less must be $\frac{1}{2}$.'

Holly is incorrect. What is the actual probability of scoring 5 or less?

Solution

The sample space diagram below shows the scores of 5 or less in yellow.

10 of the 24 cells are 5 or less so that the probability of 5 or less is $\frac{10}{24} = \frac{5}{12}$.

		Dice					
		1	2	3	4	5	6
Card	1	2	3	4	5	6	7
	2	3	4	5	6	7	8
	3	4	5	6	7	8	9
	4	5	6	7	8	9	10

Exercise 12E

Hints and tips

Drawing a sample space diagram will help you answer these questions.

1 Two fair six-sided dice are thrown and the scores added together.

  a What is the probability of scoring:

   i a total of 10?

   ii a total of 1?

   iii an even total?

   iv a total that is a prime number?

  b Which total has the same probability as a total of 9?

2 Dave throws a fair six-sided dice and a fair four-sided dice. He adds the scores together.

What is the probability of scoring:

  a a total of 10?

  b a total of 3?

  c an even total?

  d a total that is a prime number?

3 Two fair six-sided dice are thrown and the lower score subtracted from the larger to find the difference.

   a What is the probability of scoring a difference:

      i of 4?

      ii of 0?

      iii that is an odd number?

   b Which difference is the most likely? What is the probability of that difference?

4 There are two fair spinners: one with three sides numbered 1, 2, and 3, the other with seven sides numbered 1, 2, 3, 4, 5, 6, 7. The two scores are added together.

   a What is the probability that the sum is 6?

   b What is the probability that the sum is even?

   c What is the probability that the sum is less than 8?

5 Mandy flips two fair coins.

What is the probability that she gets:

   a two heads?

   b at least one tail?

6 A fair five-sided spinner numbered from 1 to 5, and a four-sided dice numbered from 1 to 4 are thrown. The scores are multiplied together.

   a What is:

      i P(1)?

      ii P(8)?

      iii P(7)?

   b Which is the most likely score? What is the probability of that score?

7 The children in class 11A have to choose two representatives, one male and one female.

There are four boys willing to stand, Alan, Bob, Charlie and Dave.

There are three girls willing to stand, Alice, Beth and Chloe.

The teacher decides to choose a boy and a girl at random.

What is the probability that:

   a Alan and Chloe get selected?

   b Charlie gets selected?

   c Both of those selected have the same initial letter in their name?

   d Either one of Bob or Beth get selected, but not both of them?

Probability: Chapter 12 Probability

C

8 Becky is playing a game. She needs to throw a double to win.

She can chose to roll two fair six-sided dice, two fair four-sided dice or one of each.

Which should she choose?

AO3

9 Denise is playing a game with these two fair spinners.

She wins if both spinners end on the same colour.

What is the probability that she wins?

B

10 Darren makes this game to raise money for charity.

Contestants pay 50p to play.

They roll two fair dice.

If they score a 3 on one dice, they win 50p.

If they score a total of 3, they win £1.

If they roll a double 3, they win £5.

Is he likely to make money or lose money?

AO3

12.6 Expectation

This section will show you how to:
- predict the likely number of successful events, given the number of trials and the probability of any one outcome.

KEY WORDS

Expect

Probability tells us what to **expect**.

If the probability of Sue being late for school is $\frac{1}{10}$, we expect her to be late one day out of every 10.

That does not mean that if she has been on time for the last 9 days, she will be late tomorrow.

It is a long-term expectation. In a school year of 190 days, we might expect her to be late on $\frac{1}{10}$ of those days, or 19 times. (Of course, she might be late more than this, or less.)

Example 9

Archie estimates the probability that he comes top in a maths test is $\frac{2}{7}$.

In the course of a year, he takes 35 maths tests.

In how many can he expect to come top?

Solution

$\frac{2}{7}$ of 35 = 10.

Example 10

Molly has 200 tracks on her MP3 player.

80 are by solo artists, and the rest are by bands.

a If she plays a track at random, what is the probability that it is by a solo artist?

b If she plays 30 tracks at random one afternoon, how many would you expect to be by bands?

Solution

a P(solo) = $\frac{80}{200} = \frac{2}{5}$.

b P(band) = $1 - \frac{2}{5} = \frac{3}{5}$.

$\frac{3}{5}$ of 30 = 18.

(This is only an expectation, and may not happen.)

Exercise 12F

1 I throw a fair dice 120 times.

How many times can I expect to get a 2?

2 A pack contains 52 cards, 13 of each suit (hearts, spades, diamonds and clubs).

I pick a card from a pack at random.

a What is the probability that I choose a heart?

b What is the probability that I choose a queen?

I pick a card at random and replace it in the pack. I do this 130 times.

c How many times do I expect to get a heart?

d How many queens do I expect?

3 When he plays darts, Phil has a probability of $\frac{1}{3}$ of hitting the bull when he aims for it, and a probability of $\frac{3}{5}$ of hitting a double.

    a In 60 attempts, how many bulls would he expect to get?

    b In 60 attempts, how many doubles would he expect to get?

4 Tina has a bag containing five red balls, three green balls and four yellow balls.

She chooses one at random, notes the colour and puts it back.

She does this 60 times.

How many of each colour does she expect to get?

5 A five-sided spinner is biased and has these probabilities of landing on each face.

Number	1	2	3	4	5
Probability	0.25	0.1	0.3	0.2	

    a What is the probability that it lands on 5?

    b If I spin the spinner 40 times, how many of each number do I expect?

6 The probability that it rains on any day in June is 0.3.

How many dry days should you expect in June?

7 Sarah often finds that when she buys a light bulb, it doesn't work.

She makes a note over a two-year period and discovers that four bulbs do not work and 52 do work.

The manufacturer makes 700 light bulbs per hour. How many might Sarah expect not to work?

8 Keith invents a game.

He charges people 20p to roll a fair dice.

He pays them back:

- nothing if they roll an even number.
- 10p if they roll a 1.
- 30p if they roll a 3.
- 50p if they roll a 5.

120 people play the game.

How much profit does Keith expect to make?

9 If I roll two fair dice 200 times, on how many occasions might I expect to score a total of 10 or more?

10 Maria buys 20 raffle tickets. She is told that she has a probability of winning of $\frac{1}{250}$.

If there is only one prize, how many tickets are there in the raffle altogether?

12.7 Two-way tables and Venn diagrams

KEY WORDS
Two-way table
Venn diagram

This section will show you how to:
- read two-way tables and Venn diagrams and use them to do probability and other mathematics.

Information can be shown in a number of ways.

Catriona has five pairs of long black socks, three pairs of short black socks, two pairs of long white socks, and seven pairs of short white socks.

She can show this information in a **two-way table**:

	Long socks	Short socks
Black	5	3
White	2	7

or she could show it in a **Venn diagram**:

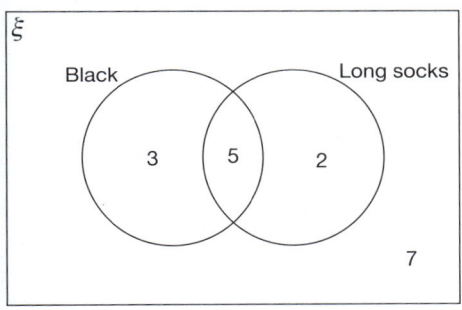

ξ

Black: 3, 5 (overlap with Long socks), 2
Outside: 7

The two-way table clearly shows the categories; in the Venn diagram we have to work out that the 7 outside the circles is the not-black, not-long section.

The Venn diagram makes it is easier to see how many are black altogether.

Another advantage of Venn diagrams is they can show three different categories, which a two-way table cannot. This Venn diagram shows the different sports played by a group of children, which cannot be shown easily in a two-way table.

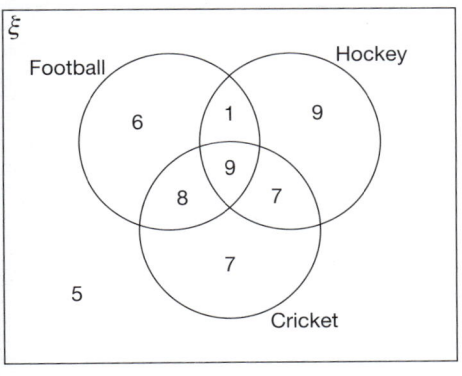

ξ

Football: 6, Hockey: 9, Cricket: 7
Football ∩ Hockey: 1
Football ∩ Cricket: 8
Hockey ∩ Cricket: 7
Football ∩ Hockey ∩ Cricket: 9
Outside: 5

Probability: Chapter 12 Probability

We can use two-way tables and Venn diagrams to summarise information, and then use them to answer questions.

Example 11

The table below shows information about the gender and age of the teachers in a school.

	Male	Female
22–35	2	4
36–45	3	7
Over 45	9	17

a How many teachers are there in the school?

b Dave chooses one of the teachers at random to interview for the school magazine.

What is the probability that he chooses:

  i a male teacher?

  ii a female teacher aged 36–45?

c Melissa knows that her form tutor next year is male.

What is the probability that he is aged 22–35?

Solution

Adding a row and column for totals will help answer many questions.

	Male	Female	Total
22–35	2	4	6
36–45	3	7	10
Over 45	9	17	26
Total	14	28	42

a There are 42 teachers.

b i $\dfrac{14}{42} = \dfrac{1}{3}$

  ii $\dfrac{7}{42} = \dfrac{1}{6}$

c $\dfrac{2}{14} = \dfrac{1}{7}$

Example 12

Connie has a container full of buttons. She categorises them as large or small, and 2-hole or 4-hole.

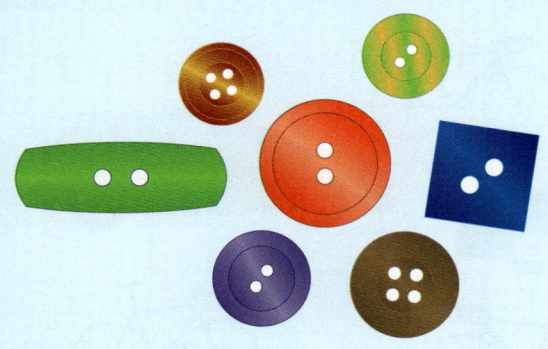

She records the information in a Venn diagram.

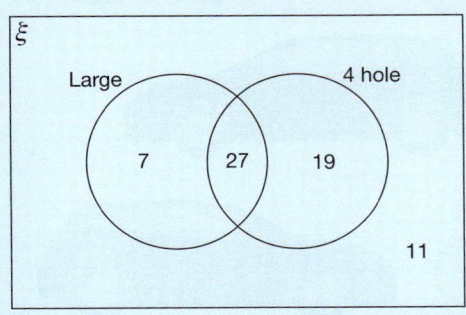

a How many large buttons does she have?
b How many small, 2-hole buttons does she have?
c She chooses a button at random. What is the probability that it is a 4-hole button?
d She chooses a large button at random. What is the probability that it has 2 holes?

Solution

a She has 34 large buttons (the red circle).
b She has 11 small, 2-hole buttons (the yellow section).
c There are 46 4-hole buttons (green circle) out of a total of 64.
So the probability is $\frac{46}{64} = \frac{23}{32}$.
d Here are 34 large buttons, 7 of which have 2 holes.
So the probability is $\frac{7}{34}$.

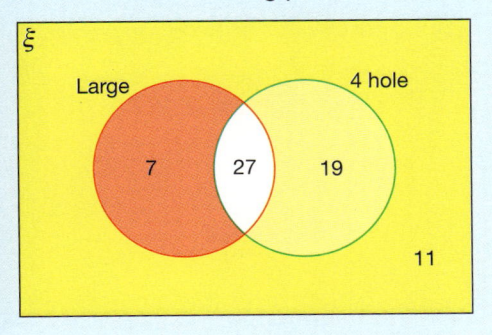

Probability: Chapter 12 Probability

Exercise 12G

1 Here are some pictures.

AO3

a Complete the table below to show the numbers of each type.

	Car	Bike
Blue		
Green		

b A picture is selected at random. What is the probability that it is a picture of a car?

2 Show the information from question 1 on a copy of this Venn diagram.

AO3

ξ

Car   Blue

344

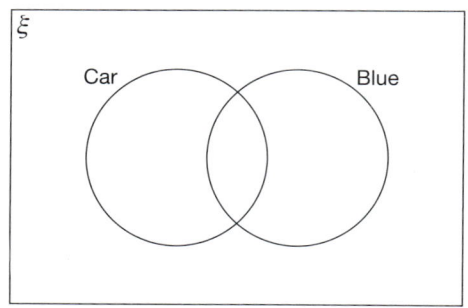

3 Corrine rolls a fair dice and flips a fair coin.

If the coin lands on heads, she doubles the score on the dice.

If the coin lands on tails, she subtracts one from the dice score.

a Copy and complete the table below to show all the scores.

		Dice score					
		1	2	3	4	5	6
Coin	Head						12
	Tails						5

b What is the probability that her final score is odd?

4 Here is a table showing information about people on a bus.

	0–3 years old	4–10 years old	11–16 years old	17–25 years old	26–50 years old	51 years or older
Male	2	3	9	2	1	9
Female	1	5	5	1	4	12

a How many of the people on the bus are less than 17 years old?

b How many of the females are 26 years old or older?

c One of the people is chosen at random. What is the probability that it is a male?

d One of the females is chosen at random. What is the probability that she is between 4 and 10 years old?

5 Oliver has some T-shirts in his wardrobe.

The table below shows the details.

	White	Grey	Red	Blue	Black
Long-sleeved	2	0	1	2	0
Short-sleeved	3	2	3	1	6

a How many T-shirts does Oliver have?

Oliver chooses a T-shirt at random. What is the probability that he chooses:

b a white shirt?

c a blue shirt?

d a long-sleeved shirt?

He decides he wants to wear a long-sleeved shirt.

e What is the probability that he chooses a white one?

6 The Venn diagram below shows information about Rosie's books.

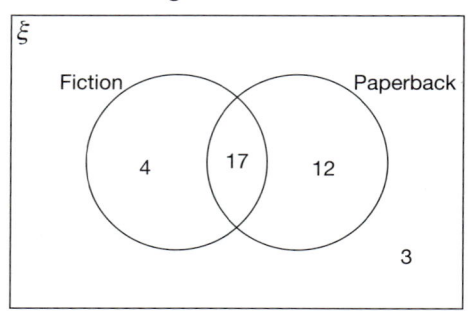

ξ
Fiction — Paperback
4 | 17 | 12
3

a How many books does Rosie have?

She chooses a book at random.

What is the probability that she chooses:

b a fiction book?

c a paperback?

She decides to read a non-fiction book.

She chooses a non-fiction book at random.

d What is the probability that she chooses a hardback?

7 A manufacturer makes flowerpots.

The numbers made in one day are shown below.

	Large	Medium	Small
Brown	65	54	34
Green	24	18	12

Tommy accidentally drops one and breaks it.

What is the probability that the broken pot was:

a brown?

b small?

c small and brown?

d not medium?

8 Harry rolls a fair six-sided dice and a fair four-sided dice.

He multiplies the scores together.

What is the probability that the answer is an odd number?

9 Andrew Owen Martin draws a Venn diagram to show the letters in each of his three names.

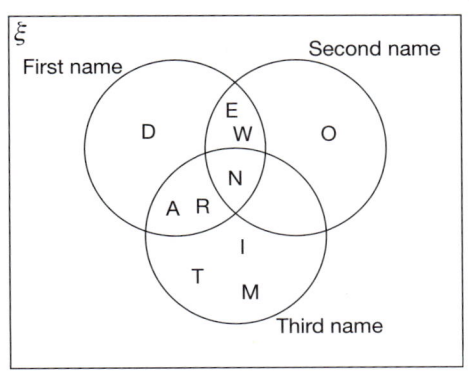

a How many different letters are there in his name?

If he chooses a letter of the alphabet at random, what is the probability that:

b it is in his name?

c it is in all three of his names?

d it is in at least two of his names?

e it is in exactly one of his names?

10 At a birthday party, children could have either a burger or a hot dog to eat, and either lemonade or cola to drink.

20 children were invited.

12 chose a burger.

9 chose lemonade.

6 chose a hot dog and cola.

a Copy and complete the Venn diagram to show their choices.

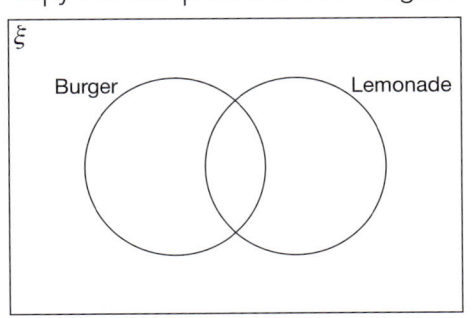

b What is the probability that a child selected at random will have chosen burger and lemonade?

Probability: Chapter 12 Probability

B **11** The number of students getting a grade C or above in their Maths, English and Science GCSEs are shown below.

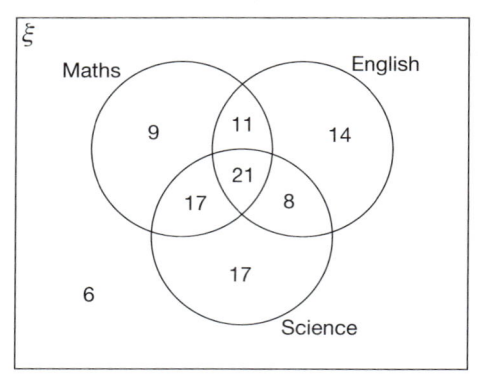

a How many students took the exams?

b Which exam (Maths, English or Science) had the highest number achieving a grade C or above?

c What is the probability that a student selected at random achieved a grade C or above in two or more subjects?

d Mary achieved a grade C in maths. What is the probability that she achieved a C or above in:

   i English?

   ii Science?

12.8 Tree diagrams

This section will show you how to:
- use tree diagrams to work out the probability of combined events.

KEY WORDS

Tree diagram
Independent events

Celia makes this game.

To win, you spin both spinners and they must land on the same colour.

Celia wants to work out the probability of winning.

She works it out like this.

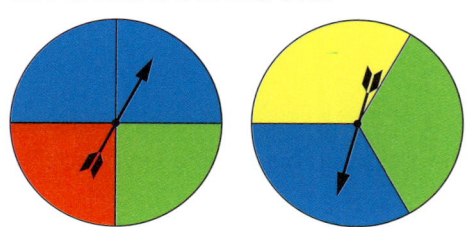

348

'If I spin the spinners 12 times, I expect the first one to land on blue six times, because P(blue) is $\frac{1}{2}$. Out of those six, I expect the second one to land on blue twice, because P(blue) is $\frac{1}{3}$. The first spinner should land on green three times, because P(green) is $\frac{1}{4}$. For the second spinner, P(green) is $\frac{1}{3}$, so out of those three, I should get another green once.

If the first spinner lands on red, I lose! If the second spinner lands on yellow I also lose! So altogether, I should win three out of 12 spins, or $\frac{1}{4}$.'

She could show this on a **tree diagram**. This is a way of showing the information in a clear, easily understood format.

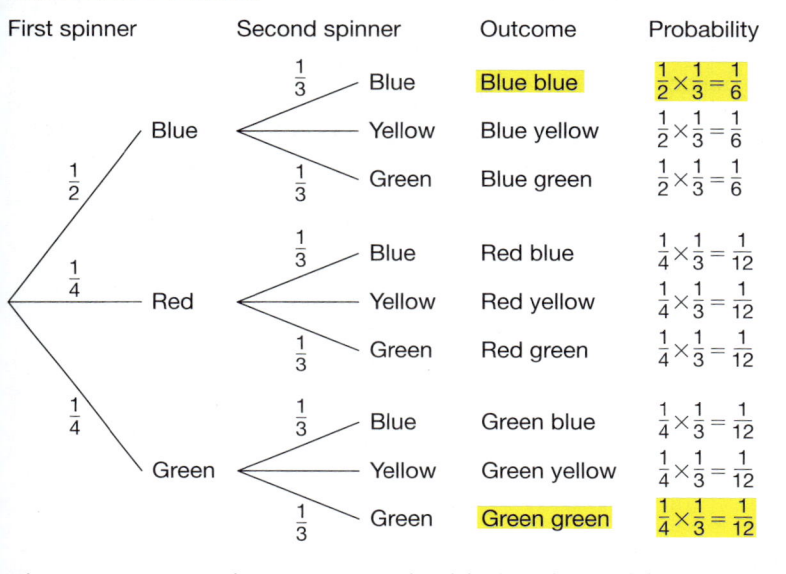

First spinner	Second spinner	Outcome	Probability
Blue ($\frac{1}{2}$)	Blue ($\frac{1}{3}$)	Blue blue	$\frac{1}{2} \times \frac{1}{3} = \frac{1}{6}$
	Yellow	Blue yellow	$\frac{1}{2} \times \frac{1}{3} = \frac{1}{6}$
	Green ($\frac{1}{3}$)	Blue green	$\frac{1}{2} \times \frac{1}{3} = \frac{1}{6}$
Red ($\frac{1}{4}$)	Blue ($\frac{1}{3}$)	Red blue	$\frac{1}{4} \times \frac{1}{3} = \frac{1}{12}$
	Yellow	Red yellow	$\frac{1}{4} \times \frac{1}{3} = \frac{1}{12}$
	Green ($\frac{1}{3}$)	Red green	$\frac{1}{4} \times \frac{1}{3} = \frac{1}{12}$
Green ($\frac{1}{4}$)	Blue ($\frac{1}{3}$)	Green blue	$\frac{1}{4} \times \frac{1}{3} = \frac{1}{12}$
	Yellow	Green yellow	$\frac{1}{4} \times \frac{1}{3} = \frac{1}{12}$
	Green ($\frac{1}{3}$)	Green green	$\frac{1}{4} \times \frac{1}{3} = \frac{1}{12}$

The winning combinations are highlighted in yellow.

$$\frac{1}{6} + \frac{1}{12} = \frac{2}{12} + \frac{1}{12} = \frac{3}{12} = \frac{1}{4}$$

We **multiply** along the branches, because **both** events must happen.

We **add** the results, because **either** combination can happen.

The probabilities for the second spinner are the same on all three sets of branches. This is because the two spinners are **independent**; the outcome of the first spinner does not influence the second.

This is not always the case in probability questions, as you will see in section 12.9.

Independent events are events where the outcome of the first event does not affect the probabilities of the subsequent events.

Example 13

On her journey to work, Cheryl has to pass two sets of traffic lights.
The probability that she gets stopped at the first set is $\frac{2}{5}$.
The probability that she gets stopped at the second set is $\frac{1}{4}$.
Find the probability that she gets stopped

a at both sets of traffic lights

b at just one set of lights.

Solution

The tree diagram will help to answer the question.

The two sets of traffic lights are independent. The probability that she gets stopped at the second set is $\frac{1}{4}$, whether she gets stopped at the first set or not.

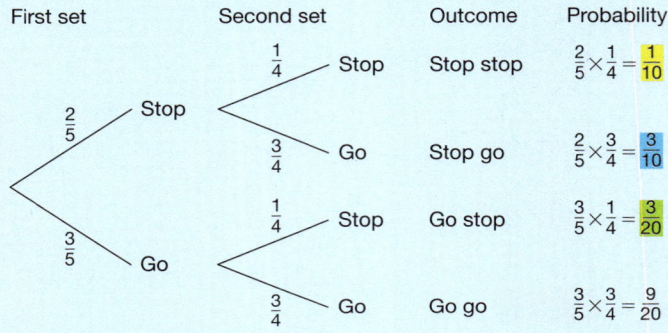

First set	Second set	Outcome	Probability
$\frac{2}{5}$ Stop	$\frac{1}{4}$ Stop	Stop stop	$\frac{2}{5} \times \frac{1}{4} = \frac{1}{10}$
	$\frac{3}{4}$ Go	Stop go	$\frac{2}{5} \times \frac{3}{4} = \frac{3}{10}$
$\frac{3}{5}$ Go	$\frac{1}{4}$ Stop	Go stop	$\frac{3}{5} \times \frac{1}{4} = \frac{3}{20}$
	$\frac{3}{4}$ Go	Go go	$\frac{3}{5} \times \frac{3}{4} = \frac{9}{20}$

a The probability that she gets stopped at both sets of traffic lights is $\frac{1}{10}$.

b The probability that she gets stopped at just one set of lights is $\frac{3}{10} + \frac{3}{20} = \frac{9}{20}$.

Example 14

Sue plays hockey for her local team.

Each week, there is a probability of $\frac{5}{8}$ that she gets picked to play, and a probability of $\frac{1}{8}$ that she is selected as a substitute, regardless of her position in the team the previous week.

a Use this information to complete the probability tree for the next two matches.
b Find the probability that she plays both matches.
c Find the probability that she plays in at least one match.

Solution

a The probability that she is dropped is $1 - \frac{5}{8} - \frac{1}{4} = \frac{2}{8} = \frac{1}{4}$.

First week	Second week	Outcome	Probability
Plays ($\frac{5}{8}$)	Plays ($\frac{5}{8}$)	Plays plays	$\frac{5}{8} \times \frac{5}{8} = \frac{25}{64}$
	Sub ($\frac{1}{8}$)	Plays sub	$\frac{5}{8} \times \frac{1}{8} = \frac{5}{64}$
	Dropped ($\frac{1}{4}$)	Plays dropped	$\frac{5}{8} \times \frac{1}{4} = \frac{5}{32}$
Sub ($\frac{1}{8}$)	Plays ($\frac{5}{8}$)	Sub plays	$\frac{1}{8} \times \frac{5}{8} = \frac{5}{64}$
	Sub ($\frac{1}{8}$)	Sub sub	$\frac{1}{8} \times \frac{1}{8} = \frac{1}{64}$
	Dropped ($\frac{1}{4}$)	Sub dropped	$\frac{1}{8} \times \frac{1}{4} = \frac{1}{32}$
Dropped ($\frac{1}{4}$)	Plays ($\frac{5}{8}$)	Dropped plays	$\frac{1}{4} \times \frac{5}{8} = \frac{5}{32}$
	Sub ($\frac{1}{8}$)	Dropped sub	$\frac{1}{4} \times \frac{1}{8} = \frac{1}{32}$
	Dropped ($\frac{1}{4}$)	Dropped dropped	$\frac{1}{4} \times \frac{1}{4} = \frac{1}{16}$

b The probability that she plays both matches is $\frac{25}{64}$.

c The probability that she plays in at least one match is $\frac{25}{64} + \frac{5}{64} + \frac{5}{32} + \frac{5}{64} + \frac{5}{32} = \frac{55}{64}$.

Probability: Chapter 12 Probability

Exercise 12H

1 A fair coin is flipped twice.

  a Copy and complete the tree diagram to show all the outcomes.

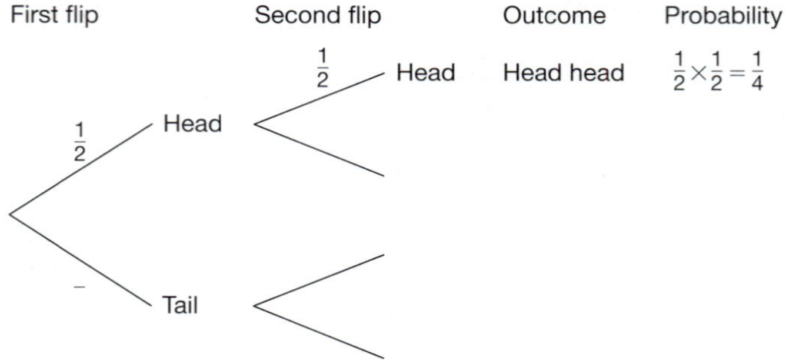

  First flip   Second flip   Outcome   Probability

  $\frac{1}{2}$ Head   Head head $\frac{1}{2} \times \frac{1}{2} = \frac{1}{4}$

  $\frac{1}{2}$ Head

  Tail

  What is the probability of

  b getting two heads?

  c getting at least one head?

2 A bag contains three blue beads and two red beads.

  Alice takes a bead out at random and then puts it back.

  Then Robert takes a bead out without looking.

  a Show this information on a tree diagram.

  b What is the probability that Alice and Robert both choose a bead of the same colour?

3 Alfie often forgets to do his Geography homework. The probability that he remembers is $\frac{1}{3}$.

  If he forgets to do his homework on both of the next two weeks, he will get a detention.

  If he remembers to do it for the next two weeks, his mother will give him £1.

  Draw a probability tree and use it to find the probability that:

  a he gets a detention.

  b he gets £1.

  c he gets neither a detention nor £1.

4 Joe has six football shirts. Four are blue and two are yellow.

He has five pairs of shorts. Two are blue, two are yellow and one is black.

He chooses a shirt and a pair of shorts at random.

  a Copy and complete the probability tree.

  Shirt   Shorts   Outcome   Probability

  $\frac{4}{6}$ Blue — Blue — Blue blue

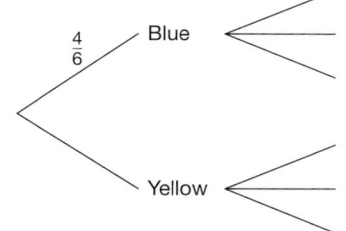

  Yellow

  b What is the probability that he chooses a shirt and shorts of the same colour?

  c What is the probability that he chooses a blue and yellow combination?

5 Teddy & The Talismen are playing a gig.

In the first song they play, there is a probability of $\frac{1}{10}$ that Simon, the bass player, will make a mistake, and a probability of $\frac{2}{5}$ that Andrew, the pianist, goes wrong.

  a Show this information on a tree diagram.

  b What is the probability that no one makes a mistake?

  c What is the probability that at least one person makes a mistake?

6 Malcolm is studying for two exams.

In his Psychology paper, he has a probability of $\frac{1}{5}$ of getting a distinction, and a probability of $\frac{7}{10}$ of being awarded a pass.

  a What is the probability that he fails?

In his Sociology paper, he has a probability of $\frac{1}{6}$ of failing, and a probability of $\frac{1}{3}$ of getting a distinction.

  b What is the probability that he gets a pass?

  c Draw a probability tree to show this information.

  d What is the probability that he does not fail either paper?

  e What is the probability that he gets at least one distinction?

Probability: Chapter 12 Probability

7 Jonathan and Will are both good athletes. They want to find out who is better.

They run the 100 m, where Jonathan has a probability of $\frac{5}{8}$ of winning.

Then they run the 1500 m, where Will has a probability of $\frac{2}{3}$ of winning.

a Copy and complete the probability tree.

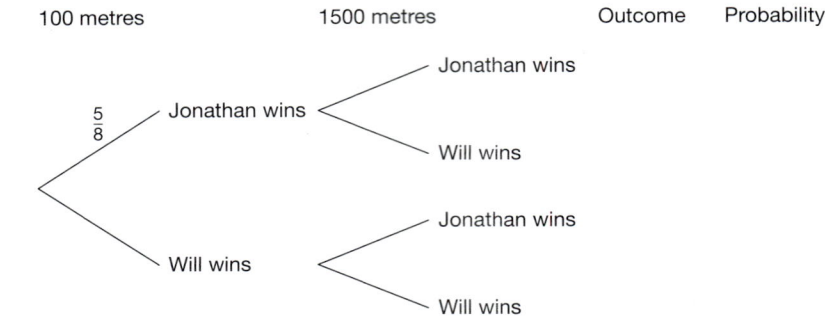

```
100 metres          1500 metres           Outcome         Probability
                                        Jonathan wins
         5/8    Jonathan wins
                                        Will wins
                                        Jonathan wins
                Will wins
                                        Will wins
```

b What is the probability that they win one race each?

They repeat this every week for 48 weeks.

c How often would you expect one of them to win both races?

8 An athletics club wants to choose a club captain. They have a choice of four males and three females.

They also want to choose a press officer. They have a choice of two males and five females.

Draw a tree diagram and use it to find the probability that they choose a captain and press officer of the same gender.

9 Phoebe and Holly are planning a meal together.

Phoebe will cook lasagne, risotto or chicken curry. The probability that she cooks lasagne is 0.6, and the probability she makes risotto is the same as the probability that she makes chicken curry.

Holly will make either a trifle or a fruit salad. The probability that she makes a fruit salad is 0.7.

a Draw a probability tree and find the probability of each combination.

b What is the probability that they have neither risotto nor trifle?

10 Alison has to drive from Ipswich to Bristol. **AO3, AO4**

She can drive on the A12, then the M25, and then the M4.

Or she could drive on the A14, M6 and M5.

The probability of a delay on each road is shown below.

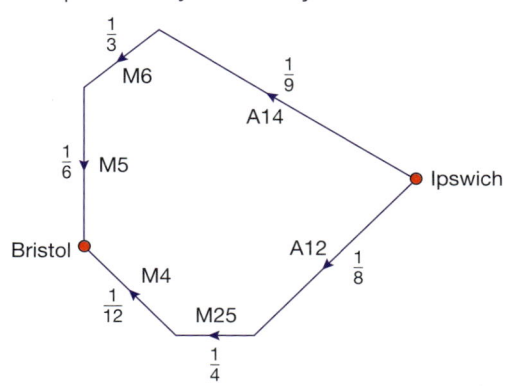

Diagram showing routes with delay probabilities:
- A14: $\frac{1}{9}$
- M6: $\frac{1}{3}$
- M5: $\frac{1}{6}$
- A12: $\frac{1}{8}$
- M25: $\frac{1}{4}$
- M4: $\frac{1}{12}$

a Draw a probability tree for the A14, M6, M5 route.

b Draw a probability tree for the A12, M25, M4 route.

c Which route should Alison take to avoid delays?

12.9 Conditional probability

This section will show you how to:
- work out the probability of combined events when the probabilities change after each event.

KEY WORDS
Conditional probability

The probability of one event is very often dependent on another event.

Millie has 12 CDs. Five of them are by boy bands.

She chooses one at random, after which she chooses one of the others at random.

The probability of choosing a boy band the first time is $\frac{5}{12}$.

For the second CD, the probability depends on her first choice, as she is going to choose one of the remaining eleven.

If she chose a boy band the first time, there are four boy band CDs left out of eleven, so the probability of choosing a boy band the second time is $\frac{4}{11}$.

However, if she did not choose a boy band CD the first time, five of the remaining eleven are by boy bands, so the probability is $\frac{5}{11}$.

355

Probability: Chapter 12 Probability

Example 15

A bag contains six strawberry sweets and three banana sweets.

Phil takes one at random and eats it.

Then Deidra takes one at random and eats it.

What is the probability that:

a Phil takes a strawberry sweet?

b They both take strawberry sweet?

c At least one of them has a banana sweet?

d Deidra takes a strawberry sweet?

Solution

a There are six strawberry sweets out of nine, so for Phil P(strawberry) is $\frac{6}{9} = \frac{2}{3}$.

b If they both take a strawberry sweet, Deidra must choose one of the five left after Phil has taken one.
So for Deidra, P(strawberry) = $\frac{5}{8}$, so P(both strawberry) = $\frac{2}{3} \times \frac{5}{8} = \frac{5}{12}$.

c P(At least one has a banana sweet) = 1 − P(they both take strawberry sweet)
= $1 - \frac{5}{12} = \frac{7}{12}$

d P(Deidra takes a strawberry sweet)
= P(both choose strawberry) + P(Phil chooses banana and Deidra chooses strawberry)

= $\frac{5}{12}$ + $\left(\frac{3}{9} \times \frac{6}{8}\right)$

= $\frac{5}{12}$ + $\frac{1}{4}$

= $\frac{8}{12} = \frac{2}{3}$

Part (d) is very difficult. Draw a tree diagram to see how it works.

Exercise 12I

A

1 George is playing a CD on random play. Once a track has been played, it is not played again. The CD has 8 tracks.

  a What is the probability that it plays track 1 followed by track 2?

  b What is the probability that it plays tracks 1 and 2 first, but in either order?

356

2 A bag contains four black balls and seven red balls.

Chris takes a ball at random to play with.

Then Amanda takes one at random to play with.

   a What is the probability that they both choose a black ball?

   b What is the probability that they both choose the same colour?

   c What is the probability that they choose one of each colour?

3 Pete has three tins of dog food and two tins of cat food.

All the labels have come off!

He feeds the dog, and then he feeds the cat.

   a What is the probability that the dog gets dog food?

   b What is the probability that the dog gets dog food and the cat gets cat food?

   c If he fed the cat first, would the probability of feeding them both the correct food be different?

4 City play United twice next season.

In the first game, the probability that City beat United is $\frac{3}{5}$.

If City win, the probability of them winning the second game is $\frac{3}{4}$.

If City do not win the first game, the probability of City winning the second game is $\frac{1}{3}$.

What is the probability that:

   a City win both games?

   b City do not win either game?

   c City win exactly one game?

5 The probability that Minnie passes the theory driving test is $\frac{2}{3}$.

If she fails, the probability of her passing at the second attempt is $\frac{5}{6}$.

   a What is the probability that she passes at the second attempt?

   b What is the probability that she will pass at either the first or second attempt?

6 In a lottery game, a player chooses three numbers from 1 to 40.

Three different numbers are then chosen at random.

If the player matches all three numbers in any order he wins, what is the probability of winning?

7 In my drawer I have six white socks and four black socks.

I choose two at random.

What is the probability that I choose a matching pair?

Probability: Chapter 12 Probability

8 A box contains six cards, numbered 1 to 6.

A card is selected at random, the number is noted, and then the card is not replaced.

A card is selected at random again.

What is the probability that:

   a a 4 is chosen the first time, and a 3 the second time?

   b the two numbers are a 3 and a 4 but in either order?

   c a 2 is chosen both times?

   d the total is 5?

   e the total is more than 10?

9 A four-sided dice has faces numbered 1, 2, 3, 4. To win a game with this dice you must throw a 4. You can have up to three throws, but you stop as soon as you win.

   a Copy and complete the tree diagram below by filling in the probabilities.

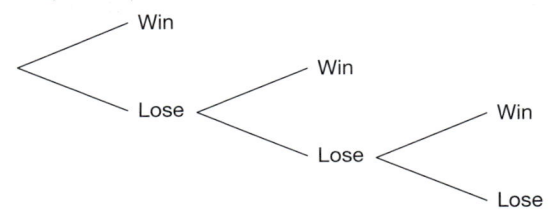

```
       Win
      /
     <         Win
      \       /
       Lose <         Win
              \      /
               Lose <
                     \
                      Lose
```

   b What is the probability of winning on your second throw?

   c What is the probability of winning any one of your 3 throws?

10 Colin the chef has accidentally put two out-of-date chicken breasts in with 8 fresh ones. **A03, A04**
He knows that if he serves one customer, the probability of serving an old chicken breast is $\frac{2}{10} = \frac{1}{5}$.
Help him answer these questions.

   a If he serves two people, what is the probability of at least one of them getting old chicken?

   b How many customers does he have to serve before the probability of serving an old one is greater than $\frac{1}{2}$?

GRADE BOOSTER

What you need to do to get this grade

G	You understand the words 'certain', 'impossible', 'likely' and 'unlikely'.
F	You can use a probability scale from 0 to 1.
E	You can draw a sample space diagram for two events.
E	You can calculate the probability of something not happening if you know the probability of it happening.
D	You understand that the total probability of all possible outcomes is 1.
C	You can use probability to predict the expected number of successes from a given number of trials.
C	You can compare relative frequency (experimental probability) with theoretical probability.
B	You can draw tree diagrams.
A	You can work out the probabilities of combined events.
A*	You can calculate probabilities of combined events where the probability of one event is dependent on the other.

What you should know now

- How to use the language of probability.
- How to calculate the probability of events using theoretical models or experiments.

Higher tier only

- How to predict outcomes, using theoretical models, and compare theoretical and experimental data.
- How to calculate probabilities for combined events.

EXAMINATION Questions

1 Here are some probability values.

0.7   1   0.5   0   0.25

Match the probabilities with the words in the table.

Word	Probability
Impossible	
Likely	
Certain	
Unlikely	
Even chance	

(3 marks)

2 a A fair six-sided dice is rolled.

The dice has numbers 1, 2, 3, 4, 5, 6 on its faces.

What is the probability that the dice shows:

  i the number 4? *(1 mark)*

  ii an even number? *(1 mark)*

b A second fair six-sided dice is also rolled.

This dice has numbers 0, 1, 2, 3, 4, 5 on its faces.

The numbers from the two dice are **multiplied** to give a score.

  i Copy and complete the table to show all possible scores.

	1	2	3	4	5	6
0					0	
1			3			
2		4				
3	3					
4						24
5				20		

(2 marks)

  ii Explain why the probability of getting a score of at least 15 is $\frac{1}{4}$. *(2 marks)*

360

3 150 students were asked which daily newspaper(s) they read.

The results are shown in the diagram.

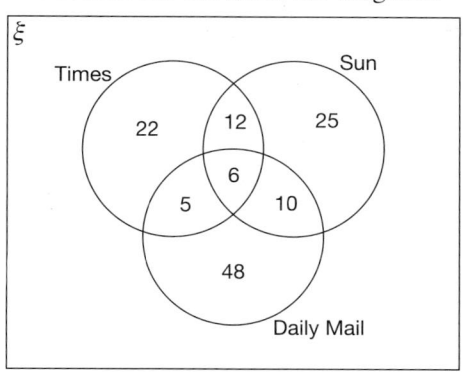

Find the probability that a student chosen at random reads

a *The Times* *(1 mark)*

b only one of the papers *(2 marks)*

c none of the three papers *(3 marks)*

d *The Sun* or *The Times* or both but not the *Daily Mail*. *(2 marks)*

Probability: Chapter 12 Examination questions

4 A dice is rolled 20 times.

The score is recorded each time.

a Leonardo draws the following diagram to show the results.

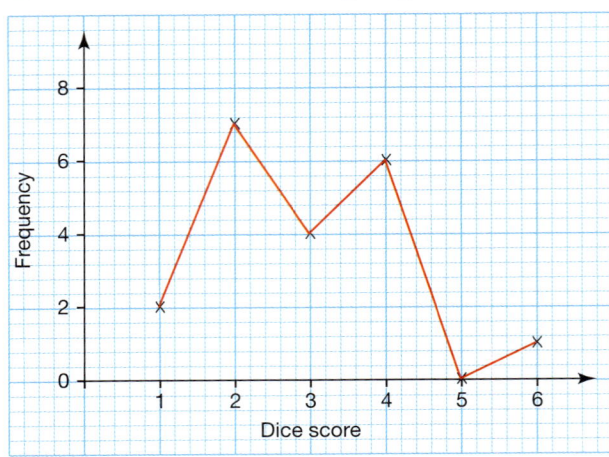

Is this diagram suitable for this data?

Explain your answer. *(2 marks)*

b Vincent draws this diagram for the same data.

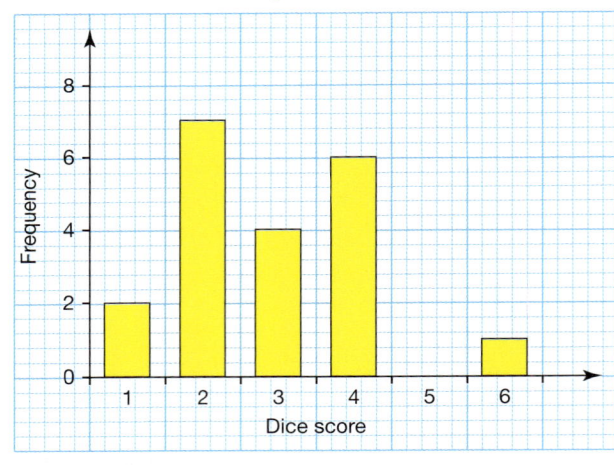

Is this diagram suitable for this data?

Explain your answer. *(2 marks)*

c i What is the relative frequency of the score 2 for this data? *(1 mark)*

  ii If this is a biased dice, use this data to estimate the probability of a score of 2 on the next roll. *(1 mark)*

  iii If this is a fair dice, write down the probability of a score of 2 on the next roll. *(1 mark)*

5 Over a long period of time a theme park has discovered that

32% of its visitors are Adults (**A**) aged 20 and over

30% of its visitors are Teenagers (**T**) aged 13–19

38% of its visitors are Children (**C**) under 13.

   a What is the probability that the next visitor is a Teenager? *(1 mark)*

   b Work out the probability that the next two visitors are both Teenagers. *(2 marks)*

   c What assumption did you make in order to answer part **b**? *(1 mark)*

6 The headteacher of a large school is concerned about the punctuality of pupils.

The pupils either walk to school (**W**), travel by bus (**B**) or go by car (**C**).

On 26 November the head teacher recorded how pupils travelled to school and whether they arrived early (**E**), on time (**T**), or late (**L**).

Her records showed that 30% of the pupils walked to school, 25% travelled by bus and the remainder by car.

Of those pupils walking to school, 20% arrived late, 15% on time and the remainder early.

For pupils travelling by bus, 65% arrived on time, 12% early and the remainder late.

Of those travelling by car, 75% arrived early, 20% on time with the remainder late.

   a Use this information to complete the following tree diagram. *(4 marks)*

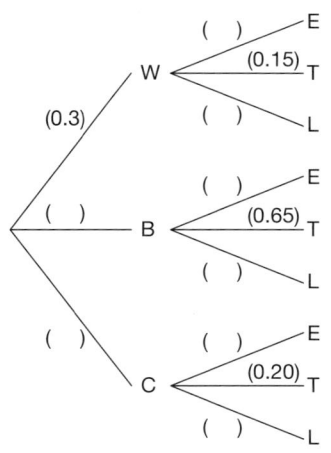

   b A pupil is chosen at random.

      Show that the probability the pupil arrived at school either early or on time is 0.86 *(4 marks)*

   c Calculate the probability that a pupil, chosen at random, arrived at school either early or on time, given that the pupil travelled by car. *(2 marks)*

   d Three pupils are selected at random with replacement.

      Calculate an estimate of the probability that two out of the three would have arrived at school late. *(5 marks)*

Probability: Chapter 12 Examination questions

7 Records for a local library show for each book whether it is in the fiction, non-fiction or classics category and whether it is a hardback or softback version.

When the library closed on Wednesday last week 2700 books were out on loan.

Of the books on loan, 72% were in the fiction category.

Of the 620 hardback books on loan, 55% were in the non-fiction category and 25% in the classics category.

In total, 176 classics books were on loan.

a Copy and complete the table, entering the number of books on loan in each case. *(4 marks)*

	Hardback	Softback	Total
Fiction			
Non-fiction			
Classics			176
Total	620		2700

b A library record for a book on loan is chosen at random.

Use the table to calculate the probability that the book is

   i   non-fiction and a softback version *(1 mark)*

   ii non-fiction or a hardback version *(2 marks)*

   iii fiction, given that it is a softback version. *(2 marks)*

c How many of the first 200 books taken out on loan on the following day would you expect to be hardback classics? *(2 marks)*

WORKED EXAMINATION Questions

1 a Give the value of the probability for an event that is certain to happen.

    An event that is certain has a probability of 1. *(1 mark)*

b Say whether these statements are true or false:

   i An event with a probability of 0.9 is very likely.

      True *(1 mark)*

   ii A probability of 0.45 means that an event is more likely to happen than not.

      False. A probability of 0.45 has a less than even chance of occurring. *(1 mark)*

   iii An impossible event has a probability of −1.

      False. An impossible event has a probability of 0. *(1 mark)*

Probability: Chapter 12 Examination questions

2 Marie has two fair spinners, A and B.

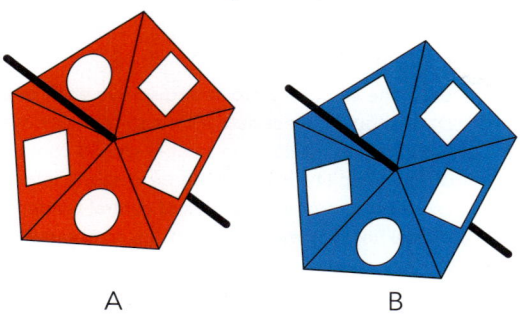

A   B

Marie spins one of the spinners. It lands on a circle.

a Marie said the probability of the spinner landing on a circle was 0.4

Was the spinner A or B? Give a reason for your answer.

Spinner A

Reason: Spinner A has 2 circles out of 5 faces, and $\frac{2}{5} = 0.4$ *(1 mark)*

> The mark will not be awarded without a reason.

b Complete the probability tree below:

Red spinner   Blue spinner

$\frac{3}{5}$ Square
 — $\frac{4}{5}$ Square
 — $\frac{1}{5}$ Circle

$\frac{2}{5}$ Circle
 — $\frac{4}{5}$ Square
 — $\frac{1}{5}$ Circle

(2 marks)

c What is the probability that both spinners land on the same symbol?

Both circle = $\frac{2}{5} \times \frac{1}{5} = \frac{2}{25}$ Both square = $\frac{3}{5} \times \frac{4}{5} = \frac{12}{25}$

Both the same = $\frac{2}{25} + \frac{12}{25} = \frac{14}{25}$

> One of these would score **1 mark**.

> Adding would score a second mark.

(2 marks)

Answers

1 Planning a strategy

Quick check

1 Check student's answer.

1.1 Data handling cycle

Exercise 1A

1   a Hypothesis: 'July is the hottest month in the UK'.
    b 'Boys are better than girls at estimating distances'.
    c 'Men make up the majority of football crowds'.
    d 'Women make up the majority of the audience for tennis matches'.
    e 'More revision leads to higher examination results'.
    f 'Marks and Spencer's attracts older shoppers'.
2   Students' answers will vary.
3   For example, Kath may carry out a survey among her friends or class mates.

1.2 Planning an investigation

Exercise 1B

1   a 'Kindle books are cheaper than ibooks' or equivalent.
    b Prices of the same books on both platforms.
    c She should compare prices of recently published books, bestsellers, books that have been published for a long time, classic books, audio books, etc., working out averages to compare the platforms.
2   Katie needs to state a hypothesis, along the lines of: 'Orange offer the cheapest tariffs'. She then needs to collect data on tariffs from several service providers, considering what phones are available on each tariff, the number of free minutes included, data plans, etc. Having gathered the information she would then need to calculate bills based on her previous usage of texts, phone calls and data on each tariff. Finally, she needs to collate her calculations and come to a conclusion. If her hypothesis is disproved she could use different hypotheses and, as she now has all the necessary data, she can easily prove or disprove each one.
3   Dave should collect data from a sample of boys' and girls' test or exam results. The sample should contain students of similar ability. He can then process the information calculating several measures of central tendency and spread before finally coming to a conclusion about his hypothesis.
4   a He should collect average rainfall data on several areas in Wales and other parts of the UK.
    b He should carefully select the regions he is collecting data from, i.e. including a mix of coastal, central and highland areas.
    c The data might be available online or directly from the Met office. If not, it will be difficult to collect.
5   a 'There are more adverts on TV shows between 7 pm and 9 pm on Saturdays compared to other days of the week.'
    b Angharad would need to note the total time of adverts between these times over a period of weeks on each day of the week.
    c This would be a very time-consuming process.
    d It may be very difficult to analyse several channels accurately over the same time period.

2 Collection of data

Quick check

1   a 18, 31, 42, 53, 69, 76, 86, 101.
    b 0.58, 0.805, 0.85, 5.08, 8.5, 50.8.
    c −21, −7, −0.3, 14.2, 16, 42.
2   Student's own answers.

2.1 Types of data

Exercise 2A

1   Colour: qualitative.
    Size: categorical.
2   Categorical
3   All of them.
4   a Cost
    b Weight
    c Type: senior, adult or puppy.

Answers: Chapter 2

5
- **a** Quantitative, discrete.
- **b** Quantitative, discrete.
- **c** Quantitative, continuous.
- **d** Quantitative, continuous.
- **e** Quantitative, discrete.
- **f** Quantitative, continuous.
- **g** Quantitative, continuous.
- **h** Qualitative.

6 Categorical: council tax band, town, post code, parking.
Quantitative, discrete: number of bedrooms, number of bathrooms, price, date of moving.
Quantitative, continuous: age of property.

7
- **a** Cost
- **b** Time spent on call.
- **c** Bivariate

8 Student's own answer, but may include:
Qualitative: Colour.
Quantitative, discrete: Price.
Quantitative, continuous: Dimensions of size, weight.
Categorical: manufacturer, whether PC or laptop.

2.2 Grouping data

Exercise 2B

1

Breed	Tally	Frequency
Boxer	//// //// //	12
Bullmastiff	//// ///	8
Dobermann	//	2
Great Dane	////	5
Mastiff	////	5
Newfoundland	//// ///	8

2

Group	Tally	Frequency
Radiohead	//// ///	8
Kasabian	/	1
Kings of Leon	////	5
Arcade Fire	//	2
Muse	////	4

3

Item	Tally	Frequency
CD	//// ////	10
Children's	//// ////	9
Non-fiction	//// ////	10
Novel	//// //// //	12
Teenage	//// //// ////	15

4

Item	Tally	Frequency
Bromley South	//// ///	8
Chatham	//// ////	9
Deal	//// /	6
Dover	////	5
Faversham	////	4
Longfield	//// /	6
Meopham	//	2
Sole Street	/	1
Swanley	//// ////	9

5 a

Amount (£)	Tally	Frequency
0–999	//// /	6
1000–1999	//// /	6
2000–2999	///	3
3000–3999	////	4
4000–4999	//	2
5000 and over	////	4

b Student's own answer of a frequency table with different class intervals and a comment. Here is an example:

Amount (£)	Tally	Frequency
0–500	/	1
501–1000	////	5
1001–1999	//// /	6
2000–2999	///	3
3000–4000	////	4
4001 and over	//// /	6

We can now see that only one booking was worth less than £500.

6 Student's own answer of a frequency table. Here is an example:

Weight, w (kg)	Tally	Frequency
$w < 40$	//// //	7
$40 \leq w < 60$	//// //// //	12
$60 \leq w < 70$	//// ////	9
$70 \leq w < 80$	///	3
$80 \leq w < 90$	//// /	6
$w \geq 90$	///	3

Answers: Chapter 2

2.3 Data sources

Exercise 2C

1 Criticism 1: overlap at £4000 and gap between £9000 and £10 000.
Criticism 2: not every make of car is covered in the table e.g. Toyota.

2 Any from:
Advantages: You know where the data has come from.
You know the questions that were asked.
You know how the data was collected.
You know who collected the data.
You know how old the data is.
Disadvantages: It can take a lot of money to source the data.
It can take a long time to acquire the data.
You may have to travel a long way to get data.

3 Any from:
Advantages: No time to collect, it's already done for you.
Data can be used from many sources where available.
Cheap to use.
Disadvantages: You do not know where the data has come from.
You do not know the original questions.
Details are likely to have been lost due to partial processing.
You may not know how old the data is.
You do not know how the data was collected.
You do not know who collected the data.

4 Data logging would be the most efficient method of data collection. The vehicles simply need to be counted as there have been no other details asked for. The data logging machine would be cheap to set up and run and would not allow for counting errors that humans may make.

5 Students' own data sheet. Here is an example:

Age, a (years) \ Hourly pay, p (£)	$p < 5$	$5 \leqslant p < 10$	$10 \leqslant p < 20$	$p \geqslant 20$
$16 \leqslant a < 18$				
$18 \leqslant a < 25$				
$25 \leqslant a < 40$				
$40 \leqslant a < 65$				
$a \geqslant 65$				

6 Primary data would be better for Elliott to use because he can survey some of the students at his own school. He could canvass opinions about stock and opening times that would directly suit his school population. If he used secondary data, the data may be old and of little relevance to his peers.

7 Hashim would have to use secondary data as he cannot go back in time to measure the height of children 50 years ago.

8 Secondary data.

9 Data logging would not provide information about the types of vehicles. The council would now need to employ people to observe the traffic and record their observations on a data collection sheet. To avoid counting errors, they could employ several people and average their results.

Examination Questions

1

Activity	Tally	Frequency
Archery (A)	///	3
Climbing (C)	////	4
Paintballing (P)	//	2
Quad biking (Q)	//// /	6

2 **i** c
  ii b

3 There is more detail in the first table; it is easier to see the shape of the distribution. The first table has equal class widths that highlight any patterns in the data more easily.

4 a (data) logging.
  b It is more accurate, there will be no human error or bias.

5

Number of televisions	Tally	Frequency
1	//// ///	8
2	//// //// //	12
3	//// /	6
4	////	4

6 a Discrete
  b Continuous

7 c

8 a

Number of meetings attended	Frequency
0–3	12
4–6	41
7–9	50
10–12	22

  b i It shows all the data.
  ii It's easier to get an overview of the data and will be easier to work with.

9 a It takes exact values.
  b Lengths and weights.

10 a

Number of items bought by each customer	Tally	Frequency
1	//// //// //// ///	18
2	//// //// //// //// //// ///	28
3	//// //// //// ///	18
4	//// /	6
5	///	3
6	//	2

  b 75
  c 179

3 Sampling

Quick check

1 a 5
 b 10.4
 c 237.9
 d 100.5
2 240
3 a 25
 b 70
 c 422
 d 271

3.1 Sampling

Exercise 3A

1 a 04, 20, 18, 14, 25
 b There would only have been 4 friends chosen: 18, 14, 20, 25, then the random number tables ends. There would not be sufficient numbers between 1 and 30 to give the full sample of 5 friends.
2 Number each of the cars 1 to 1350.
 Every 27th car is needed for the sample (1350 ÷ 50 = 27)
 Use a random number table (or the function on a calculator/spreadsheet) to find a random number between 1 and 27. Use this as the first car and then include every 27th car thereafter.
3 a Convenience sampling.
 b Shannon has not checked anyone else's samples, so the sample she takes will be biased towards Alfie's performance. If Alfie is producing good clothing, Shannon will assume that everyone is also producing good clothing. This may not be the case at all. Everyone else may be producing poor quality clothing. If Alfie is hungry just before lunchtime, he may not be producing his best work, so his sample will contain more faults.
4 a Convenience
 b Some of the teachers may have travelled together and so live a similar distance away from school. She has only asked teachers, not any of the office or cleaning staff. She has not considered anyone who works somewhere other than a school (factory workers tend to live closer to work, people who work in the City of London, tend to have a longer commute).
5 Advantage: Cheap in terms of travelling, time and money. Good for use with large populations.
 Disadvantage: If each group does not have a good mixture of different population elements, the results are likely to be biased.

6 On a map of the lake, split the lake into a grid of 200 squares. Number each square from 1 to 200.
 Use a random number table (or the function on a calculator/spreadsheet) to generate 25 random three-digit numbers. Ignore numbers higher than 200. Ignore any repeated numbers.
 Go to each section of the lake represented by the 25 squares that have been randomly selected and fill a test tube with lake water.
7 This ensures that every sector of the population is represented. With a simple random sample, it is possible for a sector to be missed out of the sample entirely which may lead to bias within the results.
8 Quota
9 10
10 a gives a systematic sample.
 b is the one to give a random sample.
 c gives a convenience sample.

Examination Questions

1 a 45
 b Number the students and then use a random number table (or function on a calculator/spreadsheet) to choose the 25 names needed.
2 a List all of the workers. Choose a random place to start from workers 1 to 9. Then choose every ninth worker.
 b Only one section of the factory has been considered; the production section. Only males have been asked, no females were included.
 c i 2
  ii 3

3 a

Student number	15	01	20	16	22	30	19	08
Gender	M	M	M	M	M	M	M	M
Number of passes	4	4	4	3	3	2	2	2

b

Student number	04	29	13	14	23	11
Gender	M	M	F	M	F	F
Number of passes	8	6	5	5	7	8

4 23 – Shah
 14 – Imeson
 01 – Anderson
 21 – Paybet
 15 – Joab
5 a Only females asked. Restricted housing type and cost (only those costing £450 000).
 b i Select 50 random numbers in the range 001 to 500 then match these numbers to actual houses and occupants.
  ii It will improve the representativeness of the sample.
  iii 10.
6 All adults in the polling area.

Answers: Chapter 4

7. Number each of the five wards and then use a random number table to choose one of the five. Number each of the subsequent six polling districts and use random numbers to choose one polling district. Number each voter in that polling district and use random numbers to select the sample.
8. **a** We are missing those who do not use the canteen so missing part of the population.
   b Excludes those with non-S surnames, siblings may have same eating habits.

4 Conducting a survey or experiment

Quick check

1. 30 students.
2. 10 boys.
3. 13 girls.

4.1 Surveys

Exercise 4A

1–5 Check students' answers and designs, which will vary.

6. **a** Possible answer: Question – Which of the following foods would you normally eat for your main meal of the day?

Name	Sex	Chips	Beefburgers	Vegetables	Pizza	Fish

   b Yes, as a greater proportion of girls ate healthy food.
7. Possible answer: Question – What kind of tariff do you use on your mobile phone?

Name	Pay as you go		Contract	
	200 or more free texts	Under 200 free texts	200 or more free texts	Under 200 free texts

(Any sheet in which choices that can distinguish one from the other have to be made will be acceptable.)

8. Possible answers: shop names, year of student, tally space, frequency.
9. A pilot study helps to correct any errors in the survey.
10. A census would involve collecting the colours of all cars in the UK, which would be impossible for David to do.
11. A census gathers information about everyone or everything in a population. A sample is a subset of this and provides information from a smaller section.
12. She should take a sample. A census would involve her asking everyone.
13. Answers should include:
    to test the design of the system and eliminate unforeseen errors.
    to prevent wasting time and money on gathering flawed data.
    can provide an indication of the final outcome of the survey.

4.2 Questionnaires

Exercise 4B

1. **a** It is a leading question, and no option to disagree with the statement.
   b Unbiased, and the responses do not overlap.
2. **a** Responses overlap.
   b Provide options: up to £2, more than £2 and up to £5, more than £5 and up to £10, more than £10.
3–6 Check students' questionnaires.
7. **a** This is a leading question with no possibility of showing disagreement.
   b This is a clear, direct question that has an answer, with good responses as only one selection can be made.
   c Check students' questions.
8. Possible questionnaire: Do you have a back problem?
   ☐ Yes   ☐ No
   Tick the diagram/text that best illustrates or describes how you sit.
   ☐ shoulders back awkwardly, curved spine.
   ☐ slumped, straining lower back.
   ☐ caved chest, pressure on spine.
   ☐ balanced, head and spine aligned.
9. The groups overlap, and the 'less than £15' is also in the 'less than £25'.
10. **a** Not all options are included, for example, a respondent may be single or widowed.
    b For example: What is your marital status?
    ☐ single
    ☐ married
    ☐ with a long-term partner
    ☐ divorced
    ☐ widowed
    ☐ other
11. **a** Needs to cover all possible age groups.
    b Random response method.
12. To get truthful responses for sensitive questions.
13. Random response method.
14. 5 people.

4.3 Experimental design

Exercise 4C

1. Use an experimental group and control group of tomato seeds, growing them under matched conditions.
2. **a** So he can compare the results with the experimental group.
   b Cows could become ill, they could stop producing milk, other foodstuffs they eat could affect production, etc.
   c The dependent variable is the outcome, whether the feed works. The independent variable is the feed.

Answers: Chapter 5

3 **a** A blind trial is one in which neither the experimental nor the control group knows who is taking the medicine.
    b The experimental group and control group keep all the variables the same, including diet, face wash, etc.

4 **a** Use two similar areas of grass. The control area and the experimental area are kept under the same conditions.
    b The results may be affected by plants being of different sizes, new seeds growing, varying weather conditions, etc.

5 This can occur when two people view things in different ways. A typical example of this might be if we wanted to collect data on the colour of people's eyes. Some observers may record brown eyes as hazel or green eyes as grey. This problem needs to be overcome if the experiment is to be successful. Observers have to be trained and examples of the correct response given as a photograph or observers are encouraged to work together when subjective decisions have to be made.

6 Grow two sets of plants, one inside the greenhouse, one outside. Give them the same feed and use identical types of plant. The weather could be an issue.

Examination Questions

1 **a** Use seven boxes or groups of boxes for responses.
    b There may be too many students to ask all of them.
    c It may not reflect the whole school population due to age and gender bias.

2 Question 1: Respondents rely on memory/There are no boxes.
    Question 2: This is a personal question.
    Question 3: This is a leading question.

3 **a i** Respondents make a choice from a given range of options.
      ii Ranges can be given as choices.
    b He could have collected them himself.
    c He could have used a pilot study.
    d No time frame.
      No response boxes.

4 **a** It is a leading question.
      People are waiting to use the vending machine. They must be happy with the cost.
    b A pilot study would have highlighted the problems.

5 **a** There is no option for < £1000.
      The responses overlap at 1500, 2000, 3500, 6000.
    b Send out reminders.
      Use another method of contact, e.g. telephone or face-to-face.

6 **a** The limits overlap.
    b The question is too personal.

7 **a** The coffee.
    b The test result.
    c Ensure students in both groups are of the same ability. Make sure none of the control group had coffee before the test.

5 Tabulation

Quick check

1 Possible answers:
    Eye colour – only qualitative data.
    Height – only continuous data.

2 Student's own answer.

5.1 Tally charts and frequency tables

Exercise 5A

1 **a** and **b**

Shoe size	Tally	Frequency
3	///	3
4	//// //	7
5	//// //// /	11
6	//// //// ///	13
7	//// ////	9
8	///	3
9	/	1

    c Size 6, because that's the most common size which was sold.
    d 47

2 **a**

No. scored	Tally	Frequency
0	//// /	6
1	//// //	7
2	//// ////	10
3	///	3
4	//	2

No. conceded	Tally	Frequency
0	//// ///	8
1	////	5
2	//// //	7
3	///	3
4	////	4

    b 1
    c You cannot come to a conclusion about this hypothesis because the information is not sufficient. You cannot tell which matches the goals were scored in.

Answers: Chapter 5

3 a

Day of the week	Tally	Frequency
Monday	HH HH ///	13
Tuesday	HH HH HH /	16
Wednesday	HH HH HH HH /	21
Thursday	HH HH HH HH ///	23
Friday	HH HH HH HH //	22

b Thursday
c Less
d As more people got to know about the new drink, more people bought it.

4 a

View	Tally	Frequency
Strongly agree	HH HH //	12
Agree	HH HH HH HH HH HH	30
Disagree	HH HH HH HH HH HH /	31
Strongly disagree	HH ////	9

b Disagree
c Any suitable comment such as the survey suggests there was a balanced view regarding value for money.

5 a

Brothers + sisters	Tally	Frequency
0	////	4
1	HH HH	10
2	HH //	7
3	////	4
4+	////	4

b 7
c 29
d

Brothers + sisters	Tally	Frequency
0	////	4
1	HH HH	10
2	HH //	7
3	////	4
4+	////	4

5.2 Grouped frequency tables

Exercise 5B

1 a

Number of hours	Frequency
0–6	4
7–12	6
13–18	10
19–24	6
25–30	3
31–36	1

b 10
c 10
d 4

2 a

Height (h) in cm	Frequency
$145 \leq h < 155$	5
$155 \leq h < 165$	4
$165 \leq h < 175$	7
$175 \leq h < 185$	9

b 20
c $165 \leq h < 175$

3 a

Time (t) (sec)	Frequency
$5 \leq t < 10$	4
$10 \leq t < 15$	9
$15 \leq t < 20$	7
$20 \leq t < 25$	7
$25 \leq t < 30$	4
$30 \leq t < 35$	7

b 38
c $10 \leq t < 15$

4 a

Rainfall (r) (mm)	Frequency
$50 \leq r < 70$	6
$70 \leq r < 90$	8
$90 \leq r < 110$	8
$110 \leq r < 130$	7
$130 \leq r < 150$	5
$150 \leq r < 170$	1
$170 \leq t < 190$	2

b Most likely rainfall between 70 and 110 mm. Least likely rainfall between 150 and 170 mm.

5 a

Pay per year to the nearest thousand (£)	Frequency
11–15	2
16–20	6
21–25	5
26–30	2
31–35	2
36–40	7
41–45	5
46–50	1

b No. There is more variation between the categories.
c The one that is in smaller groups because it more reliably shows the distribution of the data.

Answers: Chapter 5

5.3 Two-way tables

Exercise 5C

1 a

	Girls	Boys	Total
Year 7	94	80	174
Year 8	89	101	190
Year 9	22	95	117
Year 10	100	92	192
Year 11	99	102	201
Total	404	470	874

b 22 because it is so much smaller than every other number.
c 393

2 a 53
b 92
c i 8/145
  ii 11/145
d False. There were more left-handed women than men in the survey, but as the number of men and women who were asked was not equal so it is not possible to disprove the hypothesis.

3 a Chesterton United.
b Clover Town.

4 a i

	Entry (seconds, to 1 d.p.)	Stationary (seconds, to 1 d.p.)	Exit (seconds, to 1 d.p.)	Total (seconds, to 1 d.p.)
D. Wo	7.8	5.8	9.8	23.4
G. Hinchliffe	7.9	6.9	10.1	24.9
K. Patel	8.1	5.2	9.7	23.0
H. Hulsenburge	8.3	5.5	10.4	24.2
P. Terzaga	8.4	6.3	11.3	26.0
S. King	8.6	6.2	11.3	26.1

  ii K. Patel.
  iii S. King.
b i Entry: D. Wo.
    Stationary: K. Patel.
    Exit: K. Patel.
  ii 22.7 seconds.
  iii

D. Wo	Stationary
G. Hinchliffe	Stationary
K. Patel	Entry
H. Hulsenburge	Exit
P. Terzaga	Exit
S. King	Exit

5 a

	Home		Away	
	Goals for	Goals against	Goals for	Goals against
Hulse City	17	0	11	5
Liston Villa	15	5	11	10
Starns Town	15	6	9	5
Marrsfields FC	7	5	8	11
Oldridge Athletic	10	8	11	11

b i Starns Town.
  ii Starns Town.
  iii Hulse City.
c i Hulse City.
  ii Marrsfields FC.
d The teams are ordered in the table by the size of their goal difference – the bigger the difference the higher the team in the table.

Examination Questions

1 a

Number of items	Tally	Frequency
1	//// //	7
2	//// //// //// /	16
3	//// //// //// //// //	22
4	//// //// //	12
5	////	5
6	///	3

b 65
c 191

2 a

Number of times	Frequency
0–3	27
4–6	31
7–9	34
10–12	9

b i Gives more detail about individual values.
  ii Shows a more effective summary of the data.

3 a 436
b 1 adult and 3 children.
c 8
d 85

4 a 65%
b Wales, because it has the highest percentage under 10 minutes.
c 16 591
d Generally in line with the average for the county. However both percentages are slightly under which means they need to improve their times.

373

Answers: Chapter 6

6 Diagrammatic representation

Quick check

1

Shoe size	Tally	Frequency
2	## /	6
3	/	1
4	////	4
5	##	5
6	## //	7
7	## /	6
8	////	4
9	//	2
10	///	3
11	////	4
12	## //	7

2 Sizes 6 and 12.

6.1 Pictograms, bar charts and line graphs

Exercise 6A

1
5 pm, 3 pm, 1 pm, 11 am, 9 am
Key = 5 cars

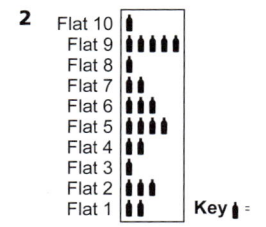

2 Flat 10 ... Flat 1 (pictogram) Key =

3 a May 9 hours, June 11 hours, July 12 hours, August 11 hours, September 10 hours.
b July
c Visual impact, easy to understand.

4 a Simon
b £165
c Difficult to show fractions of the pound symbol.

5 a i 12
ii 6
iii 13
b Check students' pictograms.
c 63

6 Use a key of 17 students to one symbol.

7 There would be too many symbols to show.

8 a–c Check students' pictograms.

9 a Swimming
b 74
c For example: limited facilities.
d No. It is likely to be biased to those people who are fit or improving their fitness and may not include people who are not fit.

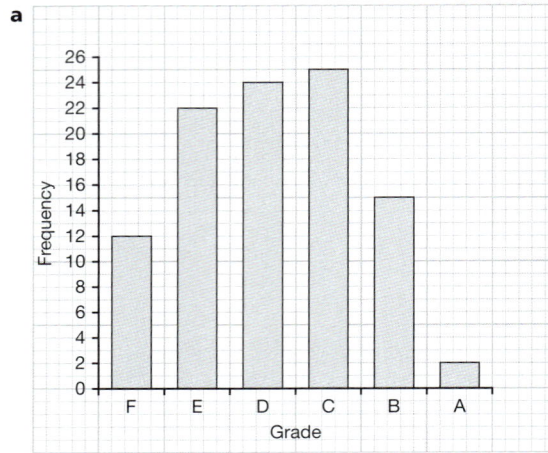

10 a (bar chart: F 12, E 22, D 24, C 25, B 15, A 2)

b $\frac{40}{100} = \frac{2}{5}$
c Easier to read the exact frequency.

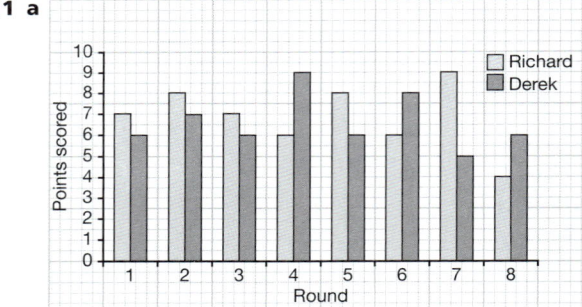

11 a (bar chart of Richard and Derek points over 8 rounds)

b Richard got more points overall and outscored Derek in five of the eight rounds.

12 a

Time (minutes)	1–10	11–20	21–30	31–40	41–50	51–60
Frequency	4	7	5	5	7	2

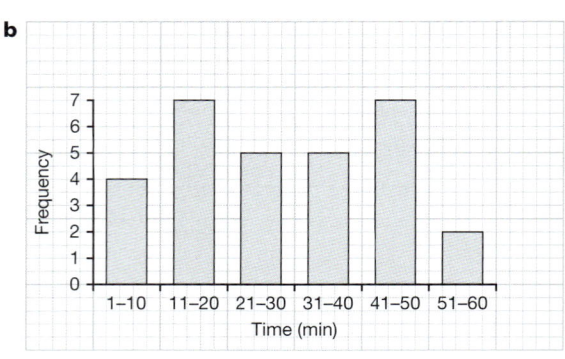

b (bar chart showing frequencies 4, 7, 5, 5, 7, 2)

c Some live close to the school. Some live a good distance away and probably travel to school by bus.

Answers: Chapter 6

13 a

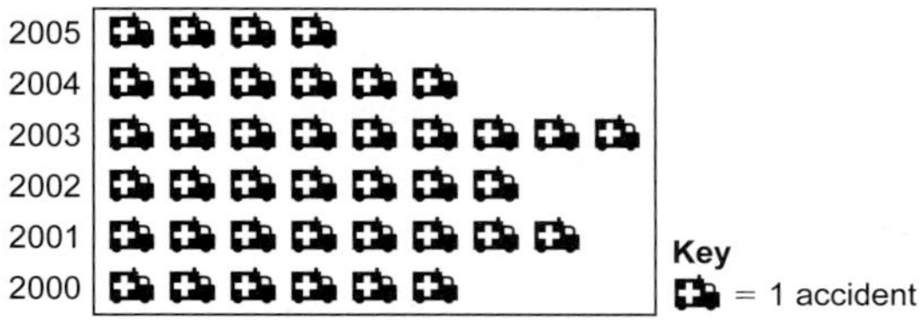

2005	🚑🚑🚑🚑
2004	🚑🚑🚑🚑🚑🚑
2003	🚑🚑🚑🚑🚑🚑🚑🚑🚑
2002	🚑🚑🚑🚑🚑🚑🚑
2001	🚑🚑🚑🚑🚑🚑🚑🚑
2000	🚑🚑🚑🚑🚑🚑

Key: 🚑 = 1 accident

b Bar chart showing number of accidents per year 2000–2005 (6, 8, 7, 9, 6, 4).

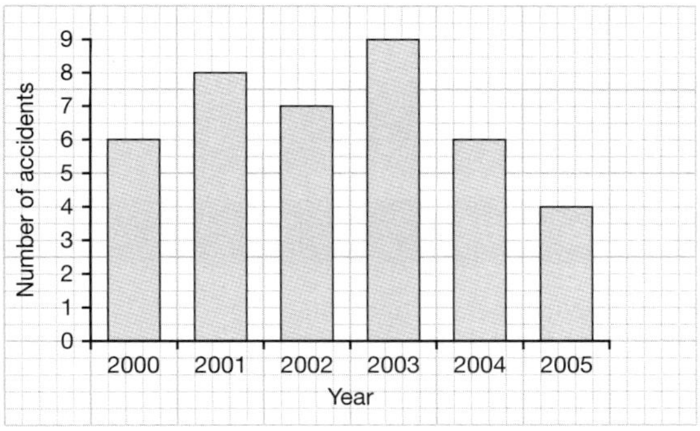

c Use the pictogram because an appropriate symbol makes more impact.

14 Yes. If you double the minimum temperature each time, it is very close to the maximum temperature in all the cities except Moscow.

15 Derek believes this is the case as he is looking at the height of the bars only. Closer inspection shows that the average temperature scale in the graph does not start at zero so he is not correct.

16 a–b Check student's survey results, pictograms and bar charts.

17 a–c Check student's frequency tables and dual bar chart. Question them about what evidence they can use to test the hypothesis.

18 a 30
 b 4
 c 8 − 1 = 7
 d Dot plot of Caterpillars (1 to 8).

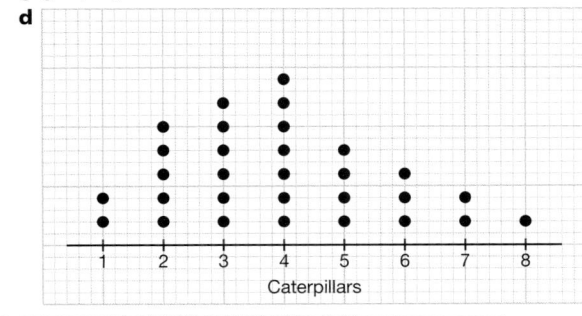

19 Dot plot of Shoe size (4 to 10).

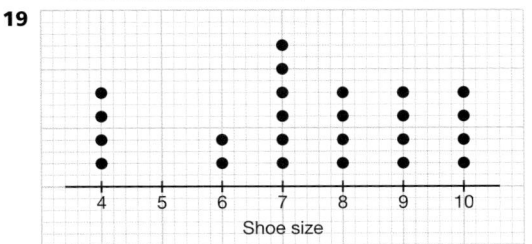

20 a 12
 b 10
 c 23
 d The number of boys absent increases as the week goes on but the number of girls absent peaks in the middle of the week.

21 a Tuesday, 52p.
 b 2p
 c Friday
 d £90

22 a Line graph of population (1000s) vs year 1941–2001.

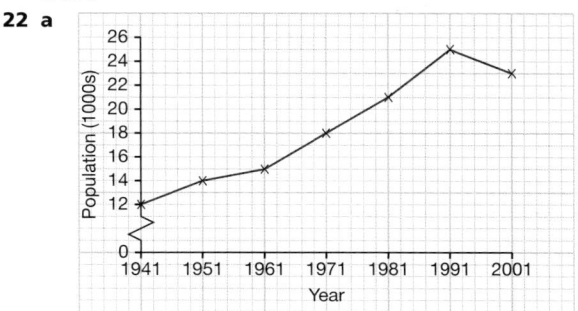

 b about 16 500.
 c 1981 and 1991.
 d No; do not know the reason why the population started to decrease after 1991.

23 a i–ii Line graph of number of ants vs week (1 to 10).

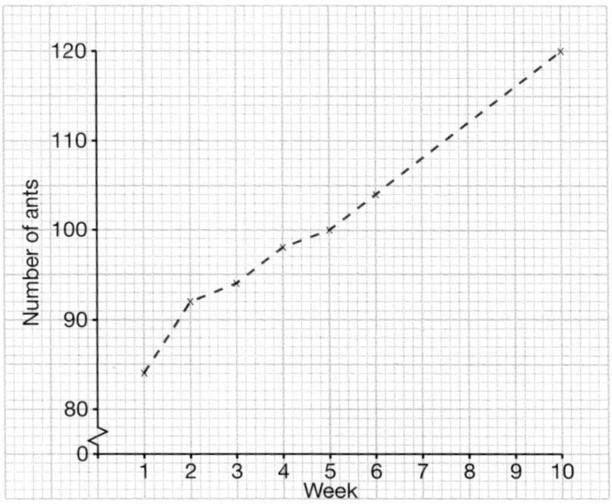

 b 112

24 a Line graph of number of tourists (millions) vs year 1970–2005.

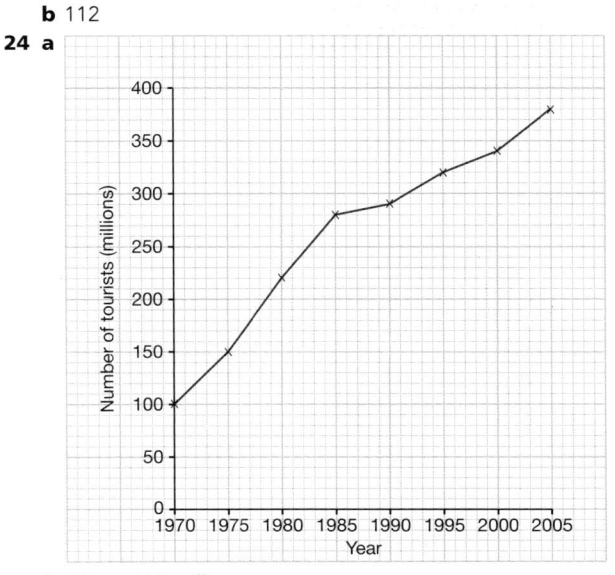

 b About 410 million.
 c 1975 and 1980.
 d Check student's explanation of trend.

Answers: Chapter 6

25 a

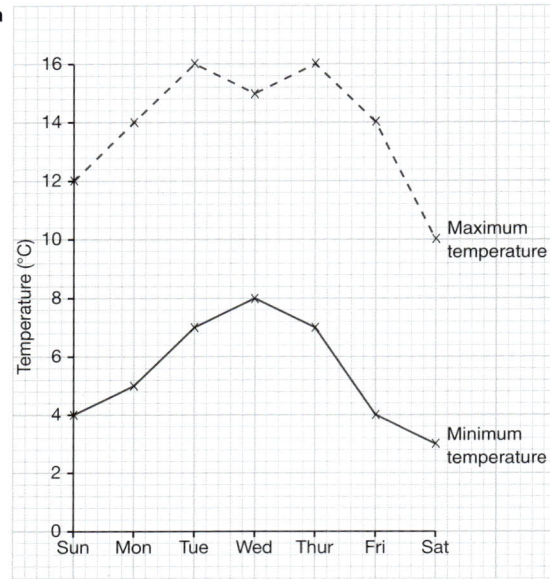

b Smallest difference = 7°C, largest difference is 10°C.

26 From a graph, about 1040 g.

27 All the temperatures were presumably higher than 20 degrees, so this scale will show more detail.

28 a

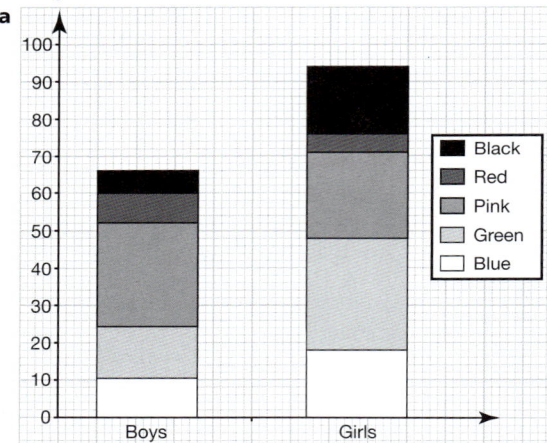

b 0–4

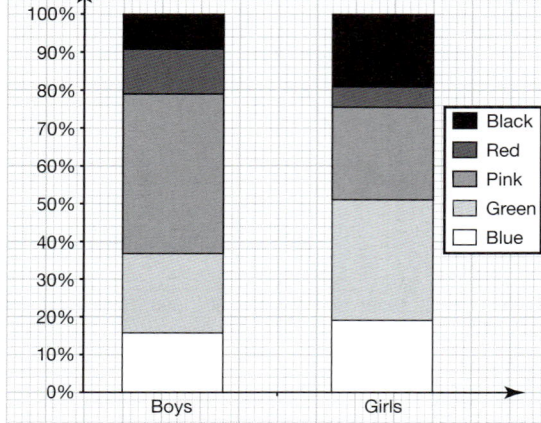

29 a 35–39
 b 0–4
 c There are more than twice as many females as males.
 d 34%

30 a 1.98 million.
 b Males, aged 80+.
 c For example; war, famine, disease.

6.2 Pie charts

Exercise 6B

1 a Favourite pets of 10 children.

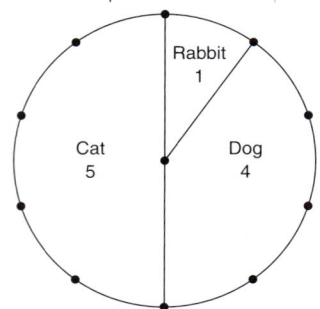

 Rabbit 1, Cat 5, Dog 4

 b Makes of cars of 20 teachers.

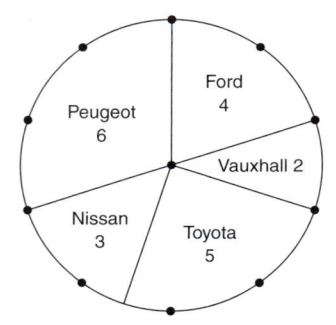

 Ford 4, Peugeot 6, Vauxhall 2, Nissan 3, Toyota 5

 c Newspapers read by 40 office workers.

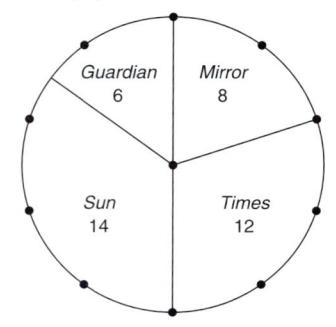

 Guardian 6, Mirror 8, Sun 14, Times 12

376

Answers: Chapter 6

2 a Numbers of children in 40 families.

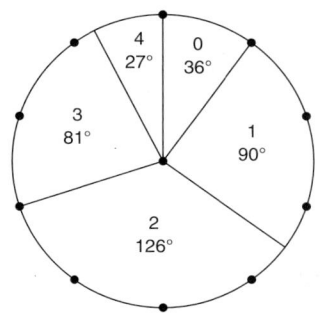

(Pie chart: 0: 36°, 1: 90°, 2: 126°, 3: 81°, 4: 27°)

b Favourite soap operas of 60 students.

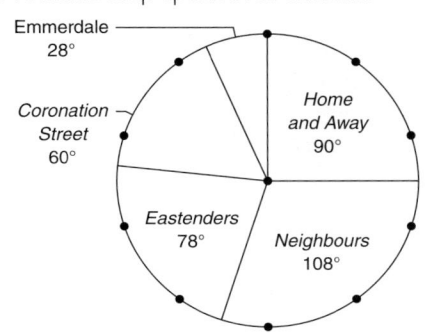

(Pie chart: Emmerdale 28°, Coronation Street 60°, Eastenders 78°, Neighbours 108°, Home and Away 90°)

c How 90 students get to school.

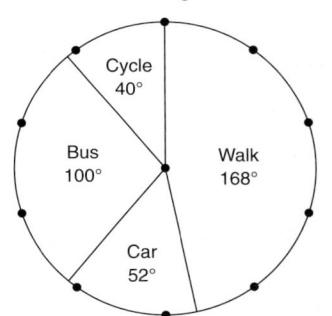

(Pie chart: Cycle 40°, Bus 100°, Car 52°, Walk 168°)

3 Favourite sport.

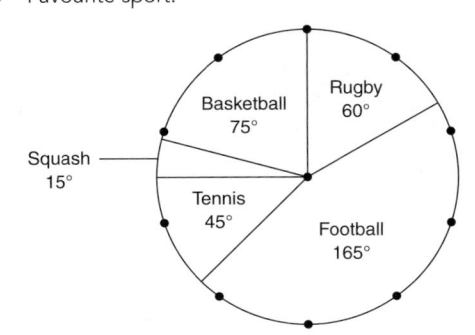

(Pie chart: Rugby 60°, Basketball 75°, Squash 15°, Tennis 45°, Football 165°)

4 a 36
b Lessons on Mandeep's timetable.

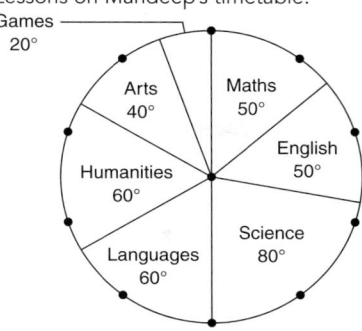

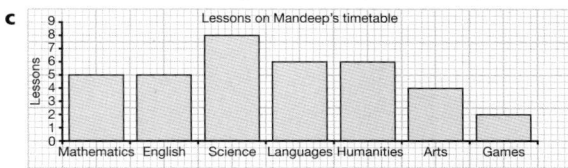

(Pie chart: Games 20°, Arts 40°, Maths 50°, English 50°, Science 80°, Languages 60°, Humanities 60°)

c (Bar chart: Lessons on Mandeep's timetable — Mathematics 5, English 5, Science 8, Languages 6, Humanities 6, Arts 4, Games 2)

d The bar chart, because it is easier to make comparisons and shows the actual number of lessons.

5 a How 720 people would vote in an election.

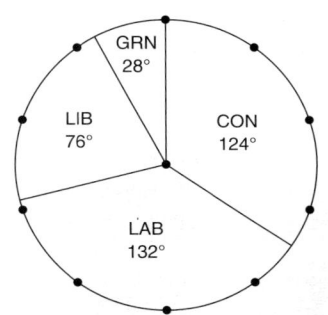

(Pie chart: GRN 28°, CON 124°, LAB 132°, LIB 76°)

b The split of the total data can be seen at a glance.

6 a 55°
b 22
c 33.3% (to 1 d.p.)

7 a Strings (Pie chart: 7: 8°, 3: 36°, 4: 118°, 5: 126°, 6: 72°)
Brass (Pie chart: 7: 23°, 3: 82°, 4: 118°, 5: 98°, 6: 39°)

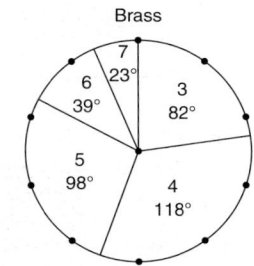

b Overall, the strings candidates did better with well over half achieving grade 5 or above. A higher proportion of Brass candidates achieved the top grade of 7.

8 1 in 9 or $\frac{1}{9}$.

9 All the possible methods of transport, and the number of students who used each method.

10 £9750

11 The radius required is 3.9 (to 1 d.p.).

Answers: Chapter 6

12

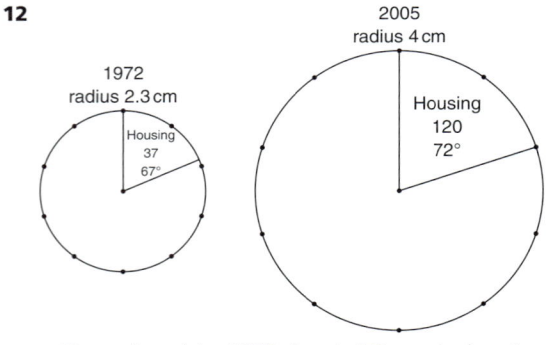

The radius of the 1972 chart is 2.3 cm, the housing angles are 67° (1972) and 72° (2005).

13

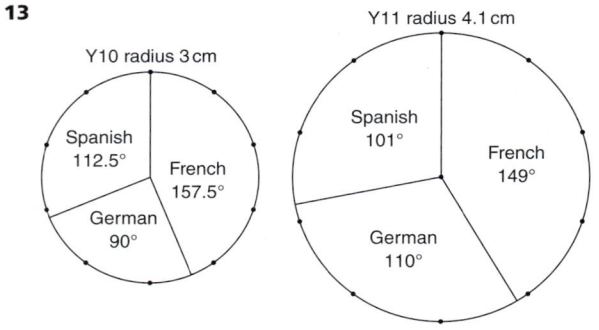

14 The total rainfall was significantly higher in 2005 than in 1976.

6.3 Misleading graphs

Exercise 6C

1. The second teddy bear appears much bigger than twice the size of the small teddy.
2. The vertical axis scale is shortened. It looks as if there were very few downloads in 2007, whereas there were far more in 2008 and 2010.
3. The shortened vertical axis makes it look as if there is a large reduction in gas bills. In fact, the bills have only reduced by approximately £30 over the four years.
4. **a** The scale on the vertical axis is shortened. The increase in area of the drawings is not in proportion to the increase in population.
   b The sheep population increases from 40 million in the 1960s to just over 45 million in the 1990s. The actual increase is only about 5 million over 40 years.
5. The larger house is about twice the size of the smaller house, which suggests that the average house price has decreased by half. The actual decrease is only £30 000 or $\frac{1}{7}$ of the value.
6. Check student's graph. It could have a shortened scale and bars that therefore aren't in proportion.
7. The graph has a shortened vertical axis and therefore the bars are not in proportion.
8. The graph has a shortened vertical axis. The actual decrease is only £2500 over three years. The graph makes the decrease look much bigger.

6.4 Choropleth maps

Exercise 6D

1. **a** London and West Midlands.
   b More people work in cities.
   c 6% to 5%.
2. **a–b**

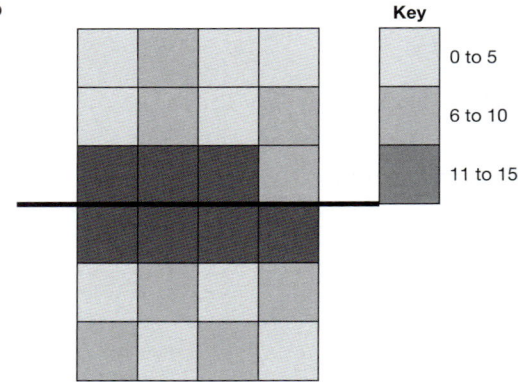

   c The stream provides sufficient water to allow more species to thrive.
3. **a**

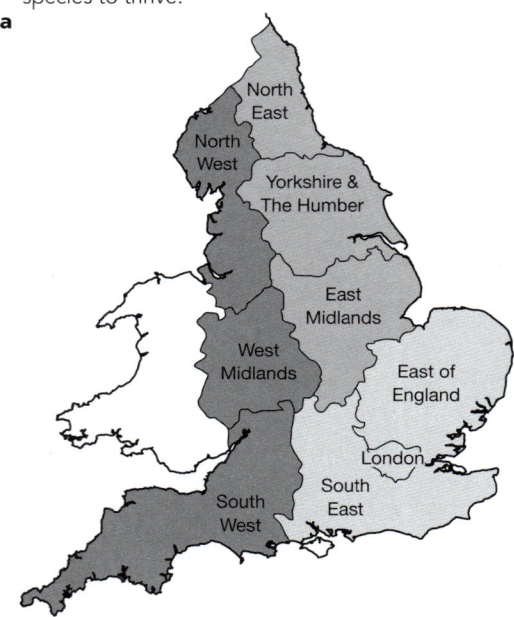

   b West side of the country.
   c Weather fronts usually move from west to east, so the west gets the most rain.
4. **a** Over 40%.
   b Under 5%.
   c Male, smoker, high cholesterol, age.
5. **a** Choropleth map.
   b Large cities or densely populated areas.

Answers: Chapter 6

6.5 Stem-and-leaf diagrams

Exercise 6E

1.
Stem	Leaves
3	5 7 8
4	3 6
5	4 7 9
6	2 2 4 5 6 7 8 9
7	2 4 5
8	1 1 5
9	2 3 8

   Key: 6 | 2 means 62 students.

2. **a**
Stem	Leaves
10	5 6 6 8 8 9 9
11	1 1 3 3 4 5 5 5 6 7 9
12	0 1 3

   Key: 12 | 2 means 12.3 seconds.

   b 1.8 seconds.
   c 11.3 seconds.

3. **a**
Stem	Leaves
1	6 9
2	1 5 6 7
3	0 1 3 4 5 5 6 6 7 7
4	1 1 2 3 5 6 7 8
5	0 2 5 8
6	2 9

   b Key: 1 | 6 means 16 years old.
   c 16 years old.
   d 69 years old.
   e 53 years old.
   f 35.5 years old.

4. **a**
Stem	Leaves
2	6 7 8 9 9
3	1 3 4 5
4	0 0 8 9 9
5	0

   Key: 3 | 1 means 31 mpg.

   b 24 mpg.
   c 34 mpg.

5.
Stem	Leaves
3	9
4	2 3 8
5	0 1 1 7 7 8 9 9
6	3 3 5 8 8
7	2 2 3 5 8
8	0 1 3 4
9	0

   Key: 6 | 1 means 6.1 grams.

6. **a** 91
   b 94
   c Class X = 67, Class Y = 53.5.
   d Overall, Class X did better, because their median mark is higher and they had significant more students scoring high marks.

7. **a**
	Boys		Girls
	9 8 8 6 4	0	1 1 2 2 2 3 5 8 9
	9 7 3 2	1	1 2 2 2 2 3 3 4 5 7 9
9 7 7 7 6 6 6 4 2 0		2	0 0 1 2 4
	5 4 4 3 3 1	3	

   Key: For the boys, 6 | 1 means 16 hours
   For the girls, 1 | 6 means 16 hours.

   b Boys: range = 31 hours; median = 26 hours, mode = 27 hours.
   Girls: range = 23 hours; median = 12 hours, mode = 12 hours.
   c Boys, in general spend considerably more time playing computer games than girls.

6.6 Histograms and frequency polygons

Exercise 6F

1. **a**

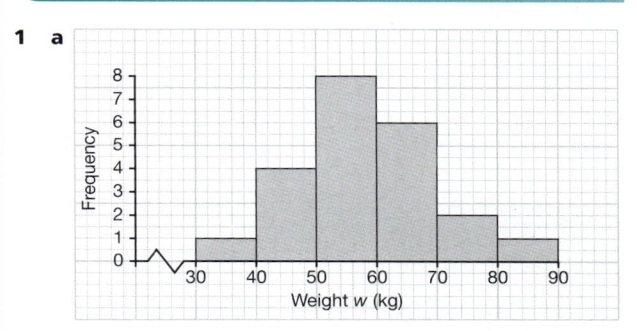

   b $50 \leq w < 60$ kg.

2. **a**
Length, l (cm)	Tally	Frequency
$10 \leq l < 12$	///// ///	8
$12 \leq l < 14$	///// /	6
$14 \leq l < 16$	///// ///// ///	13
$16 \leq l < 18$	///// /////	10
$18 \leq l < 20$	/////	5

   b

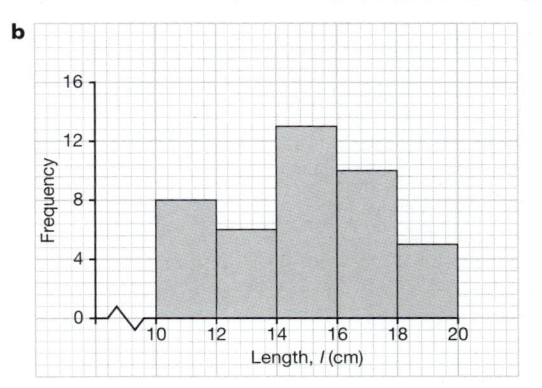

   c $14 \leq l < 16$ cm.
   d $14 \leq l < 16$ cm.

Answers: Chapter 6

3 a

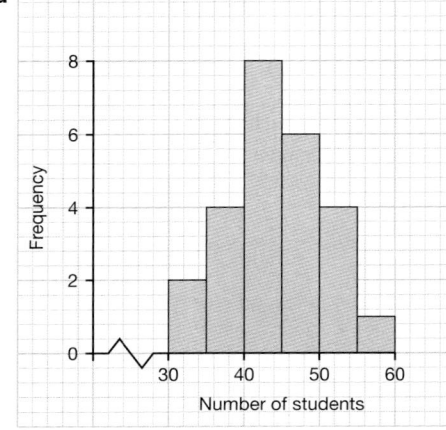

b

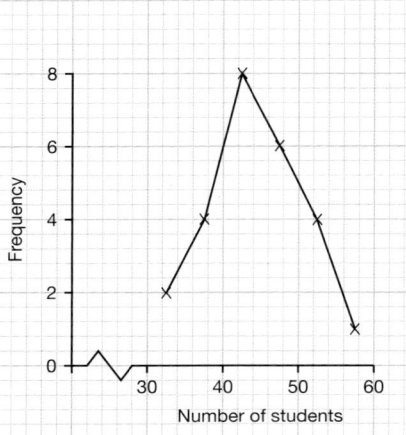

4

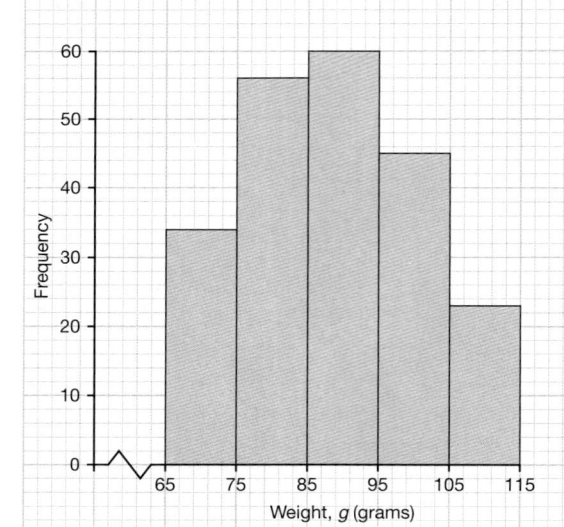

5 a

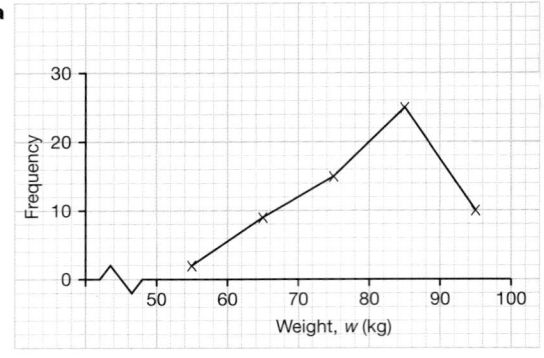

b Modal group = $80 \leq w < 90$ kg.
c Median lies within $80 \leq w < 90$ kg.

6 a

Length, l (cm)	Frequency
$0 < l \leq 2$	1
$2 < l \leq 4$	4
$4 < l \leq 6$	7
$6 < l \leq 8$	3

b 15

7 a

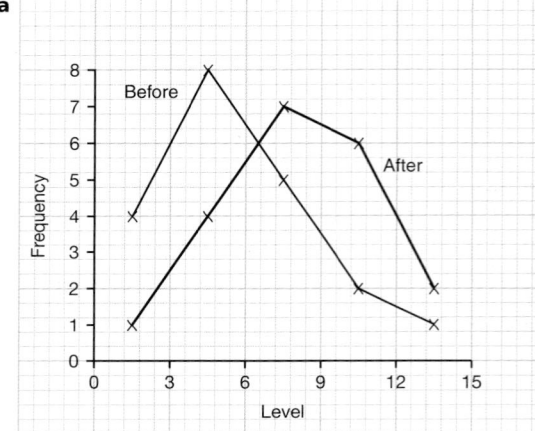

b Yes
c The polygons clearly show that the training has improved fitness levels; modal group and median has moved from 3–6 to 6–9, with fewer people in the 0–3 group.

8

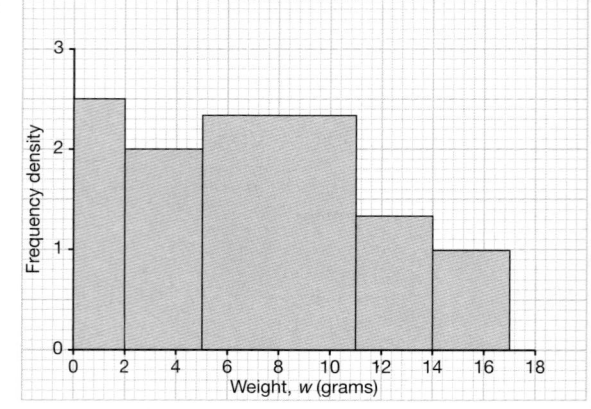

Answers: Chapter 6

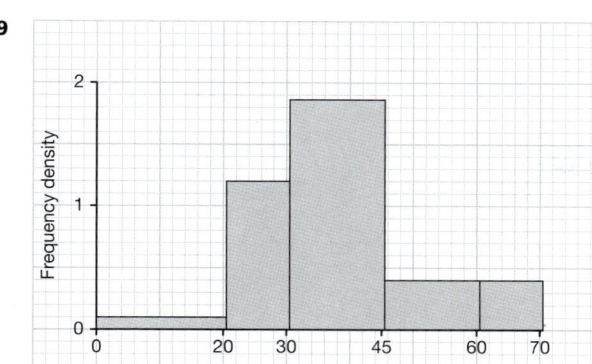

9 [histogram: Frequency density vs Results, bars at 0–20 (≈0.1), 20–30 (≈1.2), 30–45 (≈1.85), 45–60 (≈0.4), 60–70 (≈0.4)]

10 [histogram: Frequency density vs Mass, m (g), bars at 0–2 (≈1), 2–5 (≈3.5), 5–8 (≈2), 8–12 (≈2), 12–16 (≈2.5)]

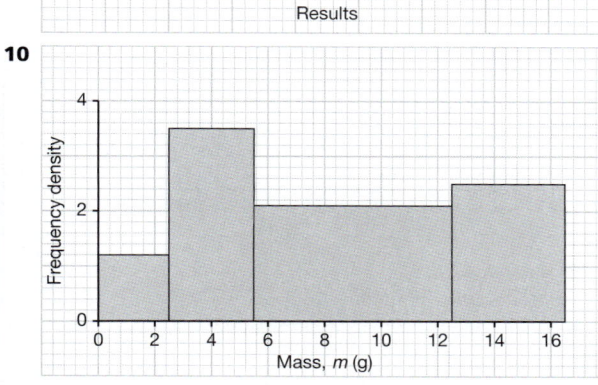

11 a

Height, h (cm)	Frequency	Frequency density
$8 \leq h < 12$	8	2
$12 \leq h < 14$	10	5
$14 \leq h < 18$	14	3.5
$18 \leq h < 24$	6	1
$24 \leq h < 30$	3	0.5

b [histogram: Frequency density vs Height, h (cm)]

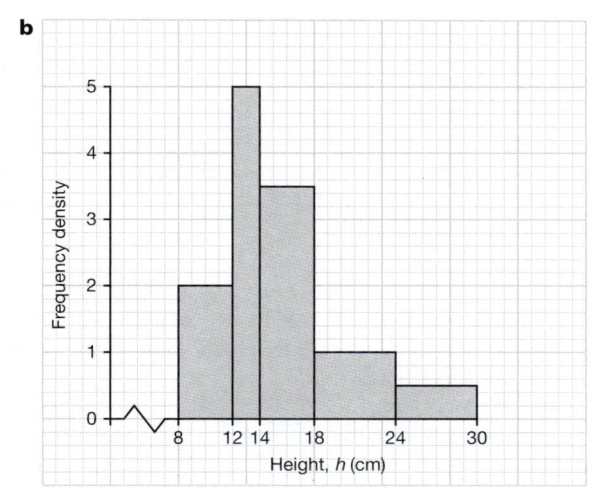

12 a [histogram: Frequency density vs Age]

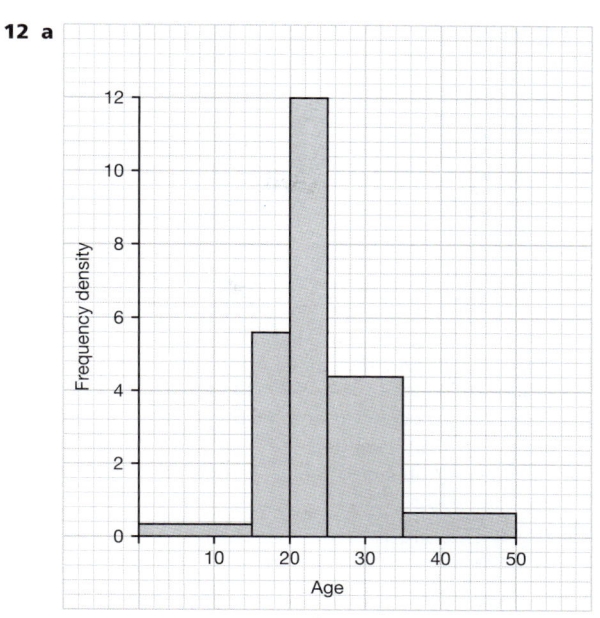

b 22 members will receive the discount.

6.7 Cumulative frequency graphs

Exercise 6G

1 a Cumulative frequency 1, 4, 10, 22, 25, 28, 30.

b [cumulative frequency curve: Cumulative frequency vs Time]

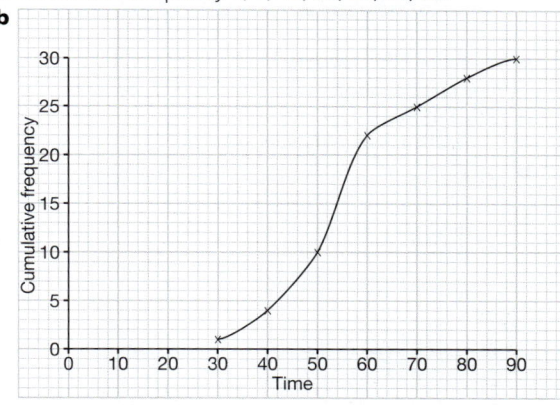

c Median = 54 seconds.
Interquartile range = 61 − 46 = 16 seconds.

Answers: Chapter 6

2 a Cumulative frequency 1, 3, 5, 14, 31, 44, 47, 49, 50.
  b [Cumulative frequency graph against Time]
  c Median = 56 seconds.
  Interquartile range = 64 – 49 = 15 seconds.
  d Pensioners, median closer to 60 seconds and slightly small interquartile range.

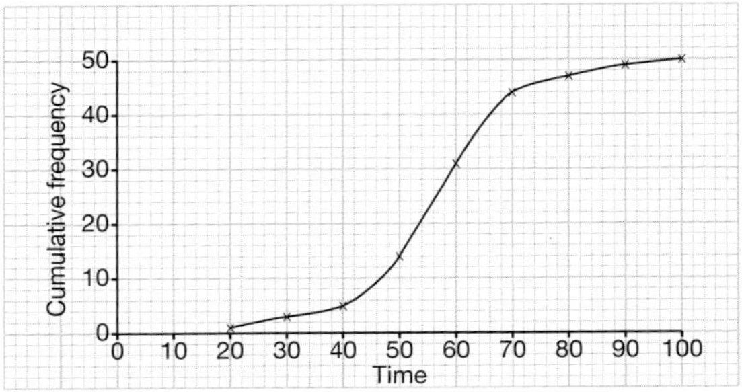

3 a Cumulative frequency 12, 30, 63, 113, 176, 250, 314, 349, 360.
  b [Cumulative frequency graph against Number of students]
  c Median = 605 students.
  Interquartile range = 730 – 460 = 270 students.
  d About 45 schools.

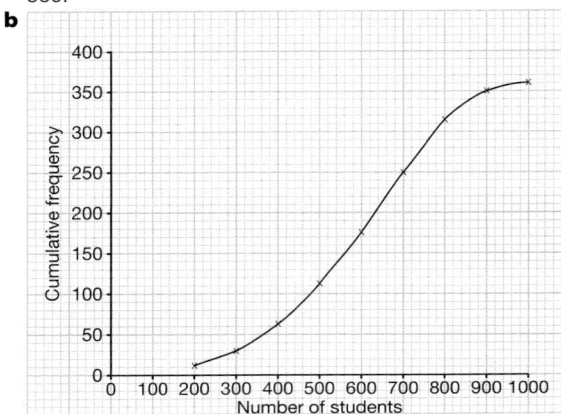

4 a Cumulative frequency 2, 5, 10, 16, 22, 31, 39, 45, 50.
  b [Cumulative frequency graph against Temperature °C]
  c Median = 20.5°C.
  Interquartile range 25 – 14.5 = 10.5°C.

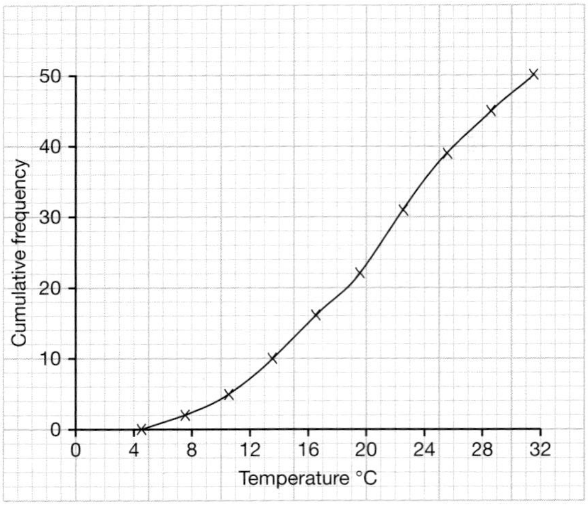

5 a [Cumulative frequency graph against Score]
  b Median = 56.
  Interquartile range 80 – 16 = 64.
  c No. of people scoring more than 90 = 80 – 66 = 14; 17.5%.

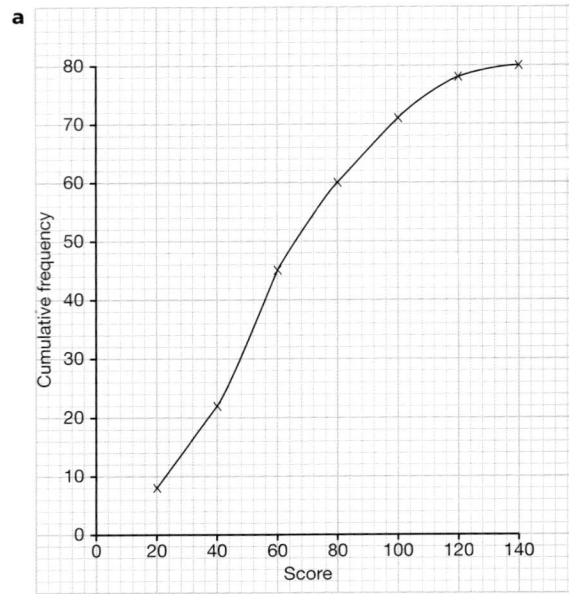

6 a Cumulative frequency 6, 16, 36, 64, 82, 93, 98, 100.
  b [Cumulative frequency graph against Pocket money (p)]
  c Median = 225p.
  Interquartile range 275 – 180 = 95p.

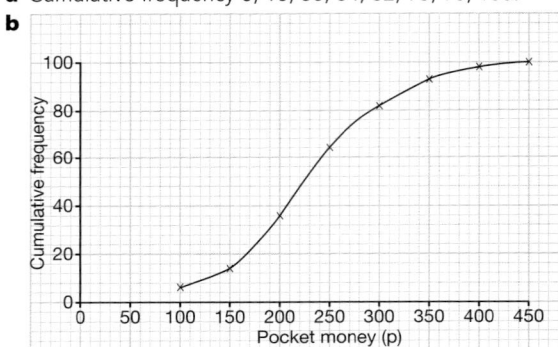

7 a Median (Paper A) = 66.
  Median (Paper B) = 56.
  b Interquartile range (Paper A) = 77 – 51 = 26.
  Interquartile range (Paper B) = 64 – 46 = 18.
  c Paper B is the harder paper, it has a lower median and a lower upper quartile.
  d i Paper A = 43, Paper B = 45.
    ii Paper A = 79, Paper B = 66.

8 9.25 minutes (create a grouped frequency chart).

9 Byron would need to calculate where on the cumulative frequency scale the 90th percentile lies (10% down from the highest value). He would then read horizontally along to the graph and then read down vertically to the marks. This mark will be the minimum mark needed for this top grade.

10 a

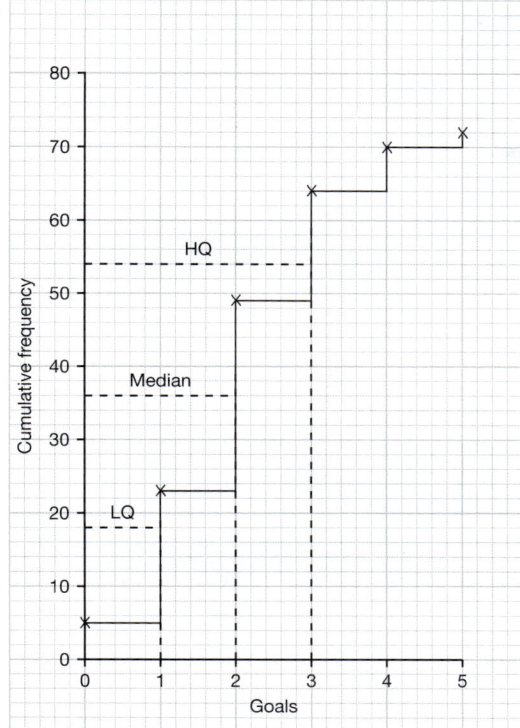

b Median = 2 goals.
Interquartile range = 3 − 1 = 2 goals.

11 a

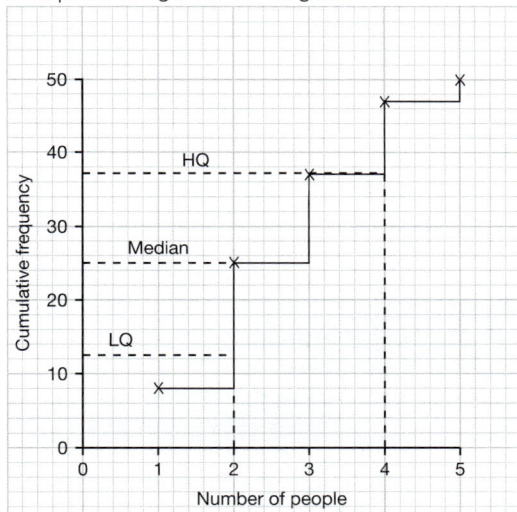

b Median = 2 people.
Interquartile range = 4 − 2 = 2 people.

12 a The median = 122 cm.
b The interquartile range = 133 − 85 = 48 cm.

13 a 80 bats.
b 23.3 cm.
c 35 − 17 = 18 cm.

Examination Questions

1 a 6 men.
b 4
c 30 women.
2 a 9 students.
b Range = 42 seconds.
c Median = 36 seconds.
d Yes, she is correct as Year 7 has a greater median (41).
3 a

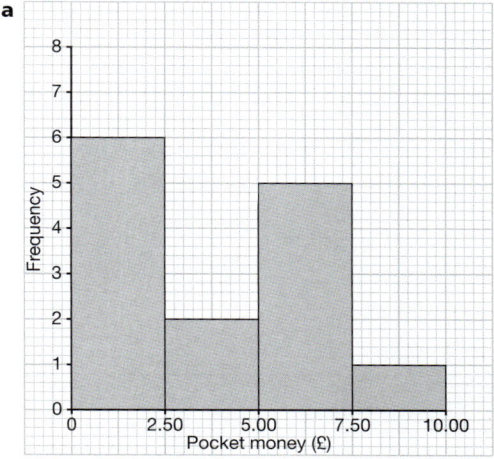

b Modal class = £0 to £2.50.
4 a

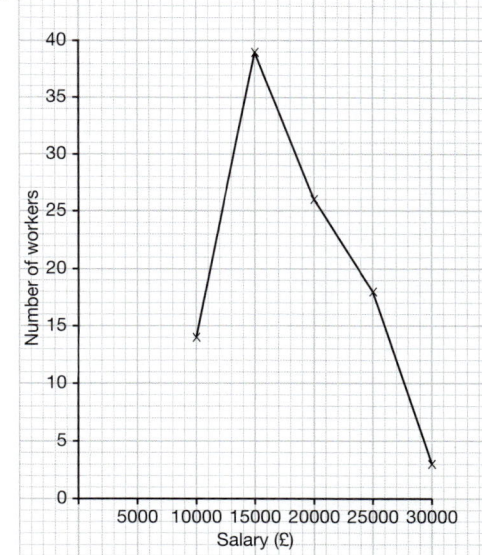

b $\frac{21}{100}$

Answers: Chapter 7

5 a Cumulative frequencies are 22, 54, 80, 95, 100.
b

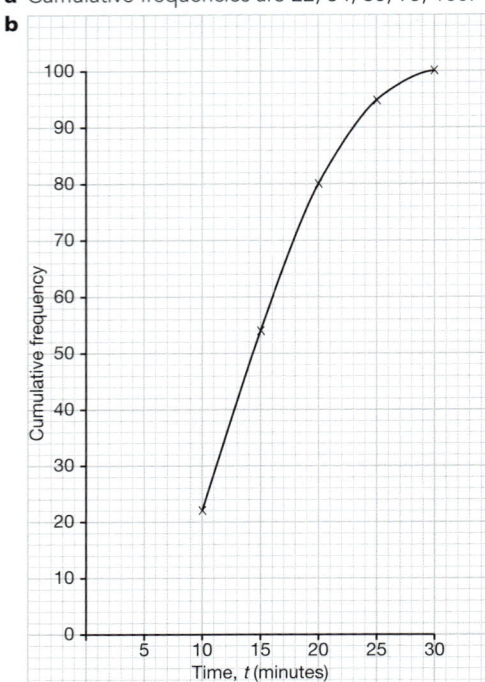

[Cumulative frequency graph: Time, t (minutes) on x-axis from 0 to 30, Cumulative frequency on y-axis from 0 to 100. Points plotted showing an S-shaped curve through approximately (5, 22), (15, 54), (20, 80), (25, 95), (30, 100).]

c i Interquartile range = 19 − 10.5 = 8.5 minutes.
  ii 34 people.
6 a 115 members.
b

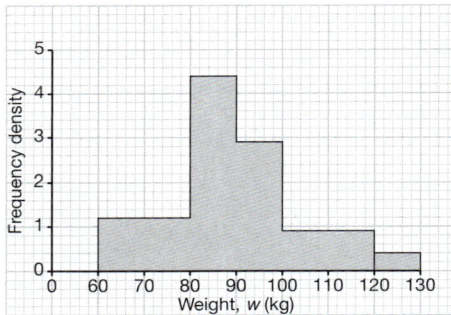

[Histogram: Weight, w (kg) on x-axis from 0 to 130, Frequency density on y-axis from 0 to 5. Bars: 60–80 at 1.2, 80–90 at 4.4, 90–100 at 2.9, 100–120 at 0.9, 120–130 at 0.4.]

7 Measures of location

Quick check

1 a 2
  b 5
  c 14

7.1 The mode

Exercise 7A

1 4
2 Blue
3 11
4 94p
5 £112 and £120.
6 36
7 4
8 6, 7 and 7.
9 Students write down three sets of numbers of the form n, n and $18 − 2n$, where $n \neq 6$. i.e. 5, 5, 8 or 4, 4, 10
10 a 15
   b 12
   c 14
   d The correct statement is **iii**. The new member is a 13-year-old male.

7.2 The median

Exercise 7B

1 a 5
  b 33
  c 28
  d 4.7
  e 108.5
2 a £34
  b £34
3 6.35 kg
4 a 4
  b 2
  c Either: the mode is better because most had this number of parts missing.
   Or: the median is better as there was only one pack with a higher number than the mode.

384

Answers: Chapter 7

5 a i 6.5
   ii 7
 b i 8.5
   ii 9
 c i 13
   ii 14
6 a 4
 b 6
7 a 4
 b 3
8 a 24.5
 b 7 and 29.
 c The median is more useful as there are two modes, which are not close together.
9 a 57 kg.
 b 56 kg.
 c 59 kg.
10 Three of the numbers must be 8, 8 and 12.
 The other number can be any value greater than 12, as the mode is 8 (it appears twice) and the median is halfway between 8 and 12, which is 10.

7.3 The mean

Exercise 7C

1 a 6
 b 49.5
 c 6.25
 d 1.5
2 All answers correct to 1 d.p. where appropriate.
 a 178.9 cm.
 b 68.3 kg.
 c 22.8 years.
 d 22 years, 70.8 kg, 182 cm.
 e 23.3 years. 66.6 kg, 176.7 cm.
3 a Mean = 11, median = 10, mode = 9.
 b Mean = 22, median = 20, mode = 18 (double the values in **a**).
 c Mean = 14, median = 13, mode = 12 (3 more than the value in **a**).
4 a 56 cars.
 b 72 cars.
 c Mean = 8.
5 Mick has £6.
6 a 18.7 to 1 d.p.
 b 18
7 5, 5, 6, 7, 8.
8 17.72
9 a The modal score is 2.
 b The median score is 2.
 c The mean number of goals per game is 2.71 (to 2 d.p.).
10 38
11 Mean = 1.28.
 Median = 1.
 Mode = 2.
12 The missing frequencies are both 4.

7.4 Which average to use

Exercise 7D

1 a

	Mean	Median	Mode
i	6	5	4
ii	15	14	12
iii	6	4	2

 b i The mode is low. The mean and median are both good; the median is central, and the mean accounts for the higher numbers.
   ii The mode is low. The mean and median are both good; the median is central, and the mean accounts for the higher numbers.
   iii The median is the best. The mode is low and the mean is influenced too much by the large number.
2 a The mode will give a good average, as it will be one of the shoe sizes.
 b The mean or median are good. The mode could be any height which two students share.
 c The mode is the only average for non-numeric data.
 d The median would allow students to find out whether they are in the top or bottom half of the class; the mean would show their standing compared to the whole class.
3 a Mean = 26, median = 14, mode = 12.
 b There are two distinct groups; weekdays and weekends. The mean takes account of both.
4 a 100.03 (to 2 d.p.).
 b 100
 c 100
 d Yes; all averages are 100 or more.
5 a The mode.
 b The mean.
 c The median.
 d The mode is too low. The mean is influenced by the high wage-earners. The median is good because it reflects the pay of the majority.
6 a True, his score is below the mean.
 b False, his score is above the median so he is in the top half.
 c False; half the students scored 54% or more.
 d True: half the class scored 54% or more.
7 a Andrew and Ed (23).
 b Andrew and Steve (34).
 c Andrew and Rob (42.7 to 1 d.p.).
 d Andrew has a high mean (so he has scored a lot of runs) and a high median, suggesting that he has a balanced set of scores.
8 a The mean will change.
 b The median will not change.
 c The mode might change.

385

Answers: Chapter 8

9	(A) Adding 10 to the largest number	(Y) The mean increases, but the mode and median are unchanged
	(B) Adding 2 to each number	(Z) The mean, median and mode all increase
	(C) Removing the highest and lowest numbers from the set	(X) The median is unchanged, but the mean and mode might change

10 They both have the same mean.
Claire has a lower mode, which suggests that she has more quick times than Sue.

7.5 Grouped data

Exercise 7E

1 a 56.9 cm.
  b $20 < l \leqslant 40$.
2 1.1 hours (to 1 d.p) or 1 hour 6 minutes.
3 29.9 g (to 1 d.p.).
4 a $175 < h \leqslant 180$.
  b 171.9 cm (to 1 d.p.).
5 a 58.6
  b 61–70
  c Fiona's mark is only just in the modal class, but is above the mean, so she had an above average score.
6 An estimate of the mean is 7.3 seconds, and the modal class is $5 < t \leqslant 10$, so the claim is justified.
7 Type A has a greater mean (23.3 cm against 22.5 cm).
8 62.1 minutes or 62 minutes and 6 seconds.
9 £374.04
10 26 times.

7.6 The geometric mean

Exercise 7F

1 a 4.64 (to 2 d.p.).
  b 3.30 (to 2 d.p.).
  c 3.31 (to 2 d.p.).
2 26.8% (to 1 d.p.).
3 1.99% (to 2 d.p.).
4 Patricia is correct. Imelda's annual increase is slightly below 4%, at 3.99%.
5 The geometric mean is 24.9% (to 1 d.p.).
It is the increase that would have to be made twice to give the same result as the 20% and 30% increase.
6 It is an annual decrease of 2%.
7 3.97% (to 2 d.p.).
8 3.8% (to 1 d.p.).
9 24
10 0.91% (to 2 d.p.).

Examination Questions

1 a £12
  b Higher
  The largest value of £225 will affect the mean.
2 a 3
  b 2.82
  c Although the theoretical probability is larger, the values are similar.
3 a 1 is the most common number in the list, occurring 8 times.
  b When put in order, 1 is in the middle:
  1 1 1 1 1 1 1 2 3 4
  c You cannot have part of a person.
4 70 minutes.
5 a 2
  b 6
  c $0 \times 21 + 1 \times 17 + 2 \times 8 + 3 \times 3 + 4 \times 2 + 5 \times 1 + 6 \times 0 + 7 \times 0 = 55$
  d 1.06 (1.057692308…)
6 a 6.23
  b The mean should be increased by 2.
7 a 8
  b 125
  c 7

8 Measures of spread

Quick check

Mean = 5.
Median = 5.
Mode = 2.

8.1 Box-and-whisker plots

Exercise 8A

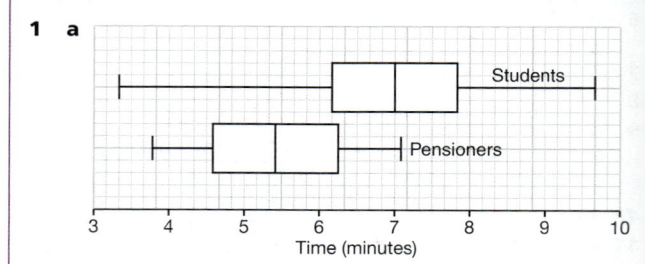

1 a

b Students are much slower than the pensioners. Both distributions have the same interquartile range, but students' median and upper quartiles are 1 minute, 35 seconds higher. The fastest person to complete the calculations was a student, but so was the slowest.

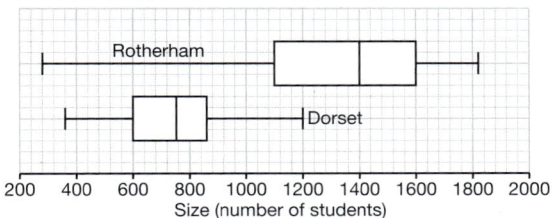

2 a [box plot: Rotherham and Dorset, Size (number of students), 200–2000]

b Schools are much larger in Rotherham than Dorset. The Dorset distribution is quite symmetrical, but the Rotherham distribution is negatively skewed – so most Rotherham schools are large.

3 a The resorts have similar median temperatures, but Resort B has a much wider temperature range, where the greatest extremes of temperature are recorded.

b Resort A is probably a better choice as the weather seems more consistent.

4 a [box plot: Men and Women, Salary (£1000s), 5–50]

b Both distributions have a similar interquartile range, and there is little difference between the upper quartile values. Men have a wider range of salaries, but the higher men's median and the fact that the men's distribution is negatively skewed and the women's distribution is positively skewed indicates that men are better paid than women.

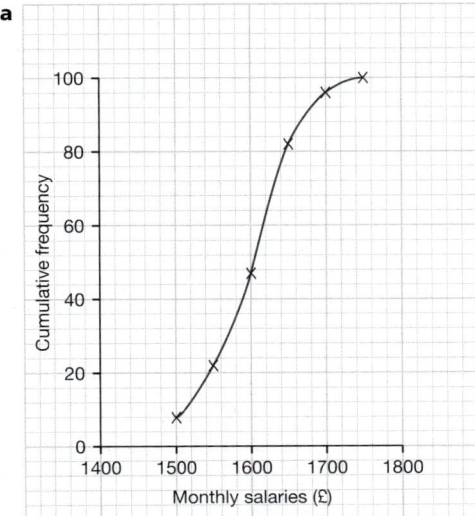

5 a [cumulative frequency graph: Monthly salaries (£), 1400–1800]

b median = £1605, interquartile range = £85.

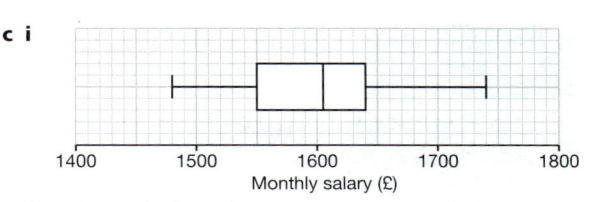

c i [box plot: Monthly salary (£), 1400–1800]

ii Negatively skewed.

6 a i 24 minutes.
ii 12 minutes.
iii 42 minutes.
b i 6 minutes.
ii 17 minutes.
iii 9 minutes.
c Either doctor with a plausible reason, e.g. Dr Excel because his waiting times are always shorter than Dr Collins', or Dr Collins because he takes more time with each patient.

7 The girls and boys have the same median results (78) and the same interquartile range (22). However, as the girls' distribution is positively skewed and the boys' distribution is negatively skewed, the girls will have a higher mean score than the boys. (Can be estimated by creating grouped frequencies using the four quartiles.)

8 Many possible answers but not including numerical values: 'Bude had a higher median than Torquay', 'Bude had a smaller interquartile range than Torquay', 'Bude had more sunshine on any one day'.

9 a Symmetric.
b Positively skewed.
c Symmetric.
d Symmetric.
e Negatively skewed.
f Positively skewed.
g Negatively skewed.
h Positively skewed.
i Positively skewed.
j Symmetric.

10 A and X, B and Y, C and W, D and Z.

8.2 Variance and standard deviation

Exercise 8B

1 a 3.53
b 3.16
c 12.97
2 Mean = 21.84, standard deviation = 0.68.
3 Mean = 2.31, variance = 1.79, standard deviation = 1.34.
4 1.02.
5 Mean = 71.4, standard deviation = 1.53.
6 4.65.
7 Mean = 112.15, standard deviation = 6.71.
8 Mean = 25, standard deviation = 8.21.
9 Standard deviation = 55.8, mean = 520.8.
No, as 95% are between 409.2 and 632.4.

Answers: Chapter 9

8.3 Using a calculator to work out standard deviation

Exercise 8C

Try the questions from the previous section, using the statistics functions you have learned.

8.4 Properties of frequency distributions

Exercise 8D

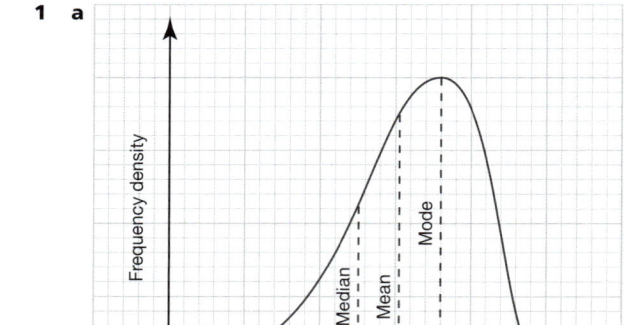

1 a [Graph: Frequency density vs Wage, showing negative skew with Median, Mean, Mode marked]

  b Negative skew.
  c −1.4 confirming negative skew.

2 a Negative skew.
  b [Graph: Frequency density vs values 0–30, with Median and Mean marked]

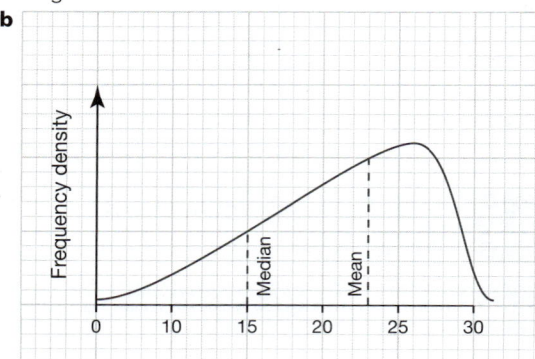

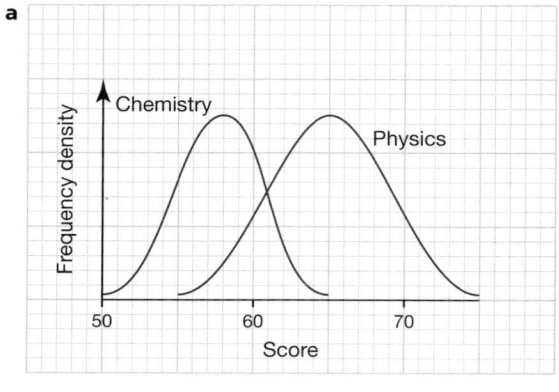

3 a [Graph: Frequency density vs Score, showing Chemistry curve peaked around 60 and Physics curve peaked around 65]

  b The physics examination had a greater spread of results and a higher mean than the chemistry examination did, which suggests it was the better examination as it differentiated between the students' ability.
  65% of the students in the chemistry examination had between 53 and 63 whereas, in the physics examination, 65% of the students had between 55 and 75.

4 2500 + (2 × 400) = 3.3 kg and 2500 − (2 × 400) = 1.7 kg.
5 2.5%
6 French 1, Welsh 0.4, Spanish 0.21. Phil did best in French.
7 74
8 a 74 and 26.
  b 8.7
  c In the second distribution, students have a higher mean and 65% achieved between 66.3 and 83.7 marks, so they are the more able class. Compare this to 65% of the first class achieving between 38 and 62 marks.
9 a 400 m: mean = 45.06 seconds and standard deviation = 0.479 seconds.
  800 m: mean = 1 minute 45.26 seconds, standard deviation = 1.444 seconds.
  b 400 m: standardised = −1.69.
  800 m: standardised = −1.22.
  Alberto performed better in the 400 m, as this was furthest from the mean.

Examination Questions

1 a Similarity: Both distributions peaked in 1999 or both distributions are negatively skewed.
  Difference: The number of freight vehicles dropped in 1997.
  b i [Box plots: London to Paris and Paris to London on Time (minutes) axis 140–210]

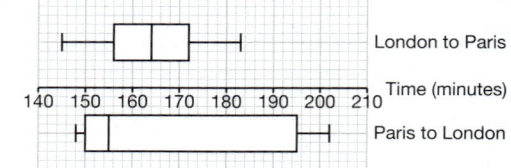

    ii London to Paris is symmetrical, Paris to London is positive skewed.
    iii 262.5 minutes.

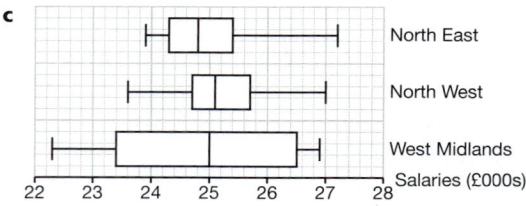

2 a £3 300
  b £1 000
  c [Box plots for North East, North West, West Midlands on Salaries (£000s) axis 22–28]

  d i North West.
    ii North East median < £25 000, West Midlands range > £4 500.

3 a Mean = 3, variance = 2.51, standard deviation = 1.58.
  b i 1.61 minutes.
    ii 24.8 minutes.
    iii 8.1 and 24.9.

388

Answers: Chapter 10

4 Jim: −1.67, Shaun: −1.5; Shaun's time is closer to the standardised mean.

5 a The data supports his claim as his standardised score in maths is −1.5 which is closer to the mean than his standardised score in statistics of −2.

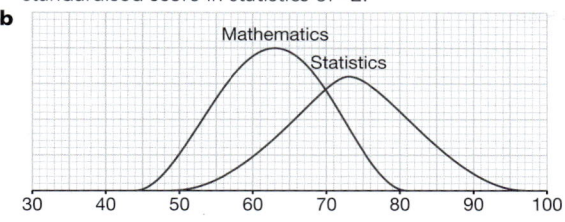

b [Graph showing two normal distribution curves labelled Mathematics and Statistics, x-axis from 30 to 100]

8 a The birth rate of Avem is 12.6 children per 1000 people when weighted according to the national standard population.

b Avem – its standardised birth rate is much higher.

c If Avem is a very small town and/or Kidlyss a big one. The age profile of Kidlyss could mean that in a few years it will have a high proportion of people who could have children, i.e. it has a high percentage of young teenagers at the moment.

Examination Questions

1 a 9.7 million.
b 4.5 years or 13.2%.
c 11.96 million.
d 9.97 million.

2 £50

3 £2.00

4 a 90%
b £152 000

5 a i Index = 194.2
ii Both the Alcohol and Tobacco categories have index values greater than the 'All groups' index so excluding this expenditure will reduce the weighted index.

b i 2003 = 109.2.
2004 = 122.7.
2005 = 95.5.
2006 = 97.7.
ii From 2002 to 2003 costs rose by 9.2%.
From 2003 to 2004 costs rose by 22.7%.
From 2004 to 2005 costs fell by 4.5%.
From 2005 to 2006 costs fell by 2.3%.

6 a 2006 index = $\frac{41034}{31560} \times 100 = 130$.
b i $\frac{140}{190} \times 100 = 73.7\%$.
ii Smaller weighting, less impact on part **a**.

7 a $(5.2 \times 3) + (2.1 \times 5) + (7.4 \times 12) = £114.90$.
b $\frac{114.9}{90.0} \times 100 = 127.7$.
c Selling price increases at a faster rate than material costs, more profitable.

9 Statistics used in everyday life

Quick check

1 1.20
2 0.80
3 £64.80

9.1 Statistics used in everyday life

Exercise 9A

1
Year	2004	2005	2006	2007	2008	2009
Index	100	102.5	107.5	108.5	112.5	120
Price (p)	80	82	86	87	90	96

2 £84.05

3 a 1.88
b The greatest drop was from June to July.
c Exchange rates cannot be predicted from past trends.

4 a 187.1
b i sweets, cake, biscuits.
ii bread.

5 The cost of living in 2010 has fallen by 3% from 2009.

6 a 2008 = 94.4.
2009 = 117.6.
2010 = 110.0.
b The cost of Jess's car insurance fell by 5.6% between 2007 and 2008, it increased by 17.6% between 2008 and 2009 and increased again by 10% between 2009 and 2010.

7 a Possible answers: holiday period, industrial action, shortage of parts.
b i 140 225 or 140 thousand (to the nearest thousand).
ii 207 229 or 207 thousand (to the nearest thousand).

Answers: Chapter 10

10 Time series and quality assurance

Quick check

a 5.5
b 7 − 2 = 5
c 5

10.1 Moving averages

Exercise 10A

1

Year	Number of visitors (1000s)	Three-point moving average (1000s)
2003	12.2	
2004	15.3	14.8
2005	16.8	17.2
2006	19.4	19.4
2007	22	22.5
2008	26.1	25.9
2009	29.7	28.7
2010	30.4	

2 a

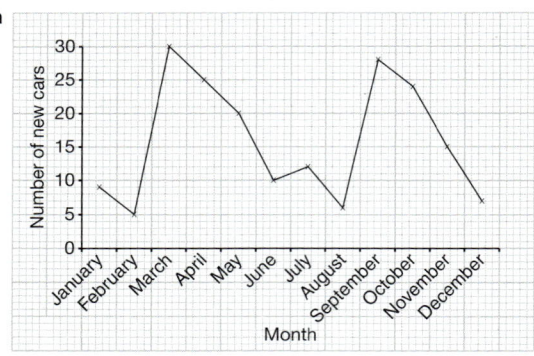

b These months are when the new registration plates are launched.
c Four-point moving averages are: 17.25, 20.0, 21.25, 16.75, 12.0, 14.0, 17.5, 18.25, 18.5.

3 a Use a four-point moving average as there are four data points per year.
b There is considerable seasonal variation with gas bills being lower in the summer months and higher in the winter months.
c First four-point moving average = $\frac{60 + 93 + 155 + 115}{4}$
= $\frac{423}{4}$ = 105.75.
d Second four-point moving average = $\frac{426}{4}$ = 106.5.

4 a, b, c

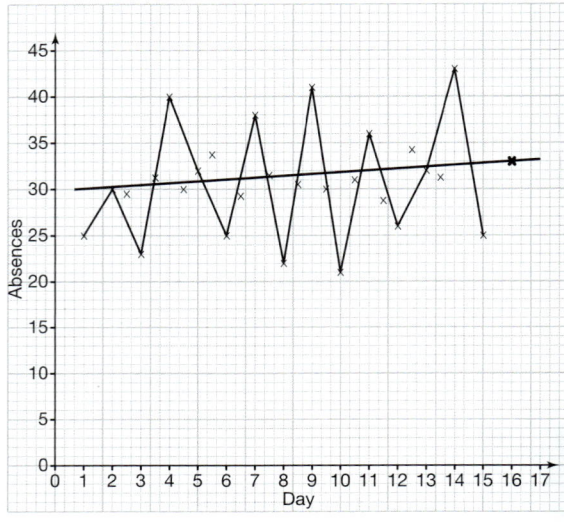

d There were 33 absences on day 16.

5 a, b, c

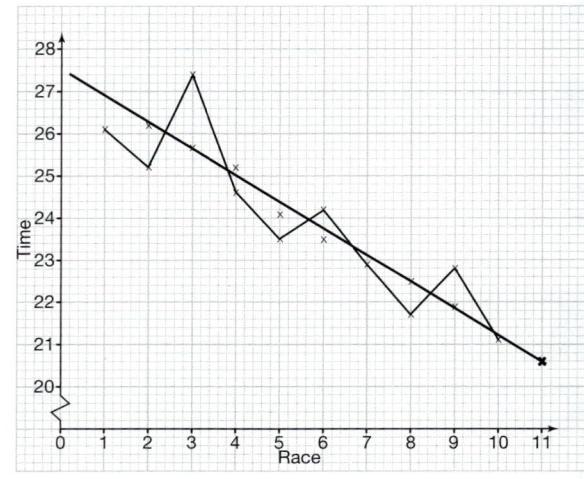

d 20.6 minutes.
e This would be extrapolation well beyond the existing data set, so there could be little certainty that the observed trend would continue.

6 a Four-point moving averages (to nearest unit): 2502, 2824, 3096, 3409, 3684, 3858, 3987, 4083, 4190.
b Use a four-point moving average as there are four data points per year.

Answers: Chapter 10

7 a, b, c

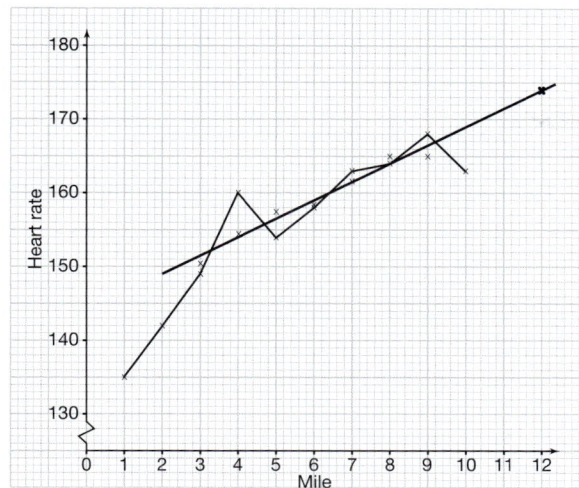

d 174 beats per minute.
e This would be extrapolation well beyond the existing data set and it would provide an estimate that was implausible.

10.2 Time series

Exercise 10B

1 a Tuesday, 200.
b 5 points.
c Thursday.

2 a

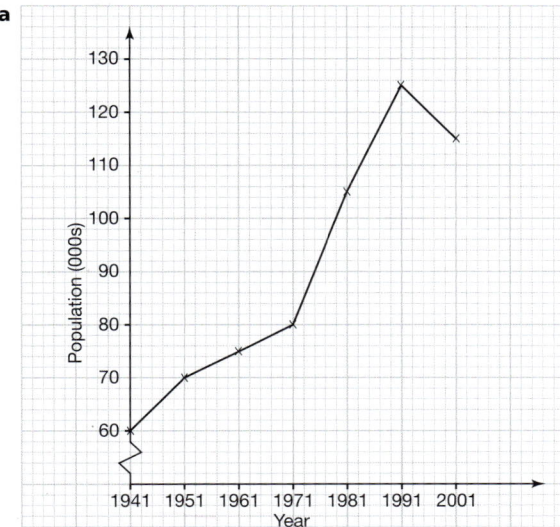

b 77 500
c 1971 and 1981.
d No; it is not known why the population started to decrease after 1991, or what will happen in subsequent years from 2001.
e No, too there are many changes in society's structure. In addition, World War I and World War II would have reduced the population.

3 a

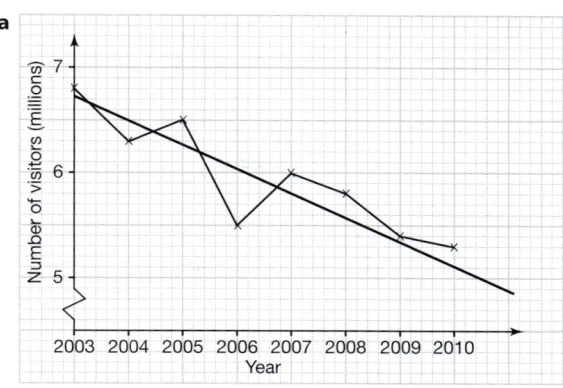

b Approximately 4.8 million (this will depend on trend line drawn).
c 2005 and 2006.
d Downward trend. Possible reasons include other similar attractions may have opened, or changing economic factors (exchange rates deterring overseas visitors, people may be feeling the effects of the recession).
e No, there are too many unknowns in the future for prediction to be possible.

4 a The four-point moving averages are:
5.23, 5.20, 5.18, 5.23, 5.43, 5.40, 5.30, 5.23, 5.43, 5.93, 6.40, 6.45, 6.13.

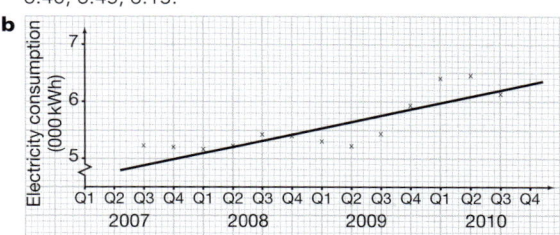

b

c There is no discernable trend but consumption increased sharply in last quarter of 2009, first quarter of 2010 due to the colder winter than previous years.

5 a

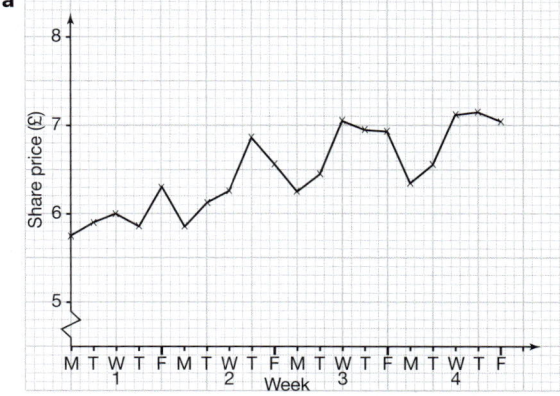

b Share prices are rising but are generally lower on a Monday.
c 5.96, 5.98, 6.03, 6.08, 6.29, 6.33, 6.41, 6.48, 6.63, 6.64, 6.72, 6.74, 6.76, 6.78, 6.82, 6.84.
Use a five-point moving average because there are 5 data points per week. A four-point moving average would not represent a week's worth of data.

391

Answers: Chapter 10

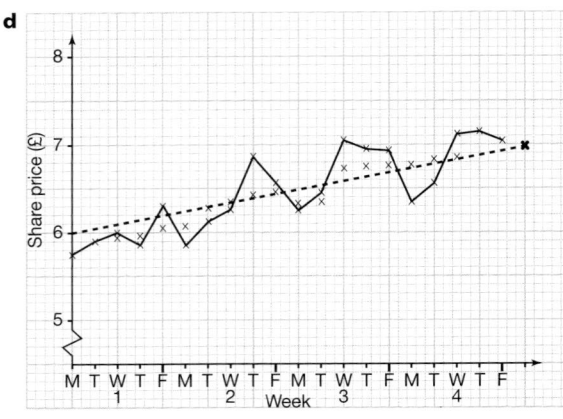

d [Graph: Share price (£) vs Week, showing weekly values M T W T F across weeks 1–4, with trend line rising from ~5.75 to ~7.0]

e 6.00 − 5.75 = 0.25.
6.25 − 5.86 = 0.39.
6.48 − 6.25 = 0.23.
6.73 − 6.34 = 0.39.
f Average seasonal effect = 0.32.
g 6.97 − 0.32 = 6.65

6 a (158), (402), 879, 1301, 1691, 2080, 2416, 2798, 3224, 3614, 4002, 4307.
b [Graph showing Monthly, Cumulative total for year, and Visits over previous 12 months by month January–December]

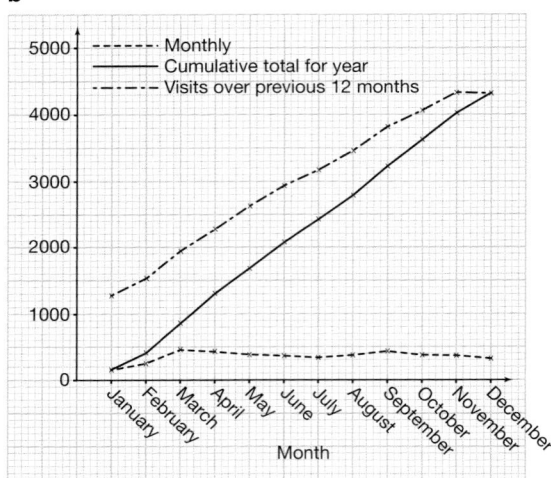

c The number of visits within 2009 is relatively consistent but, there has been a large increase in visits compared to 2008 as shown by the strong upward trend in 'Visits over the previous 12 months' line.

7 a 183, 184.25, 185.75, 187.5, 189.25, 187.5, 189.5, 191, 192.25, 191.5, 168.25, 169, 170.5.
b There are four sales figures per year.
c More sales occur during spring and summer months.

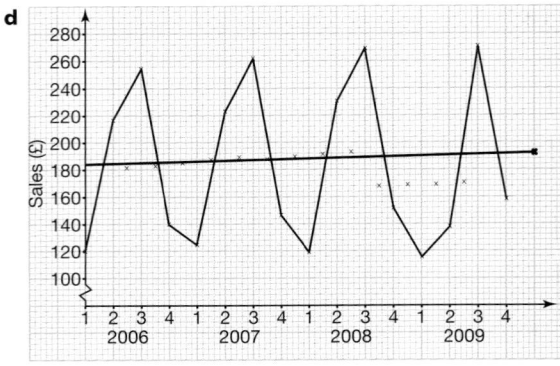

d [Graph: Sales (£) vs quarters 1–4 for years 2006–2009, showing seasonal variation with trend line]

e Seasonal variations for first quarters:
2006 = 184 − 120 = 64.
2007 = 186 − 125 = 61.
2008 = 188 − 118 = 70.
2009 = 190 − 115 = 75.
Average seasonal effect = 67.5.
Estimated sales for Q1 2010 = 192 − 67.5 = 124.5.

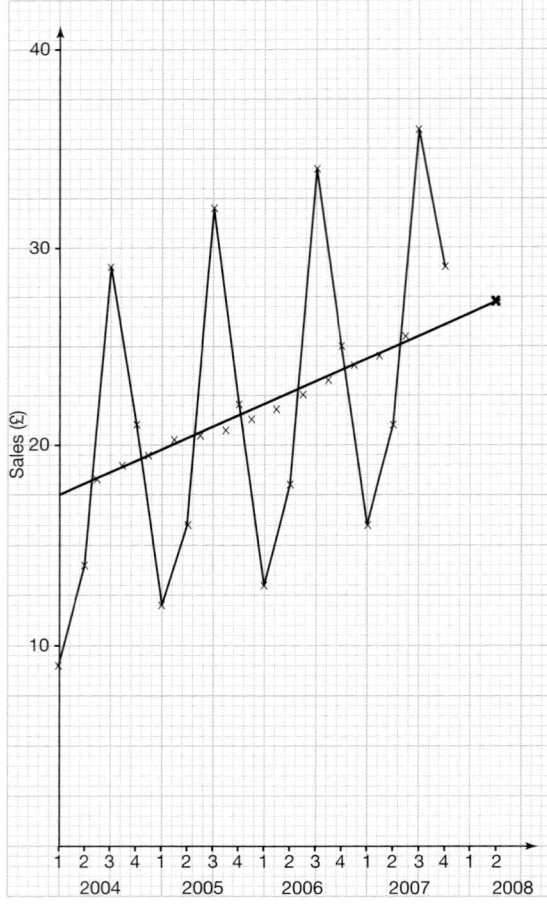

8 a, e, f
[Graph: Sales (£) vs quarters 1–4 for years 2004–2008, with trend line rising from ~17 to ~27]

b To smooth out variations, in this case seasonal variations.
c Use a four-point moving average, so that each figure contains sales from each season:
18.25, 19, 19.5, 20.25, 20.5, 20.75, 21.25, 21.75, 22.5, 23.25, 24, 24.5, 25.5.

Answers: Chapter 10

d There is a general upward trend in sales of sun cream as more people become aware of the dangers of over-exposure. There is a seasonal variation as more sun cream is sold during the summer months.

g 14 − 18.0 = −4.0.
16 − 20.4 = −4.4.
18 − 22.7 = −4.7.
21 − 25.0 = −4.0.
Average second quarter seasonal components
$$\frac{-4 + (-4.4) + (-4.7) + (-4)}{4} = -4.3.$$

h 27.2 − 4.3 = 22.9.

10.3 Quality assurance

Exercise 10C

1 a 100.04 ml.
  b Yes because the sample mean is more than the amount of toothpaste that is stated as being in the tube.
  c As the sample mean is only 0.04% above the expected value then there is not really an issue for the manufacturer. However, if the manufacturer wished to prevent the marginal overfilling then further samples need to be taken to find out if this is the case and then the machine should be adjusted if necessary.

2 a Mean = 129.9 g.
  b Yes.
  c Yes, although the sample mean is within required limits, five of the tins are below the expected value.

3 a Mean = 415 g.
  b Median = 414 g.
  c The mean should be used to compare a sample with the quality limits as its value is effected by the value of each measurement. To prevent it being influenced by points outside of the tolerance, the range of points should be used in conjunction. The median has some use as it gives the midpoint figure for the sample.

4 a Mean = 1000 g (to 3 s.f.).
  b Median = 1000 g (to 3 s.f.).
  c Both the median and the mean imply that there is not a problem with the manufacturing process. However, there is large inconsistency in the amount of rice put into the bags. The range is 11 g. This indicates that there may be a problem with the manufacturing process.

5 a, b

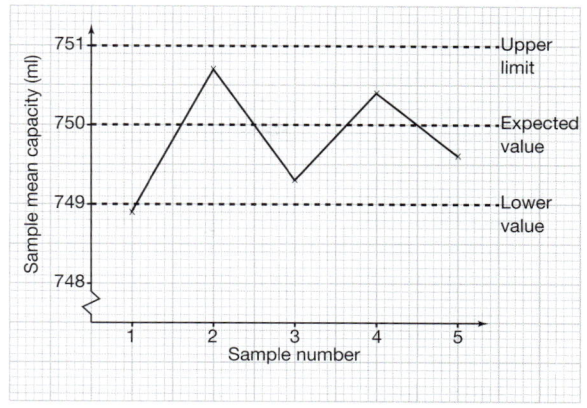

c Possibly, sample 1 is outside the tolerance limit, advice to manufacturer would be to take more samples and monitor the sample mean.
d By taking every 10th bottle it may be that the fault occurs every 10th bottle or that every 10th bottle is filled correctly when the rest are not, by nature of the process or design of the machine. It would be better to take a random sample.

6 a 1% of 30 g is 0.3 g, upper limit is 30.3 g, lower limit is 29.7 g.
  b, c

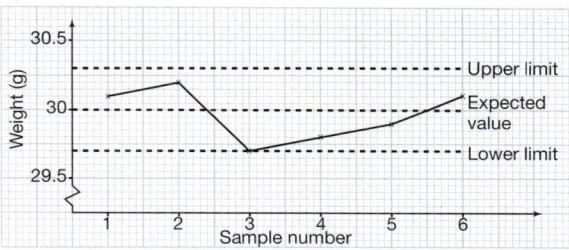

d No. All the samples are within acceptable limits for the machine but it would be advisable to continue to take further samples.

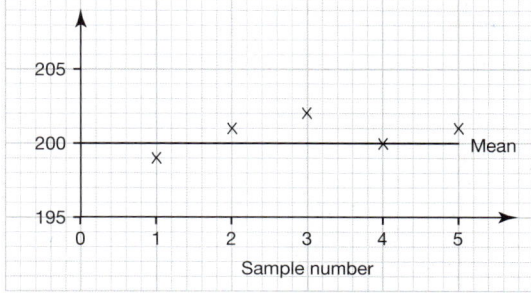

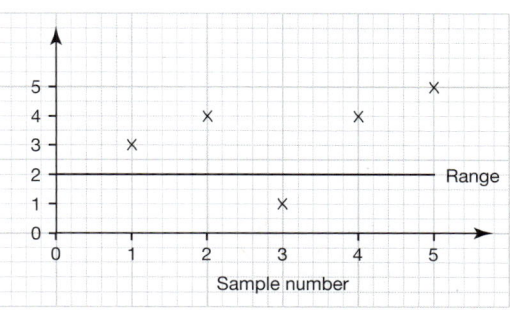

7 a

393

Answers: Chapter 10

b The mean graph does not indicate an immediate problem as all figures are with the acceptable range. There is an indication that the machine might be putting too many tablets into the containers.

The range graph confirms that there is too much inconsistency in the number of tablets put into the containers.

c The manufacturer may decide to take further samples to check the machine. However, the indications are that the machine needs to be reset to ensure greater consistency in the number of tablets being put into each container.

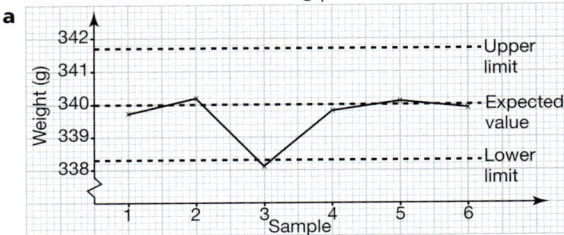

8 a [graph showing Weight (g) vs Sample with Upper limit, Expected value, Lower limit lines]

b One sample mean is outside the tolerance values. The rest are close to the mean value. Suggest taking another sample. If the mean of this sample is within the tolerance values, do nothing. If it isn't, then the machine needs to be adjusted.

Examination Questions

1 a Week 3.
 b 140.
 c Possible answer: it was just before the examination.
2 a £15.
 b 2001 and 2002.
3 a [graph of Takings (£) vs days across Week 1, Week 2, Week 3]

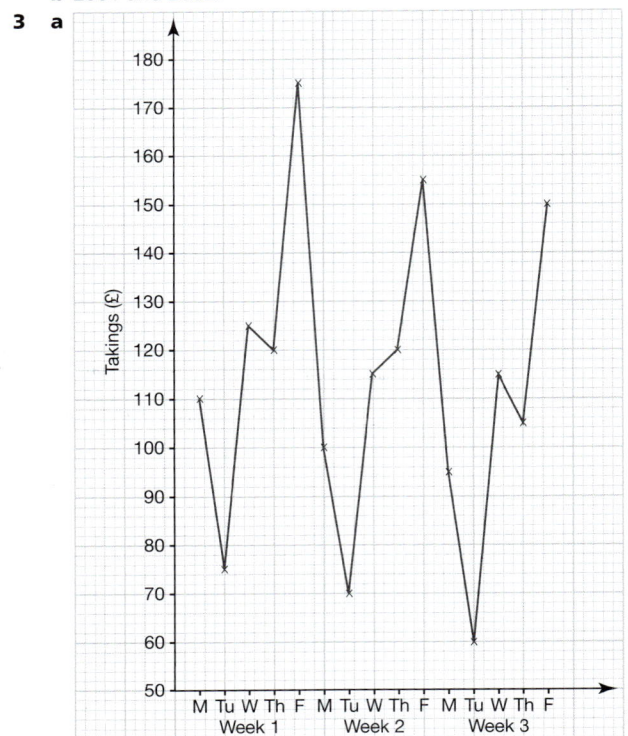

b Possible answer: the café closes early on Tuesdays.
c Takings are highest each Friday. Takings are reducing week by week.
4 a [graph of Sample mean weight (g) vs Sample number]

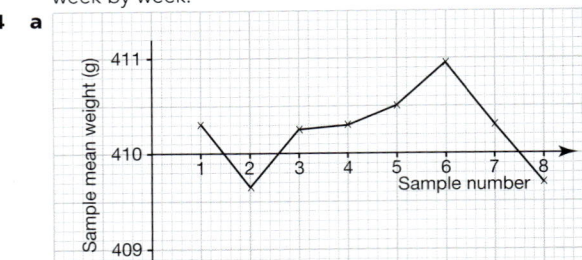

b The process was stopped and adjusted after taking sample 6 to slightly reduce the amount of food being filled into each tin.

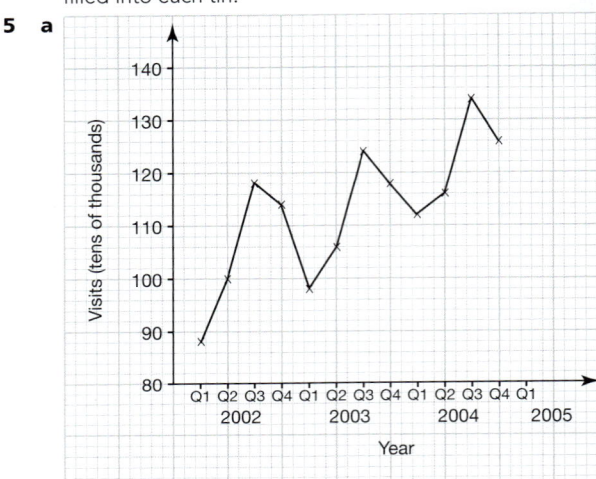

5 a [graph of Visits (tens of thousands) vs Year Q1–Q4 2002–2005]

b General increase over time. Peaks in Quarter 3 / troughs in Quarter 1.
c 112.5, 115, 117.5, 119.5.
d i, ii [graph with trend line through the quarterly data]

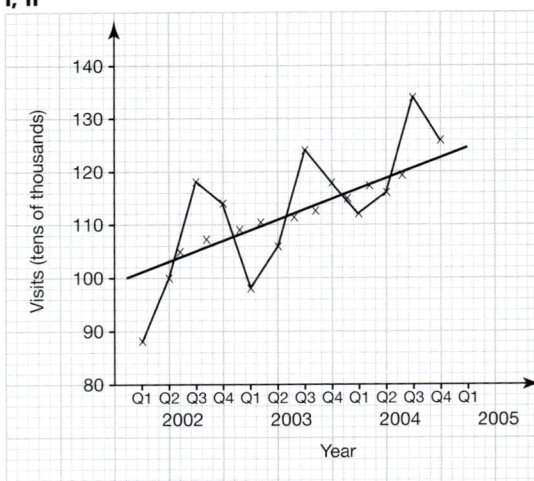

e From the trend line, the values are 14, 11 and 15, giving the average seasonal effect as 13.3.
f From the trend line, 124.5 – 13.3 = 111.2.

Answers: Chapter 11

11 Correlation and regression

Quick check

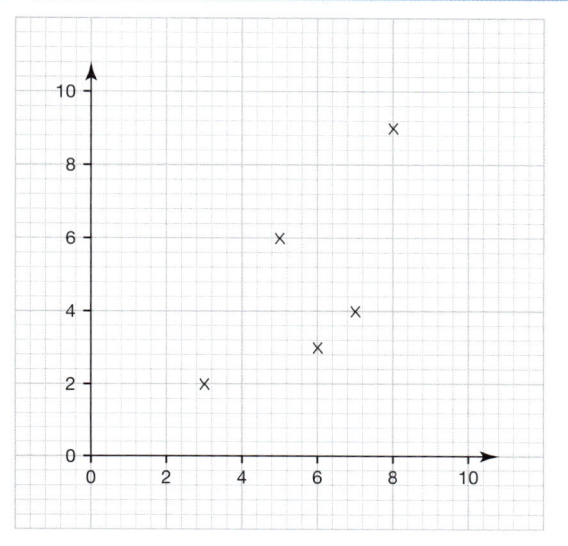

11.1 Scatter diagrams and correlation

Exercise 11A

1 **a** Positive correlation.
   b Negative correlation.
   c No correlation.
   d Positive correlation.
2 **a** A person's reaction time increases as more alcohol is consumed.
   b As people get older, they consume less alcohol.
   c There is no relationship between temperature and speed of cars on M1.
   d As people get older, they have more money in the bank.
3 **a, b**

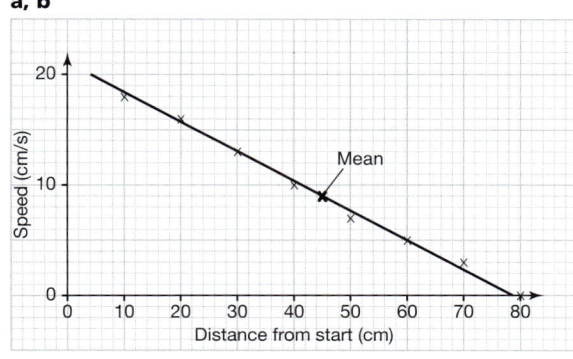

   c About 20 cm/s.
   d About 35 cm.
4 **a**

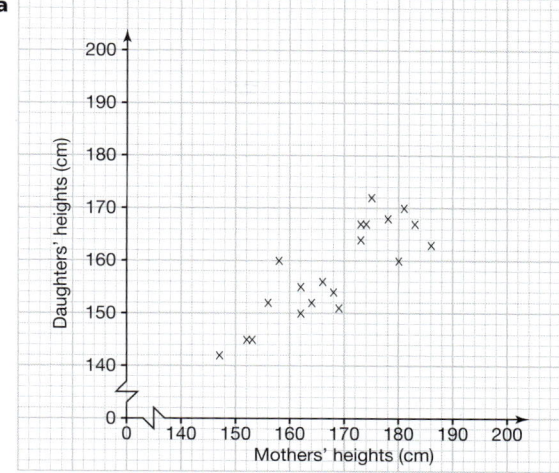

   b Yes, usually (good positive correlation).
5 **a**

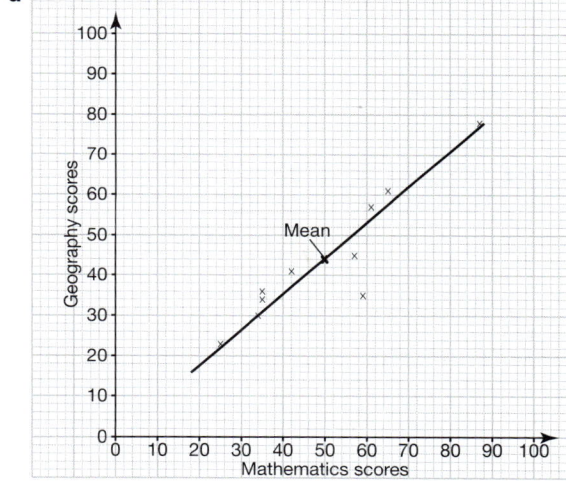

   b Mean (mathematics) = 50, Mean (geography) = 44.
   c Greta.
   d 66
   e 73
6 **a**

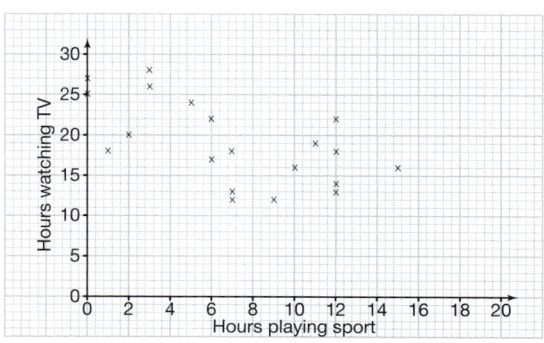

   b No, because there is little correlation (possibly a weak negative correlation).

395

Answers: Chapter 11

7 a

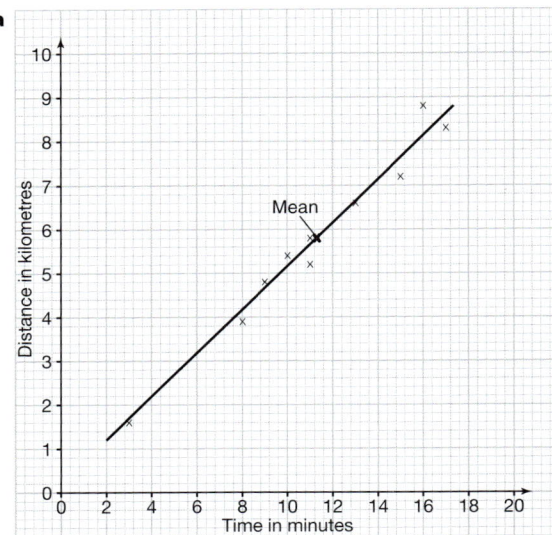

b Mean (distance) = 5.8 km, Mean (time) = 11.3 minutes.
c About 2.7 km.
d About 7.5 minutes.

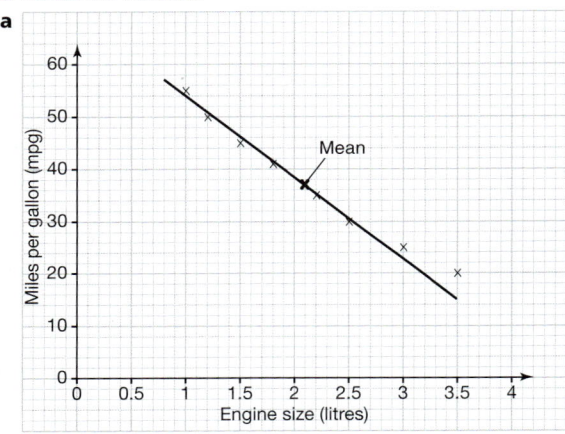

8 a

b Mean (engine size) = 2.1 litres, Mean (miles per gallon) = 37.6 mpg.
c $y = -15.5x + 70$.

9 He is not corrected to draw this conclusion as many factors could have caused the improvement, such as more training, better diet, better health. There is a correlation between his heart rate monitoring and his time trial results but that does not establish causality.

10 a

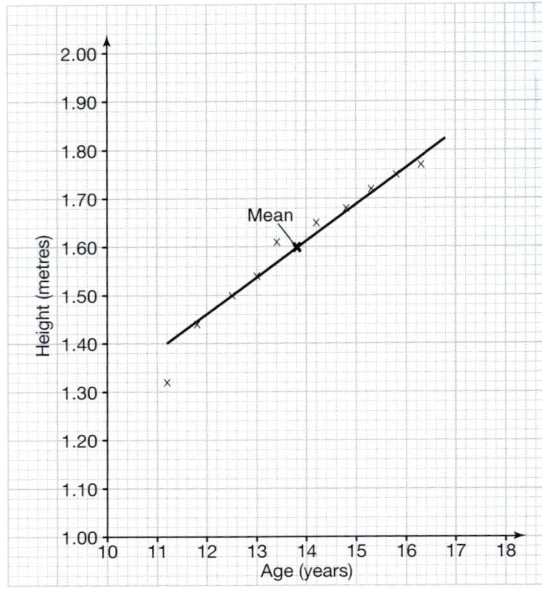

b Mean (age) = 13.8 years, Mean (height) = 1.60 metres.
c $y = 0.075x + 0.56$.
d The 25-year-old would have a height of 2.44 m, which would make him a giant. This is extrapolation, which is in this case not sensible. People do not usually continue growing after their late teens.

11.2 Spearman's rank and product moment correlation coefficients

Exercise 11B

1

Data sets	Spearman's rank correlation coefficient
Tyres: size against price	Fairly strong positive correlation (In most cases, the bigger the tyres, the higher the higher price.)
Age of car against resale value	Very strong negative correlation (The older the car, the less it's worth.)
Eye colour against IQ	Very weak positive correlation or no meaningful correlation (There is no relationship.)

2 a SRCC = 0.95.
b Very strong positive correlation – a high mark in English suggests a high mark in History, and vice versa.

Answers: Chapter 11

3 a

Hand (cm)	Shoe size	Hand rank	Shoe rank	Difference, d	d^2
12	3	10	10	0	0
16	5	8.5	8	0.5	0.25
19	10	4	3	1	1
16	4	8.5	9	−0.5	0.25
23	12	2	1	1	1
21	9	3	4	−1	1
25	11	1	2	−1	1
17	6	7	6.5	0.5	0.25
18	6	5.5	6.5	−1	1
18	7	5.5	5	0.5	0.25

b SRCC = $1 - \frac{36}{990} = 0.96$.
c Very strong positive correlation, larger hands implies larger feet.

4 a 0.78
b Strong positive correlation. Teams who concede fewer goals generally gain more points. John is correct.

5 a 0.93
b Very strong positive correlation – the theory was confirmed.

6 −0.04 so no meaningful correlation or very weak negative. Other unspecified factors as well as smoking influence life expectancy.

7 −0.87 so strong negative correlation, implying high GDP relates to low infant mortality. So yes, he is correct.

Examination Questions

1 a, d

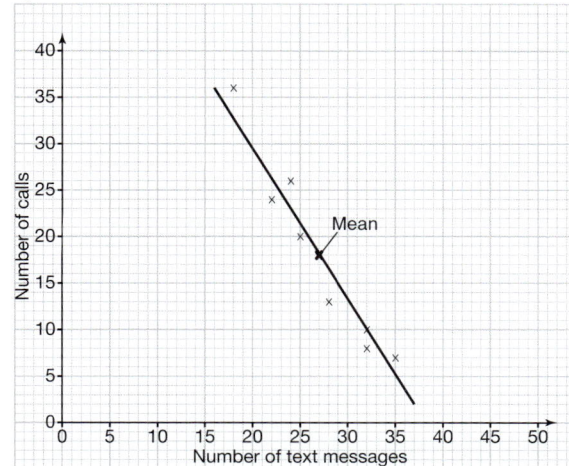

b Negative correlation.
c 144 ÷ 8 = 18 calls.
e 13 calls
f That would require extrapolation as the given value is outside the range of data.

2 a

Expert's rank	John's rank	d	d^2
1	8	−7	49
3	5	−2	4
6	2.5	3.5	12.25
7	4	3	9
8	1	7	49
3	6	−3	9
5	2.5	2.5	6.25
4	7	−3	9
		Σd^2	147.5

SRCC = $1 - \frac{885}{504} = -0.76$.

b Fairly strong negative correlation, John disagrees with the expert.
c i −0.02, 0.05.
ii 0.92

3 a Check student's graph.
b i £5300
ii For each employee, running costs increase by £5300.
c The estimate from the line of best fit is higher.

d

Number of employees	Annual running cost (£000)	Employees rank	Running costs rank	d	d^2
15	74	2	3	−1	1
13	87	3	2	1	1
17	94	1	1	0	0
8	41	5.5	6	−0.5	0.25
9	50	4	5	−1	1
8	53	5.5	4	1.5	2.25
6	25	7	8	−1	1
4	32	8	7	1	1
				Σd^2	7.5

SRCC = $1 - \frac{45}{504} = 0.91$.

4 a Check student's graph.
b 22 minutes.
c Check student's graph.
d i 41 minutes.
ii 19 minutes.
e The estimate for the bus, as it is an interpolation.
f 8 miles.
g Accept estimates anyway between 0.1 – 0.6.

h

Distance travelled	Time taken	Distance rank	Time rank	d	d^2
6	18	5	5.5	−0.5	0.25
7	23	4	4	0	0
2	11	7	7	0	0
10	36	1	1	0	0
5	18	6	5.5	0.5	0.25
9	31	2	3	−1	1
1	7	8	8	0	0
8	32	3	2	1	1
				Σd^2	2.5

SRCC = $1 - \frac{15}{504} = 0.97$.

i There is very strong correlation.

397

Answers: Chapter 12

5 a
Goal	A	B	C	D	E	F	G	H	I	J
Ahmed's rankings	9	4	6	3	10	2	8	1	5	7
Peter's rankings	7	6	1	4	8	3	9	5	2	10
d	2	−2	5	−1	2	−1	−1	−4	3	−3
d^2	4	4	25	1	4	1	1	16	9	9

SRCC = $1 - \frac{6 \times 74}{990}$ = 0.55.

b Moderate positive correlation so some agreement.

c Ahmed had a strong negative correlation to the winner so they had opposing views.
Peter had no correlation to the winner, little agreement at all.

12 Probability

Quick check

1   a $\frac{3}{4}$
    b $\frac{2}{3}$
    c $\frac{4}{7}$
    d $\frac{4}{7}$
    e $\frac{2}{3}$
2   a $\frac{5}{7}$
    b 1
    c $\frac{5}{8}$
    d $\frac{5}{12}$
    e $\frac{9}{15} = \frac{3}{5}$
3   bread – marmalade   toast – marmalade
    bread – strawberry jam toast – strawberry jam
    bread – peanut butter   toast – peanut butter

12.1 Probability scale

Exercise 12A

1   a Even chance.
    b Unlikely.
    c Likely.
    d Unlikely.
    e Certain.
    f Unlikely.
2   a Likely.
    b Impossible.
    c Unlikely.

d Even chance.

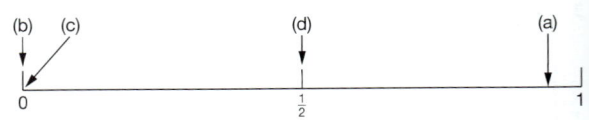

(b) (c) (d) (a)
0 — $\frac{1}{2}$ — 1

3   a Spinner A.
    b Spinner B.
    c Students draw a spinner which equal red and blue sections.

4   (a) (d) (c) (b)
0 — $\frac{1}{2}$ — 1

5
Event	Impossible	Certain	Likely	Unlikely
You will toss a coin and it lands on either heads or tails.		✓		
It will snow in London in the month of June.				✓
An athlete will run the 100 m race in less than a second.	✓			
It will rain some time in the next six months.			✓	
You will roll a dice and it lands on 7.	✓			

6   Students write down something that is likely to happen, but is not certain.
    They compare answers to decide whose event is more likely to happen.

7   Ben is wrong because the two outcomes are not necessarily equally likely.
    It is possible that his bus is on time more frequently than it is late, in which case the probability that it is late is less than 0.5. Alternatively, the bus might be late on more than half the occasions.

12.2 Equally likely outcomes

Exercise 12B

1   $\frac{1}{2}$
2   $\frac{1}{4}$
3   a $\frac{6}{11}$
    b $\frac{5}{11}$

398

4 a There are 12 blue pens.
  b i $\frac{8}{35}$
    ii $\frac{15}{35} = \frac{3}{7}$
    iii $\frac{12}{35}$
5 a $\frac{1}{6}$
  b $\frac{3}{6} = \frac{1}{2}$
  c $\frac{3}{6} = \frac{1}{2}$
  d $\frac{6}{6} = 1$
  e $\frac{1}{6}$
6 a $\frac{1}{20}$
  b $\frac{10}{20} = \frac{1}{2}$
  c $\frac{5}{20} = \frac{1}{4}$
7 a $\frac{60}{100} = \frac{3}{5}$
  b $\frac{30}{100} = \frac{3}{10}$
  c $\frac{8}{100} = \frac{2}{25}$
  d $\frac{2}{100} = \frac{1}{50}$
  e 0
8 a $\frac{1}{52}$
  b $\frac{13}{52} = \frac{1}{4}$
  c $\frac{26}{52} = \frac{1}{2}$
  d $\frac{4}{52} = \frac{1}{13}$
  e $1 - \frac{1}{13} = \frac{12}{13}$
9 a $\frac{10}{5000} = \frac{1}{500}$
  b $\frac{50}{5000} = \frac{1}{100}$
  c $\frac{150}{5000} = \frac{3}{100}$
  d $\frac{50}{5000} = \frac{1}{100}$
  e $1 - \frac{100}{5000} = \frac{49}{50}$
10 $\frac{4}{8} = \frac{1}{2}$
11 a $\frac{1}{6}$
   b By throwing a 1 or a 4; $\frac{2}{6} = \frac{1}{3}$.
   c By throwing a 2, or 6; $\frac{2}{6} = \frac{1}{3}$.

12.3 The addition rule for events

Exercise 12C

1 a $\frac{1}{6}$
  b $\frac{1}{2}$
  c $\frac{2}{3}$
2 a $\frac{1}{13}$
  b $\frac{1}{52}$
  c $\frac{5}{52}$
3 a $\frac{1}{3}$
  b $\frac{1}{4}$
  c $\frac{5}{12}$
  d $\frac{3}{4}$
4 a i $\frac{3}{5}$
    ii $\frac{2}{5}$
  b $\frac{4}{15}$

5 a 0.02
  b Fifteen times.
6 a $\frac{5}{25} + \frac{1}{5}$
  b $\frac{12}{25}$
  c $\frac{3}{25}$
  d $\frac{15}{25} = \frac{3}{5}$
7 a $\frac{1}{52}$
  b $\frac{1}{4}$
  c $\frac{1}{2}$
  d $\frac{7}{26}$
  e $\frac{27}{52}$
8 P(Mike) = 0.4, P(Debbie) = 0.3, P(Alice) = 0.3.
  Mike is the most likely to win.
9 P(Alison) = $\frac{3}{8} = \frac{15}{40}$. P(Cat) = $\frac{13}{40}$. P(Beth) = $\frac{12}{40} = \frac{3}{10}$.
  Alison is most likely to get elected.
10 a $\frac{1}{16}$
   b $\frac{3}{8}$
   c $\frac{1}{4}$
   d $\frac{5}{16}$
   e Noah is wrong because the letter 'a' is in his name and is blue, so they are not mutually exclusive.

11
Type	Probability	Number of tracks
Rock	7/30	28
Hip–hop	8/30	32
Soul	5/30	20
R&B	10/30	40

12.4 Experimental probability

Exercise 12D

1 a A dropped drawing pin will land point down is (B) using a survey or experiment.
  b The next car past the school will be blue is (B) using a survey or experiment.
  c A card chosen from a pack of cards will be a Heart is (A) using equally likely outcomes.
  d You will come top in the next maths test is (C) looking at historical data.
2 All decimals below are given to 2 decimal places.
  a $\frac{1}{6} = 0.17$.
  b i $\frac{1}{5} = 0.20$.
    ii $\frac{9}{50} = 0.18$.
    iii $\frac{31}{200} = 0.16$.
    iv $\frac{96}{600} = \frac{4}{25} = 0.16$.
  c His dice is probably fair. The experimental probability is settling on 0.16 as the number of trials increases.
3 The spinner is more likely to land on the longer sides, making even scores more likely than odd scores.

Answers: Chapter 12

4 The experimental probabilities multiplied by number of counters suggests:
RED: 0.29 × 17 = 4.93. Likely number of counters = 5
BLUE: 0.19 × 17 = 3.23. Likely number of counters = 3
BLACK: 0.4 × 17 = 6.80. Likely number of counters = 7
WHITE: 0.12 × 17 = 2.04. Likely number of counters = 2

5 a Alice's results are likely to be most accurate, as she performed the experiment the most times.
  b i $\frac{113}{257}$ = 0.4396 … = 0.44 (to 2 d.p.).
  ii $\frac{240}{547}$ = 0.4387 … = 0.44 (to 2 d.p.).

6 a The experimental probabilities are:
  1: 0.142
  2: 0.204
  3: 0.134
  4: 0.198
  5: 0.128
  6: 0.194
  The even numbers (mean = 0.199) are significantly higher than the odd numbers (mean = 0.135).
  (The even numbers all meet at a vertex on a dice, as do the odd numbers, suggesting that the dice is weighted at the odd vertex.)
  b $\frac{71 + 204 + 201 + 396 + 320 + 582}{500}$ = 3.548.
  c 3.5
  The bias is hidden because it is not just high or low scores that occur more frequently than expected.

7 Experimental probabilities in brackets:

	1	2	3	4	5	6
Tom	9 (0.225)	8 (0.200)	5 (0.125)	10 (0.250)	2 (0.050)	6 (0.150)
Sue	34 (0.159)	36 (0.168)	29 (0.136)	41 (0.192)	33 (0.154)	41 (0.192)
Jenny	29 (0.238)	19 (0.156)	18 (0.148)	22 (0.180)	23 (0.189)	11 (0.090)

Tom's sample of 40 is far too small to allow a decision to be made, despite there being very few fives.
Sue's results have experimental probabilities ranging from 0.136 to 0.192 and, given the large sample size, suggest there might be some bias. However, from a sample of 214, we might expect approximately 36 of each number. The greatest discrepancy is only 7 less than this.
Jenny's sample of 122 might still be a little small, but nearly a quarter of all throws ended on 1, and less than one tenth landed on 6. As these are on opposite sides of the dice, it suggests there is probably some bias, but more data should be collected first.

8 Tanya is correct.

9 All could suggest bias; the table shows the sample size, number of possible outcomes and theoretical and experimental probabilities.

	Sample size	Possible outcomes	Theoretical probability	Experimental probability
A	10	2	0.5	0.3
B	100	5	0.2	0.09
C	20	6	0.167	0.25

B is the experiment that suggests bias the most, due to the large sample size.

10 a $\frac{1}{4}$ = 0.25.
  b $\frac{26}{100}$ = 0.26.
  c $\frac{3}{16}$ = 0.1875.
  d $\frac{21}{100}$ = 0.21.
  e The evidence suggests that the spinner is not biased, as the experimental and theoretical frequencies are similar.

12.5 Combined events

Exercise 12E

1 a i $\frac{3}{36} = \frac{1}{12}$
  ii 0
  iii $\frac{18}{36} = \frac{1}{2}$
  iv $\frac{15}{36} = \frac{5}{12}$
  b 5

2 a $\frac{1}{24}$
  b $\frac{2}{24} = \frac{1}{12}$
  c $\frac{12}{24} = \frac{1}{2}$
  d $\frac{11}{24}$

3 a i $\frac{4}{36} = \frac{1}{9}$
  ii $\frac{6}{36} = \frac{1}{6}$
  iii $\frac{18}{36} = \frac{1}{2}$
  b 1 has a probability of $\frac{10}{36} = \frac{5}{18}$.

4 a $\frac{3}{21} = \frac{1}{7}$
  b $\frac{11}{21}$
  c $\frac{15}{21} = \frac{5}{7}$

5 a $\frac{1}{4}$
  b $\frac{3}{4}$

6 a i $\frac{1}{20}$
  ii $\frac{2}{20} = \frac{1}{10}$
  iii 0
  b 4; $\frac{3}{20}$

7 a $\frac{1}{12}$
  b $\frac{1}{4}$
  c $\frac{3}{12} = \frac{1}{4}$
  d $\frac{5}{12}$

8 She should choose two four-sided dice, as the probability is $\frac{1}{4}$. Two six-sided dice and one of each both give a probability of $\frac{1}{6}$.

9 $\frac{3}{12} = \frac{1}{4}$

Answers: Chapter 12

10 The sample space diagram shows his gains and losses in pence.

		Red dice					
		1	2	3	4	5	6
Blue dice	1	50	−50	0	50	50	50
	2	−50	50	0	50	50	50
	3	0	0	−450	0	0	0
	4	50	50	0	50	50	50
	5	50	50	0	50	50	50
	6	50	50	0	50	50	50

Over the 36 equally likely outcomes, he stands to raise £6, or an average of £1 every six throws.
Another solution would be to identify the winning throws.

		Red dice					
		1	2	3	4	5	6
Blue dice	1		£1	50p			
	2	£1		50p			
	3	50p	50p	£5	50p	50p	50p
	4			50p			
	5			50p			
	6			50p			

Income: 36 × 50p = £18.
Expenditure: £12.
Profit: £6.

12.6 Expectation

Exercise 12F

1 20
2 a $\frac{1}{4}$
  b $\frac{1}{13}$
  c About 33.
  d 10
3 a 20
  b 36
4 25 red balls, 15 green balls and 20 yellow balls.
5 a 0.15
  b 10 ones, 4 twos, 12 threes, 8 fours, 6 fives.
6 21 dry days.
7 50 light bulbs.
8 £6
9 About 33.
10 5000 tickets.

12.7 Two-way tables and Venn diagrams

Exercise 12G

1 a

	Car	Bike
Blue	2	6
Green	4	2

  b $\frac{6}{14} = \frac{3}{7}$

2

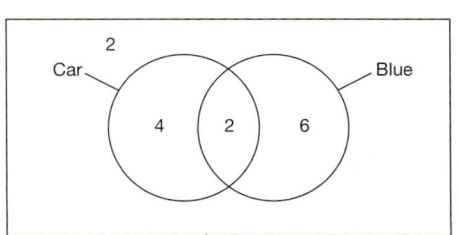

(Venn diagram: Car circle contains 4, overlap contains 2, Blue circle contains 6; outside 2)

3 a

		Dice score					
		1	2	3	4	5	6
Coin	Head	2	4	6	8	10	12
	Tails	0	1	2	3	4	5

  b $\frac{3}{12} = \frac{1}{4}$
4 a 25
  b 16
  c $\frac{26}{54} = \frac{13}{27}$
  d $\frac{5}{28}$
5 a 20
  b $\frac{5}{20} = \frac{1}{4}$
  c $\frac{3}{20}$
  d $\frac{5}{20} = \frac{1}{4}$
  e $\frac{2}{5}$
6 a 36
  b $\frac{21}{36} = \frac{7}{12}$
  c $\frac{29}{36}$
  d $\frac{3}{15} = \frac{1}{5}$
7 a $\frac{153}{207} = \frac{17}{23}$
  b $\frac{46}{207} = \frac{2}{9}$
  c $\frac{34}{207}$
  d $\frac{135}{207} = \frac{15}{23}$
8 $\frac{6}{24} = \frac{1}{4}$
9 a 10
  b $\frac{10}{26} = \frac{5}{13}$
  c $\frac{1}{26}$
  d $\frac{5}{26}$
  e $\frac{5}{26}$

401

Answers: Chapter 12

10 a

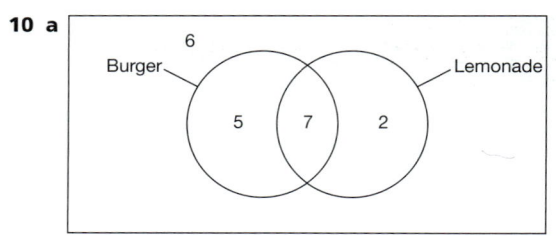

[Venn diagram: Burger circle contains 5, intersection 7, Lemonade circle contains 2, outside 6]

b $\frac{7}{20}$

11 a 103

b Science had 63.

c $\frac{57}{103}$

d i $\frac{32}{58} = \frac{16}{29}$

ii $\frac{38}{58} = \frac{19}{29}$

12.8 Tree diagrams

Exercise 12H

1 a

First flip	Second flip	Outcome	Probability
Head ($\frac{1}{2}$)	Head ($\frac{1}{2}$)	Head Head	$\frac{1}{2} \times \frac{1}{2} = \frac{1}{4}$
Head ($\frac{1}{2}$)	Tail ($\frac{1}{2}$)	Head Tail	$\frac{1}{2} \times \frac{1}{2} = \frac{1}{4}$
Tail ($\frac{1}{2}$)	Head ($\frac{1}{2}$)	Tail Head	$\frac{1}{2} \times \frac{1}{2} = \frac{1}{4}$
Tail ($\frac{1}{2}$)	Tail ($\frac{1}{2}$)	Tail Tail	$\frac{1}{2} \times \frac{1}{2} = \frac{1}{4}$

b $\frac{1}{4}$

c $\frac{3}{4}$

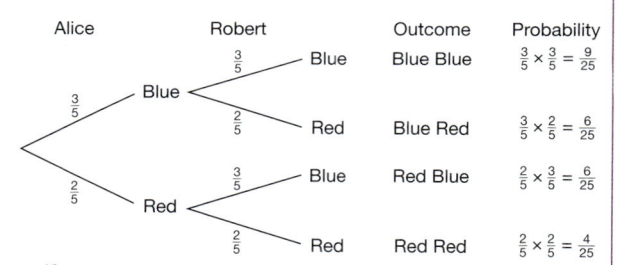

2 a

Alice	Robert	Outcome	Probability
Blue ($\frac{3}{5}$)	Blue ($\frac{3}{5}$)	Blue Blue	$\frac{3}{5} \times \frac{3}{5} = \frac{9}{25}$
Blue ($\frac{3}{5}$)	Red ($\frac{2}{5}$)	Blue Red	$\frac{3}{5} \times \frac{2}{5} = \frac{6}{25}$
Red ($\frac{2}{5}$)	Blue ($\frac{3}{5}$)	Red Blue	$\frac{2}{5} \times \frac{3}{5} = \frac{6}{25}$
Red ($\frac{2}{5}$)	Red ($\frac{2}{5}$)	Red Red	$\frac{2}{5} \times \frac{2}{5} = \frac{4}{25}$

b $\frac{13}{25}$

3

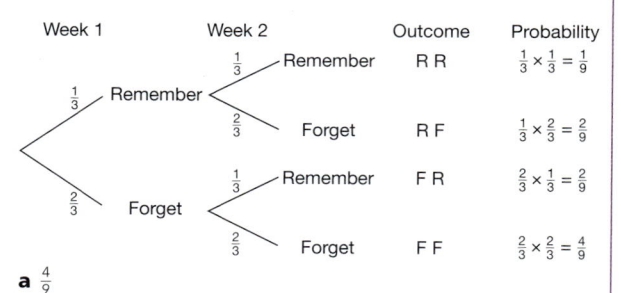

Week 1	Week 2	Outcome	Probability
Remember ($\frac{1}{3}$)	Remember ($\frac{1}{3}$)	R R	$\frac{1}{3} \times \frac{1}{3} = \frac{1}{9}$
Remember ($\frac{1}{3}$)	Forget ($\frac{2}{3}$)	R F	$\frac{1}{3} \times \frac{2}{3} = \frac{2}{9}$
Forget ($\frac{2}{3}$)	Remember ($\frac{1}{3}$)	F R	$\frac{2}{3} \times \frac{1}{3} = \frac{2}{9}$
Forget ($\frac{2}{3}$)	Forget ($\frac{2}{3}$)	F F	$\frac{2}{3} \times \frac{2}{3} = \frac{4}{9}$

a $\frac{4}{9}$

b $\frac{1}{9}$

c $\frac{4}{9}$

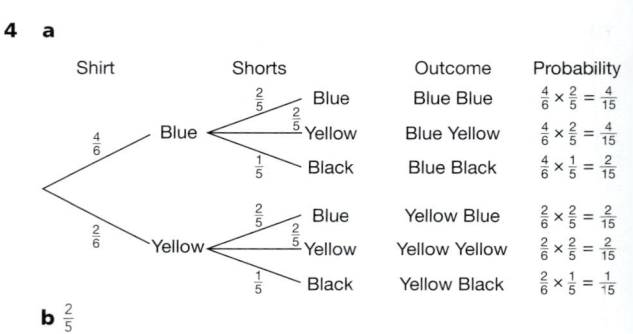

4 a

Shirt	Shorts	Outcome	Probability
Blue ($\frac{4}{6}$)	Blue ($\frac{2}{5}$)	Blue Blue	$\frac{4}{6} \times \frac{2}{5} = \frac{4}{15}$
Blue ($\frac{4}{6}$)	Yellow ($\frac{2}{5}$)	Blue Yellow	$\frac{4}{6} \times \frac{2}{5} = \frac{4}{15}$
Blue ($\frac{4}{6}$)	Black ($\frac{1}{5}$)	Blue Black	$\frac{4}{6} \times \frac{1}{5} = \frac{2}{15}$
Yellow ($\frac{2}{6}$)	Blue ($\frac{2}{5}$)	Yellow Blue	$\frac{2}{6} \times \frac{2}{5} = \frac{2}{15}$
Yellow ($\frac{2}{6}$)	Yellow ($\frac{2}{5}$)	Yellow Yellow	$\frac{2}{6} \times \frac{2}{5} = \frac{2}{15}$
Yellow ($\frac{2}{6}$)	Black ($\frac{1}{5}$)	Yellow Black	$\frac{2}{6} \times \frac{1}{5} = \frac{1}{15}$

b $\frac{2}{5}$

c $\frac{2}{5}$

5 a

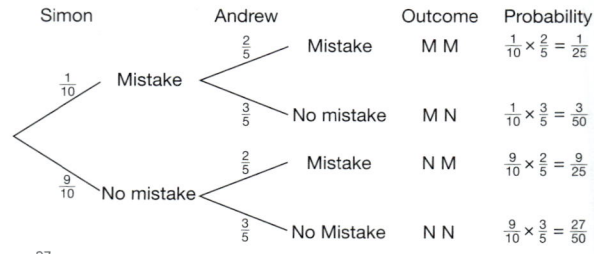

Simon	Andrew	Outcome	Probability
Mistake ($\frac{1}{10}$)	Mistake ($\frac{2}{5}$)	M M	$\frac{1}{10} \times \frac{2}{5} = \frac{1}{25}$
Mistake ($\frac{1}{10}$)	No mistake ($\frac{3}{5}$)	M N	$\frac{1}{10} \times \frac{3}{5} = \frac{3}{50}$
No mistake ($\frac{9}{10}$)	Mistake ($\frac{2}{5}$)	N M	$\frac{9}{10} \times \frac{2}{5} = \frac{9}{25}$
No mistake ($\frac{9}{10}$)	No Mistake ($\frac{3}{5}$)	N N	$\frac{9}{10} \times \frac{3}{5} = \frac{27}{50}$

b $\frac{27}{50}$

c $\frac{23}{50}$

6 a $\frac{1}{10}$

b $\frac{1}{2}$

c

Psychology	Sociology	Outcome	Probability
D ($\frac{1}{5}$)	D ($\frac{1}{3}$)	D D	$\frac{1}{5} \times \frac{1}{3} = \frac{1}{15}$
D ($\frac{1}{5}$)	P ($\frac{1}{2}$)	D P	$\frac{1}{5} \times \frac{1}{2} = \frac{1}{10}$
D ($\frac{1}{5}$)	F ($\frac{1}{6}$)	D F	$\frac{1}{5} \times \frac{1}{6} = \frac{1}{30}$
P ($\frac{7}{10}$)	D ($\frac{1}{3}$)	P D	$\frac{7}{10} \times \frac{1}{3} = \frac{7}{30}$
P ($\frac{7}{10}$)	P ($\frac{1}{2}$)	P P	$\frac{7}{10} \times \frac{1}{2} = \frac{7}{20}$
P ($\frac{7}{10}$)	F ($\frac{1}{6}$)	P F	$\frac{7}{10} \times \frac{1}{6} = \frac{7}{60}$
F ($\frac{1}{10}$)	D ($\frac{1}{3}$)	F D	$\frac{1}{10} \times \frac{1}{3} = \frac{1}{30}$
F ($\frac{1}{10}$)	P ($\frac{1}{2}$)	F P	$\frac{1}{10} \times \frac{1}{2} = \frac{1}{20}$
F ($\frac{1}{10}$)	F ($\frac{1}{6}$)	F F	$\frac{1}{10} \times \frac{1}{6} = \frac{1}{60}$

d $\frac{3}{4}$

e $\frac{7}{15}$

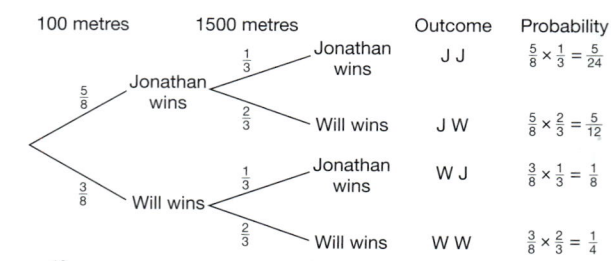

7 a

100 metres	1500 metres	Outcome	Probability
Jonathan wins ($\frac{5}{8}$)	Jonathan wins ($\frac{1}{3}$)	J J	$\frac{5}{8} \times \frac{1}{3} = \frac{5}{24}$
Jonathan wins ($\frac{5}{8}$)	Will wins ($\frac{2}{3}$)	J W	$\frac{5}{8} \times \frac{2}{3} = \frac{5}{12}$
Will wins ($\frac{3}{8}$)	Jonathan wins ($\frac{1}{3}$)	W J	$\frac{3}{8} \times \frac{1}{3} = \frac{1}{8}$
Will wins ($\frac{3}{8}$)	Will wins ($\frac{2}{3}$)	W W	$\frac{3}{8} \times \frac{2}{3} = \frac{1}{4}$

b $\frac{13}{24}$

c 22 times.

Answers: Chapter 12

8

Tree diagram:
- Captain Male 4/7 → Press Officer Male 2/7 → M M, $\frac{4}{7} \times \frac{2}{7} = \frac{8}{49}$
- Captain Male 4/7 → Press Officer Female 5/7 → M F, $\frac{4}{7} \times \frac{5}{7} = \frac{20}{49}$
- Captain Female 3/7 → Press Officer Male 2/7 → F M, $\frac{3}{7} \times \frac{2}{7} = \frac{6}{49}$
- Captain Female 3/7 → Press Officer Female 5/7 → F F, $\frac{3}{7} \times \frac{5}{7} = \frac{15}{49}$

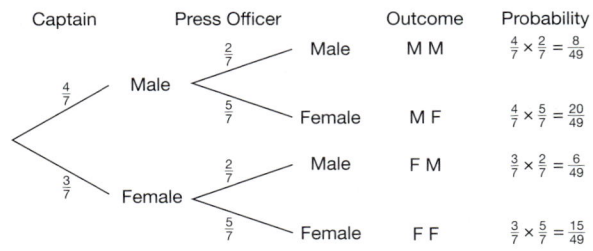

The probability that they choose a captain and press officer of the same gender is $\frac{23}{49}$.

9 a

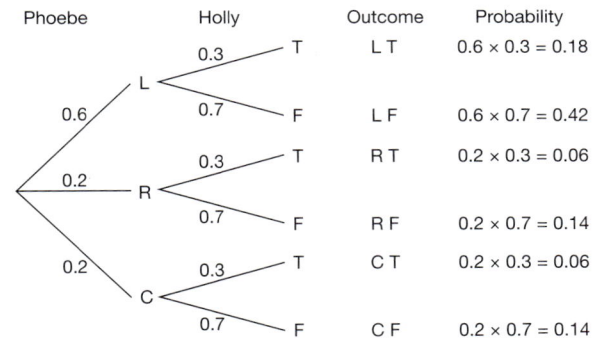

Tree diagram:
- Phoebe L 0.6 → Holly T 0.3 → L T, $0.6 \times 0.3 = 0.18$
- Phoebe L 0.6 → Holly F 0.7 → L F, $0.6 \times 0.7 = 0.42$
- Phoebe R 0.2 → Holly T 0.3 → R T, $0.2 \times 0.3 = 0.06$
- Phoebe R 0.2 → Holly F 0.7 → R F, $0.2 \times 0.7 = 0.14$
- Phoebe C 0.2 → Holly T 0.3 → C T, $0.2 \times 0.3 = 0.06$
- Phoebe C 0.2 → Holly F 0.7 → C F, $0.2 \times 0.7 = 0.14$

b $0.42 + 0.14 = 0.56$.

10 a

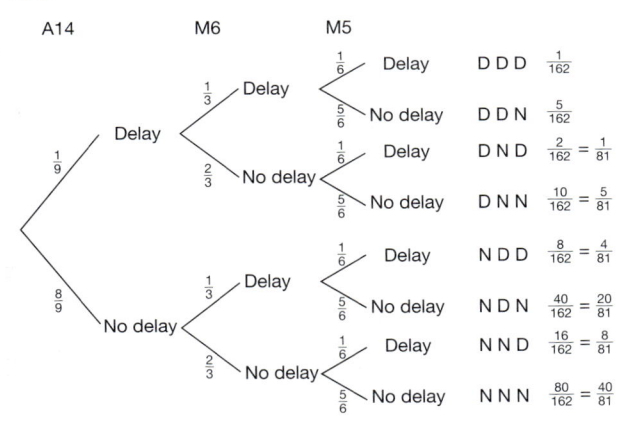

A14 → M6 → M5 tree:
- Delay 1/9 → Delay 1/3 → Delay 1/6 → D D D, $\frac{1}{162}$
- Delay 1/9 → Delay 1/3 → No delay 5/6 → D D N, $\frac{5}{162}$
- Delay 1/9 → No delay 2/3 → Delay 1/6 → D N D, $\frac{2}{162} = \frac{1}{81}$
- Delay 1/9 → No delay 2/3 → No delay 5/6 → D N N, $\frac{10}{162} = \frac{5}{81}$
- No delay 8/9 → Delay 1/3 → Delay 1/6 → N D D, $\frac{8}{162} = \frac{4}{81}$
- No delay 8/9 → Delay 1/3 → No delay 5/6 → N D N, $\frac{40}{162} = \frac{20}{81}$
- No delay 8/9 → No delay 2/3 → Delay 1/6 → N N D, $\frac{16}{162} = \frac{8}{81}$
- No delay 8/9 → No delay 2/3 → No delay 5/6 → N N N, $\frac{80}{162} = \frac{40}{81}$

b

A12 → M25 → M4 tree:
- Delay 1/8 → Delay 1/4 → Delay 1/12 → D D D, $\frac{1}{384}$
- Delay 1/8 → Delay 1/4 → No delay 11/12 → D D N, $\frac{11}{384}$
- Delay 1/8 → No delay 3/4 → Delay 1/12 → D N D, $\frac{3}{384} = \frac{1}{128}$
- Delay 1/8 → No delay 3/4 → No delay 11/12 → D N N, $\frac{33}{384} = \frac{11}{128}$
- No delay 7/8 → Delay 1/4 → Delay 1/12 → N D D, $\frac{7}{384}$
- No delay 7/8 → Delay 1/4 → No delay 11/12 → N D N, $\frac{77}{384}$
- No delay 7/8 → No delay 3/4 → Delay 1/12 → N N D, $\frac{21}{384} = \frac{7}{128}$
- No delay 7/8 → No delay 3/4 → No delay 11/12 → N N N, $\frac{231}{384} = \frac{77}{128}$

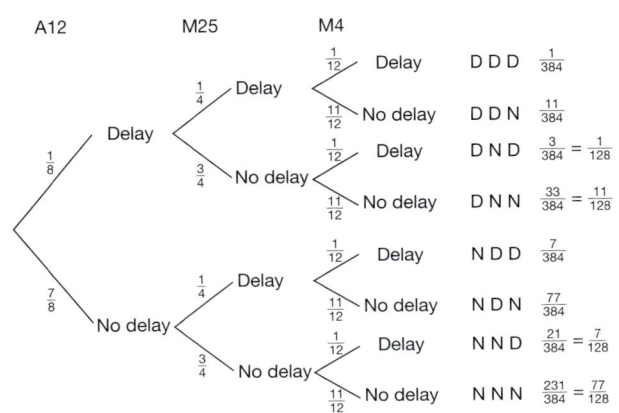

c Alison should take the A12, M25, M4 route.

12.9 Conditional probability

Exercise 12I

1 a $\frac{1}{56}$
  b $\frac{1}{28}$

2 a $\frac{6}{55}$
  b $\frac{27}{55}$
  c $\frac{28}{55}$

3 a $\frac{3}{5}$
  b $\frac{3}{10}$
  c No, it is the same.

4 a $\frac{9}{20}$
  b $\frac{4}{15}$
  c $\frac{17}{60}$

5 a $\frac{5}{18}$
  b $\frac{17}{18}$

6 $\frac{3}{40} \times \frac{2}{39} \times \frac{1}{38} = \frac{1}{9880}$

7 $\frac{7}{15}$

8 a $\frac{1}{30}$
  b $\frac{1}{15}$
  c 0
  d $\frac{2}{15}$
  e $\frac{1}{15}$

9 a

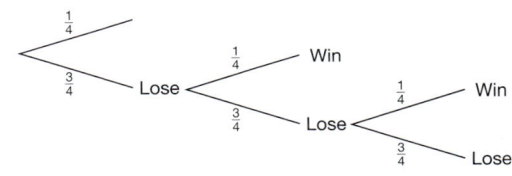

Tree diagram:
- 1/4 → Win
- 3/4 → Lose → 1/4 → Win
- 3/4 → Lose → 3/4 → Lose → 1/4 → Win
- 3/4 → Lose → 3/4 → Lose → 3/4 → Lose

b $\frac{3}{16}$
c $\frac{37}{64}$

10 a $\frac{17}{45}$
b Only 3, when the probability is $\frac{8}{15}$

Examination Questions

1

	Probability
Impossible	0
Likely	0.7
Certain	1
Unlikely	0.25
Even chance	0.5

403

Answers: Chapter 12

2 a i $\frac{1}{6}$
  ii $\frac{1}{2}$
  b i

	1	2	3	4	5	6
0	0	0	0	0	0	0
1	1	2	3	4	5	6
2	2	4	6	8	10	12
3	3	6	9	12	15	18
4	4	8	12	16	20	24
5	5	10	15	20	25	30

  ii From the sample space diagram, there are 9 scores of 15 or more out of a total of 36 scores.
  Therefore, probability of scoring 15 or more = $\frac{9}{36} = \frac{1}{4}$

3 a $\frac{45}{100} = \frac{3}{10}$
  b $\frac{95}{150} = \frac{19}{30}$
  c $\frac{22}{150} = \frac{11}{75}$
  d $\frac{80}{150} = \frac{8}{15}$

4 a No. The line graph implies continuous data whereas the score of a dice is discrete data.
  b Yes. The bar graph is ideal for discrete data as the gaps between each bar reinforces the fact that the scoring data is not continuous.
  c i 2 out of 20.
  ii 0.1
  iii 0.167

5 a P(teenager) = $\frac{3}{10}$ = 0.3
  b 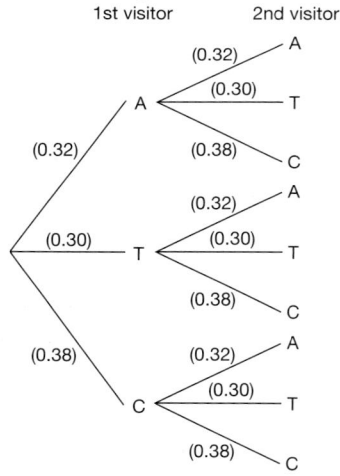

  1st visitor   2nd visitor

  (0.32) A ─ (0.32) A
         ├ (0.30) T
         └ (0.38) C
  (0.30) T ─ (0.32) A
         ├ (0.30) T
         └ (0.38) C
  (0.38) C ─ (0.32) A
         ├ (0.30) T
         └ (0.38) C

  P(both teenagers) = 0.3 × 0.3 = 0.09
  c Assumed that the order of visitors are independent events; the age of the first visitor does not influence the age of the second visitor.

6 a

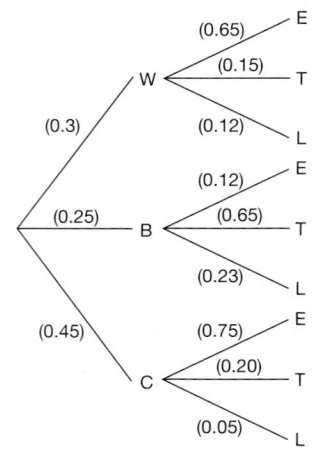

(0.3) W ─ (0.65) E
       ├ (0.15) T
       └ (0.12) L
(0.25) B ─ (0.12) E
       ├ (0.65) T
       └ (0.23) L
(0.45) C ─ (0.75) E
       ├ (0.20) T
       └ (0.05) L

  b P(early or on-time) = 1 − P(late).
  P(late) = (0.3 × 0.2) + (0.25 × 0.23) + (0.45 × 0.05)
  P(late) = 0.06 + 0.0575 + 0.0225
  P(late) = 0.14
  Therefore,
  P(early or on-time) = 1 − 0.14 = 0.86
  c P(early or on-time by car) = 1 − P(late by car) = 1 − 0.0225 = 0.9775
  d

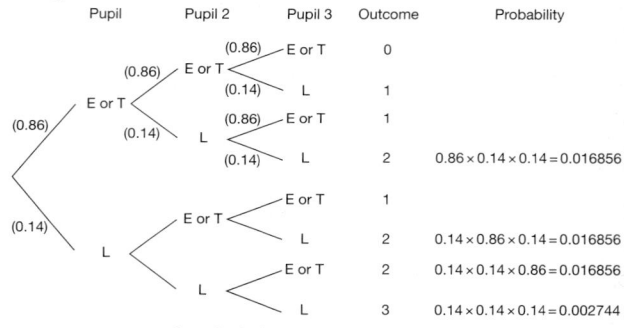

Pupil	Pupil 2	Pupil 3	Outcome	Probability
(0.86) E or T	(0.86) E or T	(0.86) E or T	0	
		(0.14) L	1	
	(0.14) L	(0.86) E or T	1	
		(0.14) L	2	0.86 × 0.14 × 0.14 = 0.016856
(0.14) L	E or T	E or T	1	
		L	2	0.14 × 0.86 × 0.14 = 0.016856
	L	E or T	2	0.14 × 0.14 × 0.86 = 0.016856
		L	3	0.14 × 0.14 × 0.14 = 0.002744

  Estimate of probability = 0.053312 = 0.05 (to 1 d.p.) = 5%

7 a

	Hardback	Softback	Total
Fiction	124	1820	1944
Non-fiction	341	239	580
Classics	155	21	176
Total	620	2080	2700

  b i $\frac{239}{2700}$
  ii $\frac{1200}{2700} = \frac{4}{9}$
  iii $\frac{1820}{2080} = \frac{7}{8}$
  c $\frac{155}{2700} \times 200 = 11.48$
  As the number of books is discrete data and can only be whole numbers, you would expect 11 hardback classics to be taken out of the first 200 books.

Glossary

Bar line graph A graph that uses lines instead of bars to represent data. A bar line graph drawn vertically is known as a vertical line graph.

Bivariate data Data sets that use two variables.

Categorical data Data that has already been put into categories or classified in some way.

Causality The relationship between an event and a second event.

Chain base method The chain base method compares current prices to those of the previous year rather than the base year.

Choropleth maps Maps in which areas are shaded differently, to illustrate a distribution.

Class width The difference between the upper and lower boundaries of any class.

Closed question Questions that have specific answers that can be chosen from a list.

Cluster sampling A sampling technique in which groups are randomly selected, used when the population can be put into (or falls naturally into) groups.

Comparative pie chart Used to compare two sets of data. The areas of the circles must be *in proportion* to the two total frequencies.

Consumer price index A measure of the cost of all goods and services to a typical consumer.

Continuous data Data that can take any value in a given range, e.g. height.

Control group A comparison group in experiments, matched as closely as possible to the experimental group, for example, with similar ages and symptoms.

Convenience sampling A type of sampling where you work with what is available to you at the time, without needing to number or order the sample frame before you begin.

Correlation A measure of the relationship between two variables or measued data values.

Cumulative frequency step polygon A form of polygon drawn to illustrate simple discrete data. Points are joined horizontally and vertically (i.e. in steps), not diagonally as in a cumulative frequency curve or polygon.

Cumulative frequency The frequency found by adding each frequency to the sum of all preceding frequencies.

Data logging The mechanical process of collecting primary data, usually just counting or storing numbers in a system to build up a history of data.

Data Factual information, particularly information organised for analysis or processing.

Discrete data A form of data with values that are specific and which cannot have in-between values, e.g. the number of cars in a car park.

Dispersion A measure of the variability or spread in a distribution. Examples include variance, standard deviation and inter-quartile range.

Dot plot A graph that shows each item of numerical data above a number line or horizontal axis. Dot plots make it easy to see gaps and clusters in a data set, as well as how the data spreads along the axis.

Explanatory variable A quantity of something that varies, which can be used to explain increases or decreases in another variable.

Extraneous variable Something that can influence the results of an experiment.

Extrapolation The process of obtaining a value that extends beyond the given data.

Field experiment A type of experiment that takes place in a natural environment where the researcher has control over the explanatory variable.

Frequency diagram A diagram used to record the number of times an event occurs.

Frequency distribution table A table where each item of data is listed alongside the number of times it occurs.

Geometric mean The single number that we can replace all the data with when multiplying. The geometric mean of n numbers is square root of the product of the n numbers. Used when numbers have been increased (or decreased) by multiplying.

Grouped frequency A type of frequency distribution in which data is grouped together, used when it is impractical to write out every single value.

Glossary

Independent events Events where the outcome of the first event does not affect the probabilities of the subsequent events.

Inter-observer bias A form of bias that occurs when two people view things in different ways.

Interpolation The process of obtaining a value from a scatter diagram or table for a point that is located within the data values shown. A line of best fit or a regression equation can be used to obtain the value.

Interview A form of research in which an interviewer asks questions to an interviewee or respondent directly.

Laboratory experiment A type of experiment that takes place in an artificial environment where the researcher is in total control of all the factors that could affect the experiment.

Leading question A question that is designed to get a particular response.

Line of regression A line that is fitted to the points on a graph; essentially a line of best fit.

Lower quartile The item one-quarter of the way up the cumulative frequency axis, given by the 1/4 *n*th value.

Matched pair A simple type of experiment using pairs of people who are as alike as possible.

Misleading Data that is presented in a way that causes confusion – either deliberately or inadvertently – is called misleading data. Graphs can sometimes deliberately show misleading data in order to gain the attention of the audience.

Moving average A sequence of averages that smooths out variations in data, and that can be used to show trends.

Multistage sampling A more cwomplex form of cluster sampling where initial clusters are still too big to be considered as the sample, and so are broken down further into new, smaller clusters. This process can be repeated until the correct sample size is reached.

Natural experiment A type of experiment that is not subject to manipulation by researchers but is simply an observation of outcomes.

Negatively skewed A distribution in which the mean is greater than the median but less than the mode because of the presence of extreme values at the negative end of the distribution. (*See* skewness.)

Normal distribution A theoretical frequency distribution for a set of variable data, represented as a symmetrical bell-shaped curve.

Observation sheet A data-collection sheet used for recording things that are observed.

Observation The most basic method of primary data collection availalble, where things that we see are simply recorded.

Open question Survey questions with no specific response. Participants might give detailed and complete responses, but each might give a completely different answer, making the data slow to collect and difficult to analyse.

Opinion scale A method used to gather opinions from a population. Scales can be discrete or continuous.

Outlier An element of a data set that stands out notably from the rest of the data.

Pilot study The collection and analysis of a small sample of data to see if meaningful results can be obtained.

Population pyramid Used to compare percentages of populations by age and gender, they look like back-to-back horizontal bar graphs.

Positively skewed A distribution in which the median value is closer to the lower quartile than to the upper quartile. (*See* skewness.)

Product moment correlation coefficient (PMCC) A measure of the correlation between two sets of data.

Qualitative data A type of data in which the values of variables differ in terms of kind rather than in number (*see* quantitative data). Examples of qualitative data include colour, texture, smell, taste or emotions.

Quantitative data A type of data that can be counted or measured. Within quantitative data are both discrete data (e.g. number of cars) and continuous data (e.g. height of children).

Quota sampling A type of sampling in which the popualrtion is first divided into classes (e.g. males and females).

Random response An information-gathering technique in which two questions are put before the respondent; one is sensitive, one is not. The respondent flips a coin. If it shows heads they answer question A, if tails question B. The interviewer has no idea which question the respondent has answered.

Glossary

Random sample These are created when each member of the population has an equal chance of being included in the sample. (Also known as simple random samples.)

Ranked data Data that has been sorted into order (or ranked).

Respondent The person who gives answers to, for example, a questionnaire or a survey.

Response variable The outcome under investigation. Also known as independent and dependent variables.

Root A number that, when multiplied by itself a given number of times produces a given quantity, e.g. 4 is the square root of 16 (4×4), and the cube root of 64 ($4 \times 4 \times 4$).

Sample frame A list that includes every item of the population from which a sample is to be taken.

Sample size The number of items in a sample.

Seasonal variation Variation in data according to the time of the year. For example, ice cream sales are higher in summer than winter.

Skewness The degree to which a distribution is balanced about the mean. A perfectly symmetrical distribution has a value of 0. (See also negatively skewed; positively skewed.)

Spearman's rank correlation coefficient (SRCC) A numerical measure of the correlation between two sets of data, used when rankings have been used or when there might be a non-linear relationship in the data.

Spreadsheets A means of recording, organising and displaying data, often automatically, using a computer system.

Standard deviation The indication of how tightly the values of a data set are clustered about the mean. The greater the standard deviation, the more spread out the data is. The actual value of standard deviation is the average distance the data values are away from the mean.

Standardised rate The weighted average that takes into account the national standard per 1 000 people, allowing two different populations to be compared wve nthough they ay be a ifferent size with a different percentage make-up of age groups.

Standardised score A test score used to compare results from different data sets. The standardised score shows how far an actual score is from the mean.

Stem-and-leaf diagrams A simple way of displaying a set of data values. The distribution of the data looks very similar to a horizontal bar graph, with the lists of numbers forming the bars.

Stratified random sample A type of sample where each group within the population is represented by the same proportion as make up the population as a whole.

Survey A method of gathering information by asking questions or observing rather than by experiment.

Systematic sampling A type of sampling where items are chosen at regular intervals (e.g. every sixth or tenth item) and the first item is chosen randomly.

Trend line A line of best fit.

Ungrouped data Raw data that has yet to be assigned to groups.

Variance The standard deviation squared.

Venn diagram A diagram using circles to represent sets. The position and overlap of the circles indicates the relationships between the sets.

Vertical line graph A form of bar line graph that uses vertical lines instead of bars to represent data.

Weighted index numbers Numbers are weighted to give an indication of their relative importance

Index

activities: board game 328
  horse race game 334
  testing hypothesis 90
  throwing a die 90
averages: choice of 185–7
  mean 172, 181–2
  median 172, 176–8
  mode 172, 174
  moving 250–1
axis, bar charts 100

bar charts 98, 100-1
  axis 100
  class intervals 100
  composite 103-4
bar line graphs 102
bias, inter-observer 70
biased: experimental data 328
  sampling 40, 47
bivariate data 17, 290
box-and-whisker plots 204–6
  median 204–5
  quartiles 204–5
  skewness 204–5

calculator: random number generator 41, 43
  standard deviation 214–16
categorical data 17
census 62
chain base method, general indexes of retail prices 234, 236
chance 314
  probability scale 316
choropleth maps 128–30
choice of averages: appropriate 185–6
  extreme values 186
  representative 185–6
class intervals, frequency tables 22, 100
class widths: equal in histograms 140–2
  frequency density 142–5
  grouping data 83–4
  unequal in histograms 142–5
closed questions, questionnaires 65
cluster sampling 47–8
combined events: conditional probability 334–6
  tree diagrams 348–51
comparative pie charts 118
composite bar charts 103–4
continuous data, frequency tables 81
continuous opinion scales 66
control group: experimental design 70
  placebo 70
convenience sampling 47
correlation 288, 290–4
  examination questions 307–13
  grade booster 306
  product moment correlation coefficient (PMCC) 299–300
  Spearman's rank correlation coefficient (SRCC) 299–302
CPI (Consumer Price Index) 232, 234
  chain base method 236
  weighted index numbers 235
cumulative frequency diagrams 150–7
  interquartile range 152–7
  median value 151
  step polygons 155–7
cumulative sales, Z-charts 262–3

data: bivariate 17
  categorical 17
  census 62
  discrete 16
  grouping 20–2
  primary 26
  qualitative 16
  quantitative 16
  ranked 21
  raw 20
  secondary 26
  ungrouped 20
data collection 14–17
  data collection sheet 28, 60–1
  examination questions 32–7
  grade booster 31
data handling cycle 8
data logging, primary data 27–8
data recording, spreadsheets 29
data sources 26–9
  primary data 26
  secondary data 26
deciles 153–4
diagrammatic representation: examination questions 164–71
  grade booster 163
discrete data 16
  frequency tables 81
  standard deviation by calculator 214–16
discrete opinion scales 66
dispersion, interquartile range 150
distribution: negatively skewed 204–5, 218
  normal 217–18
  positively skewed 204–5, 218
  symmetric 204–5
dot plot graphs 103, 105

estimated mean, grouped data 190–1
events: combined events 334–5, 348–51, 355–6
  mutually exclusive 323
  probability scale 316, 318
examination questions: correlation 307–13
  data collection 32–7
  diagrammatic representation 164–71
  measures of location 198–201
  probability 360–5
  quality assurance 279, 287
  sampling 52–7
  spread 226–31
  statistics 240–7
  surveys 74–7
  tabulation 92–5
  time series 276–8, 280–6
exhaustive response, questionnaires 65
expectation, probability 338–9
experimental design 70–1
  control group 70
  inter-observer bias 70
  matched pairs 71
  observation 70
  variables 71-2
experiments 10–11, 27, 28, 71
  experimental probability 328
  relative frequency 328
  statistical 58
  variables 16
explanatory variables 71

Index

extraneous variables 71
extrapolation, scatter diagrams 295
extreme values, choice of averages 186

Fermat, Pierre de 314
frequency density: class widths 142–5
   histograms 142–5
frequency diagrams 141–2
   cumulative 150–7
   modal class 142
   standardised scores 218–19
frequency distribution tables 21
frequency polygons 140–1
frequency tables 22, 80–1
   class intervals 22, 100
   continuous data 81
   discrete data 81
   grouped frequency 83–5
   pictograms 98–9

general indexes of retail prices 232, 234
   chain base method 236
geometric mean 194–5
   multiplier 194–5
   root 194–5
Gombaud, Antoine 314
government statistics 232
grade booster: correlation 306
   data collection 31
   diagrammatic representation 163
   experiments 73
   investigation planning 13
   measures of location 197
   probability 359
   sampling 51
   spread 225
   statistics 239
   surveys 73
   tabulation 91
   time series 275
graphs: bar charts 98, 100–1
   dot plot 103, 105
   line 101–2
   misleading 122–5
   population pyramids 106
   vertical line graphs 102–3
grouped data: estimated mean 190–1
   modal class 190–1
   standard deviation by calculator 214–16
grouped frequency tables 83–5
grouping data 20–2
   class width 84

histograms: equal class-widths 140–2
   frequency density 142–5
   frequency polygons 140–1
   unequal class-widths 142–5
hypothesis 9, 58, 60

inter-observer bias, experimental design 70
interpolation, scatter diagrams 295
interquartile range 152–7
   dispersion 150
interviews 60–1
   respondents 60
   sampling 40
investigation planning 10–11

keys: pictograms 98
   stem-and-leaf diagrams 136

leading questions, questionnaires 64
line of best fit, moving averages 251–4

line, equation of 293–5
line graphs 101–2
   line of best fit 251–4
   trends 101–2
lower quartile 152, 154–6

maps, choropleth 128–30
matched pairs, experimental design 71
mean 172, 181–2
   geometric 194–5
   quality control limits 269–71
   in skewness measures 218
measures of location 172
   examination questions 198–201
   grade booster 197
median 172, 176–8
   box plots 204–5
   in skewness measures 218
   stem-and-leaf diagrams 135–7, 177
   values 151–2
misleading graphs 122–5
   misleading scale 122–5
modal class: frequency diagrams 142
   grouped data 190–1
mode 172, 174
   in skewness measures 218
moving averages: line of best fit 251–4
   seasonal variation 253–4, 258–61
   tabulation 255
   time series 258–61
   trends 250–1
multiplier, geometric mean 194–5
multistage sampling 48
mutually exclusive events 323

negatively skewed distribution 204–5, 218
normal distribution, spread 217–18

observation: experimental design 70
   observation sheet 28–9
   primary data 28–9
open questions, questionnaires 65
opinion scales: continuous 66
   discrete 66
ordered stem-and-leaf diagrams 135–7
outcomes: experimental probability 328
   probability scale 316
   sample space diagram 335
outliers, skewness 205–6

Pascal, Blaise 314
Pearson's measures of skew 218, 220
percentiles 152–4
pictograms: keys 98
   symbols 98–9
pie charts 115–18
   comparative 118
   sector angles 115, 117
   sectors 115–16
pilot studies, surveys 11, 62
placebo, control group 70
planning investigation 10–11
population, sampling 40
population pyramids 106
positively skewed distribution 204–5, 218
primary data 26
   data logging 27–8
   observation 28–9
probability 314
   conditional 355–6
   examination questions 360–5
   expectation 338
   experimental 330
   grade booster 359

Index

probability scale 316
product moment correlation coefficient (PMCC) 299–300

qualitative data 16, 81
quality assurance 248
   examination questions 279, 287
   quality control limits 269–71
   range 269
quantitative data 16, 81
quartile method for skewness 218, 221
quartiles, box-and-whisker plots 204–5
questionnaires 60–1, 64–6
   closed questions 65
   exhaustive response 65
   leading questions 64
   open questions 65
   sampling 40
quota sampling 47

random number generator, by calculator 41, 43
random samples 41
range: spread 221
   stem-and-leaf diagrams 136–7
ranked data 21
raw data 20
regression, line of 293–5
respondents, interviews 60
response variables 71
root, geometric mean 194–5
RPI (Retail Price Index) 232, 234
   chain base method 236
   weighted index numbers 235

sample: frame 40
   size 40–1
sample space diagram, two outcomes 335
sampling: biased 40, 47
   cluster 47–8
   convenience 47
   examination questions 52–7
   grade booster 51
   interviews 40
   multistage 48
   population 40
   questionnaires 40
   quota 47
   random samples 41
   sample frame 40
   sample size 40–1
   self-selecting 49
   stratified random sample 43–4
   systematic 46
scale, misleading 122–5
scatter diagrams 290–2
   extrapolation 295
   interpolation 295
   line of best fit 292
   line of regression 293–5
   product moment correlation coefficient (PMCC) 299–300
   Spearman's rank correlation coefficient (SRCC) 299–302
seasonal variation, moving averages 253–4, 258–61
secondary data 26
sector angles, pie charts 115, 117
sectors, pie charts 115–16
self-selecting sampling 49
simple random samples 41
skewness: box-and-whisker plots 204–5
   measures of 218
   outliers 205–6
   Pearson's measures of skew 218, 220
   quartile method 218, 221

Spearman's rank correlation coefficient (SRCC) 299–302
spread: box-and-whisker plots 204–6
   examination questions 226–31
   grade booster 225
   measures compared 221
   measures of 219
   normal distribution 217–18
   standard deviation 210–12
   standardised scores 218–19
   variance 210
spreadsheets: data recording 29
   random number function 41, 43
standard deviation 210–12
   by calculator 214–16
standardised scores, spread 218–19
statistical experiments 58
statistics: examination questions 240–7
   government 232
   grade booster 239
stem-and-leaf diagrams 135–7
   median 135–7, 177
   range 136–7
step polygons, cumulative frequency diagrams 157–8
stratified random sample 43–4
surveys 10
   examination questions 74–7
   grade booster 73
   interviews 60–1
   opinion scales 66
   pilot studies 62
   questionnaires 60–1, 64–6
symbols, pictograms 98–9
symmetric distribution 204–5
systematic sampling 46

tables: frequency 22, 80–1
   frequency distribution 21
   grouped frequency 83–5, 100
   moving averages 255
   random number 41, 42–3
   two-way 61, 78, 87, 341-3
tabulation 78
   examination questions 92–5
   grade booster 91
tallies 14
   tally charts 61, 80–1
time series 248, 258–63
   examination questions 276–8, 280-69
   grade booster 275
   moving averages 258–61
tree diagrams 348–51
trends: line graphs 101–2
   moving averages 250–1, 258–61
two-way tables 61, 78, 87, 341–3

ungrouped data 20
upper quartile 152, 154–6

variables: in experiments 16
   explanatory 71
   extraneous 71
   response 71
variance, spread 210–11
Venn diagrams 341–3
vertical line graphs 102

Z-charts 262–3